LIBRARY OF NEW TESTAMENT STUDIES

659

Formerly the Journal for the Study of the New Testament Supplement series

Editor
Chris Keith

Editorial Board
Dale C. Allison, Lynn H. Cohick, R. Alan Culpepper,
Craig A. Evans, Jennifer Eyl, Robert Fowler, Simon J. Gathercole,
Juan Hernández Jr., John S. Kloppenborg, Michael Labahn,
Matthew V. Novenson, Love L. Sechrest, Robert Wall,
Catrin H. Williams, Brittany E. Wilson

Irenaeus, the Scriptures, and the Apostolic Writings

Reevaluating the Status of the New Testament Writings at the End of the Second Century

Kenneth Laing

LONDON • NEW YORK • OXFORD • NEW DELHI • SYDNEY

T&T CLARK
Bloomsbury Publishing Plc
50 Bedford Square, London, WC1B 3DP, UK
1385 Broadway, New York, NY 10018, USA
29 Earlsfort Terrace, Dublin 2, Ireland

BLOOMSBURY, T&T CLARK and the T&T Clark logo are
trademarks of Bloomsbury Publishing Plc

First published in Great Britain 2022
Paperback edition published 2023

Copyright © Kenneth Laing, 2022

Kenneth Laing has asserted his right under the Copyright, Designs and
Patents Act, 1988, to be identified as Author of this work.

For legal purposes the Acknowledgments on p. ix constitute an
extension of this copyright page.

All rights reserved. No part of this publication may be reproduced or transmitted in
any form or by any means, electronic or mechanical, including photocopying,
recording, or any information storage or retrieval system, without prior
permission in writing from the publishers.

Bloomsbury Publishing Plc does not have any control over, or responsibility for, any
third-party websites referred to or in this book. All internet addresses given in this
book were correct at the time of going to press. The author and publisher regret any
inconvenience caused if addresses have changed or sites have ceased to exist, but
can accept no responsibility for any such changes.

A catalogue record for this book is available from the British Library.

Names: Laing, Kenneth, author.
Title: Irenaeus, the scriptures, and the apostolic writings: re-evaluating
the status of the New Testament writings at the end of the second century / Kenneth Laing.
Description: London; New York: T&T Clark, 2022. |
Series: The library of New Testament studies, 2513-8790; 659 |
Includes bibliographical references and index. | Summary: "This book challenges the customary
view of Irenaeus' conception of the nature and authority of the New
Testament writings"–Provided by publisher.
Identifiers: LCCN 2021037285 (print) | LCCN 2021037286 (ebook) |
ISBN 9780567701930 (hb) | ISBN 9780567701947 (epdf) | ISBN 9780567701961 (epub)
Subjects: LCSH: Irenaeus, Saint, Bishop of Lyon. | Bible. New
Testament–Criticism, interpretation, etc. | Bible–Canon. |
Bible–Evidences, authority, etc. | Revelation.
Classification: LCC BR65.I64 L35 2022 (print) |
LCC BR65.I64 (ebook) | DDC 225.1/2–dc23
LC record available at https://lccn.loc.gov/2021037285
LC ebook record available at https://lccn.loc.gov/2021037286

ISBN: HB: 978-0-5677-0193-0
PB: 978-0-5677-0206-7
ePDF: 978-0-5677-0194-7
ePUB: 978-0-5677-0196-1

Series: Library of New Testament Studies, volume 659
ISSN 2513-8790

Typeset by Newgen KnowledgeWorks Pvt. Ltd., Chennai, India

To find out more about our authors and books visit
www.bloomsbury.com and sign up for our newsletters.

For Richard Laing
My father

Contents

Acknowledgments ix
List of Abbreviations x

Introduction 1

Part 1 Assessing the Traditional Interpretation

1   The Apostolic Writings and the Use of γραφή 13
    1.1   The Use of γραφή as a Title for the Jewish Scriptures 17
    1.2   The Traditional Interpretation: "Scripture" and the Apostolic Writings 19
    1.3   Evidence That the Use of γραφή as a Scriptural Title Excludes the Apostolic Writings 44
2   Authoritative Texts or Authoritative Authors? 51
    2.1   Use of the Jewish Scriptures 52
    2.2   Are the Apostolic Writings Used as an Inherently Authoritative Text? 63
    2.3   Do Irenaeus' Interpretations Seem Indifferent to the Intentions of the Apostolic Authors? 77
Conclusion to Part 1 91

Part 2 Constructing an Alternative Interpretation

3   The Apostolic Writings and the Tradition, the Rule of Truth, and the Jewish Scriptures 99
    3.1   The Concept of Tradition in Irenaeus' Thought 100
    3.2   The Rule of Truth in Irenaeus' Thought 115
    3.3   The Relationship between the Apostolic Writings and the Jewish Scriptures 129
4   The Question of Inspiration 139
    4.1   The Relationship between Inspiration and Authority 140
    4.2   Examining the Nature of the Inspiration of the Jewish Scriptures 150

4.3	Evaluating the Evidence for the Divine *Auctoritas* of the Apostolic Writings	156
4.4	Constructing Irenaeus' Conception of the Status of the Apostolic Writings on His Doctrine of the Word	170
Conclusion		187
Bibliography		193
Index		203
Index of References to Irenaeus' Works		208

Acknowledgments

This book represents the culmination of four years of graduate study on Irenaeus' understanding of scripture and divine revelation. It is a revised form of my PhD thesis undertaken at the University of Aberdeen. This project could not have been completed without the help and support of a great number of people who deserve credit. First and foremost among these are my PhD supervisors, Dr. Don Wood and Prof. Tom Greggs. Don worked tirelessly to guide me throughout this process, and his many profound insights have been incredibly valuable. Likewise, Tom's helpful advice, expertise, and encouragement have been of great benefit. The merits of this book are due in large part to their guidance.

I am very thankful to have been part of the community at the University of Aberdeen, which has been a great support both professionally and personally. Among the many good friends and colleagues who shared in this burden, Jake Rollison, Michael Morelli, Amy Erickson, Cole Jodon, and Declan Kelly deserve special mention. You make Aberdeen the special place that it is.

This project could never have begun without the extremely generous "Authority and Texts: Concepts and Use" scholarship from the University of Aberdeen College of Arts and Social Sciences, for which I am very grateful. Thanks is also due to Santander Universities for its Santander Mobility Award.

A special debt of gratitude is owed to the Very Reverend Doctor John Behr, whose knowledge and expertise is matched only by his willingness to take the time to share it with others. I consider my time spent learning to read Irenaeus from Fr. John to have been of immeasurable value. I am also very grateful to the community at St. Vladimir's Seminary for their kind hospitality. I won't soon forget my time there.

Most of all, I am eternally grateful for my mother's unceasing prayers, my father's steadfast encouragement, my wife's constant love and support, and my daughters' infectious joy. Ida, Richard, Ange, Alexa, and Elliott: I could never have done this without you. Thank you.

Soli Deo gloria

Abbreviations

ACW	Ancient Christian Writers series
AH	*Against Heresies/Adversus haereses*
ANF	Ante-Nicene Fathers
Dem.	*The Demonstration of the Apostolic Preaching*
Die Lehre	Hoh, Josef. *Die Lehre des hl. Irenäus über das Neue Testament*. Münster: Aschendorff, 1919.
Frg.	Fragments from lost writings
"Graphe"	Steenberg, M. C. "Irenaeus on Scripture, Graphe, and the Status of Hermas." *St. Vladimir's Theological Quarterly* 53.1 (2009): 29–66.
Harvey	Harvey, W. Wigan, ed. *Sancti Irenaei Episcopi Lugdunensis: Libros quinque adversus haereses*. 2 vols. Cambridge: Typis Academicis, 1857.
HD	Harnack, Adolf von. *Lehrbuch der Dogmengeschichte*. Vol. 2. Freiburg: Mohr, 1888. Reproduced in English from the 3rd ed. as *History of Dogma*. Vol. 2. Translated by Neil Buchanan. Boston: Roberts Brothers, 1897.
Identifying	Behr, John. *Irenaeus of Lyons: Identifying Christianity*. Oxford: Oxford University Press, 2013.
Massuet	Massuet, R., ed. *Sancti Irenaei episcopi Lugdunensis et martyris detectionis et eversionis falso cognominatae agnitionis libri quinque*. Paris: Typis Joannis Baptistae Coignard, 1710. Reprinted in *Sancti Irenaei: Episcopi Lugdunensis et Martyris*. Patrologia Graeca 7. Edited by J. P. Migne. Paris: Imprimerie Catholique, 1857.
Migne	Migne, J. P., ed. *Sancti Irenaei: Episcopi Lugdunensis et Martyris*. Patrologia Graeca 7. Paris: Imprimerie Catholique, 1857.
Nicaea	Behr, John. *The Way to Nicaea: Formation of Christian Theology Volume 1*. Crestwood, NY: SVS Press, 2001.
PG	Patrologia Graeca
PL	Patrologia Latina
PO	Patrologia Orientalis
PPS	Popular Patristics Series
Sagnard	Sagnard, F. ed. *Irénée de Lyon: Contre Les Hérésies: Livre 3*. SC 34. Paris: du Cerf, 1952.
Saint Irénée	Benoit, André. *Saint Irénée: Introduction a l'Étude de sa Théologie*. Paris: Presses Universitaires de France, 1960.
SC	Sources Chrétiennes
Visibile	Ochagavia, Juan. *Visibile Patris Filius: A Study of Irenaeus' Teaching on Revelation and Tradition*. Rome: Typis Pontificiae Universitatis Gregorianae, 1964.

Introduction

The subject of this book is the nature and basis of authority of the apostolic writings in the thought of Irenaeus of Lyons, and the ways in which these relate to his conception of divine revelation. The interpretation set forth here challenges some foundational assumptions held by Irenaeus interpreters and New Testament canon scholars who rely on the evidence he provides. This second-century patristic writer is considered to be a primary source of evidence for investigations of the early church's understanding of the New Testament writings and of the process by which they attained scriptural and canonical status—a subject of considerable debate. Despite this, however, there has been little debate over how the evidence provided by Irenaeus should be interpreted.[1] Among those who propose a first-century, second-century, or fourth-/fifth-century emergence of the New Testament canon, there is general agreement that Irenaeus' works demonstrate that by the end of the second century the church considered the majority of our contemporary New Testament to be scripture, including a closed canon of four gospels.[2] This consensus is not limited to the field of New Testament

---

[1] Debates about Irenaeus' understanding of scripture have tended to revolve around the relationship between scripture, tradition, the church, the rule of truth, etc. as sources of authority, rather than the status and basis of authority of the New Testament writings themselves, though there are a few notable exceptions.

[2] R. Laird Harris, *The Inspiration and Canonicity of the Bible: An Historical and Exegetical Study* (Grand Rapids, MI: Zondervan Publishing House, 1969), contends that the New Testament canon was formed when the final book was written, on the basis of the inspiration of its authors, and was recognized as such before 120 (208–10, 294), and he views Irenaeus as a late witness to this preexisting reality: "The Scriptures are true, according to Irenaeus, because they are apostolic and therefore inspired" (247). Hans von Campenhausen, *Die Entstehung der christlichen Bibel* (Tübingen: Mohr, 1968), translated into English as *The Formation of the Christian Bible*, trans. J. A. Baker (Mifflintown: Sigler Press, 1997), argues instead for the formation of the New Testament canon by the end of the second century, and understands Irenaeus to be a decisive figure in this process: Irenaeus is "the first catholic theologian who dared to adopt the Marcionite principle of a new 'scripture'" (186). Lee M. McDonald, *The Formation of the Christian Biblical Canon* (Peabody, MA: Hendrickson, 1995), agrees with both scholars that "Irenaeus considered the NT literature as scripture on par with the OT" (198), despite his contention that a closed canon of New Testament scriptures did not exist prior to the end of the fourth century (McDonald relies on the arguments of A. C. Sundberg, "Towards a Revised History of the New Testament Canon," *StEv* 4.1 (1968): 452–61). For additional examples of the first-century position's use of Irenaeus, see Theodor Zahn, *Geschichte des neutestamentlichen Kanons* (Erlangen: Andreas Deichert, 1888); Benjamin B. Warfield, *The Canon of the New Testament: How and When Formed* (Philadelphia, PA: American Sunday-School Union, 1892). For additional examples of the second-century position's use of Irenaeus, see Adolf von Harnack, *Lehrbuch der Dogmengeschichte*, vol. 2 (Freiburg: Mohr, 1888); reproduced in English from the 3rd ed. as *History of Dogma*, vol. 2, trans. Neil Buchanan (Boston, MA: Roberts

canon scholarship but extends also to Irenaean scholarship more broadly. Most studies of Irenaeus' thought devote little attention to the status of the New Testament writings, instead (implicitly or explicitly) uncritically adopting the conclusions of New Testament canon scholarship. Among the few treatments concerned specifically with Irenaeus' view of the New Testament writings, increased engagement has not led to substantially different conclusions.[3]

The consensus interpretation of Irenaeus' view of the New Testament[4] may be broadly summarized. Irenaeus is held to consider the New Testament writings that he knows and uses to be "scripture," understood to be equivalent to the status of the Old Testament scriptures, on the basis of three substantiating claims: Irenaeus utilizes the scriptural title γραφή in reference to the New Testament writings alongside the Old Testament; he uses the New Testament writings as a scriptural *text* equivalent to his manner of use of the Old Testament; and he treats the New Testament writings as if they possess equal *authority* to the Old Testament. As a corollary to this, the New Testament writings are often understood to acquire their scriptural status for Irenaeus on the basis of their inspiration by the Spirit, mirroring the basis of the scriptural status of the Old Testament.[5]

Alongside this trajectory, there exists a minority of interpreters who have questioned certain elements of the traditional interpretation and have sought to propose alternative readings of Irenaeus on the subject of the status of the apostolic writings and the nature of their authority. Irenaeus has been argued to hold a more restricted[6] or a more expansive[7] conception of scripture than is typically recognized.

Brothers, 1897); *Das Neue Testament um das Jahr 200* (Freiburg: Mohr, 1889); and Tomas Bokedal, *The Formation and Significance of the Christian Biblical Canon* (London: Bloomsbury, 2014). For additional examples of the fourth-/fifth-century position's use of Irenaeus, see A. C. Sundberg, "Canon of the NT," in *The Interpreter's Dictionary of the Bible* (Nashville, TN: Abingdon, 1976), 136–40; "Canon Muratori: A Fourth Century List," *HTR* 66 (1973): 1–41; "The Bible Canon and the Christian Doctrine of Inspiration," *Int* 29 (1975): 352–71; Craig Allert, *A High View of Scripture?* (Grand Rapids, MI: Baker Academic, 2007); Harry Y. Gamble, *The New Testament Canon: Its Making and Meaning* (Philadelphia, PA: Fortress Press, 1985); Bruce M. Metzger, *The Canon of the New Testament* (Oxford: Clarendon Press, 1987); Geoffrey M. Hahneman, *The Muratorian Fragment and the Development of the Canon* (Oxford: Clarendon Press, 1992).

[3] Most prominent among these are Josef Hoh, *Die Lehre des hl. Irenäus über das Neue Testament* (Münster: Aschendorff, 1919); John Lawson, *The Biblical Theology of Saint Irenaeus* (London: Epworth Press, 1948); and André Benoit, *Saint Irénée: Introduction a l'Étude de sa Théologie* (Paris: Presses Universitaires de France, 1960). Cf. also F. R. Montgomery Hitchcock, *Irenaeus of Lugdunum: A Study of His Teaching* (Cambridge: Cambridge University Press, 1914); Damien van den Eynde, *Les Normes de l'Enseignement Chretien dans la littérature patristique des trois premiers siècles* (Paris: Gabalda & Fils, 1933); Ellen Flesseman-van Leer, *Tradition and Scripture in the Early Church* (Assen: Van Gorcum, 1954), 100–44. The only dedicated study on this subject to appear within the last fifty years is Yves-Marie Blanchard, *Aux Sources du Canon, le Témoignage d'Irénée* (Paris: du Cerf, 1993). In this and the majority of recent broader studies on Irenaeus, the conclusions of these previous interpreters are repeated.

[4] This interpretation will be referred to as "the traditional interpretation" throughout this book.

[5] Seen, for example, in Harnack, HD 2; Harris, *Inspiration and Canonicity*; and Bokedal, *Significance*.

[6] Johannes Werner, *Der Paulinismus des Irenaus: Eine Kirchen- und Dogmengeschtliche Untersuchung uber das Verhaltnis des Irenaus zur Paulinischen Briefsammlung und Theologie* (Leipzig: J.C. Hinrichs'sche Buchhandlung, 1889), esp. 16–46. He argues that the Pauline epistles do not possess full scriptural status in Irenaeus' writings.

[7] M. C. Steenberg, "Irenaeus on Scripture, Graphe, and the Status of Hermas," *SVTQ* 53.1 (2009): 29–66, contends that Irenaeus' conception of scripture is in fact much wider than the later scriptural

Objections have been raised against the view that Irenaeus speaks fluently of the New Testament as scripture[8] and seeks to establish the canonical status of the four gospels.[9] Distinctions between Irenaeus' conception of the Jewish scriptures and the apostolic writings have been emphasized.[10] The notion that Irenaeus locates the authority of the New Testament writings in their inspiration has received sustained critique,[11] and the authority of these writings has been traced instead to their position as a central means of transmission of the apostolic tradition.[12]

In what follows, I seek to critically extend this minority interpretative current. This project is motivated by the contention that the traditional interpretation of Irenaeus—by interpreting him through a post-Reformation lens in which demonstrating a (more or less) canonized two-part Scriptural text is treated as a controlling motif[13]—has imposed foreign categories onto Irenaeus' thought and overlooked central elements of his understanding of the nature of revelation. This widespread practice has resulted

---

canon, including also the *Shepherd of Hermas* and other writings that authentically witness the apostolic teaching.

[8] Bernard Sesboüé, "La Preuve par les Ecritures chez S. Irenee: A propos d'un texte difficile du livre III de l'*Adversus haereses*," *NRTh* 103 (1981): 872–87. He finds substantial evidence that γραφή almost always refers exclusively to the Old Testament in *Adversus haereses*, though this does not lead him to the conclusion that the New Testament was not considered to be scripture.

[9] Annette Yoshiko Reed, "ΕΥΑΓΓΕΛΙΟΝ: Orality, Textuality, and the Christian Truth in Irenaeus' *Adversus haereses*," *VC* 56.1 (2002): 11–46. She argues that the intention of his defense of the four Gospel accounts was "to defend the singular Gospel message against a multiplicity of heretical deviations" (14–15).

[10] John Behr, *Irenaeus of Lyons: Identifying Christianity* (Oxford: Oxford University Press, 2013). Behr, perhaps the most notable of these minority interpretations, has presented an in-depth account of Irenaeus' understanding of the New Testament writings, which includes the contention that Irenaeus meant by "the scriptures" specifically the Old Testament. While Behr accepts the conclusions of the traditional interpretation that the New Testament is also considered scripture by Irenaeus, he believes that Irenaeus nonetheless perceives a strong distinction between the Old Testament and the New, "not seeing the latter simply as a continuation of the former, treating them simply as more books of Scripture" (*Identifying*, 110). For Behr, the New Testament represents the apostolic interpretation and recapitulation *of* the scriptures in Irenaeus' thought. Cf. also *St Irenaeus of Lyons: On the Apostolic Preaching* (Crestwood, NY: SVS Press, 1997); "Irenaeus on the Word of God," *StP* 36 (2001): 163–7; *The Way to Nicaea: Formation of Christian Theology Volume 1* (Crestwood, NY: SVS Press, 2001).

[11] Everett R. Kalin, *Argument from Inspiration in the Canonization of the New Testament* (ThD Diss., Harvard University Press, 1967). Kalin published a summary of his findings in "The Inspired Community: A Glance at Canon History," *CTM* 42 (1971): 541–9. He contends that according to Irenaeus inspiration is neither unique to the New Testament writings nor the basis of their scriptural status.

[12] Juan Ochagavia, *Visibile Patris Filius: A Study of Irenaeus' Teaching on Revelation and Tradition* (Rome: Typis Pontificiae Universitatis Gregorianae, 1964). Ochagavia also emphasizes the primary role of the Word in the impartation of revelation.

[13] John Friesen, on the basis of his illuminating work *A Study of the Influence of Confessional Bias on the Interpretations in the Modern Era of Irenaeus of Lyons* (Ann Arbor, MI: University Microfilms International, 1977), has concluded that

> most of the interpretations were strong in the area of asking questions from the perspective of the present, especially from the standpoint of the confessional bias of interpreters … [while being] weak in the matter of placing Irenaeus into his own cultural and intellectual context. Very few studies made a serious attempt to do this … The result of this lack has been a view of Irenaeus which suggests that his concerns were the concerns of today which are of significance to the various confessions. (147)

in an inaccurate picture of Irenaeus' understanding of the nature and status of the apostolic writings.[14] When Irenaeus is allowed to be his own interpreter, it becomes evident that his theology of the Word decisively controls his understanding of all forms of revelation, and when he is interpreted in light of this Irenaeus exhibits an understanding of the apostolic writings that contrasts in a number of significant ways from his understanding of the Jewish scriptures.[15] Such a distinction has up to this point gone largely unacknowledged.

[14] In order to avoid anachronism, I have elected to refer to the collection of writings currently referred to as the New Testament as the "apostolic writings" throughout the remainder of this book when I am speaking of Irenaeus' understanding of them. This phrase is used to refer specifically to those writings that Irenaeus takes to have been apostolic, not specifically to the documents in the later canonized New Testament—though the overlap is almost complete. Irenaeus makes use of all of the New Testament writings except Philemon, 3 John, and Jude, with some uncertainty regarding Hebrews and 2 Peter (cf. Hoh, *Die Lehre*, 1–59; Blanchard, *Sources du Canon*; Benoit, *Saint Irénée*, 103–47). My decision to use the phrase "apostolic writings" also avoids imposing the modern categories of Old Testament and New Testament scripture, which would have been foreign to Irenaeus. It is worth noting, however, that Irenaeus himself did not use the phrase "apostolic writings" in reference to the whole of the New Testament documents he used. His rare use of the phrases "λόγους ἀποστολικούς [*sermones apostolicos*]" (1.8.1) and "*apostolicis epistolis*" (5.pre) appears to refer to only the epistles, and perhaps only to those of Paul (cf. Campenhausen, *Formation*, 203 n. 80, 206 and n. 291). Irenaeus had no term for the entirety of the New Testament writings he knew and used, though he conceptually grouped together the gospels and epistles as "evangelical and apostolic" words (1.3.6) or as the teachings of "the Lord and the apostles" (2.2.6).

[15] The phrase "Old Testament" is also replaced with "the Jewish scriptures" when discussing Irenaeus' conception. This phrase is not without baggage, but it has been considered to be the least confusing and unhelpful phrase within the context of this book. It is worth briefly discussing the content of the Jewish Scriptures for Irenaeus. There are two primary views of the process of "Old Testament" canonization. One view holds that the canon had been closed within Judaism prior to the emergence of Christianity, with the result that Christianity received from Judaism a closed canon of scriptures at its inception, and therefore had no need of subsequent clarification (this view is represented by E. Earle Ellis, *The Old Testament in Early Christianity: Canon and Interpretation in the Light of Modern Research* [Grand Rapids, MI: Baker Academic, 1992]; Stephen G. Dempster, "Torah, Torah, Torah: The Emergence of the Tripartite Canon," in *Exploring the Origins of the Bible: Canon Formation in Historical, Literary, and Theological Perspective*, ed. Craig A. Evans and Emanuel Tov [Grand Rapids, MI: Baker Academic, 2008], 87–127). In contrast, the current majority view holds that while the scriptural categories of "Law" and "Prophets" had been precisely delineated well before the advent of Christianity, it would be premature to speak of a closed canon at any time prior to Christianity's split from Judaism, as a third category of "Writings" still had not been precisely defined and canonized (this view is exemplified by A. C. Sundberg, *The Old Testament of the Early Church* [Cambridge, MA: Harvard University Press, 1964]; and McDonald, *Formation*). According to most proponents of this view, the existence of a closed canon of Jewish scriptures *within Christianity* is not seen prior to at least the fourth century (with the regional Council of Laodicea in 363 or the Council of Carthage in 397). Yet even according to this view, in the absence of a closed canon of Jewish scriptures at the end of the second century, Irenaeus nonetheless has a clear conception of what "the scriptures" are—just as Jesus, the apostles, and the early church before him did (on the history of the concept of "canon" and its distinction from "scripture," see especially John Barton, *Holy Writings, Sacred Text: The Canon in Early Christianity* [Louisville, KY: Westminster John Knox Press, 1997], 1–14). The contents of the Jewish scriptures are determined for Irenaeus by the Septuagint translation he has access to (3.21.1-3). A number of interpreters have attempted to determine precisely which books Irenaeus considers to be part of the Jewish scriptures based on his citations (cf. especially Benoit, *Irénée*, 74–102), yet Irenaeus' lack of concern for delineating the precise canonical boundaries of the Jewish scriptures indicates he does not consider such an exercise to be of much importance, if he has considered the notion at all. In any case, the precise contents of the Jewish scriptures for Irenaeus (beyond consisting of the canonical Law and Prophets along with an amorphous collection of Writings) are a matter of indifference for the argument of this thesis.

The central argument advanced in this book, stated negatively, is that the unique revelatory authority of the apostolic writings in Irenaeus' thought does not arise from (or lead to) a notion of their scriptural status. In positive terms, it is contended that the apostolic writings are conceived of instead as the written record of the *apostolic tradition*, acquiring their unique revelatory authority on this basis as a result of their perceived apostolic origin. It is the testimony of the apostles, directly accessed through the writings they left behind, that is primarily in focus for Irenaeus. For this reason apostolicity, not inspiration, is the foundation of the unique authority of the apostolic writings (though Irenaeus also affirms their inspiration by the Spirit) because the Word of God—as Revealer of the Father and the sole source of divine revelation—has in the consummation of his revelation become incarnate as a human being and by this has fully revealed to humanity both himself and the Father. Within this consummate revelatory act, the incarnate Word's unparalleled relationship to his apostles grants their preaching unique revelatory authority, from which their subsequent writings derive their status as the *authoritative written record of the divinely sanctioned mediation of the Word's consummate revelation to humanity*. This conception of the apostolic writings provides the basis for Irenaeus' consistent use of them as a uniquely authoritative source of divine revelation alongside yet distinct from the Jewish scriptures throughout his works.

The demonstration of this thesis proceeds by way of a close, contextual analysis of Irenaeus' surviving works, utilizing an interpretative strategy characterized by what has been called "the principle of contextuality—contextual coherence as a key interpretative standard."[16] It is held that key statements within Irenaeus' works can only be properly interpreted when they are considered within their larger contexts: within the greater theological arguments of the works in which they appear, within the overall theological agenda maintained across his works, and within the historical and linguistic context in which he lived and wrote.[17] This analysis is organized into two major parts. It begins with a critical assessment of the traditional interpretation of Irenaeus' conception of the nature and status of the apostolic writings, undertaking a careful analysis of Irenaeus' claims within the context of his wider theological project and polemical agenda to test the evidence for and against the contention that Irenaeus considered the apostolic writings to be "scripture." The findings of this assessment then inform the construction of an alternative interpretation of Irenaeus' conception of the apostolic writings on the basis of his concepts of tradition and revelation in the final two chapters.

In Part 1, the first two chapters assess the traditional interpretation's first two substantiating arguments for its claim that Irenaeus considered the apostolic writings to be "scripture" equivalent to the Jewish scriptures. Chapter 1 undertakes a systematic analysis of Irenaeus' relevant statements, interpreted within their wider contexts, to evaluate the claim that Irenaeus' use of γραφή indicates that he assigns a scriptural title to the apostolic writings alongside the Jewish scriptures. This analysis suggests

---

[16] Nicholas Rescher, *Interpreting Philosophy: The Elements of Philosophical Hermeneutics* (Frankfurt: Ontos Verlag, 2007), 25.
[17] Rescher identifies these three levels of context as "Immediate," "Proximate," and "Peripheral" (155).

the conclusion that Irenaeus refrains from using γραφή as a scriptural title for the apostolic writings, reserving its use as a title for the Jewish scriptures. These findings are understood to suggest a previously unrecognized conceptual distinction between the apostolic writings and the Jewish scriptures in Irenaeus' thought.

Building on the findings of Chapter 1, Chapter 2 assesses the traditional interpretation's argument that Irenaeus uses the apostolic writings as a scriptural text equivalent to his manner of use of the Jewish scriptures. Through a careful investigation of his references to texts and authors and of his principles of interpretation within the contexts of his arguments, it is concluded that while Irenaeus treats the Jewish scriptures as an inherently authoritative scriptural text, he uses the apostolic writings as a record of the testimony of authoritative human authors. This indicates that the apostolic writings do not possess their unique revelatory authority on the basis of perceived scriptural status as the Jewish scriptures do, but on the basis of the derived authority of their apostolic authors. These findings are understood to confirm the existence of the conceptual distinction which was previously suggested, and to indicate a possible basis for it.

Part 1 concludes by assessing the implications of the traditional interpretation's third argument, which correctly identifies the unique authoritative status of the apostolic writings in Irenaeus' thought. This assessment leads to the conclusion that the argument has failed to recognize that Irenaeus' attribution of authority does not require the implication that they are therefore assigned scriptural status. This judgment on the traditional interpretation's final substantiating argument suggests that its central claim lacks adequate grounds. This indicates the need for an alternative interpretation of Irenaeus' conception of the nature and status of the apostolic writings, to be constructed in Part 2.

Chapter 3 begins this constructive task by investigating the relationship between the apostolic writings and Irenaeus' concepts of tradition and the rule of truth. It is contended that the rule of truth and the apostolic writings are twin elements of the apostolic tradition, which is itself understood to be the content of the apostolic preaching. The apostolic writings are the primary means of accessing this content, as the authoritative written record of the tradition. The apostolic tradition, the rule of truth, and the apostolic writings are therefore united by *apostolicity* as the overarching authoritative basis upon which they derive their unique revelatory authority. This leads to an examination of the relationship between the apostolic writings and the Jewish scriptures. Utilizing a number of key passages in which Irenaeus describes the apostolic preaching of the Gospel as a "demonstration" and a "recapitulation" of the scriptures, this section argues that the apostolic writings relate to the Jewish scriptures as the record of the *apostolic interpretation* of these scriptures. For Irenaeus, the Gospel itself is not properly understood merely as a description of the life and teachings of Christ but as the new reading of the (Jewish) scriptures in light of the Incarnation. These findings confirm that the distinction that has been observed arises because apostolicity is the basis for the unique revelatory authority of the apostolic writings.

Chapter 4 builds upon the conclusions of Chapter 3, beginning with an assessment of the traditional interpretation's corollary claim that the apostles or their writings acquire their unique revelatory authority for Irenaeus on the basis of their inspiration by the Spirit. On the basis of a systematic analysis of Irenaeus' patterns of introducing the Jewish scriptures and the apostolic writings and his comments concerning their inspiration, it is concluded that Irenaeus gives no indication that inspiration plays a defining role in the unique status of the apostles or their writings. Instead, the unique revelatory authority of the apostolic writings appears to be tied directly to the apostles' relationship to Christ. This leads to an examination of Irenaeus' overarching theology of the Word as Revealer of the Father, in order to determine why apostolicity functions for Irenaeus as a second category of unique revelatory authority, equal to but distinct from that of the Jewish scriptures. This investigation culminates in a definitive determination of Irenaeus' conception of the nature and status of the apostolic writings, which constitute the authoritative written record of the divinely sanctioned apostolic mediation of the Word's consummate revelation to humanity.

Notes on Procedure

The analysis undertaken in this book begins with the presumption that Irenaeus is predominantly coherent in his thought. It is here assumed, in contrast to a number of works in previous generations of Irenaean scholarship,[18] that Irenaeus expresses a

---

[18] After his rediscovery by Erasmus in the sixteenth century, Irenaeus' reputation as a capable systematic thinker began to erode toward the end of the nineteenth century, initiating a period of largely negative assessment of his writing. H. H. Wendt, *Die christliche Lehre von der menschlichen Vollkommenheit* (Gottingen: Vandenhoeck & Ruprecht, 1882), was the first to question the unity of Irenaeus' thought, pointing out contradictions and incompatible lines of thought, particularly concerning the effects of the Fall (21–9; cf. Anthony Briggman, *Irenaeus of Lyons and the Theology of the Holy Spirit* [Oxford: Oxford University Press, 2012], 4–5). This criticism would be taken up by Harnack in his *Lehrbuch der Dogmengeschichte*, as well as "Der Presbyter-Prediger des Irenaus (IV,27,1-32,1)," in *Philotesia: Paul Kleinert zum 70. Geburtstag dargebracht* (Berlin: Trowzisch, 1907), 1–37. Harnack denied the presence of a single theological system in *Adversus haereses*, attempting instead to identify a number of individual strains of tradition that had been compiled by Irenaeus, organized around the principles of the one Creator God and Christ as the incarnate Son of God. Harnack would prove to have a lasting influence. Similar assessments soon became standard, as exemplified by Paul Beuzart, *Essai sur la Theologie d'Irenee* (Paris: Ernest Leroux, 1908); Wilhelm Bousset, *Judisch-christlicher Schulbetried in Alexandria und Rom: Literarische Untersuchungen zu Philo und Clemens von Alexandria, Justin und Irenaus* (Gottingen: Vandenhoeck & Ruprecht, 1915), 272–82; and H. Koch, "Zur Lehre vom Urstand und von der Erlösung bei Irenäus," *ThStK* 96-7 (1925): 183–214. The most significant of these critiques, however, is found in Friedrich Loofs, *Theophilus von Antiochien Adversus Marcionem, und die anderen theologischen Quellen bei Irenaeus* (Leipzig: J. C. Hinrichs, 1930). Building on the critiques of Harnack and Bousset, Loofs employed the use of source criticism in his analysis of *Adversus haereses* in order to account for inconsistencies of thought by identifying a number of different mutually incoherent sources—unknown and thus inferred from subject matter—that Irenaeus was said to have merely compiled, and to differentiate these sources from what he took to be Irenaeus' own meager contributions in *Adversus haereses*. Far from a first-rate systematic theologian, in Loofs' presentation Irenaeus was a mere compiler of sources who lacked the ability to unite them into a coherent theological system. Commenting on the figure that emerged from his study, Loofs concluded, "As a theological writer, Irenaeus was much less important than previously supposed ... Even slighter a figure was Irenaeus as a theologian" (27; cited in Behr, *Identifying*, 15). This devastating critique proved incredibly influential, and despite immediate criticism from D. B. Reynders, "La polemique de Saint Irenee: Methode et principes," *RThAM* 7 (1935): 5–27; and Hitchcock's subsequent detailed critique in "Loofs' Theory of Theophilus of Antioch as a Source of Irenaeus I/II," *JTS* 38 (1937): 130–9, 255–66; and "Loofs' Asiatic Source

coherent and consistent system of thought across his writings. Despite languishing for a number of decades in disrepute, Irenaeus' works have since earned a reputation for their depth, unity, and coherence,[19] as it has become recognized that although Irenaeus does not always present his thought in a systematic manner, he was nonetheless a deeply coherent thinker. For this reason, apparent contradictions among his many statements are treated as opportunities to discover previously obscured areas of his thought, rather than dismissed as examples of inconsistency in his thinking.

Beyond the assertion of the overall coherence of Irenaeus' thought, this book does not represent an attempt either to defend or to critique Irenaeus' claims. The purpose of this investigation is to determine what Irenaeus believed about the nature and status of the apostolic writings, rather than to make a determination as to the accuracy of his claims or the merits of his ideas. There is ample opportunity to critique elements of his thought and call certain of his historical claims into question, but these criticisms lie outside the scope of this work.[20]

(IQA) and the Ps-Justin De Resurrectione," *ZNW* 36 (1937): 35–60; the overall effect of Loofs' work was a virtual suspension of study of the thought of Irenaeus for the next few decades.

[19] This reversal would begin in 1947 with Gustaf Wingren, who took up the criticisms of Hitchcock and produced an influential systematic treatment of Irenaeus' thought in direct response to Loofs in his *Människan och Inkarnationen enligt Irenaeus* (Lund: C.W.K Gleerup, 1947). Benoit also took up this critique of Loofs a decade later in *Irénée*, though while he rejected Loofs' conclusions he also questioned the possibility of giving a full systematic account of Irenaeus given the lack of coherence of his work. Finally, in 1978, P. Bacq recovered Irenaeus' status as an original and systematic thinker, as he convincingly demonstrated the overall unity and structure of his thought, including the coherence of the different streams of thought, in his *De l'ancienne a la nouvelle alliance selon S. Irenee: Unite du livre IV de l'Adversus haereses* (Paris: Lethielleux, 1978). D. Jeffrey Bingham has applied Bacq's methodology to Book 1 in "The Bishop in the Mirror: Scripture and Irenaeus's Self-Understanding in *Adversus haereses* Book One," in *Tradition & the Rule of Faith in the Early Church*, ed. Ronnie J. Rombs and Alexander J. Hwang (Washington, DC: Catholic University of America Press, 2010), 48–67. Mary Ann Donovan has likewise applied his methodology to her analysis of the whole of *Adversus haereses* in *One Right Reading? A Guide to Irenaeus* (Collegeville, MN: Liturgical Press, 1997). Since that time, Irenaean scholarship has grown substantially and the unity and coherence of his theology has been largely accepted as a given. Cf. Briggman, *Holy Spirit*, 4–5; Behr, *Identifying*.

[20] There are a number of works in existence that include critical evaluations of aspects of Irenaeus' writings. His descriptions of Valentinian and Ptolemaic teachings are critiqued by Elaine Pagels, "Conflicting Versions of Valentinian Eschatology: Irenaeus' Treatise vs. the Excerpts from Theodotus," *HTR* 67 (1974): 35–53; *The Gnostic Gospels* (London: Penguin, 1980); Karen King, *What Is Gnosticism?* (Cambridge, MA: Belknap Press, 2003); and "Which Early Christianity?," in *The Oxford Handbook of Early Christian Studies*, ed. Susan Ashbrook Harvey and David G. Hunters (Oxford: Oxford University Press, 2008), 66–84; David Brakke, *The Gnostics: Myth, Ritual, and Diversity in Early Christianity* (Cambridge, MA: Harvard University Press, 2010); Rowan Greer, "The Dog and the Mushrooms: Irenaeus's View of the Valentinians Assessed," in *The Rediscovery of Christian Gnosticism: Proceedings of the International Conference on Gnosticism at Yale*, ed. Bentley Layton (Leiden: Brill, 1980–1), 1:146–75; etc. In similar fashion, Irenaeus' assumption of a single continuous apostolic form of Christianity against a multitude of late false teachers has been challenged by Walter Bauer, *Rechtglaubigkeit und Ketzerei im altesten Christentum* (Tubingen: Mohr, 1934); reproduced in English as *Orthodoxy and Heresy in Earliest Christianity*, trans. R. Kraft and G. Krodel (Philadelphia, PA: Fortress Press, 1971); Bart D. Ehrman, *Lost Christianities: The Battles for Scripture and the Faiths we Never Knew* (Oxford: Oxford University Press, 2003); Brakke, *Gnostics*; etc. Irenaeus' purpose for writing to refute the "heretics" is itself critiqued by Pagels, *Gnostic Gospels*; Gérard Vallée, "Theological and Non-Theological Motives in Irenaeus' Refutation of the Gnostics,"

Interpreting Irenaeus' thought often proves especially difficult because of the state in which his writings are preserved. Because his two extant works have survived primarily through (often unsatisfactory) translations,[21] interpreting his thought often requires textual reconstruction or careful evaluation of the reconstructive decisions made by editors and interpreters. The combination of fragments and manuscripts, combined with the level of dedicated scholarship that has gone into piecing together *Adversus haereses*, lends support for the belief in its overall accuracy, and in many places of the precision of finer details of his writing. However, there are many gaps in this knowledge, and as Dennis Minns describes, "so little of what he wrote survives in the language in which he wrote, an educated guess at what the original Greek might have been is often crucial to the interpretation of his thought."[22] Because of this, in a project of this sort where a slight change in vocabulary can significantly impact the plausibility of an interpretation or argument, it is at times necessary to settle for tentative conclusions.

Throughout this book, the five books of *Adversus haereses* are accessed primarily through the *Sources Chrétiennes* (SC) edition edited by Adelin Rousseau et al.,[23] and all Latin and Greek citations (and suggested retroversions) and French translations are reproduced from here, unless otherwise noted. The editions of Harvey,[24] Sagnard,[25] and Massuet[26] are also consulted, as is the Armenian translation of Books 4 and 5

---

in *Jewish and Christian Self-Definition, Volume One: The Shaping of Christianity in the Second and Third Centuries*, ed. E. P. Sanders (London: SCM Press, 1980), 174–85; etc.

[21] Other than a lengthy section of Book 1 copied by Epiphanius (Adelin Rousseau et al. note [SC 263:61] that it covers 74% of the book), there are only minimal surviving Greek fragments of Irenaeus' works, which can often be shown by comparison with the Latin and Armenian translations to be rather imprecise (cf. SC 263:61–100). The Latin translation—the only complete translation of *Adversus haereses*—is of such poor quality that Erasmus, analyzing it in 1526 and assuming that Irenaeus himself had written it in Latin, believed it must not have been his first language (P. S. and H. M. Allen, eds., *Opus Epistolarum Des. Erasmi Roterdami, Vol. 6, 1525-1527* [Oxford: Clarendon Press, 1926], 384–91; summarized by Paul Parvis, "Packaging Irenaeus: Adversus Haereses and Its Editors," in *Irenaeus: Life, Scripture, Legacy*, ed. Sara Parvis and Paul Foster [Minneapolis, MN: Fortress Press, 2012], 184). However, because the translation is believed to have been produced by c. 200, within twenty years of the original (cf. Hitchcock, *Irenaeus*, 44; ACW 55:14–15), it may be supposed that the translator worked off of a very accurate Greek manuscript. In addition, while stilted, the translation is also quite literal, often making it possible to determine the exact Greek words being translated (cf. ACW 55:14). The Armenian translation of Books 4 and 5 (along with a few brief fragments from the other three books) and *the Demonstration* dates to the sixth century (cf. ACW 55:15). However, Behr explains that it was a product of the "Hellenistic School" of translation that sought "to reproduce the Greek original exactly, both in syntax and in the construction of compound verbs and nouns" (PPS 17:33). This resulted in an "over literal accuracy," which allows for a complete reconstruction of the original Greek text (PPS 17:33-4). An extended discussion of all the translations and fragments for each book can be found in SC 263:9-111, 293:17-115, 210:11-48, 100:15-104, 152:27-165, and 406:16-49.

[22] Dennis Minns, *Irenaeus: An Introduction* (London: T&T Clark International, 2010), x.

[23] Adelin Rousseau, Bertrand Hemmerdinger, Louis Doutreleau, and Charles Mercier, eds., *Irénée de Lyon: Contre les hérésies*, Books 1–5, SC 100, 152–3, 210–11, 263–4, 293–4 (Paris: du Cerf, 1965–82).

[24] W. Wigan Harvey, ed., *Sancti Irenaei Episcopi Lugdunensis: Libros quinque adversus haereses*, 2 vols. (Cambridge: Typis Academicis, 1857).

[25] F. Sagnard, ed., *Irénée de Lyon: Contre Les Hérésies: Livre 3*, SC 34 (Paris: du Cerf, 1952).

[26] R. Massuet, ed., *Sancti Irenaei episcopi Lugdunensis et martyris detectionis et eversionis falso cognominatae agnitionis libri quinque* (Paris: Typis Joannis Baptistae Coignard, 1710); reprinted in PG 7, ed. J. P. Migne (Paris: Imprimerie Catholique, 1857).

edited by Karapet Ter-Mekerttschian and E. Ter-Minassiantz.[27] English translations for Books 1–3 are reproduced from the *Ancient Christian Writers* (ACW) series edited by Dominic J. Unger,[28] and of Books 4 and 5 from the *Ante-Nicene Fathers* (ANF) series edited by Alexander Roberts and James Donaldson,[29] unless otherwise noted. In all instances where translation is at issue or effects the argument, my own translation is provided. This is always noted.

Irenaeus' second surviving work, *The Demonstration of the Apostolic Preaching*, is accessed through the *Patrologia Orientalis* (PO) edition of Ter-Mekerttschian and S. G. Wilson,[30] and all Armenian citations are reproduced from here. English translations are reproduced from the *Popular Patristics Series* (PPS) edited by John Behr,[31] unless otherwise noted. French and Latin translations (and suggested Greek retroversions) are reproduced from Rousseau's SC edition.[32] Fragments from lost works of Irenaeus are primarily accessed through the edition of Harvey, whose numbering is used. Eusebius' *Historia Ecclesiastica*[33] and the *Sacra Parallela*[34] are also consulted. English translations are reproduced from the ANF translation, unless otherwise noted.[35] Citations of all other ancient works provide full bibliographic information of the original work, edition used, and translation cited in a footnote. Abbreviations conform to Lampe's *Patristic Greek Lexicon*.[36]

---

[27] Karapet Ter-Mékérttschian and E. Ter-Minassiantz, eds., *Irenäus, Gegen die Häretiker* [Ἔλεγχος καὶ ἀνατροπὴ τῆς ψευδωνύμου γνώσεως], *Buch IV u. V in armenischer Version*, TU 35.2 (Leipzig: Hinrichs, 1910).

[28] Dominic J. Unger, ed., *St. Irenaeus of Lyons: Against the Heresies*, Books 1–3, ACW 55, 64, 65 (New York: Paulist Press, 1992–2012).

[29] Alexander Roberts and James Donaldson, eds., *The Apostolic Fathers, Justin Martyr, Irenaeus*, ANF 1 (Edinburgh: T&T Clark, 1989).

[30] Karapet Ter-Mékérttschian and S. G. Wilson, eds., *Saint Irénée*: Εἰς Ἐπίδειξιν τοῦ Ἀποστολικοῦ Κηρύγματος. *The Proof of the Apostolic Preaching, with Seven Fragments*, PO 12.5 (Turnhout: Editions Brepols, 1989).

[31] John Behr, ed., *St Irenaeus on Lyons: On the Apostolic Preaching*, PPS 17 (Crestwood, KY: SVS Press, 1997).

[32] Adelin Rousseau, ed., *Irénée de Lyon: Démonstration de la Prédiction Apostolique*, SC 406 (Paris: du Cerf, 1995).

[33] Eusebius, *Historia Ecclesiastica*, ed. E. Schwartz (Berlin: GCS, 1952); English trans. Paul L. Maier, *Eusebius: The Church History* (Grand Rapids, MI: Kregel, 2007).

[34] K. Holl, ed., *Fragmente vornicänischer Kirchenväter aus den Sacra Parallela*, TU 20.2 (Leipzig: Hinrich, 1899).

[35] Discrepancies in numbering between Harvey's edition and the ANF translation are noted where they occur.

[36] G. W. H. Lampe, ed., *A Patristic Greek Lexicon* (Oxford: Oxford University Press, 1961).

Part 1

Assessing the Traditional Interpretation

1

The Apostolic Writings and the Use of γραφή

The evaluation of the traditional interpretation's claim that Irenaeus considers the apostolic writings to be scripture begins in this chapter with a critical assessment of its first substantiating argument: Irenaeus uses γραφή as a title for the apostolic writings, analogous to his references to the Jewish scriptures. This usage, it is claimed, demonstrates that the apostolic writings enjoy equivalent scriptural status in his thought. Ochagavia's assertion is broadly representative: "Irenaeus uses the expression ἡ γραφή to refer to a New Testament writing," and this demonstrates that "the New Testament was regarded as 'Scripture.'"[1] To assess the plausibility of this argument, this chapter undertakes a systematic analysis of Irenaeus' uses of γραφή throughout his writings—interpreted within the contexts of his immediate polemical agenda, his overarching theological arguments, and his historical milieu—in order to discover its particular meanings, intended referents, and possible scriptural significance. The results of this analysis will determine whether and to what extent Irenaeus applies γραφή as a scriptural title to the apostolic writings.

My contention is that the traditional interpretation has consistently misinterpreted either the intended referent or the implications of Irenaeus' terminology within those passages that have commonly been used as evidence, and has therefore misconstrued his intentions. Despite the assertions of the traditional interpretation, Irenaeus in fact refrains from giving a scriptural title to the apostolic writings, instead reserving this title for the Jewish scriptures. If my contention is correct, this would substantially weaken the claim of the traditional interpretation that the apostolic writings are considered by Irenaeus to be scripture alongside the Jewish scriptures, and would

---

[1] Ochagavia, *Visibile*, 176. Cf. Hoh, *Lehre*, 60; Metzger, *Canon*, 155; McDonald, *Formation*, 168; Sesboüé, "Preuve," 875; van den Eynde, *Normes*, 111; etc. While some interpreters caution against drawing conclusions solely on the basis of the use of γραφή in reference to a specific writing (Lawson, *Biblical Theology*, 50–1; Hitchcock, *Irenaeus*, 226; Campenhausen, *Formation*, 188; Steenberg, "Graphe," 33–6), this hesitancy is often expressed in order to deny that the *Shepherd of Hermas* was considered to be scripture by Irenaeus (Lawson), or to argue that the Pauline writings are to be considered scripture despite the lack of reference to them as γραφή (Hitchcock). In most cases, γραφή is nonetheless used as evidence for the scriptural status of the apostolic writings. Only Campenhausen sees Irenaeus' inconsistent use of γραφή as a reason not to interpret his use of the term in reference to the apostolic writings as proof of their scriptural status (*Formation*, 188 n. 204). Campenhausen ultimately affirms the scriptural status of the apostolic writings, but he does so primarily on the basis of the level of authority granted to them, which parallels that of the Jewish scriptures (discussed in the conclusion to Part 1).

suggest the existence of a largely unacknowledged conceptual distinction between the apostolic writings and the Jewish scriptures in his thought.

Interpreting Irenaeus' Use of γραφή

The analysis of Irenaeus' use of γραφή undertaken in this chapter is distinguished by a commitment to the principle that the meaning of a word is to be determined on the basis of its function within the particular context in which it occurs.[2] Following Wittgenstein's rejection of what he calls the "craving for generality" in interpretation,[3] I take it as axiomatic that words are not to be understood as static carriers of meaning but as "instruments characterized by their use."[4] The task of interpretation, then, is not to identify a stable meaning for a given term, which may then be applied to each particular situation in which it occurs, but to determine the particular meaning that arises within its use in a specific context.

According to this interpretative strategy, attempts to determine how γραφή functions for Irenaeus must resist the temptation to regard "the *word, rather than the sentence or speech-act*, [as] the basic unit of meaning to be investigated."[5] Previous analyses of Irenaeus have exhibited a certain vulnerability at this point: because γραφή is repeatedly used by Irenaeus to refer to those writings that possess scriptural status for him, the term is often treated as if it had inherent scriptural connotations (except perhaps in specific exceptional cases). In contrast to this tendency, the following analysis attempts to discover the meaning of Irenaeus' particular uses of γραφή within their immediate, proximate, and peripheral contexts.[6]

The peripheral context influencing Irenaeus' own use(s) of γραφή includes the standard usage and particular Christian significance of the term before Irenaeus, which should indicate the semantic range he inherited. This usage is often helpfully expressed in standard lexicons of ancient Greek, so long as Thiselton's advice is kept in mind: "Dictionary-entries about words are rule-of-thumb generalizations based on assumptions about characteristic contexts."[7] Γραφή, from the Greek root γραφ, meaning "to draw or write," is the term most commonly used within Greek antiquity to designate a "writing," and to refer specifically to the Jewish and Christian scriptures. *A Greek English Lexicon* defines γραφή as "representation by means of lines," and

---

[2] This semantic principle is associated especially with the linguistic philosophy of Ludwig Wittgenstein, observable in *The Blue and Brown Books* (Oxford: Basil Blackwell, 1969); and *Philosophical Investigations* (Oxford: Basil Blackwell, 1967).
[3] "The Blue Book," in *Blue and Brown Books*, 17. Wittgenstein also describes this attitude as "the contemptuous attitude towards the particular case" (18).
[4] Ibid., 67. As he explains, "We are inclined to forget that it is the particular use of a word only which gives the word its meaning" (69).
[5] Anthony Thiselton, "Semantics Serving Hermeneutics: 'Semantics and New Testament Interpretation,'" in *Thiselton On Hermeneutics: Collected Works with New Essays* (Grand Rapids, MI: Eerdmans, 2006), 193.
[6] Utilizing the three levels of context identified by Rescher, *Interpreting Philosophy*, 155.
[7] Thiselton, "Semantics," 196. However, he also notes, "words do indeed possess a stable core of meaning without which lexicography would be impossible."

therefore (1) "drawing or painting," and (2) "writing" or "that which is written";[8] and lists many substantiations of the varied uses of γραφή, commonly referring to registrations, letters, spurious writings, published writings, a written law, a catalogue, an inscription, and "the Holy Scripture" or, in the singular, "a particular passage" of scripture.[9] According to *The Greek Lexicon of the Roman and Byzantine Periods*, the use of γραφή during this period signifies "a writing," as well as "Scripture, the holy writ," a "passage of Scripture," and a reading, letter, or epistle.[10] Within the Christian culture of the Roman empire in the following centuries after Christ, γραφή becomes increasingly correlated with the concept of "scripture," though its original use signifying "a writing" is not diminished.

The Latin term *scriptura* and the Armenian term գիր (*gir*)—the standard translations of γραφή in the Latin and Armenian translations of Irenaeus' works—are both used similarly to γραφή. *Scriptura* is virtually synonymous with γραφή, commonly used to signify "a writing; written characters," while also having among its more specific uses "the Scriptures" or "a passage of Scripture," especially as it is used within a Christian context.[11] Whenever the Greek New Testament or other Greek Christian writings are translated into Latin (including *Adversus haereses*), γραφή is overwhelmingly translated as *scriptura* regardless of context.[12] Գիր is used similarly, signifying "script" or "writing," as well as "book" or "Scripture," often when used in plural form (գիրք).[13]

These catalogued uses of γραφή (and *scriptura* and գիր) suggest that while it is routinely used to refer to "the scriptures" in Christian writing, its use as a scriptural title is essentially a contextual reference, in the same way that in English the phrase "the book" can clearly refer to scripture in one context, while in other contexts it can refer to *any* book, lacking any religious significance (this analogy would be closer if contemporary English operated without a distinct word for "scripture," as is the case in Greek, Latin, and Armenian). The mere occurrence of the term "book" does not indicate scriptural status for its referent; only context and textual clues (e.g., *this* book) will determine its meaning. The same is true for γραφή. This term is what Thiselton has identified as a "polymorphous concept,"[14] whose meaning must be determined within the context of its use in each particular instance.

---

[8] Henry George Liddell and Robert Scott, *A Greek-English Lexicon*, 9th ed. (Oxford: Clarendon Press, 1983), 359–60.
[9] Ibid.
[10] E. A. Sophocles, *Greek Lexicon of the Roman and Byzantine Periods* (Cambridge, MA: Harvard University Press, 1914), 339–40. Cf. the similar definition in G. Abbott-Smith, *A Manual Greek Lexicon of the New Testament* (Edinburgh: T&T Clark, 1922), 95.
[11] Charlton T. Lewis and Charles Short, *A Latin Dictionary*, rev. ed. (Oxford: Clarendon Press, 1962), 1648–9.
[12] There are limited exceptions where γραφή is translated as another term (e.g., *litteras* in *Adv. haer.* 3.3.3), as well as instances where another term is translated as *scriptura* (e.g., ἀντιγράφοις in *Adv. Haer.* 5.30.1).
[13] Robert W. Thomson, *An Introduction to Classical Armenian* (Delmar: Caravan Books, 1975), 169. Cf. Matthias Bedrossian, *New Dictionary: Armenian-English* (Venice: S. Lazarus Armenian Academy, 1875–9), 121.
[14] "'Faith,' 'Flesh,' and 'Truth' as Context-Dependent Concepts: 'Language-Games and Polymorphous Concepts,'" in *Thiselton on Hermeneutics*, 183–4.

M. C. Steenberg's investigation of Irenaeus' use of γραφή represents the most comprehensive and nuanced attempt to create a logical and consistent framework for accurately interpreting his meaning to date.[15] On the basis of his analysis of every occurrence of γραφή in *Adversus haereses*, Steenberg proposes a rule for determining the meaning of the term in any specific instance based on his principle of "delimited" versus "non-delimited" use. According to this rule, when γραφή is delimited by specifying words and phrases like "this," "of the prophets," and so on, these references are less likely to be scriptural titles and must be determined by context.[16] In this way he is able to account for obvious non-scriptural uses of the term that have proved problematic for prior interpreters.[17] On the other hand,

> what is eminently clear in Irenaeus is that non-delimited use of the term is *always* scriptural in its implication. To refer simply to "the writings" (αἱ γραφαί) or "the writing" (ἡ γραφή), without further qualification, is *always and without exception* to indicate a passage or concept drawn from a book of scriptural authority ... Never does he use an unqualified instance of γραφή in reference to a text that he does not regard as of Christian scriptural possession in accord with the apostolic tradition.[18]

Founded on his opening assumption that the Jewish scriptures and apostolic writings together are considered to be scripture for Irenaeus,[19] Steenberg's resulting principle of "delimited" versus "non-delimited" use allows him to analyze Irenaeus' use of γραφή in reference to less certain texts. This analysis results in the identification of a scriptural title assigned to the *Shepherd of Hermas*. This leads Steenberg to the conclusion that Irenaeus' understanding of scripture extended much more widely beyond the Jewish scriptures and apostolic writings to include many other writings that authentically expressed the "Christocentric vision of the cosmos,"[20] despite the fact that this is at odds with Irenaeus' uniform insistence on "the prophets, the Lord, and the apostles" as the only sources of revelatory authority.[21] This improbable conclusion

---

[15] M. C. Steenberg, "Irenaeus on Scripture, Graphe, and the Status of Hermas," *SVTQ* 53.1 (2009): 29–66.
[16] Somewhat problematically, in these instances Steenberg advocates that a determination can be made based on whether the reference "refers to a title from a commonly accepted canon" (52).
[17] Cf. the opening discussion in Section 1.2B.
[18] Ibid., 52–3; emphasis added. Hoh, *Lehre*, has also set out a rule for interpreting γραφή similar to Steenberg's. He explains,

> Allein wenn Ir. von den "Lesern dieser (sc. seiner) Schrift" spricht, so ist der Unterschied von einem Zitate wie etwa: "die Schrift" sagt, doch nicht zu verkennen. Ir. Gebraucht ἡ γραφή = Hl. Schrift, ohne Autornamen oder sonst nähere Bestimmungen beizufügen, also absolut, wie einen terminus technicus. Man vergegenwärtige sich die 135 Fälle, wo die Schrift, ἡ γραφή, als etwas Bekanntes angerufen wird; durch ein paar Stellen wird der sonstige Sprachgebrauch nicht aufgehoben. (62)

Cf. Werner, *Paulinismus*, 36–7.
[19] Steenberg briefly defends this assumption by claiming that the apostolic writings are seen to be "of equal merit and stature" with the Jewish scriptures (32). The plausibility of this claim is evaluated in the conclusion to Part 1.
[20] Ibid., 65–6.
[21] Cf. 1.8.1., for example. See p. 31 n. 89, below.

arises as a result of constructing his principle of "delimited" versus "non-delimited" use upon a prior assumption that Irenaeus considers both the Jewish scriptures and apostolic writings to be scripture. His principle is therefore clearly unsuitable as a methodological device for determining Irenaeus' uses of γραφή in reference to the apostolic writings themselves. However, when "delimited" versus "non-delimited" use is properly mapped on to the immediate, proximate, and peripheral contexts in which γραφή occurs it may provide a useful guide, which contributes to the interpretation of Irenaeus' use of γραφή undertaken in this chapter.

1.1. The Use of γραφή as a Title for the Jewish Scriptures

The investigation into the implications of Irenaeus' uses of γραφή begins in this section with a brief examination of his use of γραφή in reference to the Jewish scriptures. The conclusions of the traditional interpretation concerning this aspect of Irenaeus' use of γραφή are not contested; rather, the findings of this examination provide a baseline of Irenaeus' use of γραφή in reference to a written collection that he unquestionably believed to possess scriptural status, against which his use of the term in reference to the apostolic writings may be compared in the following section.

Irenaeus is not concerned with demonstrating the scriptural status of the Jewish scriptures, and he neglects to give a deliberate defense of their authoritative status in his writings. Such a defense would be unnecessary, as their unique scriptural status is a necessary assumption within the proto-orthodox Christian community to which Irenaeus belongs. The Jewish scriptures had been inherited by the Christian movement at its inception from its parent Jewish religion. Jesus attests to and even requires acceptance of the divine status of the Jewish scriptures by his followers throughout the canonical gospels,[22] and Paul and the other apostolic authors similarly attest to this reality throughout their writings.[23] Even the Valentinians, Marcionites, and other opponents that Irenaeus is writing against, though they alter their interpretation or claim that they originate from a different God, nevertheless acknowledge the scriptural status of the Jewish scriptures, to be reinterpreted or ascribed to lesser deities.[24] Irenaeus' argument in *Adversus haereses* is a response to his opponents' acceptance of the Jewish scriptures as scripture and resulting reinterpretation of them to demonstrate their own systems, and his arguments against them are consistently based on the presumption of a shared belief in the divine authority of these scriptures. He writes that his opponents "select passages from the Scriptures [τῶν γραφῶν] in order to prove that Our Lord announced another Father besides the Creator of the universe," and demonstrates how

---

[22] Mt. 21:42, Mt. 22:29, Mt. 26:54, Mk 14:49, Lk. 4:21, Lk. 24:27, Jn 5:39, Jn 7:42, Jn 10:34-36, Jn 13:18, etc.

[23] Acts 1:15-17, Acts 17:2-3, Acts 18:28, Rom. 1:2, 1 Cor. 15:3-4, Gal. 3:8, 2 Tim. 3:15-16, Js. 2:8, 2 Pet. 1:20, etc.

[24] 3.12.12: "All the rest who are puffed up with a false knowledge indeed recognize the Scriptures, but they pervert their interpretation." Cf.1.pre.1, 1.8.1, 1.9.4, 1.20.2-3, 1.30.11, 2.27.3, 3.pre.1, 3.11.7, 4.35.1, etc.

"they violently stretch" the passages they cite from the prophets and "make believe" and "lie" when they apply them to their own system (1.19.1).

These Jewish scriptures that function as scripture for Irenaeus are consistently designated αἱ γραφαί (*Scripturae*), as in his statement that "the treasure hid in the scriptures [ταῖς γραφαῖς] is Christ" (4.26.1). Similarly, citations from individual passages of the Jewish scriptures are often introduced as ἡ γραφή (*Scriptura*), as in his citation of Genesis 2:2 that is introduced, "φησιν ἡ γραφή" (5.28.3). Throughout Irenaeus' writings, he uses the term γραφή a total of 172 times,[25] the majority of which are explicit references to the Jewish scriptures.[26]

Many of Irenaeus' citations of and allusions to the Jewish scriptures use γραφή in such a way as to indicate that it is not intended to signify merely "(a) writing" in these instances but is functioning as a title for this scriptural collection, just as it has previously functioned within the apostolic writings and other early Christian works. The majority of Irenaeus' citations of the Jewish scriptures introduced with γραφή conform to Steenberg's principle of "non-delimited" use, signifying the generic "*the writings*" instead of specifying "*this* writing," "*Isaiah's* writings," "the *holy* writings," and so on. Irenaeus is confident that simply saying "*quemadmodum Scriptura ait*"

---

[25] This total does not include fourteen instances of γραφή that occur within quotations of other writings, and are therefore considered not to reflect Irenaeus' own usage (3.12.1, 3.16.3, 3.16.5, 3.18.3 [twice], 4.5.1, 4.5.2, 4.10.1, 4.21.1, 4.23.1, 5.32.2, *Dem*. 67, *Dem*. 90, *Dem*. 97). A number of scholars have compiled lists of Irenaeus' use of γραφή and related phrases. Reynders, *Lexique Comparé du Texte Grec et des Versions Latine, Arménienne et Syriaque de l'"Adversus Haereses" de saint Irénée* (Leuven: Peeters, 1954), lists 119 instances of *scriptura* in *Adversus haereses* (2:291); and in *Vocabulaire de la "Démonstration" et des fragments de S. Irénée* (Louvain: Éditions de Chevetogne, 1958), lists nine instances of ḳhp in the *Demonstration* (16). Hoh, *Lehre*, presents 135 instances of γραφή used as a term for "scripture" throughout Irenaeus' writings (190–7), fifty-seven of which he believes refer to the Jewish scriptures, a few to the apostolic writings, and the majority to both collections as a unified whole (62). Steenberg, "Graphe," has compiled the most complete list to date, listing 171 instances of γραφή (or *scriptura*) within *Adversus haereses*, as well as other related phrases he considers to have scriptural significance (37–51). His list does not include eleven instances in the *Demonstration* and fragments from lost writings, and does include eleven occurrences of γραφή in *Adversus haereses* within quotations. In addition, his list has missed three instances of γραφή (a second instance in 3.1.1, a second instance in 3.3.3, and a seventh instance in 3.21.2), and has added two instances (he repeats the same "*Scriptura*" twice in 3.12.12, and opts to include an instance where *scriptura* is a translation of ἀντίγραφος in 5.30.1).

[26] Ninety-six explicit references to the Jewish scriptures are found in 1.18.2, 1.18.3, 1.19.1, 1.22.1, 2.2.5, 2.9.1, 2.13.3, 2.22.2, 2.28.3, 2.28.4, 2.28.7, 2.30.7, 2.35.3, 3.6.1, 3.6.3, 3.12.8, 3.19.2 (four times), 3.20.1, 3.21.1 (three times), 3.21.2 (seven times), 3.21.3 (five times), 3.21.5, 3.23.2, 3.23.3, 4.10.1 (twice), 4.11.1 (twice), 4.11.3, 4.16.1, 4.16.4, 4.20.1, 4.23.1, 4.23.2, 4.24.1, 4.24.2 (three times), 4.25.2, 4.26.1 (four times), 4.26.5, 4.27.1 (four times), 4.30.2, 4.31.1 (four times), 4.33.15, 4.35.1, 4.35.4 (three times), 4.40.3, 5.5.1 (twice), 5.5.2, 5.15.2, 5.15.4, 5.16.1, 5.17.1, 5.21.2 (three times), 5.23.1 (twice), 5.28.3, *Dem*. 24, *Dem*. 32, *Dem*. 44, *Dem*. 52 (twice), *Dem*. 62, *Dem*. 71, *frg*. 19, *frg*. 39 (ANF 40). In thirty-eight instances the referent of γραφή cannot be conclusively identified from within its immediate context: 1.1.3, 1.9.4, 1.10.3, 2.pre.1, 2.10.1, 2.10.2, 2.24.3 (twice), 2.27.1, 2.27.2 (twice), 2.28.2 (twice), 2.28.3 (four times), 2.28.4, 2.28.7 (four times), 2.30.6, 2.35.2, 2.35.4 (twice), 3.12.9 (twice), 3.12.12 (twice), 3.16.4, 4.pre.4, 4.32.1, 4.33.8 (twice), 4.34.5, 5.14.4, and *frg*. 2. In twenty-eight instances γραφή initially appears to refer to the apostolic writings: 1.6.3, 2.30.6, 2.35.4 (twice), 3.pre, 3.5.1, 3.12.9, 5.20.2 (twice), discussed in Section 1.2A; and 1.8.1, 1.8.2, 1.9.1, 1.9.3, 1.27.4, 2.24.4 (twice), 2.27.2, 3.1.1 (twice), 3.2.1 (twice), 3.2.2, 3.4.1, 3.12.5, 3.12.12, 4.41.2, 5.30.1, 5.30.2, discussed in Section 1.2B. In ten instances it appears to refer to other writings outside of the Jewish scriptures and apostolic writings: 1.20.1, 3.3.3 (twice), 3.6.4, 3.11.9, 3.17.4, 4.20.2, 5.pre, 5.33.4, and *Dem*. 1, discussed in Section 1.2B.

(4.30.2)²⁷ is sufficient to indicate which "writing" he is referring to. Thus, for instance, he can say, "the Scriptures do teach us [*Scripturae nos docent*] that this world was made complete by God" (2.28.3) in an allusion to Genesis 2:4,²⁸ indicating that *Scripturae* is functioning as a title for the Jewish scriptures. Similarly, in the *Demonstration* a passage from Genesis 15:6 is introduced, "God testified of him, by the Holy Spirit, saying in Scripture [Գիրս]" (*Dem.* 24).

The same patterns of use may be observed in the way he discusses the Jewish scriptures. In Book 5 Irenaeus urges, "let [these heretics] read the Scriptures [*Scripturas*], and they will find that our predecessors advanced beyond seven hundred, eight hundred, nine hundred years of age" (5.5.1). In this passage, Irenaeus' use of γραφή makes sense only if it is intended as a specific reference to the Jewish scriptures, and he feels no need to specify *which* writings he is referring to, indicating that αἱ γραφαί is functioning as a title for the Jewish scriptures. This is similarly evident when, speaking of the prophets foreseeing the advent of Christ, he asks, "how do the Scriptures [*Scripturae*] testify of Him, unless all things had ever been revealed and shown to believers by one and the same God?" (4.11.1). Comments of this type are common for Irenaeus,²⁹ indicating that he regularly uses γραφή as a title for the Jewish scriptures.

Particular uses of γραφή in reference to the Jewish scriptures may also lack evidence that it functions as a title for them or even exhibit evidence that the term is *not* functioning in this way. Thus, for example, when Irenaeus refers to the Jewish scriptures as "ἡ θεία γραφή" (*frg.* 39),³⁰ this delimited use of γραφή as "the *divine* writings" gives no indication that γραφή itself is meant to signify anything beyond "writing," as Irenaeus has here specified which writings he is referring to. Similarly, in Irenaeus' claim that "the son of God is implanted everywhere throughout [Moses'] writings [*Scripturis ejus*]" (4.10.1), *Scripturis* refers to (part of) the Jewish scriptures, yet it is clearly intended to signify only the generic "writings" in this instance, as the translators indicate. Irenaeus' use of γραφή, even when in reference to the Jewish scriptures, does not automatically indicate that it is functioning as a title. However, the majority of Irenaeus' particular uses of γραφή in reference to the Jewish scriptures demonstrate that he does intend it as a title for them, indicating his common practice.

1.2. The Traditional Interpretation: "Scripture" and the Apostolic Writings

Having examined Irenaeus' use of γραφή in reference to the Jewish scriptures in the previous section and concluded that his frequency and methods of use indicate that γραφή often functions as a title for the Jewish scriptures, the subject of investigation in this section is the traditional interpretation's claim that Irenaeus' use of γραφή as a

---

²⁷ Cf. 1.22.1, 3.6.1, 3.21.1, 3.23.2, 3.23.3, 4.11.1, 4.16.1, 4.16.4, 4.20.1, 4.27.1, 4.31.1, 5.5.1, 5.5.2, 5.15.2, 5.16.1, 5.23.1, *Dem.* 32.
²⁸ This allusion is confirmed by Unger (ACW 65:155).
²⁹ Cf. 1.18.1-3, 1.19.1, 2.35.3, 3.21.1-3, 4.10.1, 4.23.1, 4.23.2, 4.24.1-2, etc.
³⁰ *Frg.* 40 in ANF.

title ("*the writings*") also includes the apostolic writings, thereby extending to them the same scriptural status possessed by the Jewish scriptures. There are a number of passages that are routinely offered as evidence that Irenaeus uses γραφή as a title for the apostolic writings. These may be divided into two categories: there are passages in which (A) it is questionable whether the apostolic writings are in fact the intended referent of γραφή; and those in which (B) it is questionable whether γραφή is intended as a scriptural title, rather than signifying the specific "writing" he is discussing. The following investigation takes place in two parts, following these categories.

This chapter is not concerned with the question of whether the apostolic writings possess similar authority to the Jewish scriptures in Irenaeus' thought.[31] It is beyond doubt that the apostolic writings and Jewish scriptures are both of utmost authority for Irenaeus, to the extent that the question as to which collection is more authoritative becomes nonsensical.[32] The entirety of his argument throughout *Adversus haereses* is based on consistent appeals to both the Jewish scriptures and the apostolic writings, as observed when he proves the first article of the rule of truth—that "There is one God Almighty, who created all things through His Word"—by appealing to both:

> Just as Scripture [*Scriptura*] says, "For by the word of the Lord the heavens were made, and all their host by the breath of His mouth" [Ps. 32:6]. And again: "All things were made through Him and without Him was made not a thing" [Jn 1:3]. (1.22.1)

The unique revelatory authority of the apostolic writings is therefore not in question, and does not impact the question posed by this chapter as to whether the traditional interpretation's substantiating argument that Irenaeus uses γραφή as a scriptural title for the apostolic writings is correct.

A. Passages in Which the Apostolic Writings May Not Be the Referent of γραφή

This examination begins with a series of analyses of passages that traditionally have been considered to indicate that γραφή functions as a title for the apostolic writings alongside the Jewish scriptures, but which invite further evaluation as to the intended referent of γραφή. These passages include an apparent citation of a Pauline passage as αἱ γραφαί in 1.6.3; the use of the phrase "*ostensiones ex Scripturis*" in relation to the apostolic writings in 2.35.4, 3.pre, 3.5.1, and 3.12.9; and the use of "*Scripturis dominicis*" in 2.35.4, 2.30.6, and 5.20.2.

---

[31] This question represents the third claim of the traditional interpretation used as evidence of the scriptural status of the apostolic writings identified in the introduction (p. 2). The relation between authority and scriptural status is discussed in detail in the conclusion to Part 1.

[32] As Lawson, *Biblical Theology*, notes, "It would never have occurred to Irenaeus … to estimate the position of the Apostolic writings apart from the ancient Scriptures or, for that matter, to contrast the words of Jesus with the words of either the Prophets or of the Apostles. To him, all God-ordained authority is one" (52).

1.6.3: Αἱ γραφαὶ and Galatians 5:21

The first passage under investigation is found near the beginning of Book 1. In ch. 6 Irenaeus describes the Valentinian anthropology, consisting of three classes of people, and their resulting system(s) of salvation. He explains that while the ensouled persons (the category in which Christians find themselves) must perform good works and demonstrate faith, the spiritual persons (the Valentinians, according to their own teaching) are saved by nature, and therefore do not require good works. Irenaeus offers the illustration of a piece of gold being dipped in mud and nevertheless remaining gold, being unable to lose the beauty it has by nature—a metaphor that the Valentinians believe describes themselves. On this basis there is no need for good works, as salvation is assured regardless of what practices they engage in. Commenting on this system and its implications, Irenaeus says,

> Because of this doctrine, the most perfect among them shamelessly do all the forbidden things, about which the Scriptures give guarantee that "those who do such things shall not inherit the kingdom of God"[33] [περὶ ὧν αἱ γραφαὶ διαβεβαιοῦνται τοὺς ποιοῦντας αὐτὰ βασιλείαν Θεοῦ μὴ κληρονομήσειν]. Food sacrificed to idols they eat without scruple, thinking they in no way defile themselves by it. And they are the first to assemble at every heathen festival held in honor of the idols for the sake of pleasure, with the result that some do not abstain even from the spectacle loathsome to God and men where men fight wild beasts and each other in homicidal fashion. (1.6.3)

On the basis of the reference to Galatians immediately following "αἱ γραφαὶ διαβεβαιοῦνται," this passage has been understood to demonstrate that Irenaeus uses γραφή as a scriptural title for the Pauline writings. Hitchcock, for example, comments, "in I.6.3 we have a quotation from Gal. v.21 ascribed to the Scriptures."[34] Upon closer examination, however, this interpretation suffers from a number of difficulties.

In this passage, Irenaeus' claim is that "the Scriptures" promise that those who eat food sacrificed to idols, attend festivals and gladiator games, or commit fornication or adultery as the Valentinians do will not inherit the kingdom of heaven. If Galatians 5:21 is indeed the "Scripture" that Irenaeus describes, it is puzzling that this passage bears such little resemblance to the description he gives on the basis of it. No injunction against eating meat sacrificed to idols appears in the passage Irenaeus has quoted,[35] or indeed anywhere else in Galatians, and Paul in fact explicitly permits the practice in other places.[36] The examples of attending pagan festivals and gladiator games are also absent. Only fornication and adultery are consistent with Paul's admonition in

---

[33] Gal. 5:21.
[34] Hitchcock, *Irenaeus*, 227. Cf. Robert M. Grant, *The Formation of the New Testament* (New York: Harper & Row, 1965), 153; Blanchard, *Sources*, 125; Benoit, *Irénée*, 140; Lawson, *Biblical Theology*, 51. Werner, *Paulinismus*, argues against this that Irenaeus only referred to the Pauline letters as "scripture" because the Gnostics did so (43–4).
[35] Cf. Gal. 5:16-21.
[36] Cf. 1 Cor. 8:1-10.

Galatians, and many of the additional transgressions listed by Paul are absent from Irenaeus' description.³⁷

An alternative interpretation is plausible, in which, rather than referring directly to the Galatians verse, Irenaeus is understood to state that the Jewish scriptures prohibit these things, while referencing the apostolic writings in support of his contention about the Jewish scriptures. According to this interpretation, Αἱ γραφαὶ functions as the title of the Jewish scriptures, which are better equipped to make sense of the examples he gives,³⁸ and his citation of Galatians acts as a secondary source to support his interpretation of "the Scriptures." In similar fashion one could write, "All the gospels declare that 'the Lord discoursed with the disciples after His resurrection from the dead' (4.26.1)," using a citation from Irenaeus to support the contention that the gospels in fact make this claim. This sentence, though justified, could be misinterpreted as a claim that the writings of Irenaeus are part of the gospels, if the writer's position on the subject were not already known. Irenaeus does precisely the same thing more explicitly in 4.26.1, where he writes, "The Lord discoursed with the disciples ... proving to them from the Scriptures themselves [*ex ipsis Scripturis*] 'that Christ must suffer, and enter into his glory,'" citing Luke 24:26 and 47, and unquestionably in this instance using *Scripturis* to refer to the Jewish scriptures known to Jesus rather than the passage he immediately cites from Luke. The direct parallel to 1.6.3 in this passage, in which *Scripturis* introduces a citation from the apostolic writings that Irenaeus is unquestionably not titling "scripture," suggests the same intention in 1.6.3 to cite the apostolic writings in support of the Jewish scriptures, which alone are titled αἱ γραφαί.

This alternative interpretation of 1.6.3 receives additional support from the fact that Irenaeus uses the plural αἱ γραφαὶ in both passages. In every other instance outside of 1.6.3 and 4.26.1 where Irenaeus introduces a citation as γραφή he uses the singular "ἡ γραφή φησιν" ("*Scriptura ait*"),³⁹ indicating a single passage. His consistency in this matter indicates that his use of the plural αἱ γραφαὶ in 1.6.3 is not intended as a title for the next passage he cites, as 4.26.1 demonstrates. Benoit, who is otherwise convinced that the Pauline writings were considered scripture by Irenaeus, nevertheless states that "the term *Scriptura* itself is never directly applied to a pauline passage," for he believes that 1.6.3 is best described as an "allusion" to Paul that lacks a formal introductory formula.⁴⁰

Given the similarity between Irenaeus' use in 1.6.3 and 4.26.1, as well as his consistent history of use of the singular γραφή when citing scriptural passages, it is unlikely that his use of the plural form in 1.6.3 is intended as a descriptive title for the Galatians verse. The alternative interpretation that αἱ γραφαί refers instead to the

---

[37] The Galatians examples of "sorcery, enmities, strife, jealousy, anger, quarrels, dissensions, factions, envy, drunkenness, carousing" (Gal. 5:20-21; NRSV) are left entirely unaddressed.
[38] Cf. Hos. 11:2; Isa. 2:6; Ps. 11:5; Isa. 33:15; Exod. 20:14; Hos. 4:18, etc.
[39] Cf. 3.6.1, 4.11.1, 4.16.1, 5.15.2, 5.16.1, etc. I have not discovered a single instance where a plural from of *scriptura*/γραφή is used to introduce a single scriptural citation.
[40] Benoit, *Irénée*, 140; my trans. Nevertheless, he is convinced that "'γραφή' désigne sans aucun doute l'Épître aux Galates (5/21)." Campenhausen, *Formation*, also maintains that the letters of Paul are never termed "scripture," and directs the reader to Benoit's section on Irenaeus' use of Paul (188 n. 204).

Jewish scriptures is compatible with these findings, and is able to avoid the problems of consistency in the traditional interpretation by shifting the subject of the injunction from the specific verse in Galatians to the whole of the Jewish scriptures in order to make sense of the examples Irenaeus gives. If this interpretation is correct, this passage does not provide evidence for the traditional interpretation's claim that Irenaeus uses γραφή as a title for the apostolic writings alongside the Jewish scriptures.

"Ostensiones ex Scripturis"

Irenaeus' use of the phrase *"ostensiones ex Scripturis"* is also commonly understood as evidence that he uses γραφή as a title for the apostolic writings. Because his "proofs from the Scriptures" are frequently composed of citations from both the Jewish scriptures and the apostolic writings, this phrase is often understood to constitute the claim that the apostolic writings are part of the "Scriptures" referred to. Campenhausen remarks that for Irenaeus, the New Testament writings "serve to construct a formal 'proof from scripture,' such as had previously been drawn only from the Old Testament."[41] The most commonly adduced passages occur in the conclusion to Book 2 and the preface to Book 3. At the end of Book 2 Irenaeus declares,

> Since the Scriptures themselves [*ipsis Scripturis*] preach this very doctrine much more obviously and clearly, for such as do not have a depraved mind toward them, we will supply a special book, which will utilize these Scriptures [*has Scripturas*], and so, for all who love the truth, we will bring into clear light proofs from the divine Scriptures [*reddentes ex Scripturis diuinis probationes apponemus in medio omnibus amantibus ueritatem*]. (2.35.4)

He restates in the beginning of Book 3, "*In hoc autem tertio ex Scripturis inferemus ostensiones*" (3.pre). Then, after spending the first five chapters defending the validity of the apostolic preaching, Irenaeus dedicates the remainder of Book 3 to demonstrating that only one God is declared in scripture using both the Jewish scriptures and the apostolic writings to prove his contention. This evidence leads many to the seemingly straightforward conclusion that the apostolic writings for Irenaeus are part of "the Scriptures" from which he gives his proof.[42] Thus Steenberg, for example, argues on

---

[41] Campenhausen, *Formation*, 185, cf. 187.
[42] Benoit, *Irénée*, claims that Irenaeus' promise of "proofs from the divine Scriptures" in 2.35.4, which is fulfilled using numerous citations from the Gospel accounts, shows that "les évangiles sont également des Écritures divines" (121). Similarly, Hoh, *Lehre*, includes 2.35.4 and 3.pre as evidence of the gospels as scripture because Irenaeus' promise of "Beweis aus den 'Schriften'" in Book 3 includes "besonders die vier Evv" (64). Everett Ferguson, "Factors Leading to the Selection and Closure of the New Testament Canon: A Survey of Some Recent Studies," in *The Canon Debate*, ed. Lee Martin McDonald and James A. Sanders (Peabody, MA: Hendrickson, 2002), also claims that the "proofs from the Scriptures" mentioned in 3.pre refer to the Gospel accounts (314). Lawson, *Biblical Theology*, claims on the basis of Irenaeus' announcement of his task in 3.pre to give proofs from the scriptures, and subsequent defense of the authority of the four apostolic Gospel accounts, that "The Four Gospels are to Irenaeus in consequence clearly authoritative Scripture" (42). Cf. also Denis. M. Farkasfalvy, "Theology of Scripture in St. Irenaeus," *RBén* 78 (1968): 325 n. 1; Hitchcock, *Irenaeus*, 226; Eric Osborn, *Irenaeus of Lyons* (Cambridge: Cambridge University Press, 2001), 178.

the basis of these two passages above that "it is clear that Irenaeus here means the 'scriptures of the Lord,' i.e., the Gospels and apostolic writings."[43]

However, this conclusion has been questioned by Bernard Sesboüé,[44] who argues on the basis of Irenaeus' use of the same phrase in 3.5.1 that his "proof from the Scriptures" is not a proof from the apostolic writings and Jewish scriptures but a proof from the Jewish scriptures *by* the apostolic writings. Irenaeus writes,

> *Traditione igitur quae est ab apostolis sic se habente in Ecclesia et permanente apud nos, reuertamur ad eam quae est ex Scripturis ostensionem eorum qui Euangelium conscripserunt apostolorum, in quibus*[45] *conscripserunt de Deo sententiam, ostendentes quoniam Dominus noster Iesus Christus ueritas est et mendacium in eo non est.* (3.5.1)

Unger translates the relevant clause in this passage, "let us return to the proof from the Scriptures of the apostles, of those who wrote the Gospel," and the evident connotations are often taken as proof that Irenaeus applies the scriptural title γραφή to the apostolic writings.[46] Commenting on this passage, Benoit states, "This text is clear: the proof from the Scriptures consists in relying on the written Gospel, that is to say the text of the four gospels."[47] However, Sesboüé proposes that a different translation of this passage is necessary. Noting that both the current SC edition and the earlier edition of Sagnard had difficulty in translating this passage,[48] and that Rousseau–Doutreleau even resorted to amending the Latin text in order to make it say more clearly what they believed it should say (influencing all subsequent translations),[49] Sesboüé argues against them that this passage "becomes, in our opinion, entirely clear, without need of correction, if one considers that the Scriptures designate here in the thought of Irenaeus that which we name the Old Testament."[50] Interpreted in this way, the passage

---

[43] Steenberg, "Graphe," 40–1.
[44] Bernard Sesboüé, "La preuve par les Ecritures chez S. Irenee: A propos d'un texte difficile du livre III de l'*Adversus haereses*," *NRTh* 103 (1981): 872–87.
[45] Rousseau–Doutreleau have amended *ex quibus* to *in quibus* here (SC 211:52-3; discussed in 210:245).
[46] ACW 64:36. Roberts-Donaldson translate, "let us revert to the Scriptural proof furnished by those apostles who did also write the Gospel" (ANF 1:417), with similar connotations. Rousseau–Doutreleau translate "revenons à la preuve tirée des Écritures qui nous viennent de ceux d'entre les apôtres qui ont mis par écrit l'Évangile" (SC 211:53), which could be taken in either sense, though their comment on this passage (SC 210:245 n. 2) suggests the implication that the gospels are being called "*Scripturis.*" Unger agrees with Rousseau–Doutreleau's conjecture (ACW 64:36 n. 1). Campenhausen, *Formation*, cites 3.5.1 as proof that Irenaeus' purpose in Book 3 is "providing scriptural proof from the New Testament" (190). Cf. similar claims made by Hoh, *Lehre*, 64; Blanchard, *Sources*, 126; Charles Hill, "The Truth above All Demonstration: Scripture in the Patristic Period to Augustine," in *The Enduring Authority of the Christian Scriptures*, ed. D. A. Carson (Grand Rapids, MI: Eerdmans, 2016), 76.
[47] Benoit, *Irénée*, 121; my trans.
[48] Cf. Sagnard's SC 34:121; SC 211:52-3 and 210:245.
[49] Sesboüé, "Preuve" (872–3), describes that in their translation of 3.5.1, Rousseau–Doutreleau sought to relate "*ex quibus*" to "*ex Scripturis*," and, finding that they could not do so, proposed the correction "*in quibus*" (SC 210:52-3, 211:245). Unger states that he has accepted Rousseau–Doutreleau's emendation (ACW 64:36 n. 1).
[50] Ibid., 873; my trans.

becomes much easier to translate,⁵¹ with the implication that "The evangelical writings consist of a proof drawn from the Scriptures."⁵²

If Sesboüé is correct, this also makes sense of the intended referent of "*ostensiones ex Scripturis*" in 2.35.4 and 3.pre and other places he uses it.⁵³ Irenaeus is not titling the apostolic writings "*Scripturis*," but is making use of the apostolic writings in order to prove the teachings of the Jewish scriptures, for the apostolic writings provide their proper interpretation.⁵⁴ It is for precisely this reason that Behr also agrees with Sesboüé's translation and its implications. Behr believes that Irenaeus considers the apostolic writings themselves to constitute the true interpretation of the Jewish scriptures; this is both their conscious purpose and a central reason for their unique authority for Christianity.⁵⁵ The apostolic writings are the true interpretation of the Jewish scriptures in light of the Christ event, which illuminates their true objective. Because of this understanding, Behr believes that the "proofs from the Scriptures" that Irenaeus refers to are in fact "expositions of the apostolic demonstrations from Scripture."⁵⁶ "The Scriptures" in these passages refers to the Jewish scriptures, and Irenaeus is seeking to present the apostolic demonstrations from these scriptures to show that both the scriptures and the apostolic writings proclaim one and the same God.⁵⁷

Echoing the implications of Sesboüé's translation, Behr maintains that the relevant clause in 3.5.1 should be translated, "let us revert to the demonstration from the Scriptures provided by those apostles who wrote the Gospel."⁵⁸ He explains that for Irenaeus, the preaching of the apostles is nothing more or less than "the Gospel proclaimed in accordance with the Scriptures."⁵⁹ His translation clarifies Irenaeus' intention to prove his claims from the apostolic demonstrations of the scriptures, showing how they present the proper interpretation of the Jewish scriptures, which is of course the Gospel. I would suggest a similar translation:

> Therefore, the tradition which is from the apostles thus being held in the Church and persevering among us, we may return to the previously-mentioned [3.pre] demonstration from the Scriptures, which is from those of the apostles who have put the Gospel into writing, in [or "from"]⁶⁰ which they have written the teaching of God.

---

⁵¹ Sesboüé proposes the following translation: "revenons à la preuve tirée des Ecritures qui nous vient de ceux d'entre les apôtres qui ont mis par écrit l'Evangile; à partir de ces Ecritures ils ont exposé la doctrine sur Dieu" (873).
⁵² Ibid; my trans.
⁵³ Cf. 3.12.9, 4.24.1, 4.34.5.
⁵⁴ Further analysis of 3.5.1 occurs in Sections 3.1B and 3.3A.
⁵⁵ Behr, *Identifying*, 132–9.
⁵⁶ Behr, *Nicaea*, 113, Cf. 45; *Identifying*, 76, 88.
⁵⁷ Cf. the discussion of the apostolic writings as the true interpretation of the Jewish scriptures in Section 3.3.
⁵⁸ Behr, *Identifying*, 126. Steenberg, "Graphe," agrees with this translation and its implications for the referent of *Scripturis* here, stating that "proofs from the Scriptures" is "a reference to the apostolic writers forming their arguments from the OT" (41).
⁵⁹ Ibid., 125.
⁶⁰ If Rousseau–Doutreleau's emendation of the Latin text is correct, then *in quibus* refers to the written account of the Gospel; if Sesboüé is correct and *ex quibus* was not a mistake in the Latin edition, then it refers back to *ex Scripturis*. In either case, the implications are the same.

This translation remains faithful to the Latin text, and most closely aligns with what Irenaeus intended to accomplish within 3.pre-3.4.3, summarized in 3.5.1. It clarifies that in Irenaeus' claim that he would "introduce proofs from the Scriptures" (2.35.4; 3.pre) in Book 3, the proofs that he intended to introduce were the apostolic proofs from the scriptures. This interpretation also receives further confirmation in Book 4, where Irenaeus writes that the task of the apostles to preach the Gospel to the Jews was easier, "because they could allege proofs from the Scriptures [*ex Scripturis haberent ostensiones*]" (4.24.1), referring to the LXX revered by Jews but unhelpful for preaching to Greeks. This passage demonstrates both that in "proofs from the Scriptures," *Scripturis* refers solely to the Jewish scriptures, and that it was the apostles who made these proofs. The phrase "*ex Scripturis ostensiones*" and the related claim "*ex Scripturis demonstrauimus*" are also used in four other passages, each time using *Scripturis* exclusively in reference to the Jewish scriptures, and using the apostolic writings to demonstrate their proper interpretation,[61] while in 2.32.5 Irenaeus uses the related phrase "*ex prophetis ostensionibus*," further demonstrating his intended referent. Irenaeus' use of the phrase "*ostensiones ex Scripturis*" therefore does not provide evidence for the claim that the apostolic writings are given the scriptural title γραφή.

"Scripturis dominicis"

There are also a number of passages that contain the phrase *Scripturis dominicis*, commonly translated as "the Lord's Scriptures" and often believed to refer either to the gospels or to the whole of both the Old and New Testaments, in both cases granting the New Testament the title "scripture." Campenhausen, for example, contends that Irenaeus refers to the Old and New Testaments "without differentiation by the long-hallowed names of 'scriptures of the Lord.' "[62] The most commonly cited passage occurs in the conclusion to Book 2. Here Irenaeus says,

> We believe that we have sufficiently proved that the preaching of the apostles, the teaching of the Lord, the announcement of the prophets, the spoken message of the apostles, and the service of the law all harmonize with what we have said and prove that there is one and the same God of all things ... But lest we seem to be avoiding the proof from the Lord's Scriptures [*illam quae ex Scripturis dominicis est probationem*], since the Scriptures themselves preach this very doctrine much more obviously and clearly [*ipsis Scripturis multo manifestius et clarius hoc ipsum praedicantibus*], for such as do not have a depraved mind toward them, we will

---

[61] "*Ex Scripturis ostensiones*" appears in 3.12.9 and 4.34.5, and in both passages *Scripturis* refers to the Jewish scriptures. Hitchcock, *Irenaeus*, 228; and Norbert Brox, "Irenaeus and the Bible," in *Handbook of Patristic Exegesis: The Bible in Ancient Christianity*, by Charles Kannengiesser (Leiden: Brill, 2004), 1:485; both claim that in 3.12.9 Irenaeus is calling the Pauline letters "*Scripturis*," but it is clear that Paul's letters are called a proof *from* the scriptures. The claim "*ex Scripturis demonstrauimus*" is made in 2.35.2 and 3.19.2.

[62] Campenhausen, *Formation*, 188. Cf. Brox, "Irenaeus," 1:485; Hitchcock, *Irenaeus*, 194 and 226; Ferguson, "Selection and Closure," 314; Steenberg, "Graphe," 40–1; Flesseman-van Leer, *Tradition*, 132 and 141.

supply a special book, which will utilize these Scriptures, and so, for all who love the truth, we will bring into clear light proofs from the divine Scriptures [*proprium librum qui sequitur has Scripturas reddentes ex Scripturis divinis probationes apponemus in medio omnibus amantibus ueritatem*]. (2.35.4)

If *Scripturis dominicis* is translated as "the Lord's Scriptures,"[63] it appears to be a straightforward reference to the apostolic writings as scripture by Irenaeus, and this claim is often made.[64] Hitchcock claims that "when promising to give proofs from the Gospels in II.35.4 [Irenaeus] describes the latter as *Scripturae Dominicae*."[65] It has already been demonstrated in the previous section that the *Scripturis* mentioned here in 2.35.4 as the subject of the following book refers to the Jewish scriptures, the proper interpretation of which is demonstrated by the apostles.[66] In addition to this, the genitive singular noun *domini* would be expected if "Scriptures *of the Lord*" was intended, rather than the dative/ablative plural adjective *dominicis*. These factors indicate that the traditional translation and interpretation of this phrase require reevaluation.

Behr suggests an alternate translation of *Scripturis dominicis* as "dominical oracles," as he believes it to be a rendering of λογίων κυριακῶν, and a reference to the Jewish scriptures, rather than to the gospels.[67] His conclusion has the advantage of more closely aligning with Irenaeus' intention in this passage,[68] as well as the other passages in which this phrase occurs,[69] though Behr does not provide an account of how λογίων would have come to be translated as *Scripturis*. Behr's rejection of the traditional translation and interpretation is also supported by Irenaeus' use of the equivalent phrase *dominicis Scripturis* in 2.30.6, which is translated by Roberts–Donaldson as "authoritative Scriptures" and by Rousseau–Doutreleau and Steenberg as "the divine

---

[63] In addition to ACW (65:111-12), a translation of *Scripturis dominicis* as "the Lord's Scriptures" or "Scriptures of the Lord" is also given in ANF 1:413; SC 294:367 ("*des Écritures du Seigneur*"); Flesseman-van Leer, *Tradition*, 141; Ferguson, "Selection and Closure," 314; Campenhausen, *Formation*, 188; Hitchcock, *Irenaeus*, 194; Steenberg, "Graphe," 40; etc. The only alternative translation of this passage has been suggested by Behr, *Identifying*, 76, discussed below.

[64] Ferguson, "Selection and Closure," states that Irenaeus "declares that he will devote a special book to the 'scriptures of the Lord' (2.35.4), referring to the immediately mentioned preaching and teaching of the apostles, Lord, prophets, and law" (314). Similarly, Steenberg, "Graphe," maintains that *Scripturis dominicis* in 2.35.4 refers to "the writings of the Gospels and the apostles" (40–1). Cf. Campenhausen, *Formation*, 188; and Osborn, *Irenaeus*, 178. Farkasfalvy, "Theology," agrees that this phrase refers to "the Lord's Scriptures," although he holds that this is intended as a reference to the Old Testament (325–6).

[65] Hitchcock, *Irenaeus*, 226; cf. 194.

[66] In addition, had the referent of "*Scripturis dominicis*" been the Gospel accounts, it is not clear that this phrase should be translated as "Scriptures of the Lord," rather than "writings of the Lord," which would be a logical title for the Gospel accounts and conforms to Steenberg's principle of "delimited use" for ruling out the use of γραφή as a scriptural title.

[67] Behr, *Identifying*, 76 n. 4. His hypothesis is based in part on the similar phrase κυριακῶν λογίων in 1.8.1, discussed below.

[68] Cf. the discussion of 2.35.4 in the previous section, as well as Behr, *Identifying*, in which he gives his translation and explanation of the meaning of this passage (76).

[69] Cf. 2.30.6, 5.20.2, and possibly 1.8.1 (Behr conjectures that the Greek phrase is identical; the Latin translation is *dominicis eloquiis*), in addition to 2.35.4.

Scriptures,"⁷⁰ on the basis of Harvey's conjecture that *dominicis Scripturis* is based on κυρίων γραφῶν.⁷¹ Steenberg also states that it is a reference to the Jewish scriptures,⁷² and while he does not explain his reasoning, it is evident from the context of the passage. It reads,

> We have proved first from the dominical Scriptures [*ex dominicis Scripturis ostendimus*] that all the things which have been mentioned, visible and invisible, have been made by one God. For these men are not more sufficient than the Scriptures [*Scripturae*], nor, forsaking the utterances of the Lord [*eloquia Domini*] and Moses and the rest of the prophets who have proclaimed the truth [*et Moysen et reliquos prophetas qui ueritatem praeconauerunt*], is it necessary to believe these men who certainly say nothing sound, but rave insensibly. (2.30.6)⁷³

Within this passage, *dominicis Scripturis* does not refer to the Gospel accounts. The referent throughout this section is to the Jewish scriptures, and Christ is here included among the prophets as the basis of their prophecies.⁷⁴ This lends further support to Behr's contention that Irenaeus' use of the phrase *Scripturis dominicis* in 2.35.4 is also meant as a reference to the Jewish scriptures rather than the gospels, though a translation of "dominical writings" may be preferable to either Behr's "dominical oracles" or the SC and ANF translations of "authoritative" or "divine" scriptures.⁷⁵ The appearance of the same phrase in 5.20.2 is also best understood according to this interpretation.⁷⁶

Irenaeus also uses the similar phrase "κυριακῶν λογίων [*dominicis eloquiis*]," which occurs only once in *Adversus haereses*. Here, upon finishing his initial description of

---

⁷⁰ ANF 1:405; SC 294:311; Steenberg, "Graphe," 40. Unger, however, elects to translate the phrase as "the Lord's Scriptures" in this passage (ACW 65:97). The Latin passage runs, "*primo quidem ex dominicis Scripturis ostendimus omnia quae pradicta sunt*" (2.30.6).

⁷¹ Harvey 1:365. However, the Latin *dominicis* suggests κυριακῶν γραφῶν.

⁷² Steenberg, "Graphe," 40. Blanchard, *Sources*, 127; Hitchcock, *Irenaeus*, 226; and Campenhausen, *Formation*, 188, take *dominicis Scripturis* in 2.30.6 to be a reference to the apostolic writings.

⁷³ My trans.

⁷⁴ Cf. 4.2.3:

> But since the writings [*literae*] of Moses are the words of Christ, He does himself declare to the Jews, as John has recorded in the Gospel: "If ye had believed in Moses, ye would have believed Me: for he wrote of Me. But if ye believe not his writings, neither will ye believe My words." He thus indicates in the clearest manner that the writings of Moses are His words. If, then, [this be the case with regard] to Moses, so also, beyond a doubt, the words of the other prophets are His [words], as I have pointed out.

> And 4.2.5: "He shows that all are from one essence, that is, Abraham, and Moses, and the prophets, and also the Lord Himself." Cf. also 3.6.2, 4.5.2, 4.7.4, 4.9.1, 4.10.1, 4.20.9, etc.

⁷⁵ However, if Behr is correct in his contention that *Scripturis Dominicis* is a rendering of λογίων κυριακῶν, "dominical oracles" would be preferable.

⁷⁶ Though there is nothing within 5.20.2 itself to indicate that *dominicis Scripturis* refers to the apostolic writings, Rousseau et al. translate *dominicis Scripturis* in 5.20.2 as "*des Écritures du Seigneur*" (SC 153:259), offering a Greek rendering of κυριακαῖς γραφαῖς. Hitchcock, *Irenaeus*, 226; and Flesseman-van Leer, *Tradition*, 132, suggest similar translations, along with the implication that Irenaeus is referring to the apostolic writings.

the Valentinian cosmology and resulting anthropology and salvation system, Irenaeus writes,

> They disregard the order and connection of the Scriptures [τῶν γραφῶν] and, in as much as in them lies, they disjoint the members of the Truth. They transfer passages and rearrange them; and, making one thing out of another, they deceive many by the badly composed phantasy of the Lord's words that they adapt [ἐξαπατῶσι πολλοὺς τῇ τῶν ἐφαρμοζομένων κυριακῶν λογίων κακαοσυνθέτῳ φαντασίᾳ]. (1.8.1)

Both Unger and Rousseau–Doutreleau translate κυριακῶν λογίων as "the Lord's words"[77] while Roberts–Donaldson translate it as "the oracles of the Lord."[78] However, Behr contends that it should instead be translated "dominical oracles," just as *Scripturis dominicis* has been, as he believes the two Latin phrases are translations of the same Greek phrase κυριακῶν λογίων, and that both refer to the Jewish scriptures.[79] The adjective κυριακῶν/*dominicis* indicates that neither κυριακῶν λογίων nor *Scripturis dominicis* refer straightforwardly to "the Lord" as Unger and Roberts–Donaldson suggest. Behr's decision to use "dominical" in reference to messianic texts from the Jewish scriptures therefore seems preferable, for its reference to the Jewish scriptures is supported by the passage. Explaining his decision, Behr says, "the reference in *haer.* 1.8.1 is to the writings we now speak of as the Old Testament, and so I have translated the phrase as 'dominical oracles' rather than 'words of the Lord,' which is often done, but which would have easily been expressed straightforwardly in Greek."[80]

Behr's contention that "words of the Lord" could have been more easily expressed using different language is well supported by Irenaeus' own use. Whenever Irenaeus refers to "the words of the Lord" (referring to the statements of Jesus recorded in the gospels) as he does in the conclusion to Book 3 and the preface and conclusion of Book 4, the Latin translator consistently uses the phrase *Domini sermones*,[81] for which Rousseau et al. provide the Greek retroversion λόγια τοῦ Κυρίου.[82] If "the Lord's words"

---

[77] ACW 55:41, cf. 125 n. 5; SC 264:115: "des paroles du Seigneur."
[78] ANF 1:326.
[79] Behr, *Identifying*, 76 n. 4.
[80] Ibid.
[81] 3.25.7; 4.pre.1; 4.41.4 (twice as *Domini sermones*, once as *sermones Domini*). Additional examples can be found at 1.27.2 (though not in the Armenian translation which Rousseau–Doutreleau and Unger follow, cf. SC 264:350-1, 263:295; ACW 55:91 n. 7), 1.27.4, 2.2.6, 2.11.2, 3.5.3, 3.11.9, and 4.30.3 (listed by Reynders, *Lexique Comparé*, 2:298). Irenaeus also uses the similar phrase *uerba Domini*, which is identical in Greek (τὰ λόγια τοῦ Κυρίου), in 1.pre.1 and 2.11.1, with the same meaning.
[82] Cf. SC 211:491, 100:383 and 992-4. The Greek of *Domini sermones* is conjectured by Rousseau et al. in each instance to be Κυρίου λόγους, Κυρίου ... λογίων, λόγια τοῦ Κυρίου, Κυρίου λογίων, and λόγια τοῦ Κυρίου. Unger disagrees with Behr and Rousseau et al. here, positing instead that *Domini sermones/uerba Domini* and *dominicis eloquiis* have the same meaning and refer to the same Greek phrase (ACW 55:21 n. 5). However, *uerba Domini* (1.pre.1), and *dominicis eloquiis* (1.8.1) refer to the Greek phrases τὰ λόγια τοῦ Κυρίου and κυριακῶν λογίων, which both the Latin translator and most contemporary translators understand to convey different meanings. Similarly, though the Greek referred to by *Domini sermones* is lost, the adjective *dominicis* weighs against Unger's contention, as Rousseau et al. demonstrate in their retroversions.

in the gospel had been the meaning Irenaeus wished to communicate in 1.8.1, this frequently used phrase would much more clearly express it, avoiding the unnatural use of the adjective κυριακός for this role. These findings therefore offer additional support for the conclusion that *Scripturis dominicis* and κυριακῶν λογίων (*dominicis eloquiis*) are references to the Jewish scriptures in Irenaeus' use, and therefore that *Scripturis dominicis* is not evidence of the use of γραφή as a scriptural title for the apostolic writings.

B. Passages in Which γραφή May Not Be Intended as a Scriptural Title

In addition to those passages in which the apostolic writings do not appear to be the intended referent of γραφή, there are also a number of passages, routinely used as evidence that Irenaeus assigns a scriptural title to the apostolic writings, in which it may be questioned whether Irenaeus intends γραφή to function as a scriptural title. The primary passages under examination in this section are found in 1.8-9, 3.1-4, and 2.27.2; while the findings of these analyses suggest similar conclusions for other less prominent passages that conform to similar patterns.[83]

While γραφή can, and often does, function as a title for those writings that Irenaeus considers to be "scripture," this is not his only use of the term. There are a number of instances where Irenaeus unquestionably uses γραφή as a reference to specific "writings," without any scriptural significance. He is comfortable, for example, referring to a number of non-apostolic orthodox writings using γραφή. Describing Clement's first letter to the Corinthians, he says, "The Church of Rome wrote a very forceful letter to the Corinthians [γραφὴν[84] τοῖς Κορινθίοις]," and continues, "from this writing [*ex ipsa scriptura*], whoever wishes can learn" (3.3.3).[85] In similar fashion, he says of Papias that "he bore witness in writing in his four books [ἐγγράφως[86] ἐπιμαρτυρεῖ ἐν τῇ τετάρτῃ τῶν ἑαυτοῦ βιβλίων]" (5.33.4). Even more explicitly, Irenaeus introduces a passage from the *Shepherd of Hermas* by saying, "Therefore the writing spoke well, which says [Καλῶς οὖν ἡ γραφὴ ἡ λέγουσα]" (4.20.2).[87] This passage is especially notable because Irenaeus never once uses a direct introductory formula comparable to "ἡ γραφὴ ἡ λέγουσα" in any of his citations of the apostolic writings, which number over a thousand.[88] This passage also violates Steenberg's "delimited use" rule, prompting him to declare that Irenaeus

---

[83] These less prominent passages are 1.27.2-4, 2.20-24, 3.12.5, 3.12.12, 4.41.2, and 5.30.1-2. See below p. 36 n. 110.

[84] The Latin has *litteras*, but Rousseau–Doutreleau consider γραφὴν to be original.

[85] My trans. Rousseau–Doutreleau argue that Clement's letter is not called "Scripture" in this passage (SC 210:237), and Steenberg, "Graphe," 41, appears to agree. Benoit, *Irénée*, maintains that while Clement is cited as γραφή, this does not signify that it is considered to be Scripture, but rather "une 'écrit très important'" (147), citing the translation offered by Sagnard in his edition of Book 3 (SC 34:116).

[86] The Latin translation gives *scripturam*, supported by the Armenian (SC 153:416).

[87] My trans. Roberts–Donaldson translate this passage, "Truly, then, the Scripture declared, which says" (ANF 1:488). Steenberg, "Graphe," translates, "Therefore Scripture rightly says" (33).

[88] Blanchard, *Sources*, counts 1,800 New Testament references (950 of which are direct citations) from the indexes of the SC editions for *Adversus haereses* alone (122–3). Hoh, *Lehre*, catalogues 1,778 New Testament references (1,122 of which are direct citations) across all of Irenaeus' works (198; cf. 189–99).

considered the *Shepherd of Hermas* to be scripture—an unlikely contention given Irenaeus' strict standard of apostolic authorship as a criterion for authority.[89]

In addition to these examples, Irenaeus also uses γραφή in reference to his own work on four separate occasions. In 3.6.4 he asks God to grant that "everyone who reads this writing may know You [*omni legenti hanc scripturam cognoscere te*]." He also writes of his own work, "Consequently, it will be incumbent on you, in fact, on all who read this writing [*omnes qui intendunt huic Scripturae*]" (3.17.4). In Book 5 he similarly writes, "It will be incumbent upon thee, however, and all who may happen to read this writing [*omnes lecturos hanc scripturam*]" (5.pre), once again in reference to his own work. He also introduces the *Demonstration* by saying, "we have not hesitated to speak a little with you, as far as possible, by writing [գրելյ[90]]" (*Dem.* 1).

On at least one occasion, Irenaeus even refers to heretical writings using γραφή. He says in Book 1, "they adduce an untold multitude of apocryphal and spurious writings [ἀμύθητὸ πλῆθος ἀποκρύφων καὶ νόθων γραφῶν]" (1.20.1).[91] A second occurrence may also be found in Book 3:

> They give the title *Gospel of Truth* to a work written not long ago, and agreeing in no way with the gospels of the apostles, so that among them even the Gospel would not be without blasphemy. For if the gospel which is produced by them is a gospel of the Truth, but is unlike those which have been handed down to us by the apostles, whoever wishes can learn, as is shown by the writings themselves [*ex ipsis Scripturis*], that what is handed down by the apostles is no longer the Gospel of Truth. (3.11.9)[92]

In this passage, Irenaeus' use of *Scripturis* only makes sense as a reference to the heretical *Gospel of Truth* in comparison with the apostolic gospels. Benoit interprets this passage the same way as a second instance of γραφή used in reference to heretical writings,[93] here without delimitation.

---

[89] Whenever Irenaeus discusses authoritative teachings or writings he refers exclusively to "the prophets, the Lord, and the apostles" and similar phrases (1.3.6, 1.8.1, 2.28.7, 2.35.4, 3.6.1, 3.8.1, 3.9.1, 4.1.1, 5.pre, etc.), and his detailed defense of the church's tradition and of the authoritative written sources of it in 3.pre-3.5.1 is based solely on its apostolic origin. The same focus on apostolic authorship as the authority behind the apostolic writings will continue throughout the rest of *Adversus haereses*. There is no indication of other authorities outside of "the prophets, the Lord, and the apostles" and no indication that Irenaeus believes *Hermas* was of apostolic origin. However, this has not stopped Steenberg and many others (Metzger, *Canon*, 155; McDonald, *Formation*, 198; Gamble, *New Testament*, 49; Hahneman, *Muratorian Fragment*, 61; Ochagavia, *Visibile*, 37; Hitchcock, *Irenaeus*, 20; Hoh, *Lehre*, 56–8) from asserting that Irenaeus' use of γραφή in this passage demonstrates that he considered *Hermas* to be scripture, even if only in a limited sense (Benoit, *Irénée*, 146–7). Rousseau et al. translate γραφή in this passage as "l'ecrit" (SC 100:629), and explain in detail why it is unlikely that Irenaeus is calling *Hermas* scripture in this passage (SC 100:248-50).

[90] Գրելյ is the genitive singular form of գիր, the typical Armenian translation of γραφή. Rousseau offers *scriptum* in his Latin translation (SC 406:82), presupposing instead a form of γράμμα.

[91] Unger (ACW 55:76); Roberts–Donaldson (ANF 1:344); Steenberg, "Graphe," 38; and F. F. Bruce, *The Canon of Scripture* (Downers Grove: InterVarsity Press, 1988), 173; all translate γραφῶν as "writings" here.

[92] My trans.

[93] Benoit, *Irénée*, 75 n. 1. Yet Unger (ACW 64:58), Roberts–Donaldson (ANF 1:429), and Rousseau-Doutreleau (211:175) all translate *Scripturis* as "the Scriptures" here.

On the basis of these ten passages, it is impossible to maintain the position held by Blanchard, who acknowledges six occasions in which the term *scriptura* is used in reference to non-biblical texts, yet nevertheless argues that "the portion is tiny (scarcely 4%) and not sufficient to alter the assessment according to which Irenaeus reserves the notion of the Scriptures for the biblical corpus as a whole."[94] On the contrary, these passages provide conclusive proof that the term γραφή itself possesses no inherent scriptural significance in Irenaeus' usage. It may be used in reference to any specific "writing" under discussion just as easily as it can function more generally as a title for the Jewish scriptures. It must therefore be determined, in the few passages where γραφή is used in reference to the apostolic writings,[95] whether Irenaeus intends to signify the "writings" he is discussing or to use an already widely recognized scriptural title, "*the writings*," encompassing both the apostolic writings and the Jewish scriptures. This question is asked in the analysis of each passage below. In doing so, it becomes evident that Steenberg's principle of "delimited" versus "non-delimited" use, while a useful guide, has been too narrowly applied to adequately reflect Irenaeus' meaning.

1.8.1-1.9.4 and Related Passages

There is an extended section in Book 1 in which Irenaeus' use of γραφή in reference to the apostolic writings alongside the Jewish scriptures is routinely considered to function as a scriptural title. This section spans chs. 8 and 9, which function as the culmination of his detailed description of the teachings and methods of the Valentinians spanning the first nine chapters of Book 1. Throughout this description, Irenaeus explains that they misuse both the Jewish scriptures and the apostolic writings to prove their teachings. After describing the "sayings" (εἰῆσθαι/*dicta*) of the Lord and the apostles that they misuse (1.3.1-5), Irenaeus continues,

> Such indeed is what they say concerning their pleroma and of the formation of all, doing violence to things well said to adapt them to their wicked inventions; and not only from the evangelical and the apostolic [sayings] do they attempt to make proofs, perverting the interpretations and falsifying the explanations; but also from Law and Prophets. (1.3.6)[96]

Then, after completing his description of their systems (chs. 4–7), he concludes,

> Such is their system [ὑποθέσεως] which neither the prophets preached nor the Lord taught nor the apostles handed down [ἥν οὔτε προφῆται ἐκήρυξαν οὔτε ὁ Κύριος ἐδίδαξεν οὔτε ἀπόστολοι παρέδωκαν] …, they attempt to adapt to their sayings either the Lord's parables, or the prophets' sayings, or the apostles' discourses [ἤτοι παραβολὰς κυριακὰς ἢ ῥήσεις προφητικὰς ἢ λόγους ἀποστολικούς] in a plausible

---

[94] Blanchard, *Sources*, 127–8; my trans.
[95] 1.8.1, 1.8.2, 1.9.1, 1.9.3, 1.27.4, 2.24.4 (twice), 2.27.2, 3.1.1 (twice), 3.2.1 (twice), 3.2.2, 3.4.1, 3.12.5, 3.12.12, 4.41.2, 5.30.1, and 5.30.2.
[96] My trans.

manner, so that their fabrication might not seem to be without witness, indeed disregarding the order and connection of the writings [τὴν μὲν τάξιν καὶ τὸν εἱρμὸν τῶν γραφῶν ὑπερβαίνοντες] and, as much as depends on them, dismembering the truth. (1.8.1)[97]

Τῶν γραφῶν is often understood to function as a title for both the Jewish scriptures and the apostolic writings in this passage,[98] and this interpretation is reinforced when it appears in translation as "the Scriptures" and is separated from the previous clauses by periods that do not appear in the Greek.[99] However, the structure of this passage indicates that Irenaeus uses γραφή here to refer directly back to the "writings" he has just mentioned—his two three-part descriptions of the Lord, the prophets, and the apostles. As described in the introduction, γραφή functions as a title only when Irenaeus does not specify *which* writings he is referring to; in these cases the general reference to "*the writings*" is a title, corresponding to (at least) the Jewish scriptures. However, this function is ruled out when Irenaeus identifies specific "writings," as he does in this passage.

The same principle is at work at the end of this paragraph. Immediately following his use of the metaphor of rearranging a mosaic of a king into the likeness of a fox, Irenaeus continues to describe the Valentinians' misuse of scripture. He begins by claiming,

wresting sayings and discourses and parables [ῥήματα καὶ λέξεις καὶ παραβολὰς] from one place or another, they seek to apply these discourses of God [τὰ λόγια τοῦ Θεοῦ] to their fables. And indeed we have said how many [of these discourses] they apply to the things within the pleroma [Καὶ ὅσα μὲν <τοῖς> ἐντὸς τοῦ Πληρώματος ἐφαρμόζουσιν εἰρήκαμεν]. (2) But the following is how much they attempt to appropriate from these writings also to the things outside of their pleroma ['Ὅσα δὲ καὶ τοῖς ἐκτὸς τοῦ Πληρώματος αὐτῶν προσοικειοῦν πειρῶνται ἐκ τῶν γραφῶν ἔστιν τοιαῦτα]. (1.8.1-2)[100]

This description is immediately followed by a number of examples of the Valentinian interpretations of the words and actions of Jesus, the words of Paul, and the actions of Moses. Because of this, "τῶν γραφῶν," commonly translated as "the Scriptures,"

---

[97] My trans.
[98] Ferguson, "Selection and Closure," states that in this passage Irenaeus identifies "the triple authority of prophets, Lord, and apostles as 'scriptures'" (314). Hitchcock, *Irenaeus*, also indicates that this passage refers to both the Old and New Testaments (196; cf. 213), as does Flesseman-van Leer, *Tradition*, 134–5. Steenberg, "Graphe," similarly takes it to be a reference to "scripture" (37), though he does not indicate whether he believes the apostolic writings are part of the scriptures referred to.
[99] Unger's translation, for example, reads,

They try to adapt to their own sayings in a manner worthy of credence, either the Lord's parables, or the prophets' sayings, or the apostles' words, so that their fabrication might not appear to be without witness. They disregard the Order and connection of the Scriptures and, as much as in them lies, they disjoint the members of the Truth. (ACW 55:41)

Cf. SC:264:112-13; ANF 1:326.
[100] My trans.

appears to be a title for both the apostolic writings and Jewish scriptures.[101] However, both this passage and the rest of 1.8.1 indicate that τῶν γραφῶν refers to the "ῥήματα καὶ λέξεις καὶ παραβολάς," echoing "the Lord's parables, or the prophets' sayings, or the apostles' discourses" of the previous passage,[102] and summed up as the "discourses of God." Γραφή is therefore once again functioning as a specific reference to *these writings* currently under discussion, rather than as a title.

Irenaeus continues to describe the Valentinian use of these writings for the rest of ch. 8, before concluding at the beginning of ch. 9,

> You see, dear friend, the method which they use to deceive themselves, misusing the writings [ἐπηρεάζοντες ταῖς γραφαῖς], attempting to set up their fabrication out of them. (1.9.1)[103]

Then, two paragraphs later, after pointing out some errors in their exegesis, he concludes, "their entire system [ὑπόθεσις] fails, this false dream for which they misuse the writings [τῶν γραφῶν]" (1.9.3).[104] Here once again the standard translation of "the Scriptures" in both passages suggests the conclusion that γραφή functions as a title that includes the apostolic writings.[105] Steenberg's rule specifically supports this interpretation, as γραφή is not directly delimited in either passage by specifying words such as οὗτος or ἀποστόλων. Despite this, however, it remains the case that Irenaeus is using γραφή in both instances to refer to all the writings he has just adduced throughout the previous two chapters, as introduced in 1.8.1-2, indicating that γραφή functions as a specific reference to *these writings* he has been discussing. In these particular instances γραφή therefore cannot function as a title, despite conforming to Steenberg's principle of "non-delimited use."[106] All instances of γραφή within 1.8.1-1.9.3 fit this pattern.

Throughout these two chapters, Irenaeus' use of γραφή refers to both the apostolic writings and the Jewish scriptures that are under discussion. However, the Jewish scriptures nevertheless remain his primary focus. The Valentinians make use of both collections, but their method is to take statements from the apostolic writings in order to reinterpret the Jewish scriptures as an account of the work of the Demiurge in which the higher pleroma may be glimpsed. The authority of Jesus and the apostles is thus

---

[101] Cf. ACW 55:41; ANF 1:326. Rousseau–Doutreleau translate it instead as "les textes" (SC 264:117). This passage is translated as "the scriptures" and taken to indicate the scriptural status of the following examples by Steenberg, "Graphe," 37; and supplied as evidence for the scriptural status of the apostolic writings by Hoh, *Lehre*, 64; and Blanchard, *Sources*, 125.

[102] The Latin translation makes this echo explicit, as "*uel parabolas dominicas, uel dictiones propheticas, aut sermones apostolicos*" at the beginning of 1.8.1 becomes "*sermones et dictiones et parabolas*" at the end. The Greek text exhibits only slight differences: "παραβολὰς κυριακὰς ἢ ῥήσεις προφητικὰς ἢ λόγους ἀποστολικούς" becomes "ῥήματα καὶ λέξεις καὶ παραβολάς."

[103] My trans.

[104] My trans.

[105] Cf. ACW 55:45 and 47; ANF 1:329-30; SC 264:137 and 147. Steenberg, "Graphe," takes both to be references to the apostolic writings as "scripture" (37). 1.9.1 is adduced as evidence that Irenaeus gives New Testament writings the title "Scripture" by Hoh, *Lehre*, 64; Blanchard, *Sources*, 126; and Flesseman-van Leer, *Tradition*, 135.

[106] Cf. Steenberg, "Graphe," 51-3. This illustrates that Steenberg's principle of "delimited use" is not broad enough to include delimitation occurring outside the direct phrase in which γραφή occurs.

co-opted in order to prove the Valentinians' interpretation of the Jewish scriptures. For this reason Irenaeus' use of γραφή throughout this section includes both sets of writings used by the Valentinians (as described by Irenaeus in 1.8.1), yet the Jewish scriptures are the primary subject. This has already been noted in the previous section in reference to his use of the phrase "κυριακῶν λογίων," most accurately defined as "dominical oracles," used in reference to the Jewish scriptures: "they deceive many by this badly composed phantasy of the dominical oracles they adapt" (1.8.1).[107] In both his metaphor of the mosaic of the king and in his metaphor of the poems of Homer in 1.9.4, it is the Jewish scriptures that have been reinterpreted, using the statements of Jesus and the apostles as proof.[108]

This shifting focus also occurs because although he has both the apostolic writings and Jewish scriptures in view when discussing the writings that the Valentinians misuse, when he turns to positively describing the proper interpretation of these writings his primary concern is the Jewish scriptures. This can be seen at the end of ch. 9, where, concluding his critique of their use of these writings, Irenaeus uses the metaphor of rearranging the lines of Homer to make an entirely different poem, which any expert would recognize to be a fraud despite its accurate citations on the basis of its foreign theme. He then continues,

> In the same way, anyone who keeps unchangeable in himself the Rule of the Truth received through baptism will recognize the names and sayings and parables from the Scriptures [τῶν γραφῶν], but this blasphemous theme of theirs he will not recognize. (1.9.4)

Here, discussing proper Christian interpretation, Irenaeus is now concerned specifically with the Jewish scriptures, which must be interpreted by the rule of truth that comes from the apostles in their writings. The apostolic writings cannot be included alongside the Jewish scriptures as τῶν γραφῶν here,[109] for the apostolic writings are the source of the rule of truth by which αἱ γραφαί are interpreted. Irenaeus sets out the rule of truth immediately following this passage, which he begins by saying that the church "received from the apostles and their disciples [παρά τε τῶν ἀποστόλων καὶ τῶν ἐκείνων μαθητῶν] the faith in one God the Father Almighty, the Creator" (1.10.1). This aptly describes how the apostolic writings relate to the Jewish scriptures for Irenaeus. By setting out the rule of truth, the apostles through their writings provide the key

---

[107] My trans. Cf. Behr's interpretation: "the reference in *haer.* 1.8.1 is to the writings we now speak of as the Old Testament, and so I have translated the phrase as 'dominical oracles' rather than 'words of the Lord,' which is often done, but which would have easily been expressed straightforwardly in Greek" (*Identifying*, 76 n. 4).

[108] Joseph Trigg, "The Apostolic Fathers and the Apologists," in *A History of Biblical Interpretation*, ed. Alan Hauser and Duane Watson (Grand Rapids, MI: Eerdmans, 2003), also appears to hold this interpretation, as he maintains that Irenaeus' mosaic analogy in 1.8.1 refers exclusively to the Jewish scriptures: "Implicit in Irenaeus' image is the assumption that, while the *hypothesis* of the Old Testament would not have been fully apparent until the coming of Christ, the Rule of Faith now makes it plain" (1:329).

[109] As claimed by McDonald, *Formation*, 168.

for interpreting "the Scriptures," as Irenaeus describes in 1.9.4, here using γραφή specifically in reference to the Jewish scriptures.

In light of this examination of 1.8.1-1.9.4, the conclusion is suggested that despite initial appearances Irenaeus' use of γραφή throughout this section does not function as a title for the apostolic writings alongside the Jewish scriptures, but is instead used by Irenaeus to refer to *those writings* that he has identified as having been misused by the Valentinians whenever it includes the apostolic writings. The pattern of use of γραφή identified here can also be used to clarify a few less prominent passages that fit this pattern.[110] Irenaeus' identifiable pattern of use of γραφή suggests the conclusion that in each of these passages, despite being characterized by Steenberg as "non-delimited use," γραφή functions as a reference to specific writings under discussion that have been explicitly identified, rather than functioning in a general sense as the title "*the writings*" and by this granting the apostolic writings equivalent status to the Jewish scriptures.

3.1-4: "In Scripturis nobis tradiderunt"

Two of the passages most commonly cited as evidence that Irenaeus uses γραφή as a scriptural title for the apostolic writings are found within the first four chapters of Book 3. Within this section, having explained in the preface that he will refute the Valentinians using "proofs from the Scriptures,"[111] Irenaeus presents a defense of the unique authority of the apostles and their writings, the relation of their writings to the apostolic tradition, and the apostolic origin of the contemporary church through

---

[110] In 1.27.2-4, Irenaeus discusses Marcion's misuse of "the prophets and the law" that he abolished, the accounts of "the Gospel" that he divided (keeping only "the Gospel according to Luke"), and "the Letters of Paul" that he edited (1.27.2), before commenting on Marcion's practice by saying that he "truncated the writings [*circumcidere Scripturas*]" (1.27.4; my trans.). This description is echoed in 3.12.12: Irenaeus claims that his opponents are "rebelling against the Mosaic Law" and claim to be "wiser than the apostles" who "proclaimed the Gospel." He continues, "Marcion and those who follow him have turned to mutilating the writings [*ad intercidendas conuersi sunt Scripturas*]" (my trans.), and repeats his description of the Marcionite use of the Jewish scriptures and apostolic writings in 1.27.4. In 2.20-24, Irenaeus discusses his opponents' use of "the parables and deeds of the Lord" (2.20.1), "the prophet" (2.22.1-2), "Paul" (2.22.2), "the Gospels" (2.22.3-5), "the Lord's deeds" (2.23.1-2), the heretical practice of counting up "numbers and letters" in written words of "the Hebrew and Greek languages" (2.24.1-3), and "proofs from the law" (2.24.3), before explaining that by these methods of interpretation anything at all could be proven from the writings ("*ex Scripturis*") they use (2.24.3), and then demonstrating this by using their methods to "prove" the importance of the number five "*ex Scripturis*" (2.24.4). In 3.12.5, as Irenaeus is discussing the words and actions of Peter and the other apostles as presented in Acts, he writes, "Therefore having been confounded both by the healing—'for the man,' the writing states [*inquit Scriptura*], 'was over forty years in whom this sign of healing was made'—and by the doctrine of the apostles and [their] exposition of the prophets" (my trans.). In 4.41.2 Irenaeus says, "the writing justly speaks of those who always persist in separation as 'sons of the devil' and 'angels of the evil one' [*juste Scriptura eos qui in abscessione perseverant semper filios diaboli et angelos dixit maligni*]" (my trans), in reference to the two parables he has been describing. In 5.30.2, as Irenaeus is discussing the fact that some manuscripts of John's Revelation have the number 666, while some have the erroneous number 616, he mentions, "the number which has been announced by the writing [*numerum qui a Scriptura annuntiatus est*], that is, six hundred sixty six" (my trans.; cf. 5.30.1).

[111] Recall the discussion in Section 1.2A in which it has been determined that the apostolic writings are the "proofs from the [Jewish] Scriptures" to which he is referring.

its possession of this same apostolic tradition, traced back to the apostles through its origin and through the succession of bishops. Within this section, the first passage under consideration occurs as he begins his demonstration of the authority of the apostles and their writings in ch. 1, where he says,

> In point of fact, we received the knowledge of the economy of our salvation through no others than those through whom the Gospel has come down to us. This Gospel they first preached orally, but later by God's will they handed it on to us in the Scriptures [*postea uero per Dei uolontatem in Scripturis nobis tradiderunt*], so it would be the foundation and pillar of our faith [*"fundamentum et columnam fidei nostrae" futurum*]. (3.1.1)

The primary issue at stake in the investigation of this passage concerns whether *Scripturis* is intended as a scriptural title for the apostolic writings, as Unger has suggested in his translation here,[112] or whether its use is intended to communicate only that the apostles put their preaching of the Gospel into *writing*. Among editors and interpreters of Irenaeus, the consensus is that *Scripturis* is here intended as a scriptural title for the apostolic writings, and this passage is among the most commonly cited passages in favor of the view that the apostolic writings are given a scriptural title by Irenaeus. Hitchcock, for example, cites this passage as evidence that Irenaeus "applied the term 'Scriptures' to the gospels and epistles of the N.T., thereby coordinating them with the O.T."[113] McDonald similarly claims, "Irenaeus believed that the four gospels and other NT literature, along with the OT writings, were normative for the church, and he clearly called these writings 'Scripture,'" citing 3.1.1 as proof.[114] Many examples of similar claims can be found.[115] However, it is equally plausible that Irenaeus' use of γραφή does not have any scriptural implications in this passage, just as it lacks such implications when used twice in reference to the epistle of Clement later in this section (3.3.3).

Irenaeus' purpose within this section supports the interpretation according to which γραφή is used for the purpose of conveying that the apostolic preaching has been put into *written form*. In order to proceed with his purpose in this chapter to present the apostolic "proofs from the Scriptures" (3.pre), Irenaeus must first defend the authority of the apostolic writings he intends to use. He therefore sets out to present his defense in 3.1-4, first by tracing the authority of the Gospel from Christ to the apostles: "For the Lord of all things gave to His apostles the power of the Gospel" (3.pre), and then

---

[112] ACW 64:30. Roberts-Donaldson (ANF 1:414) and Rousseau-Doutreleau (SC 211:21) agree with Unger's translation.
[113] Hitchcock, *Irenaeus*, 213. Cf. 227.
[114] McDonald, *Formation*, 168.
[115] Cf. Steenberg, "Graphe," 41, 56–7; Blanchard, *Sources*, 126; Behr, *Nicaea*, 39; *Identifying*, 124–5; Lawson, *Biblical Theology*, 42; Flesseman-van Leer, *Tradition*, 129; Metzger, *Canon*, 154; Ferguson, "Selection and Closure," 315; Bokedal, *Significance*, 167–8; Sesboüé, "Preuve," 875; Benoit, *Irénée*, 119. While Lawson cautions that definite conclusions should not be made simply because of Irenaeus' use of the term γραφή (42), Campenhausen, *Formation*, 189; Ochagavia, *Visibile*, 177; and Farkasfalvy, "Theology," 329; are the only interpreters who translate *Scripturis* in this passage as "writings."

by contending that the apostles handed down this Gospel in their writings: "For we know the economy of our salvation through no others than those through whom the Gospel has come to us: at one time they certainly proclaimed this Gospel publicly, but afterwards through God's will they handed it down to us in writings [*postea uero per Dei uoluntatem in Scripturis nobis tradiderunt*]" (3.1.1),[116] followed by a description of the processes by which each of the four authoritative statements of the Gospel was created.

Within this context, there is no indication that γραφή is simultaneously functioning as a scriptural title in this passage, thereby necessitating a translation of "Scriptures" on this basis.[117] γραφή is undoubtedly being used here to describe the process by which the authoritative Gospel of Christ came to be authentically represented by the apostolic writings that Irenaeus intends to make use of, as Irenaeus guarantees this authentic representation by explaining that the apostles who authoritatively preached the Gospel also handed it down in their writings (*Scripturis*). These factors suggest that this passage does not constitute evidence of Irenaeus using γραφή as a scriptural title for the apostolic writings.

Irenaeus makes use of γραφή a second time in 3.1.1 in a similar way and for the same purpose, yet here it consistently receives a different translation and interpretation. Irenaeus comments that "Matthew, accordingly, produced a writing of the Gospel among the Hebrews in their own language [Ματθαῖος ἐν τοῖς Ἑβραίοις τῇ ἰδίᾳ αὐτῶν διαλέκτῳ καὶ γραφὴν ἐξήνεγκεν εὐαγγελίου]" (3.1.1). Irenaeus' use of γραφή here, though directly related to his use at the beginning of 3.1.1, is rarely translated as "Scripture" or adduced as evidence of Irenaeus' use of a scriptural title for the apostolic writings.[118] The probable reason for this is that it is evident that γραφήν lacks any scriptural connotations, indicating instead the process of putting the *Euangelium* into

---

[116] My trans.

[117] It has been suggested by Behr, *Nicaea*, that the phrase "*fundamentum et columnam fidei nostrae futurum*" that occurs immediately after "*in Scripturis nobis tradiderunt*" refers to *Scripturis*, rather than *Euangelium*. Behr suggests that the referent here is to *Scripturis*, and therefore that "it is the Scripture which is the 'ground and pillar' of the faith" (9). Cf. Bokedal, *Significance*, 167–8; van den Eynde, *Normes*, 120; Briggman, *Holy Spirit*, 51; Steenberg, "Graphe," 57. If accurate, this could indicate that *Scripturis* does imply a scriptural connotation, as the unique authority of these writings would then be the emphasis of the sentence. The grammatical construction of the sentence is ambiguous in this regard, as *futurum* leaves the subject unclear. However, in the first four clauses of 3.1.1, *Euangelium* is stated as the subject of the sentence in the first clause and then left as the unstated subject in each subsequent clause, indicating that it is still the subject of the final clause, "*fundamentum et columnam fidei nostrae futurum*"—despite the fact that *Scripturis* has been mentioned immediately before it. *Euangelium* continues to be the primary subject after this passage throughout the rest of 3.1.1. This interpretation is supported by Irenaeus' use of the same phrase in 3.11.8, where he states that the "*columna et firmamentum*" of the church is the Gospel: "στῦλος δὲ καὶ στήριγμα τῆς ἐκκλησίας τὸ εὐαγγέλιον καὶ Πνεῦμα ζωῆς." Unger (ACW 64:30) and Rousseau-Doutreleau (SC 211:21) agree that *Euangelium* is the referent of the phrase, and Unger explains that Irenaeus "ascribes this function to the Gospel, as itself the foundation of the Church," and notes that "The priority of the oral Gospel, 'traditioned' and handed on, over the written Gospel as a conduit of revelation is here clearly enunciated" (ACW 64:117 n. 1).

[118] Γραφὴν εὐαγγελίου is variously translated as "a writing of the Gospel" (ACW 64:30), "a written Gospel" (ANF 1:414), and "une forme écrite d'Évangile" (SC 211:23). Sesboüé, "Preuve," stands as an exception, identifying this passage as evidence that "Irénée désigne explicitement le NT par le terme d'Ecriture" (875).

written form, as the parallel descriptions of the process of creation of the other three accounts of the Gospel in this passage illustrate.[119] It is difficult to account for the disparity in translations and interpretations between this passage and Irenaeus' first use of γραφή in this chapter.

A similar pattern of use of γραφή is exhibited a few chapters later in 3.4, providing further illumination of the intent of Irenaeus' use of γραφή within this section.[120] After having described the process by which the church received the authoritative written forms of the Gospel from the apostles in 3.1, Irenaeus turns in 3.2 to describing how his opponents assent neither to the apostles' writings nor to their public teachings, first contending that their writings were not correct and then claiming that even the apostles and the Lord himself mixed in teachings from the Demiurge with those of the Savior. This is followed in 3.3 by a defense of the church's tradition having been passed from the apostles to the entire church through the succession of bishops, to whom the apostles would certainly have taught any "secret traditions" if they had them. On the basis of this demonstration, Irenaeus concludes in 3.4 that the tradition held by the church preserves the truth, pointing out that if the apostles had not left their writings then recourse could just as easily be given to the teachings of the church, as is often done by "barbarian" churches who do not possess writings but nonetheless hold firmly to the same tradition of the church. It is in the process of making this point in 3.4 that Irenaeus writes,

> What if the apostles had not left us the Scriptures [*Quid autem si nec apostoli quidem Scripturas reliquissent nobis*]; ought we not, then, to follow the disposition of tradition, which they handed down to those to whom they entrusted the Churches? (3.4.1)

The occurrence of *Scripturas* in this passage is commonly translated as "Scriptures"[121] and considered as evidence that Irenaeus uses γραφή as a scriptural title for the apostolic writings. Steenberg, for example, holds up this passage as a claim that the gospels and apostolic texts are scripture, noting that this passage is among those that are "of significant merit in determining Irenaeus' understanding of Scripture."[122]

---

[119] Mark "ἐγγράφος ἡμῖν παραδέδωκεν" the Gospel preached by Peter; Luke "εὐαγγέλιον ἐν Βίβλῳ κατέθετο" preached by Paul; and John "αὐτὸς ἐξέδωκεν τὸ εὐαγγέλιον" (3.1.1).

[120] Irenaeus also uses γραφή in reference to the apostolic writings in ch 2. However, because that chapter is rarely adduced as evidence for the claims of the traditional interpretation, and because a detailed explanation of Irenaeus' intentions in that chapter—including the significance of his use of γραφή—occurs in Section 3.1B, that explanation is not reproduced here in order to reduce repetition. In brief, the conclusion reached is that γραφή within 3.2.1-2 refers to the apostolic accounts of the Gospel identified in 3.1.1, not as a title but in order to distinguish them from the supposed private *oral* teachings of the apostles that Irenaeus' opponents claim take precedence over their *writings*.

[121] Unger's translation here (ACW 64:35 and n. 3) is in agreement with Rousseau-Doutreleau (SC 211:47), though Roberts-Donaldson choose instead to translate *Scripturas* as "writings" in this instance (ANF 1:417).

[122] Steenberg, "Graphe," 41 and 37. Similar claims are made by Blanchard, *Sources*, 126; Sesboüé, "Preuve," 875; Farkasfalvy, "Theology," 320; Bokedal, *Significance*, 168-9; Flesseman-van Leer, *Tradition*, 144; Hoh, *Lehre*, 64; and Campenhausen, *Formation*, 190. McDonald, *Formation*, 167, and Behr, *Nicaea*, 43; both translate *Scripturas* instead as "writings" in this passage.

However, Irenaeus' argument in this passage calls the traditional translation and interpretation into question. As he has previously done in 3.1.1, Irenaeus uses γραφή in order to refer to the "writings" of the apostles, here describing the agreement between what the apostles put into writing and what they taught to the leaders of the churches they initiated: "But what if the apostles had not in fact left behind writings for us, would it not be necessary to follow the arrangement of the tradition which they handed down to those to whom they committed the Churches?"[123] His question concerns what Christians would do if the apostolic preaching had not been left behind *in writing*, and he brings up this question in order to answer that the church would simply look to the apostolic tradition that has been passed down in the church. The agreement between these two forms of apostolic teaching is such that the apostolic tradition is sufficient without any written record, for there are "barbarian" Christians who have no writings but keep the apostolic tradition that they have been given:

> To this disposition many nations of the barbarians who believe in Christ give assent, having salvation "written in their hearts through the Spirit, without paper and ink," ["*sine charta et atramento scriptum habentes per Spiritum in cordibus suis" salutem*][124] and guarding carefully the ancient tradition ... Those who believed this faith, without writings [*litteras*], are barbarians with respect to their language; but as regards doctrine and practices and conduct they are most wise. (3.4.2)

Irenaeus confirms that his use of γραφή in 3.4.1 is intended to refer to the written form of the apostolic preaching of the Gospel by his use of "*sine charta et atramento*" and "*litteras*" for the same purpose in 3.4.2.

Throughout the section spanning 3.1-4, Irenaeus' use of γραφή performs the specific role of signifying the written form of the apostolic preaching.[125] There is no indication within this section that γραφή simultaneously functions as a scriptural title for the apostolic writings, and therefore no basis for concluding that these passages provide evidence that Irenaeus uses γραφή in this way.

2.27.2: "*Uniuersae Scripturae et propheticae, et euangelicae*"

The final passage to be investigated in this section is perhaps the most significant passage cited as evidence by the traditional interpretation for its claim that Irenaeus used γραφή as a title for the apostolic writings alongside the Jewish scriptures. It occurs in Book 2, as Irenaeus is describing the proper method of interpretation of the Jewish scriptures and apostolic writings that his opponents misuse to prove their doctrines. In the midst of his explanation, Irenaeus states,

---

[123] My trans.
[124] Cf. 2 Cor. 3:2; Rom. 2:15; Heb. 8:10.
[125] The exception to this is 3.3.3 where it is Clement's letter, rather than the apostolic preaching, which is referred to using γραφή.

Since therefore, the entire Scriptures, both the prophets and the Gospels, clearly and unambiguously [*Cum itaque uniuersae Scripturae et propheticae, et euangelicae in aperto et sine ambiguitate*]—so they can equally be heard by all, even though all do not believe that there is only one God to the exclusion of others—preach that through his own Word God made all things. (2.27.2)

On the basis of the phrase "*uniuersae Scripturae et propheticae, et euangelicae*" and its usual translation of "the entire Scriptures, both the Prophets and the Gospels,"[126] this passage has been widely held up as the prime example of Irenaeus defining the scriptures as both "Prophets" and "Gospels." Unger comments on this passage, "Note that the Gospels are put on equal footing with the Prophets as Scripture."[127] However, the extent to which this encompasses the apostolic writings is not agreed upon. This passage is understood by some to refer to the whole of the Jewish scriptures and the apostolic writings as scripture,[128] while according to others only the gospels are included with the Jewish scriptures in this passage.[129] This ambiguity stems from the fact that Irenaeus does not use εὐαγγέλιον on its own to refer to the apostolic writings as a whole,[130] yet he considers the Pauline epistles and the other apostolic treatises he knows to be of equivalent status to the gospels.[131] The incongruity between these two

---

[126] Unger (ACW 65:86), in agreement with Roberts–Donaldson (ANF 1:398). Rousseau–Doutreleau's translation differs, but suggests similar implications: "toutes les Écritures, tant prophétiques qu'évangéliques" (SC 294:267).

[127] ACW 65:153 n. 7.

[128] Flesseman-van Leer, *Tradition*, states, "Scripture for Irenaeus consists of the Old and New Testament … He indicates the two parts by 'the prophets' and 'the gospel(s)' respectively" (128–9), citing 2.27.2. Similarly, Campenhausen, *Formation*, finds in 2.27.2 evidence that Irenaeus groups together the gospels, Acts, and the Pauline epistles "with the Old Testament, and refers to the whole without differentiation by the long-hallowed names of 'scriptures of the Lord,' 'the scriptures,' or 'the scripture'" (188). Ferguson, "Selection and Closure," lists various types of scriptural formulations encompassing both the Old Testament and the New, and cites 2.27.2 as an example of such a scriptural formulation (306); it is the only one he lists that is claimed to use "gospels" to refer to the entirety of the New Testament. Similar claims are made by Sesboüé, "Preuve," 875; Farkasfalvy, "Theology," 329; Bokedal, *Significance*, 67; and Osborn, *Irenaeus*, 54.

[129] In addition to Unger, Benoit, *Irénée*, writes, "Il ressort clairement de cette formule que l'ensemble des Écritures comprend à la fois prophéties et les évangiles. Ceux-ci sont donc considérés comme Écriture" (120). Hoh, *Lehre*, similarly holds this passage up as evidence for the scriptural status of the gospels only (64). McDonald, *Formation*, says, "the Scriptures, for Irenaeus, were evidently made up of the still fluid collections of OT writings and *at least* the four Gospels" (198), citing 2.27.2 as proof. Werner, *Paulinisimus*, finds evidence from this passage that Irenaeus' notion of scripture explicitly excludes the Pauline epistles (43).

[130] When Irenaeus (infrequently) refers to the whole of the apostolic writings as a written collection, he uses the twofold formula "the Lord and the apostles" (1.8.1, 1.27.4, 2.2.5, 2.30.9, 2.35.4, 3.9.1, 3.17.4, 4.36.6), or occasionally just "the apostles" (3.8.1, 3.9.1, 3.19.2, 3.21.4, 3.24.1, 5.pre), but never "the gospels." There are a small number of instances where Irenaeus uses εὐαγγέλιον on its own in comparison with "law" or "prophets" (3.9.2, 3.10.6, 4.12.3, 4.34.1), but in these instances it is not the apostolic writings but the Gospel itself that is being referred to. Reed, "ΕΥΑΓΓΕΛΙΟΝ," reaches the same conclusion in her discussion of these passages (25–34). Cf. Robert H. Gundry, "ΕΥΑΓΓΕΛΙΟΝ: How Soon a Book?," *JBL* 115 (1996): 324.

[131] In his defense of the authority of the four Gospel accounts, Irenaeus identifies the basis of Luke's authority as his status as a follower of Paul (3.1.1), demonstrating that the Pauline epistles must possess authority equal to that of the gospels. Equivalent authority would presumably also extend to any other writings shown to be apostolic in origin. Cf. Lawson, *Biblical Theology*, 30–1.

considerations in this passage creates an uncomfortable tension, as it is difficult to account for why Irenaeus would give only the gospels the title "scripture" alongside the Jewish scriptures if he considers the other apostolic treatises to possess the same status.[132] This tension is the cause of the widespread disagreement as to whether the four gospels alone or a much larger collection of the apostolic writings are being referred to, even while it is agreed that whatever is referred to is being given a scriptural title.

Translational issues have added to the difficulty of interpreting this passage. The adjectives *propheticae* and *euangelicae* have proven problematic enough that a number of editors and translators decided to treat them as corruptions in the text. Massuet first elected to alter them to the nouns *prophetiae* and *euangelia* in his 1710 edition of *Adversus haereses*,[133] and defended his choice by maintaining, "This reading, which is cod. Clarom., is more agreeable than *et propheticae et euangelicae*, as contained in other transcripts."[134] No further justification is given for why this reading is more agreeable, and it appears he was mistaken about which manuscript his preferred reading was found in. Rousseau-Doutreleau note that *prophetiae* is not found in any of the three primary Latin manuscripts, but only in the fifteenth-century Vatican manuscript,[135] while *euangelia* is not found in *any* existing manuscripts, originating only in Massuet's 1710 edition.[136] Nonetheless, Massuet's editorial decision would be followed by all the major editions and translations of *Adversus haereses*,[137] until in 1982 the *Sources Chretiennes* edition returned to *propheticae* and *euangelicae*.[138] In spite of Massuet's claim, the SC rendering should be preferred on the basis of its overwhelming manuscript evidence.

On this basis, I propose the following translation:

Therefore, since the whole of both the prophetic and evangelical writings can be perceived openly, and without ambiguity, and similarly by all—although not all believe [*Cum itaque uniuersae Scripturae et propheticae, et euangelicae in aperto et sine ambiguitate, et similiter ab omnibus audiri possint etsi non omnes credunt*]. (2.27.2)

---

[132] Werner, *Paulinismus*, is the only one to have advanced the argument that Irenaeus considered the gospels but not the rest of the apostolic writings to be scripture (16–45), and his conclusions have not been met with agreement. Cf. Lawson, *Biblical Theology*, 31, 46–8, 52; Hitchcock, *Irenaeus*, 226–9; Benoit, *Irénée*, 139–40.

[133] PG 7:803.

[134] Ibid.; my trans.

[135] Vatican manuscript Latin 187, written around 1429. Cf. ACW 55:12-3; W. Sanday and C. H. Turner, *Novum Testamentum Sancti Irenaei* (Oxford: Clarendon Press, 1923), 25–35.

[136] SC 294:266.

[137] Harvey adopted Massuet's emendations in his 1857 edition (1:348), without offering any justification for this decision. Roberts-Donaldson's translation, based on Harvey's edition of the text, also follows this pattern, rendering this passage "the entire Scriptures, the prophets, and the Gospels" (ANF 1:398). Unger's translation also follows Harvey and Roberts-Donaldson (ACW 65:86; cf. ACW 55:16), despite the availability of Rousseau-Doutreleau's SC edition and translation.

[138] SC 294:266-7; cf. 293:311-12. Steenberg, "Graphe," 39, and Blanchard, *Sources*, 127, also adopt this rendering; they are the only interpreters to date to have done so.

This translation, by taking into account the adjectival function of *propheticae et euangelicae*, clarifies the intention of the sentence to contend that the specific writings that Irenaeus' opponents misuse (the Jewish scriptures and the gospels) can be clearly seen by any reasonable person to speak of the one God over all things whom his opponents deny. The Jewish scriptures and the gospels are specifically mentioned because Irenaeus has just finished spending four chapters discussing "the parables and acts of the Lord" (2.20.1), which his opponents pervert in order to reinterpret the Jewish scriptures to fit their teachings (2.20-24). It is these "prophetic and evangelical writings" to which Irenaeus now refers in order to contend that they clearly teach what his opponents try to deny with their "obscure explanations of the parables" (2.27.2). This translation has a dual advantage over the traditional translation and interpretation in that it conforms more closely to the manuscript evidence of the original Latin text, and its resulting interpretation is able to account for why it is only the gospels, rather than the apostolic writings as a whole, that are mentioned.

The implication of this translation is that Irenaeus is now seen not to be making a claim that "the entire Scriptures" are made up of "the Prophets and the Gospels," but rather is saying that the "prophetic and evangelical writings" that he has been discussing clearly teach what his opponents deny. In this interpretation γραφή cannot be understood to function in a general sense as a title ("*the writings*") for the apostolic writings alongside the Jewish scriptures, as Irenaeus has delimited precisely *which* "*Scripturae*" he is discussing. Irenaeus certainly seems to imply for the Gospel accounts a similar level of authority or importance to that of the Jewish scriptures; however, there is no indication of a corresponding transfer of scriptural status. His use of γραφή in this passage is therefore equivalent to its use in reference to the apostolic writings in the other passages that have been examined. If this proposed translation is accurate, this passage does not constitute evidence of the traditional claim that Irenaeus used γραφή as a scriptural title for the apostolic writings.

Conclusion

A closer examination of each of the passages that could be interpreted as evidence for the traditional interpretation's claim that Irenaeus used γραφή as a scriptural title for the apostolic writings within their immediate, proximate, and peripheral contexts has failed to turn up a single instance where the most plausible interpretation is that Irenaeus uses γραφή as a scriptural title for them. Every passage under discussion in this section finds its most probable interpretation either as a reference to the Jewish scriptures rather than the apostolic writings (Section 1.2A) or as the use of γραφή in reference to the specific *writing* under discussion, rather than as a scriptural title (Section 1.2B). Irenaeus' use of γραφή in reference to the apostolic writings matches his references to other non-scriptural and even heretical writings, and bears no resemblance to his clear and consistent use of γραφή as a title for the Jewish scriptures. These findings weigh heavily against the traditional interpretation's claim that Irenaeus used γραφή as a scriptural title for the apostolic writings alongside the Jewish scriptures.

1.3. Evidence That the Use of γραφή as a Scriptural Title Excludes the Apostolic Writings

In addition to the negative findings of the previous section, there are also a number of passages within Irenaeus' writings that support the positive assertion that his use of γραφή as a title in fact *excludes* the apostolic writings. The first group of passages exhibits the use of γραφή for the Jewish scriptures alone in which it appears that Irenaeus is speaking of the *entirety* of the scriptures as he understands them, and the second group indicates that the title αἱ γραφαὶ can be directly contrasted with the apostolic writings.

A. Γραφή Can Refer to the Jewish Scriptures while Indicating the Whole of the Scriptures

There are a number of instances in which Irenaeus uses γραφή as a title for the Jewish scriptures in such a way as to indicate that this collection constitutes the whole of the scriptures as he understands this concept. This pattern can be observed throughout Book 4. In one instance, in ch. 26, Irenaeus writes,

> If any one, therefore, reads the Scriptures with attention, he will find in them an account of Christ, and a foreshadowing of the new calling [*Si quis igitur intentus legat Scripturis, inveniet in eisdem de Christo sermonem et novae vocationis praefigurationem*]. For Christ is the treasure which was hid in the field, that is, in this world (for "the field is in the world"); but the treasure hid in the Scriptures is Christ, since He was pointed out by means of types and parables [*Hic enim est is "thesaurus absconsus in agro," hoc est in isto mundo—"ager" enim "mundus est"—absconsus vero in Scripturis, quoniam per typos et parabolas significabatur*]. (4.26.1)

In this passage Irenaeus uses γραφή as a title solely for the Jewish scriptures, and it is evident that "*Scripturis*" here includes the whole of αἱ γραφαὶ as he understands them. This interpretation receives further confirmation from his statement at the end of this chapter that the presbyters of the church who have received the apostolic succession,

> expound the Scriptures to us without danger [*Scripturas sine periculo nobis exponunt*], neither blaspheming God, nor dishonoring the patriarchs, nor despising the prophets [*neque Deum blasphemantes, neque patriarchas exhonorantes, neque prophetas contemnentes*]. (4.26.5)

Scripturas include only the writings of the patriarchs and prophets; no mention is made of the apostles. There are a number of additional examples of exclusive use of the title αἱ γραφαὶ by Irenaeus throughout Book 4.[139]

---

[139] Other examples of γραφή being used as a title to describe the whole of the scriptures and referring exclusively to the Jewish scriptures are found in 4.10.1-2, 4.11.1, 4.23.2, 4.24.2, 4.27.1, 4.31.1, 4.35.1, 4.35.4, etc.

Irenaeus' use of the title αἱ γραφαί as a reference solely to the Jewish scriptures is found also throughout the other books of *Adversus haereses*. Sesboüé identifies five passages in Book 3 in which "The *Scriptures* designate The Old Testament alone,"[140] the most explicit of which occurs in ch. 21. Irenaeus sets himself to proving the divinity of Christ from the scriptures beginning in ch. 19, as part of which ch. 21 is concerned to demonstrate that Christ was born of a *virgin*, rather than a *young girl*, as some of his opponents have translated the applicable typological text of Isaiah 7:14 (3.21.1). In the course of defending his own translation of this passage by explaining that it agrees with the Septuagint translation, Irenaeus defends the authority of the LXX as an inspired translation of the scriptures, before concluding, "The Scriptures, then, have been translated with such fidelity by God's grace [*Cum tanta igitur ueritate et gratia Dei interpretatae sint Scripturae*], and from these God has prepared and prefashioned our faith in His Son" (3.21.3). Here and throughout this chapter, Irenaeus repeatedly uses αἱ γραφαί as a title for the Jewish scriptures that were translated in the LXX, and indicates that it is the whole of the scriptures that have been translated.[141] He goes on to say,

> But our faith is firm and not fictitious, and alone true. This can be proved clearly from these Scriptures [*his Scripturis*], which were translated in the manner we described. Furthermore, the preaching of the Church is without additions. For since the apostles are much earlier than all these [heretics], they agree with the above mentioned translation, and the translation agrees with the tradition of the apostles [*Etinem apostoli, cum sint his omnibus uetustiores, consonant praedictae interpretationi, et interpretatio consonat apostolorum traditioni*]. For Peter and John and Matthew and Paul, and the rest after them, and also the followers of these, preached all the prophetical writings [*prophetica omnia*], just as they are contained in the translation of the elders. (3.21.3)

After using γραφή as a title for the Jewish scriptures numerous times throughout ch. 21, Irenaeus now adds the testimony of the apostles as a distinct witness, which *agrees* with the Greek translation of the scriptures, making the distinction explicit.

This identifiable pattern in Irenaeus' use of γραφή indicates that its function as a scriptural title is exclusive to the Jewish scriptures, suggesting the conclusion that the apostolic writings are considered to be distinct from αἱ γραφαί, contrary to the claim of the traditional interpretation. While such a conclusion remains tentative on the basis of the analysis of the above passages, these findings receive additional support from a number of passages where Irenaeus is more explicit.

---

[140] Sesboüé, "Preuve," 875; my trans. He identifies 3.12.8, 3.16.3, 3.16.4, 3.19.2, and 3.21.1-5 as examples (877–8).

[141] Lawson, *Biblical Theology*, 51; and Hitchcock, *Irenaeus*, 226; also conclude that αἱ γραφαί is used as a title for the Jewish scriptures alone in this chapter.

B. Αἱ γραφαί Are Contrasted with the Apostolic Writings

The passages in which Irenaeus most explicitly distinguishes between αἱ γραφαί and the apostolic writings are found in Books 1 and 2. In these passages "the Scriptures" are directly contrasted with the apostolic writings or with some part of them, indicating a definite distinction in Irenaeus' thought between those writings titled αἱ γραφαί and the apostolic writings. The first instance occurs in chs. 19 and 20 of Book 1, where Irenaeus sets out to demonstrate the methods by which his opponents prove their teaching of another God besides the Creator: "I considered it necessary to add to these things also whatever they attempt to persuade us of concerning their First-Father, who was unknown to all before Christ's coming" (1.19.1). His demonstration is in three parts, corresponding to the three sources used by his opponents. First, he explains,

> They select passages from the Scriptures [ἐκλέγοντες ἐκ τῶν γραφῶν] in order to prove that our Lord announced another Father beside the Creator of the universe, who, as we have already mentioned, they impiously say was a product of degeneracy. For instance, the words of the prophet Isaiah: "But Israel does not know me, and the people do not understand me," they adapt to refer to the ignorance about the invisible Profundity. (1.19.1)

Immediately after citing the verse from Isaiah, he cites verses from Hosea, the Psalms, Exodus, and Daniel in succession in order to prove his contention that "τῶν γραφῶν" are being perverted by his opponents. No verses from the apostolic writings are cited in this chapter. Next, he describes the second source:

> Besides those passages, they adduce an untold multitude of apocryphal and spurious writings [ἀμύθητον πλῆθος ἀποκρύφων καὶ νόθων γραφῶν], which they have composed to bewilder foolish men and such as do not understand the letters of the Truth [τῆς ἀληθείας μὴ ἐπισταμένων γράμματα]. (1.20.1)

This claim is demonstrated by one quotation, which is from an apocryphal gospel. After this Irenaeus describes the third source used by them:

> Further, they falsely fit to that standard some of the things put in the Gospel [ἐν τῷ Εὐαγγελίῳ κειμένων]; for example, the answer he [the Lord] gave to his Mother when he was twelve years old: "Did you not know that I must be about my Father's business?"[142] (1.20.2)

The verse from Luke in this passage is followed by seven more verses from the gospels to end his description of their arguments. Irenaeus' threefold classification of the sources used by his opponents is therefore comprised of "τῶν γραφῶν," "ἀποκρύφων καὶ νόθων γραφῶν," and "Εὐαγγελίῳ," indicating that αἱ γραφαί consist only of the

---

[142] Lk. 2:49.

Jewish scriptures, in this instance to the exclusion of the gospels and apocryphal writings.

This pattern becomes more explicit in Book 2, as Irenaeus attempts to demonstrate the errors of the Valentinian systems and methods of interpretation. In ch. 9 he says,

> That God is the Maker of the world is clear even to those people who talk against him in many ways, and they acknowledge him by calling him Maker and styling him an Angel, without mentioning that all the Scriptures acclaim [him], and the Lord teaches this "Father who is in heaven" and not some other [*ut non dicamus quoniam omnes clamant Scripturae et Dominus hunc Patrem qui est in caelis docet et non alium*], as we shall show in the course of this treatise. (2.9.1)

In this passage Irenaeus proclaims that the scriptures *and* the Lord's words in Matthew are in agreement, making a two-part case that the Jewish scriptures and the Gospel accounts proclaim one and the same God. Irenaeus' use of αἱ γραφαί here in differentiation from the gospels constitutes an implicit yet direct statement that he conceives of the apostolic writings as separate and distinct from "the Scriptures." While the existence of one such passage could perhaps be a mistake or a scribal error, this passage is not unique. Irenaeus makes a virtually identical statement in 2.28.4:

> The Father alone is called God, as he truly is, whom you call Demiurge. The Scriptures know only this God; and the Lord acknowledges only him as his own Father and knows of no other, as we shall prove from his very words [*sed et cum Scripturae hunc solum sciant Deum, sed et cum Dominus hunc solum confitetur proprium Patrem et alterum nesciat, sicut ex ipsis uerbis eius ostendemus*]. (2.28.4)

Once again, "the Scriptures" are explicitly distinguished from the words of the Lord in the Gospel accounts. It is evident from this that the scriptures and the words of the Lord represent two distinct sources for Irenaeus.

It is not only the words of the Lord in the gospels that he directly contrasts with αἱ γραφαί. Only a few chapters further he writes,

> All the Scriptures loudly proclaim that there are spiritual creatures in heaven. Paul, too, testifies that these are spiritual beings [*Quoniam enim sunt in caelis spiritales conditiones, uniuersae clamant Scripturae, et Paulus autem testimonium perhibet quoniam sunt spiritalia*]. (2.30.7)

In this passage "*uniuersae Scripturae*" are directly contrasted with the writings of Paul as Irenaeus establishes the agreement of two witnesses to make his case, in the same way that the scriptures were contrasted with the words of the Lord in the examples above.[143] Paul—and presumably also the other apostolic epistles—therefore appears to be considered alongside the gospels as a separate witness from the scriptures.

---

[143] Werner, *Paulinismus*, also concludes that 2.30.7 demonstrates that "die Paulusbriefe eine ausserhalb der Summe der *universae scripturae* stehende Instanz sind" (44). Hitchcock, *Irenaeus*, agrees that

Irenaeus' understanding that αἱ γραφαὶ comprise only the Jewish scriptures and are distinct from the apostolic writings is perhaps most directly expressed at the end of ch. 28, as he explains that full knowledge containing all things is unattainable. Using the example of the problem of God's foreknowledge, Irenaeus explains,

> The Lord told us plainly, and the rest of the Scriptures prove [*Dominus manifeste dixit, et reliquae demonstrant Scripturae*], that eternal fire is prepared for sinners ... But neither does any Scripture relate, nor does the Apostle tell us, nor did the Lord teach [*neque Scriptura aliqua retulit neque Apostolus dixit neque Dominus docuit*] what the cause of the nature itself of sinners is. And so we ought to leave such knowledge of this to God, just as the Lord did the knowledge of the hour and day. (2.28.7)

Irenaeus' claim at the beginning of this passage that "The Lord told us plainly, and the rest of the Scriptures prove" that eternal fire has been prepared for sinners has often been understood to suggest that he envisions a certain equivalence between the gospels and the scriptures, contrary to his statements in the other passages above.[144] However, his understanding of this relationship is immediately clarified, as he states concerning the cause of the nature of sinners that "neither does any Scripture relate, nor does the Apostle tell us, nor did the Lord teach." This statement demonstrates a clear distinction in Irenaeus' thought between the scriptures, the apostolic teaching, and the words of the Lord, which comprise three distinct sources of authority for him.[145] This passage parallels a number of other statements such as 1.8.1:

> Such is their system which neither the prophets preached, nor the Lord taught, nor the apostles handed down [οὔτε προφῆται ἐκήρυξαν, οὔτε ὁ Κύριος ἐδίδαξεν οὔτε ἀπόστολοι παρέδωκαν].[146]

---

this passage is best interpreted as distinguishing between Paul's writings and "the Scriptures," although he finds counter evidence in other places (225). He is followed by Farkasfalvy, "Theology," 332. Lawson, *Biblical Theology*, disagrees with Werner, arguing that the passage is inconclusive: "A contrast between 'the Scriptures' and 'Paul' may certainly be read into the first sentence, but equally the passage may be taken as treating Paul as an example of Scripture" (47). Benoit, *Irénée*, also argues against Werner that this passage could also be interpreted as including Paul among "the Scriptures" (139); while Hoh, *Lehre*, gives this passage as evidence *for* Paul's scriptural status (65).

[144] Cf. Hoh, *Lehre*, 75; Steenberg, "Graphe," 40. Unger and Roberts–Donaldson suggest that the gospels are to be considered part of "the Scriptures" in their translations (ACW 65:91; ANF 1:401). Rousseau–Doutreleau interpret this clause instead as distinguishing between the Lord and the scriptures: "le Seigneur l'a dit clairement et toutes les Écritures le démontrent" (SC 294:287).

[145] Hitchcock, *Irenaeus*, agrees that scripture is distinguished from the Lord here, but takes this as evidence that Irenaeus' use of γραφή is "too vague or loose" for establishing scriptural status, for the purpose of arguing that Irenaeus' lack of use of γραφή in reference to passages from the Pauline writings does not mitigate against their scriptural status (226). Similarly, Blanchard, *Sources*, notes that 2.28.7 "allows us to identify the word 'Scripture' as covering the whole of the Old Testament by differentiation from the new testament traditions" (125; my trans.), yet he contends that this represents an exception, and that only the plural *scripturae* refers exclusively to the Jewish scriptures.

[146] Cf. 2.30.9, 2.2.5, 2.35.4, 3.8.1, 3.9.1, 3.9.2, 3.17.4, 5.pre, etc.

It is significant that "προφῆται" here is replaced by "*Scriptura*" in the above passage, indicating that the prophetic writings are considered to be identical to αἱ γραφαί, while the apostolic writings are distinguished.

Taken together, the passages examined in this section combine to form a compelling case that Irenaeus' use of the title αἱ γραφαί refers exclusively to the Jewish scriptures, and therefore excludes the apostolic writings, in direct contradiction to the claim of the traditional interpretation. These findings also support the accuracy of the alternative interpretations of the passages analyzed in Section 1.2, which the traditional interpretation utilizes as evidence.

Chapter Conclusion

The purpose of this chapter has been to evaluate the traditional interpretation's claim that Irenaeus used γραφή as a title for the apostolic writings alongside the Jewish scriptures, one of the central proofs for the traditional view that Irenaeus considers the apostolic writings to possess equivalent scriptural status. This investigation, utilizing Wittgenstein's concept of words as "instruments characterized by their use" as an interpretative strategy by which to analyze Irenaeus' uses of γραφή in reference to the Jewish scriptures and the apostolic writings, found a consistent pattern of use. While a brief investigation of Irenaeus' references to the Jewish scriptures found that they are consistently referred to using γραφή as a scriptural title (Section 1.1), his references to the apostolic writings were found to differ significantly. Many passages which have traditionally been interpreted as evidence that Irenaeus uses γραφή as a scriptural title for the apostolic writings were found instead to have been references to the Jewish scriptures (Section 1.2A), while a number of other passages in which γραφή was used in reference to the apostolic writings were found to have exhibited the use of γραφή as a reference to a specific *writing* under discussion, rather than as the scripturally significant title "*the writings*" (Section 1.2B). No evidence of unquestionable use of γραφή as a title that included the apostolic writings was discovered, in sharp contrast to Irenaeus' consistent use of γραφή as a title for the Jewish scriptures. These findings received further confirmation from a number of additional references to αἱ γραφαί, which demonstrate that Irenaeus explicitly distinguishes between αἱ γραφαί and the apostolic writings (Section 1.3).

The findings of this investigation lead to the conclusion that Irenaeus does not initiate a new practice of extending the scriptural title αἱ γραφαί to include the apostolic writings, and therefore that his use of γραφή does not provide evidence for the traditional interpretation that Irenaeus considered the apostolic writings to be scripture equivalent to the Jewish scriptures. Irenaeus' practice of reserving the title αἱ γραφαί for the Jewish scriptures to the exclusion of the apostolic writings suggests the existence of a significant conceptual distinction between the two collections in his thought—a distinction widely underappreciated in the standard account of Irenaeus' scriptural consciousness.

2

Authoritative Texts or Authoritative Authors?

In this chapter, the evaluation of the traditional interpretation's claim that Irenaeus considers the apostolic writings to be scripture continues with an assessment of the second of its substantiating arguments: Irenaeus uses the apostolic writings in the same manner as he uses the Jewish scriptures, that is, as a *scriptural text*. This argument is often unstated, running implicitly through accounts of Irenaeus' use of the apostolic writings, although occasionally an explicit endorsement of this argument is given. Benoit, commenting on the lack of attributions to the Gospel accounts as γραφή in Irenaeus' works, maintains, "If there is hesitation when it comes to the terminology, and if a little embarrassment is found to speak of 'Scripture' concerning the gospels, there is no doubt in substance: the gospels are used in the same manner as the Old Testament and their authority is identical."[1] He likewise comments on Irenaeus' use of the Pauline epistles that "there is no difference between their utilization and that of the Old Testament," demonstrating that "they are part of the *Scripturae*."[2] A number of other interpreters have made equivalent claims,[3] and a similar implication is entailed by Campenhausen's argument that for the first time in Irenaeus the apostolic writings "now serve to construct a formal 'proof from scripture' such as had previously been drawn only from the Old Testament."[4]

---

[1] Benoit, *Irénée*, 122; my trans. Here Benoit utilizes both the second argument of undifferentiated use and the third argument of equivalent authority.

[2] Ibid., 141; my trans.

[3] Benoit is echoed by Steenberg, "Graphe," who also utilizes both the second and third claims of the traditional interpretation's argument to cover any possible deficiencies in the first claim. He argues that while Irenaeus' use of γραφή might seem to rule out the New Testament as part of "the scriptures," Irenaeus uses the New Testament "in the same manner" as the Old, and assigns it the same authoritative status (32). For Hoh, *Lehre*, these two arguments are one: the same manner of use of the apostolic writings and Jewish scriptures indicates that they possess the same level of authority, and therefore the same scriptural status. As he explains, "sind ntl Schriften ohne Unterschied der Wertung neben Propheten Moses, lex gestellt. Wenn man bedenkt, was für hohe Vorstellungen Ir. vom AT hat, so liegt in dieser Nebeneinanderstellung eine offenkundige Gleichachtung des NT mit dem AT" (75), thus demonstrating their scriptural status. Among Harnack's reasons for declaring that the New Testament writings were canonical scripture by the time of Irenaeus is his contention that the New Testament "is used exactly like the Old Testament" (HD 2:44). A similar sentiment appears to be expressed by McDonald, *Formation*, when he claims that Irenaeus "freely employed the four canonical Gospels and the letters of Paul in a scriptural fashion" (167).

[4] McDonald, *Formation*, 185. He claims that Irenaeus "was the first catholic theologian who dared to adopt the Marcionite principle of a new 'scripture' " (186; cited approvingly by McDonald, *Formation*, 166), and maintains, "Adversus haereses is nothing less than a comprehensive and continuous proof from Scripture, and the Scripture in question is 'New Testament' " (187). However, Campenhausen

In order to assess the plausibility of this argument, this chapter begins with a brief description of two core characteristics of Irenaeus' use of the Jewish scriptures (Section 2.1), followed by a detailed analysis of Irenaeus' patterns of use of the apostolic writings in the following two sections for the purpose of determining whether Irenaeus' treatment of the apostolic writings is equivalent. First, the question of whether the apostolic writings are treated as an inherently authoritative text, as the Jewish scriptures are, is evaluated (Section 2.2). Following this, an examination of whether Irenaeus' principle of interpretation of the apostolic writings matches that of the Jewish scriptures is undertaken (Section 2.3). My argument is that Irenaeus' use of the apostolic writings differs significantly from his use of the Jewish scriptures. While the Jewish scriptures are used straightforwardly as an inherently authoritative scriptural text, the apostolic writings are used instead as a record of the testimony of authoritative authors, contrary to the traditional interpretation's claim that Irenaeus uses the apostolic writings as scripture equivalent to the Jewish scriptures. This would suggest the further conclusion that in Irenaeus' conception the apostolic writings possess their unique revelatory authority on the basis of the derived authority of their apostolic authors, rather than perceived scriptural status, as the Jewish scriptures do. This significant difference would seem to confirm the existence of the conceptual distinction suggested in the previous chapter between the apostolic writings and the Jewish scriptures, and to indicate a possible basis for it.

2.1. Use of the Jewish Scriptures

In order to determine to what extent Irenaeus' use of the apostolic writings parallels his use of the Jewish scriptures, it is worth briefly describing two core characteristics of his use of the Jewish scriptures, in order to create a baseline for comparison. This description focuses on his treatment of the Jewish scriptures as an authoritative *text*, and his principle of interpretation that (initially) appears indifferent to authorial intent.

A. The Jewish Scriptures Are Treated as Authoritative Texts

The first characteristic of Irenaeus' use of the Jewish scriptures is his treatment of them primarily as an inherently authoritative *text*,[5] rather than as the testimony of an

---

does not view the scriptural use of the apostolic writings as the result of transferring the status of the Jewish scriptures to them: "Irenaeus does not proceed simply by putting the new Scripture alongside the old, and then asserting its authority by analogy. He does not start from a general 'principle of scripture,' which would carry over from the Old Testament to the New" (188). Similarly, Lawson, *Biblical Theology*, though he believes that the Pauline letters and the gospels are used "in the same manner as the prophets" (46–7), nonetheless notes that the apostolic writings and Jewish scriptures are not conceived of identically: "in the case of the Apostolic writings he always bases their authority on the fact of the authorship, not on the simple circumstance that the book occurs in the Canon. The argument is always that the books were written by the Apostles, or by those who had trustworthy recollection of the Apostles" (35).

[5] The use of the terminology of "text" risks implying additional connotations that are not intended. George Aichele, *Biblical Meaning: Canon as Semiotic Mechanism* (Harrisburg: Trinity Press International, 2001), differentiates between two different uses of "text." He notes, "the word 'text'

authoritative *author*. In other words, in Irenaeus' use the text of the Jewish scriptures itself functions authoritatively, without requiring an appeal to its prophetic authors. This use can be observed both in the way he introduces citations from the Jewish scriptures and in his references to and discussions about the Jewish scriptures.

Introductions to Citations from the Jewish Scriptures

Irenaeus' references to the Jewish scriptures when introducing citations from them demonstrate that they are treated as an authoritative text whose authority does not rely upon their authorship. This statement operates on the basis of the presumption that when a given passage of writing is declared (or assumed) to be authoritative in its claims, without appeal to its own interior logic that is meant to convince the reader of the truth of these claims,[6] its perceived authority must therefore reside in the authoritative status of either the author of the passage or the textual unit of which it is a part. In Irenaeus' introductions to citations, passages taken from the Jewish scriptures can at various times be described either as the testimony of authoritative authors (the prophets) or as belonging to an authoritative textual unit (the scriptures), indicating that either referent can function authoritatively on its own, without reference to the other (though the authority of both is undoubtedly interconnected).

A brief examination of Irenaeus' frequent citations from the Pentateuch may be used as a case study by which to illustrate his patterns of use of citations from the Jewish scriptures as a whole. Each of these citations is used authoritatively in his arguments, and his methods of introducing each are understood to provide an indication of whether its authoritative status is being established with reference to the identity and status of its human author or to the scriptural status of the text itself.[7] Irenaeus often introduces citations from the first five books of the Jewish scriptures as the attestation of Moses; in these instances the authority of the prophetic writer appears as the basis of authority for the passage. Thus, quoting a passage from Deuteronomy as evidence for his position in 5.18.3, Irenaeus introduces it with the words, "as Moses declared this very thing among the people." Direct references of this kind are not uncommon for

---

often stands in a special relationship to writing," while it can also be used "to refer to the materiality of *any sign*, written or otherwise" (15; italics added). Within this book, the use of the term "text" corresponds to his first definition, referring specifically to the *written-ness* of a particular writing, the physical document itself, in differentiation from the *message* it communicates and its function as the communication of an author. Cf. the similar use of this term in Lewis Ayres, " 'There's Fire in That Rain:' On Reading the Letter and Reading Allegorically," *MoTh* 28.4 (2012): 616–34, esp. 618–20.

[6] There are a number of times within *Adversus haereses* where Irenaeus appeals to the quality or persuasiveness of the cited claim itself, rather than the authority of its author or the status of the text. He introduces a quotation from Justin Martyr with "Justin does well say" (4.6.2); a quotation from the *Shepherd of Hermas* is introduced with "Therefore the writing spoke well, which says" (4.20.2); a quotation from Plato begins, "Plato is shown to be more religious than these men, since he acknowledged that one and the same God is both just and good ... Thus he said" (3.25.5); etc.

[7] Patterns of citation do not necessarily indicate underlying conscious determinations; it is likely that these patterns are largely habitual, rather than deliberate attributions of authority. However, if Irenaeus' habitual preferences of terminology arose as a result of his underlying understanding of the nature of the authority of the Jewish scriptures, then it should be possible to infer this understanding from his introductions to citations even if he is not always conscious of communicating it.

Irenaeus: he introduces passages from the Pentateuch as the words of Moses twenty-six times throughout *Adversus haereses* and the *Demonstration*.[8] Each instance can be interpreted as an implicit claim that the authority of the scriptural passage being cited is founded to some degree on the authority of the prophet who wrote it.

On the other hand, Irenaeus often cites passages from the Pentateuch without reference to their human author, introducing a text simply as "Scripture," or by the title of the individual book (Genesis, etc.), or as words spoken by God, the Word, or the Spirit. Thus, for example, within a few chapters of the passage above Irenaeus introduces quotations from Genesis with the words, "as the Scripture tells us [*Scriptura dicit*] that the serpent said to the woman" (5.23.1), "as it holds in Genesis [*habet in Genesi*] that God said to the serpent" (5.21.1),[9] and "therefore says the Spirit of God [*ait Spiritus Dei*]" (5.20.2). In *Adversus haereses* and the *Demonstration* Irenaeus refers to passages from the Pentateuch as "Scripture" twenty-three times;[10] he identifies a passage by the title of the book in which it is found twelve times;[11] and in eighteen instances he characterizes a passage from the Pentateuch as having been given by "the Spirit," "the Word," or "God."[12] Together, these are approximately double his references to Moses as author.

Irenaeus' use in these instances suggests that in these citations the Jewish scriptures are being used primarily as an authoritative *text* rather than as the words of an authoritative human author, with authority therefore established on the basis of scriptural status in order to prove his assertions.[13] If this inference is correct, the authority of the prophetic writers is not required for the passages themselves to function authoritatively. The Jewish scriptures are able to function as a scriptural *text*, without the requirement of appealing to the authority of a human author—though the prophetic writers still can be and often are the stated authority behind a given passage.

These findings of the number and type of referenced authorities in introductions to scriptural citations of the books of the Pentateuch are generally applicable to the citations of all the books of the Jewish scriptures throughout Irenaeus' writings, having only variations in emphasis.[14]

---

[8] Cf. 1.18.1, 1.20.1, 2.2.5, 3.12.10, 3.18.7, 4.2.1, 4.8.3, 4.10.2, 4.15.1, 4.16.2, 4.16.3, 4.16.4, 4.16.5, 4.18.1, 4.20.6, 4.20.8, 4.31.2, 4.32.1, 5.18.3, *Dem.* 43, *Dem.* 44, *Dem.* 55, *Dem.* 57, *Dem.* 58, *Dem.* 79, and *Dem.* 95.

[9] My trans.

[10] 2.2.5, 3.6.1, 3.23.2, 3.23.3, 4.11.1, 4.16.1, 4.16.4, 4.20.1, 4.25.2, 4.30.2, 4.31.1, 4.40.3, 5.5.1, 5.15.2, 5.15.4, 5.16.1, 5.17.1, 5.23.1 (twice), 5.28.3, *Dem.* 24, *Dem.* 32, *Dem.* 44.

[11] 4.2.1, 4.8.3, 4.15.1 (twice), 4.16.1, 4.16.2, 4.16.3, 4.20.6, 5.21.1, *Dem.* 55, *Dem.* 57, and *Dem.* 95. In a number of these instances Moses is also mentioned by name, but is mentioned as a speaker within the story, rather than as the author of the passage.

[12] Authorship by "the Spirit": 3.6.5, 5.20.2, *Dem.* 2, *Dem.* 24, and *frg.* 20 (ANF 22). Authorship by "the Word": 2.34.4, 4.7.4, 4.20.9 (twice), 4.29.2, *Dem.* 2, and *Dem.* 46. Authorship by "God": 4.16.1, 4.18.3, 5.23.1, *Dem.* 24, *Dem.* 26, and *Dem.* 29.

[13] Although emphasized in a different way, this is also the case with passages introduced as having been spoken by "the Spirit," "the Word," or "God." In these instances of stated divine authorship, the human element is similarly minimized, here treated as incidental to the more central process of divine communication. Cf. Section 2.1B.

[14] In the books of the prophets, for example, Irenaeus appears less likely to use the title ἡ γραφή, often preferring to introduce a given passage as having been spoken by the Word or the Spirit. Variations of this sort are explained by differences in subject matter and Irenaeus' polemical needs.

References to the Jewish Scriptures

Similar patterns are found in Irenaeus' references to the Jewish scriptures. On occasion he refers to the Jewish scriptures as "the writings of Moses" (4.2.3),[15] "the testimony of the prophets" (3.21.1),[16] and so on.[17] However, it is much more common for him to refer to "the Law and the Prophets [ὁ νομός καὶ αἱ προφῆται]"[18] or "the Scriptures [αἱ γραφαί],"[19] without any reference to a human author. He often argues that the Lord acknowledges the same Father "who was announced by the Law and the Prophets [*a lege et prophetis adnuntiatus sit*]" (2.11.1) and declares that "the Scriptures know only this God" (2.28.4). Irenaeus also consistently refers to the Jewish scriptures as authoritative scriptural *texts* in discussions of their authority. It is the *Scriptures* that are called "perfect," "given by God's Word and Spirit" (2.28.2), declared to be "Spiritual" (2.28.3), claimed to be "translated through the inspiration of God" (3.21.2), and said to testify of the Lord because "they were from one and the same Father" (4.10.1). In similar fashion to his patterns of introducing citations, when Irenaeus discusses the Jewish scriptures he often does so specifically in reference to the text itself, indicating that its authority is able to function independently from the authority of its prophetic authors.

The existence of a large number of instances of scriptural citations and references without attributed human authorship in Irenaeus' writings does not negate his practice of introducing and discussing the Jewish scriptures as having been spoken by the specific prophet who wrote them, and the attribution of authority this presupposes. It does, however, demonstrate that the authority of the Jewish scriptures does not *require* reference to them. The point that will become relevant in Section 2.2 is that the Jewish scriptures are able to function as an authority for Irenaeus specifically as *texts*, and on the basis of the scriptural status of these texts, without reference to a human author and therefore without the requirement of the authority such an author would provide. Authoritative human authorship does not appear to be a necessary component of the authoritative status of the scriptural text, even if Irenaeus does believe and often illustrates that the prophetic authors themselves are authoritative.

---

[15] Irenaeus also alludes to the Pentateuch as having been written by Moses in 2.22.3 and 2.24.4.

[16] Cf. 3.21.2, 3.24.1, 4.2.3, 4.17.1, 4.20.5. Irenaeus often refers to the Jewish scriptures as "the prophets," but in many cases αἱ προφῆται functions as a conventional title for the Jewish scriptures themselves, rather than as a reference to the prophetic authors, and in many other cases his intent cannot be determined.

[17] Irenaeus can speak of "reading Isaiah the prophet" (3.12.8), but it is exceedingly rare for him to refer to the "writings of Isaiah" or of any other prophet outside of introductions to citations.

[18] 1.3.6, 1.27.1, 1.27.2 (twice), 2.11.1, 3.1.2, 3.10.2, 3.10.4, 3.12.7, 4.5.1, 4.6.6, 4.9.3, 4.12.12, 5.17.2. Irenaeus also often speaks of "ὁ νομός" or "αἱ προφῆται" in isolation to refer to the Jewish scriptures, but it is difficult to determine whether Irenaeus' use of ὁ νομός is a reference to the mosaic law itself or the scriptures in which they are found, and whether ἁι προφῆται functions as a title or a reference to the prophetic authors themselves.

[19] See especially 2.9.1, 2.28.4, 2.28.7, 2.30.7, 4.10.1, 4.11.1, 4.23.1, 4.31.1, 4.35.4, 5.5.1, etc. All Irenaeus' uses of γραφή have been catalogued and listed in 1.1, p. 18 nn. 25–6.

B. Irenaeus' Principle of Interpretation Appears Indifferent to Authorial Intent

The second significant characteristic of Irenaeus' use of the Jewish scriptures is his principle of interpretation, which is closely related to his treatment of them as authoritative texts. There are many aspects of Irenaeus' method of interpretation that merit careful discussion, and a number of works have already attempted this task in one form or another.[20] This section focuses on one particular aspect of his interpretative method that is considered to be an overarching principle: the Jewish scriptures are consistently interpreted seemingly without consideration of their authors' own intended meanings, in order to demonstrate that the Jewish scriptures prophesied the coming of Christ according to God's economy of salvation. This type of interpretation is commonly described using the categories of "allegorical" and/or "typological" (in contrast with "literal") interpretation, but these categories often prove unhelpful and may actually serve to obscure Irenaeus' intentions.[21] The more relevant contrast is between concern for the meaning intended by the author (regardless of whether the author uses allegorical or literal language to communicate his or her intention) and concern for what the text itself, in isolation from its historical context, may be interpreted to say (utilizing any of a number of possible interpretative methods).

As a scriptural text, the Jewish scriptures are understood by Irenaeus to possess a single unified meaning that can be understood by reading them according to the correct ὑπόθεσις and that therefore does not ultimately depend on the intentions of the various prophetic authors in their original contexts. In his description of the proper understanding of the Jewish scriptures, Irenaeus maintains,

> If any one, therefore, reads the Scriptures with attention, he will find in them an account of Christ ... since He was pointed out by means of types and parables

---

[20] Lawson, "On the Exegesis of the Bible," in *Biblical Theology*, 55–86; Jacques Fantino, *La Théologie d'Irénée: Lecture des Écritures en réponse à l'exégèse gnostique: Une approche trinitaire* (Paris: du Cerf, 1994); Rolf Noormann, *Irenäus als Paulusinterpret: zur Rezeption und Wirkung der paulinischen und deuteropaulinischen Briefe im Werk des Irenäus von Lyon* (Tubingen: J. C. B. Mohr, 1994); Frances Young, *Biblical Exegesis and the Formation of Christian Culture* (Cambridge: Cambridge University Press, 1997); D. Jeffrey Bingham, *Irenaeus's Use of Matthew's Gospel in Adversus Haereses* (Louvain: Peeters, 1998); Charles Kannengiesser, "The 'Speaking' God and Irenaeus's Interpretative Pattern: The Reception of Genesis," *ASEs* 15.2 (1998): 337–52; Brox, "Irenaeus," 1:483–505; Thomas Holsinger-Friesen, *Irenaeus and Genesis: A Study of Competition in Early Christian Hermeneutics* (Winona Lake, IN: Eisenbrauns, 2009); Lewis Ayres, "Reading the Letter"; "Irenaeus vs. the Valentinians: Toward a Rethinking of Patristic Exegetical Origins," *JECS* 23.2 (2015): 153–87; David W. Jorgensen, *Treasure Hidden in a Field: Early Christian Reception of the Gospel of Matthew* (Berlin: De Gruyter, 2016).

[21] A useful critique of these terms and summary of their use is found in Young, *Biblical Exegesis*, esp. chs. 6–9. She notes, in her description of methods of patristic exegesis of scripture, that "The usual categories of literal, typological and allegorical are clearly inadequate to describe most of what we have observed" (99). Cf. Lewis Ayres, "Patristic and Medieval Theologies of Scripture: An Introduction," in *Christian Theologies of Scripture: A Comparative Introduction*, ed. Justin S. Holcomb (New York: New York University Press, 2006); who notes that the term "literal" "is frequently associated in modern discussion with the sense intended by the human author of a text or the sense that a text had for its initial readers" (14), despite the fact that this is not what early Christian exegetes meant by the term. Cf. also "Reading the Letter" and "Irenaeus vs. the Valentinians."

[*quoniam per typos et parabolas significabatur*]. Hence His human nature could not be understood, prior to the consummation of those things which had been predicted ... for every prophecy, before its fulfillment, is to men [full of] enigmas and ambiguities [*Omnis enim prophetia priusquam habeat effectum, aenigmata et ambiguitates sunt hominibus*]. (4.26.1)[22]

Irenaeus believes that the proper reading of the Jewish scriptures is as an account of Christ, given by types and parables that could not be understood prior to his Incarnation. It appears that whatever original meaning may have been intended by the prophetic writers in their own contexts is simply not relevant to the proper interpretation of the Jewish scriptures.

In practice, Irenaeus' interpretations of the Jewish scriptures are consistent with his description of their proper interpretation. Two examples illustrate his practice. In ch. 21 of Book 4 Irenaeus sets out a number of interpretations of stories from Genesis without concern for historical context in order to demonstrate that they prophesied the coming of Christ. In 4.21.3 he turns to the story of Jacob, which he begins by saying, "If any one, again, will look into Jacob's actions, he shall find them not destitute of meaning, but full of import with regard to the dispensations [*sed plenos dispositionum*]," before going on to explain the true prophetic meaning of the events of that story. He describes that Jacob's birth holding his brother's heel represents striving and conquering, and is therefore a type of Christ and his purpose to be born to conquer his adversary. In similar fashion, Jacob receiving the rights of the firstborn occurred in order to represent the younger nation receiving Christ, the "first-begotten," when the older nation rejected him. Jacob begetting sons from two sisters represents Christ being born of two laws from the same Father, while Jacob's patience for Rachel prefigures the church for whom Christ patiently endured. In this interpretation the events of the story themselves are understood to prophesy about the Incarnation.[23] As a unified scriptural text, every part of the Jewish scriptures is concerned with the same overall prophetic message, and can be interpreted accordingly.

In the *Demonstration* Irenaeus frequently makes use of similar interpretations.[24] In the midst of a lengthy section of interpretations of the prophets of this type, spanning *Dem.* 53-89, Irenaeus interprets a passage from the Psalms describing God's covenant with David as referring ahead to Christ's Passion. He says,

> And concerning the Passion of Christ, moreover, the same prophet says: "You, you have rejected and despised us, you have cast forth your Anointed<>, you have broken the covenant with <your> Servant, you have cast down His sanctuary, you have broken down all His hedge[s], you have put His strongholds in trepidation—those who pass by the way despoiled Him, He is become a reproach to His

---

[22] Cf. 4.25.3 and 4.33.10.
[23] Interpretations of this kind that take events occurring in the Jewish scriptures to be types of Christ or of realities that are fulfilled at his advent are common for Irenaeus. Cf. 3.17.3, 3.21.8, 4.31.1-3, 5.17.4, etc.
[24] Cf. *Dem.* 9, 43, 47–50, 53–89, 92, etc.

neighbours; you have exalted the right hand of His oppressors, you have made His enemies glad over Him, you have turned away the help of His sword and not given Him a hand in battle; you have removed Him from purification, you have cast down His throne to the earth, you have shortened the days of His time, and you have poured shame [down] upon Him."[25] Both that He would suffer these things, and that [it would be] by the will of the Father, he clearly shows, for by the will of the Father He was going to undergo the passion. (*Dem.* 75)

Though this passage and the context of the psalm suggest (to modern readers) that the author was speaking of David and his kingdom, Irenaeus feels justified in asserting that this is in fact a prophecy of Christ's passion. This is permitted because the true purpose of the Psalms, as with all the Jewish scriptures, is to point forward to the Incarnation.

The Rule of Scriptural Interpretation

Despite his consistent practice, however, many interpretations using similar methods are disallowed by Irenaeus. He repeatedly takes issue with his opponents' interpretations of the Jewish scriptures by which they prove their own systems. In one instance, criticizing their interpretation of the creation account, he says,

> And while they affirm such things as these concerning the creation, every one of them generates something new, day by day, according to his ability; for no one is deemed "perfect," who does not develop among them some mighty fictions. (1.18.1)[26]

He then goes on to describe their method of interpretation of Genesis 1 in demonstration of their error:

> Moses, then, they declare, by his mode of beginning the account of the creation, has at the commencement pointed out the mother of all things when he says, "In the beginning God created the heaven and the earth;" for, as they maintain, by naming these four,—God, beginning, heaven, and earth,—he set forth their Tetrad. Indicating also its invisible and hidden nature, he said, "Now the earth was invisible and unformed." They will have it, moreover, that he spoke of the second Tetrad, the offspring of the first, in this way—by naming an abyss and darkness, in which were also water, and the Spirit moving upon the water. Then, proceeding to mention the Decad, he names light, day, night, the firmament, the evening, the morning, dry land, sea, plants, and, in the tenth place, trees. Thus, by means of these ten names he indicated the ten Aeons. The power of the Duodecad, again, was shadowed forth by him thus:—He names the sun, moon, stars, seasons, years, whales, fishes, reptiles, birds, quadrupeds, wild beasts, and after all these, in the

---

[25] Ps. 88:39-46 (LXX).
[26] ANF 1:343.

twelfth place, man. Thus they teach that the Triacontad was spoken of through Moses by the Spirit. (1.18.1)[27]

The interpretation Irenaeus describes here bears resemblance to Irenaeus' own interpretations, similarly uninterested in the context of the passage and the observable intention of the prophetic writer.[28] This similarity of interpretative methods has led some to question whether Irenaeus is guilty of the same thing he accuses his opponents of.[29] It is not the interpretation itself that Irenaeus takes issue with, however. His problem with his opponents' interpretations has less to do with their specific styles or methods than it does with the overarching system that guides their interpretations, and with their practice of ignoring plain passages of the Jewish scriptures in favor of more ambiguous ones for this reason. As he explains,

> Since many parables and allegories have been spoken [ἄτε πολλῶν παραβολῶν καὶ ἀλληγοριῶν εἰρημένων] and can be made to mean many things, what is ambiguous they cleverly and deceitfully adapt to their fabrication by an unusual explanation [τὸ ἀμφίβολον διὰ τῆς ἐξηγήσεως [ἕτεροι δὲ] δεινῶς τῷ πλάσματι αὐτῶν καὶ δολίως ἐφαρμόζοντες]. Thus they lead away from the Truth into captivity. (1.3.6)

Irenaeus is in agreement that there are many passages in the Jewish scriptures that have been spoken in "parables and allegories," and takes issue instead with the fact that his opponents use only these ambiguous and difficult to understand passages, ignoring the plain passages that make clear the true message of the scriptures.[30] This strategy is employed by them because they interpret the Jewish scriptures according to a false ὑπόθεσις or system,[31] which they get from non-scriptural sources (1.8.1).

This notion of a false ὑπόθεσις[32] is central to Irenaeus' critiques of his opponents and arguments for correct methods of interpretation throughout *Adversus haereses*,

---

[27] Ibid.
[28] Other descriptions of his opponents' interpretations can be observed in 1.14.8, 1.18.1-19.1, 2.22.1-2, 2.24.3, etc.
[29] Brox, "Irenaeus," writes, "It is all the more astonishing and significant, in view of the basic hermeneutical principles which he formulates and after he has repeatedly disqualified and exposed allegory, that Irenaeus himself to a large extent and in the most varied ways makes use of allegory" (1:489). Cf. Hitchcock, *Irenaeus*, 185-6; M. C. Steenberg, *Irenaeus on Creation: The Cosmic Christ and the Saga of Redemption* (Leiden: Brill, 2008), 202-3; etc.
[30] 2.27-28. Cf. 2.pre.1, 2.9.2, 2.10.1-2, etc.
[31] Cf. Young, *Biblical Exegesis*:

> What distinguishes Irenaeus and the Gnostics is not so much allegory in itself, as the task to which allegory is put. Irenaeus recognized a coherent overarching narrative within which the signs and symbols made sense; the Gnostics had no interest in the *hypothesis*, only (as Irenaeus saw it) in piecemeal abstraction of hidden enigmas which point to their own perspective on God and the world. (292)

[32] The Greek term ὑπόθεσις (usually translated in the Latin edition as *argumentum* or *argumentatio*) is important for apprehending Irenaeus' understanding of the proper method of interpretation of the Jewish scriptures. However, translating it in order to properly capture the concept intended by Irenaeus has proven difficult. Unger and Roberts-Donaldson render ὑπόθεσις variously as "system," "hypothesis," "subject," "theme," or "narrative." Rousseau et al. are generally consistent in translating it as "système," although in at least one instance as "doctrine fondamentale." Irenaeus'

and provides insight into his understanding of the nature of the Jewish scriptures. Irenaeus refers to his opponents' ὑπόθεσις most frequently in the section spanning 1.8.1-1.9.5,[33] in order to explain the problems with their interpretations. He believes that individual passages must be interpreted in light of the overall ὑπόθεσις (plot) of the Jewish scriptures; however, his opponents exchange this ὑπόθεσις for their own independently derived ὑπόθεσις, which they then use to manipulate various passages of the Jewish scriptures into conformity with it. Beginning in 1.8.1 he uses his famous analogy of the mosaic of a king that is rearranged into the likeness of a dog, yet argued to be the true likeness of the king on the basis of its individual jewels, which are genuine. By this deceit the ignorant could be deceived into believing the new image was in fact a likeness of the king, but those who knew the king would not accept it. This describes the process of Irenaeus' opponents,

> disregarding the order and connection of the writings and, as much as depends on them, dismembering the truth. They transfer passages and rearrange them, and making one thing out of another, they deceive many by the badly composed phantasy which they adapt from the dominical oracles. (1.8.1)[34]

Irenaeus' opponents disregard the true ὑπόθεσις of the Jewish scriptures,[35] which is sufficiently clear when they are read in proper order and connection. Instead, they bring a foreign ὑπόθεσις to the Jewish scriptures and interpret them according to this system, resulting in a perversion of the meaning of the scriptures, which misleads many because of how similar it sounds.[36]

Latin translator also had difficulty, usually rendering ὑπόθεσις as *argumentum* but also occasionally using *controversia* (1.9.4) or *regula* (1.20.3). *Regula* is also used to refer to the systems of the heretics in 2.pre.2, 2.12.8, 2.18.4, 2.19.8, 2.25.1, 4.pre.2, and 4.pre.3, though it is unknown whether *regula* is a translation of κανών or ὑπόθεσις. Irenaeus himself also substituted various other terms to express the same meaning. Within a single section from 1.8.1-1.9.5, in addition to his preferred term ὑπόθεσις, he also employed μέθοδος (*adinventionem*); πλάσμα (*fictio/figmentum*); παραποίησις (*transfictio*); and μῦθος (*fabula*) to express roughly the same concept. While urging that there is no sufficient direct translation, Richard Norris, "Theology and Language in Irenaeus of Lyon," *ATR* 76.3 (1994), believes it is best understood as signifying the "plot" or "coherent story structure" through which to interpret scripture (289–90). Norris finds evidence for this in Sextus Empiricis, who explains in his treatise *Adversus Mathematicos* that one of the uses of ὑπόθεσις refers to "the development of events in a drama," which Norris interprets to mean "the plot, in short, or argument of a play." Norris believes this is the sense in which it is used by Irenaeus. It is useful to keep all these possible translations in mind when interpreting this concept as Irenaeus uses it.

[33] Other instances of use of this term include 1.4.4, 2.12.3, 2.14.1, 2.25.1, 4.pre.2, etc.

[34] My trans.

[35] It is notable that Irenaeus never, so far as can be verified, uses ὑπόθεσις to refer to the true plot or presupposition of the scriptures. (In 1.10.3 the term is used to designate the "doctrine of the truth," though not directly in reference to the church or the scriptures, and it is possible—though impossible to verify—that one or more of the occurrences of the term *regula* without a parallel Greek text could be a translation of ὑπόθεσις, just as it is at 1.20.3 in reference to heretical teachings.) Instead, the true plot of the scriptures is consistently referred to using the language of κανών τῆς ἀληθείας.

[36] As he explains in 3.17.4: "though they speak words that sound like those of the believers, they understand not only different doctrines but even contrary ones, and such as are made up wholly of blasphemies." Cf. 1.pre.2, 1.9.4, 3.15.2, 3.16.6, 3.16.8.

In the following chapter, after describing his second analogy of an imposter taking various verses from the poems of Homer and manipulating them to create an entirely different poem, Irenaeus argues that this is how his opponents treat the scriptures:

> Collecting a set of expressions and names [λέξεις καὶ ὀνόματα] scattered here and there, they twist them, as we have already said, from a natural to a non-natural sense [ἐκ τοῦ κατὰ φύσιν εἰς τὸ παρὰ φύσιν]. (1.9.4)[37]

However, anyone who:

> retains unchangeable in his heart the rule of the truth [τὸν κανόνα τῆς ἀληθείας] which he received by means of baptism, will doubtless recognise the names, the expressions, and the parables taken from the Scriptures, but will by no means acknowledge the blasphemous use which these men make of them. For, though he will acknowledge the gems, he will certainly not receive the fox instead of the likeness of the king. But when he has restored every one of the expressions quoted to its proper position, and has fitted it to the body of the truth, he will lay bare, and prove to be without any foundation, the figment of these heretics. (1.9.4)[38]

The κανών τῆς ἀληθείας (*regula veritatis*), preserving the true ὑπόθεσις of the Jewish scriptures, guards against the distorted interpretations of the heretics, and is the lens through which the Jewish scriptures are correctly understood.[39] Interpretation of the Jewish scriptures can be properly undertaken only according to this rule of truth.[40] This understanding is central to Irenaeus' entire interpretative scheme. The rule of truth ensures that the Jewish scriptures are interpreted according to their own ὑπόθεσις and intended message. This remains true even if an interpretation goes against what would appear to be the intended meaning of the prophetic writer.

The Basis for Irenaeus' Principle of Interpretation of the Jewish Scriptures

The reason such interpretations are permissible, so long as they conform to the rule of truth, is that Irenaeus understands the true author of the Jewish scriptures to be

---

[37] ANF 1:330.
[38] Ibid. Cf. ACW 55:48.
[39] Cf. 2.27.1 and 2.25.1. As Trigg, "Apostolic Fathers," explains, "while the *hypothesis* of the Old Testament would not have been fully apparent until the coming of Christ, the Rule of Faith now makes it plain" (329).
[40] As John Behr, "Scripture, the Gospel, and Orthodoxy," *SVTQ* 43.3–4 (1999); explains,

> The canon of truth, then, is not so much a list of obligatory beliefs, but a hypothesis or presupposition for reading Scripture *as Scripture*—to see in it the image of the King, rather than simply as a curious collection of ancient texts which might be interesting for what they say, but do not have much to do with our relationship with God. The canon, in this sense, and this is its primary sense, is equivalent to the Christocentric reading of Scripture, seeing the whole of Scripture in the light of Christ and as speaking of Christ. (246)

the Word of God who spoke to the prophets through the Spirit.[41] The rule of truth summarizes God's intended purpose and in so doing provides the proper context for interpretation. Therefore Irenaeus can say, "by the law and the prophets did the Word preach both himself and the Father alike" (4.6.6), and also say:

> It is not David nor any other one of the prophets, who speaks from himself—for it is not man who utters prophecies—but [that] the Spirit of God, conforming Himself to the person concerned, spoke in the prophets. (*Dem.* 49)[42]

This is the ground of the self-evident authority of the Jewish scriptures. On this basis, because the Word (through the Spirit) is their author, and because the rule of truth describes the Word's intended message, any interpretation that corresponds to the rule of truth also corresponds to the (divine) author's context and intended meaning.[43]

In light of this, it is evident that what initially appeared to be indifference to authorial intent is in fact the opposite. Irenaeus' principle of interpretation of the Jewish scriptures is characterized by an overriding commitment to seeking the meaning intended by the Word, as primary author. Various methods of interpretation of the Jewish scriptures are permissible to the extent that they do not stray from this principle. Likewise, Irenaeus does not consider his interpretations to be at odds with the intentions of the prophets themselves, for he believes that they were aware of and active in proclaiming the Word's own revelation of his future advent. Irenaeus speaks of the prophets "foreseeing through the Holy Spirit His advent," and asks,

> How could they have foreknown it, unless they had previously received foreknowledge from Himself? And how do the Scriptures testify of Him, unless all things had ever been revealed and shown to believers by one and the same God through the Word? (4.11.1)[44]

The prophets intend the messages described in Irenaeus' interpretations, whether or not such interpretations would make sense within the prophets' own historical contexts. Irenaeus is not unaware of the possible historical issues with his interpretations; he is merely convinced that the Jewish scriptures were spoken through the Spirit for his present time, rendering historical considerations irrelevant.[45] Irenaeus' concern for the

---

[41] A full discussion of this point is reserved for Chapter 4, where the subject of inspiration as it relates to revelatory authority is discussed.

[42] Cf. 2.28.2-3, 2.33.3, 3.9.3, 4.11.1, 4.20.4, 4.20.8, 4.34.3, *Dem.* 6, *Dem.* 30, etc.

[43] Irenaeus describes the proper method of interpretation of the scriptures in terms of recognizing one author of all the varied passages, using the metaphor of one artist playing many notes, which must all be understood as a single composition (2.25.2). As W. S. Reilly, "L'inspiration de l'A.T. chez Saint Irénée," *RB* 14 (1917), notes, "D'après saint Irénée … l'action de Dieu dans la composition des livres de l'A.T. est telle que chacune des propositions qu'ils renferment doit être considérée comme un oracle divin. Pour en mesurer la profondeur théologique et la valeur religieuse, il ne suffirait pas de leur appliquer les règles employées usuellement pour déterminer le sens des paroles humaines" (506). Cf. Lawson, *Biblical Theology*, 55–6.

[44] Cf. 2.22.1, 4.5.5, 4.20.5, 4.20.10-12, 4.27.1, 4.33.10-15, etc.

[45] In *Dem.* 67, Irenaeus acknowledges that Isaiah's prophecies concerning the advent of Christ have the historically inaccurate past tense instead of the future tense—"Isaiah says thus, 'He took our

Authoritative Texts or Authoritative Authors? 63

intended message of the prophets is solely a function of his commitment to discovering the message given by the Word, which Irenaeus believes the prophets simply record for the benefit of later generations.[46]

Conclusion

The two characteristics of Irenaeus' use of the Jewish scriptures identified in this section—his treatment of them as a written text whose authority does not depend on its human authors, and his principle of interpretation according to the rule of truth, indifferent to the various contexts of its prophetic authors—indicate that he conceives of the Jewish scriptures as an *inherently authoritative scriptural text*, which has ultimately been given by God and acquires its scriptural status on this basis. In the following two sections, in order to assess the traditional interpretation's claim that the apostolic writings are used in the same manner, and are therefore also conceived as an *inherently authoritative scriptural text* equivalent to the Jewish scriptures, an analysis of Irenaeus' use of the apostolic writings seeks to determine to what extent the apostolic writings are treated as authoritative *texts* (Section 2.2), and are interpreted without regard for the apparent intentions of the apostolic authors in their own contexts (Section 2.3).

2.2. Are the Apostolic Writings Used as an Inherently Authoritative Text?

My assessment of the traditional interpretation's claim that the apostolic writings are used in the same manner as the Jewish scriptures, as a scriptural text, begins in this section with an investigation of the extent to which Irenaeus describes them as a written text and bases their authority on the status of the text itself, as he does with the Jewish scriptures. This investigation involves analyses of his descriptions of the apostolic writings in his introductions to citations from them (A) and in his references to them (B), as well as an examination of a number of statements in which the *text* of the Jewish scriptures is contrasted with the *testimony* of the apostles (C).

A. Introductions to Citations from the Apostolic Writings

When Irenaeus' citations of the apostolic writings are analyzed, it becomes evident that they are introduced almost exclusively as the words of the apostolic author or of the

---

infirmities and bore our diseases,' that is, 'He will take,' and 'will bear'"—and explains this by stating that "the Spirit of God, through the prophets, relates things that would come to pass as having happened," because "the Spirit employs words considering and regarding the time in which the fulfillment of prophecy is accomplished."

[46] Reilly, "L'inspiration," states, "Une étude de l'exégèse de l'A.T. chez saint Irénée montre que, quelle que soit à ses yeux la grandeur du personnage, le prophète n'avait après tout qu'un rôle très secondaire dans la prophétie. Les paroles du prophète sont les paroles de Dieu purement et simplement." The prophecies speak "non pas aux contemporains du prophète, mais à tous less hommes, aux chrétiens en particulier" (499).

Lord, or are not introduced at all. This indicates a divergence from his citations from the Jewish scriptures, which may be equally introduced as either a scriptural text or as the message of a prophet. In his approximately 1,800[47] references to the apostolic writings, Irenaeus introduces a citation as γραφή on only a single occasion. As he is describing the preaching mission of Peter and the apostles as presented in Acts, he says,

> Therefore having been confounded both by the healing—"for the man," the writing states [*inquit Scriptura*], "was over forty years in whom this sign of healing was made"[48]—and by the doctrine of the apostles and [their] exposition of the prophets. (3.12.5)[49]

Even here, however, it is not the text of Acts that is primarily in focus. Irenaeus' use of Acts, spanning 3.12.1-10, begins with the words,

> Now that we have examined, from the capital points themselves, the doctrine of those who handed the Gospel down to us [*sententia eorum qui nobis tradiderunt Euangelium*], let us go also to the other apostles [*ad reliquos apostolos*] and investigate their doctrine of God. (3.11.9)

Irenaeus is concerned to present the teachings of the apostles. Acts itself is never explicitly mentioned throughout this section, and among his numerous citations from it, the citation above is the only direct indication Irenaeus gives that he is using it. As he ends his account, he maintains,

> That the entire doctrine of the apostles announced one and the same God ... all who are willing can learn from the very sermons and deeds of the apostles [*ex ipsis sermonibus et actibus apostolorum*]. (3.12.11)

Acts has functioned for Irenaeus as a record of what the apostles said and did. His use of γραφή to introduce one of his citations from it indicates the written record he used to access these authoritative testimonies, without suggesting an appeal to an authoritative *text*. Later in Book 3, Irenaeus will defend his use of Acts specifically as "the testimony [*testificatio*] of Luke" (3.13.3).[50]

---

[47] Blanchard, *Sources*, counts 1,800 New Testament references (950 of which are direct citations) from the indexes of the SC editions for *Adversus haereses* alone (122–3). Hoh, *Lehre*, catalogues 1,778 New Testament references (1,122 of which are direct citations) across all of Irenaeus' works (198; cf. 189–99).

[48] Acts 4:22.

[49] My trans.

[50] Here Irenaeus sets out to defend the accuracy of Paul's accounts:

> Now if anyone diligently examines the Acts of the Apostles about the period under discussion, when [Paul] went up to Jerusalem on account of the aforementioned dispute, he will find that the years that Paul mentioned agree. Thus, the preaching of Paul agrees with and is the same as the testimony of Luke [in Acts] in regard to the apostles.

Irenaeus also occasionally refers to a written εὐαγγέλιον when introducing citations. Of his abundant citations from the apostolic writings, there are nine instances of a citation or paraphrased reference being introduced in some way as "the Gospel" in reference to the written gospels.[51] Of these, five occur as εὐαγγέλιον is used to introduce a citation in order to convey that the apostolic author has "said in his account of the Gospel" the cited passage. Irenaeus may, for example, introduce a quotation from the Gospel of Mark by saying, "Mark too, Peter's translator and follower, began his Gospel account thus [*initium Euangelicae conscriptionis fecit sic*]" (3.10.6).[52] In these passages it is the apostolic author rather than the text itself that functions authoritatively, in spite of the use of εὐαγγέλιον as a title. Similar treatment is observed in a further three passages in which "the Lord" is the subject, as in Irenaeus' introduction of a citation from Matthew's account of the Gospel with the words, "The Lord says in the Gospel [*Dominus in Euangelio ... ait*]" (3.23.3).[53] In the final remaining instance, directly between a citation of "Moses" (Genesis) and a citation of "the Apostle Paul" (Ephesians), Irenaeus introduces a quotation from John's Gospel account by saying, "*in Evangelio legimus*" (4.32.1). This is the only passage where Irenaeus' use of εὐαγγέλιον as a title to introduce a citation includes no reference to apostolic authorship, therefore appearing to treat a Gospel account as a written text in similar fashion to his frequent descriptions of the Jewish scriptures. Yet even this passage is not understood primarily as a reference to the written gospels themselves by Blanchard, who states in reference to this passage that "nothing permits us to say that the word 'Gospel' has a more precise meaning than that of the Tradition referred to Christ as a whole."[54]

In addition to his occasional use of εὐαγγέλιον as a title for the Gospel accounts, Irenaeus may also refer to the specific letter (ἐπιστολή) from which he is reciting an apostolic statement. He may, for example, introduce a passage from Galatians by saying: "The apostle Paul, too, in his letter to the Galatians, says plainly [*Et apostolus autem Paulus in epistola quae est ad Galatas manifeste ait*]" (3.22.1). This occurs more frequently than his use of εὐαγγέλιον for the same purpose,[55] though there is evidence

---

Luke's own authority is then defended at length in 3.14.1-4. As Gamble, *New Testament*, describes, "The authority of Acts for Irenaeus rests on the belief that its author was an inseparable companion of Paul" (47).

[51] These are found in 3.10.6, 3.11.2, 3.11.8, 3.16.8, 3.23.3, 4.29.1, 4.32.1, 5.18.2, and 5.22.1. Two further possible instances, 4.2.3 and 4.20.6, are contradicted by the Armenian translation, leading Rousseau et al. (SC 100:400–1, 646–7) and Reed, "ΕΥΑΓΓΕΛΙΟΝ," 19 and 54, to conclude that these represent interpolations by the Latin translator. These instances also suggest the possibility that other unattested occurrences may also be interpolations.

[52] This is also the case in 3.11.2, 3.11.8, 3.16.8, and 5.18.2. Irenaeus' use of εὐαγγέλιον in 3.11.8 comes closest to treating the gospels as written texts, introducing a citation as "Τὸ μὲν γὰρ κατὰ Ἰωάννων," referring back to εὐαγγέλια in the previous sentence. This citation occurs within a unique section whose implications are discussed in the following section.

[53] Cf. 4.29.1 and 5.22.1.

[54] Blanchard, *Sources*, 154; my trans.

[55] There are thirty-six direct references to an apostolic ἐπιστολή in introductions to citations from the apostolic writings: 1.8.2, 2.22.2, 3.3.3, 3.11.9, 3.12.12, 3.13.1, 3.13.3, 3.14.1, 3.16.3, 3.16.5, 3.16.8, 3.16.9, 3.22.1, 4.9.2, 4.21.1, 4.21.2, 4.27.3, 4.27.4, 4.32.1 4.34.2, 4.36.6, 4.37.1, 5.2.3, 5.6.1, 5.8.1, 5.10.2, 5.11.1, 5.11.2, 5.12.3, 5.12.4, 5.12.5, 5.13.3, 5.13.4, 5.14.2, 5.14.4, and 5.21.1; as well as fourteen similar but unstated allusions to an apostolic ἐπιστολή in introductions to citations: 3.7.1, 3.7.2, 3.16.3, 3.16.8, 3.16.9, 4.28.3, 4.29.1, 5.3.1, 5.7.1, 5.24.1, 5.25.1, 5.25.3, 5.32.1, and 5.32.2.

to suggest that the majority of these may be interpolations by the Latin translator or a later scribe.[56] However, these references never occur in the absence of a direct reference to the apostle who wrote the letter. In every single instance, Irenaeus states *what an apostle has said* in a specific letter. The mention of an ἐπιστολή is used to tell his reader *where* and *in what context* an apostolic author has said something, never to tell what an ἐπιστολή says. In the same way, Irenaeus cites eight passages from Revelation as "the Apocalypse,"[57] in every instance using a form of "John says in the Apocalypse [*Johannes in Apocalypsi ait*]" (4.21.3).

This analysis demonstrates that the vast majority of Irenaeus' 1,800 apostolic citations or allusions are introduced as the words of the apostolic author (or as the words of the Lord, or are not introduced at all), rather than as a written text. Of the few documented instances of γραφή, εὐαγγέλιον, ἐπιστολή, or Ἀποκάλυψις being used as a title in an introduction to a citation from the apostolic writings, virtually all represent instances of referring to the words of an apostolic author and citing where his comments can be found. In only a single instance is an apostolic citation introduced as τό εὐαγγέλιον without direct reference to the apostolic author,[58] and here it is debatable whether εὐαγγέλιον is intended as the title for a written gospel.[59] These findings demonstrate a contrast with his frequent practice of introducing citations from the Jewish scriptures as the words of an authoritative text.

B. References to the Apostolic Writings

Irenaeus' numerous references to and discussions of the apostolic writings illustrate a similar pattern. In distinction from his references to the Jewish scriptures, Irenaeus

---

[56] The majority of these references occur in sections of the Latin translation for which there is no surviving Greek original. Only three instances of *epistola* are conclusively supported by a Greek fragment (1.8.2, 3.3.3, and 3.16.8), while in three instances a Greek fragment demonstrates that the Latin translator has in fact added the reference to the written work in which an apostolic statement occurs (5.2.3, 5.3.1, and 5.13.3). Thus, for example, a passage in 5.13.3 states, "*Et propter hoc ait in secunda ad Corinthios*" while the corresponding Greek fragment instead reads, "Καὶ διὰ τοῦτό φησιν." This occurrence has led Harvey to claim, "The interpolation of the Scriptural reference by the translator, suggests the suspicion that the greater number of such references have come in from the margin" (2:357). The subsequent recovery and publishing of the Armenian fragments has largely confirmed his suspicions. Rousseau et al.'s references to the variances in the Armenian fragments throughout the SC editions of *Adversus haereses* show that an additional twenty-one instances of *epistola* or similar unstated allusions in the Latin translation are omitted in the Armenian (4.21.1, 4.21.2, 4.27.3, 4.27.4, 4.36.6, 4.37.1, 4.37.1, 5.2.3, 5.6.1, 5.8.1, 5.10.2, 5.11.1, 5.12.3, 5.12.4, 5.12.5, 5.14.4, 5.21.1, 5.24.4, 5.25.1, 5.32.1, and 5.32.2), while only eight instances of *epistola* (4.9.2, 4.41.4, 5.pre, 5.11.2, 5.12.3, 5.13.3, 5.13.4, and 5.14.3) and six unstated allusions (4.28.3, 4.29.1, 4.34.2, 5.3.1, 5.7.1, and 5.23.3) are supported by it. These supported references to an apostolic *epistola* are often found where the word or allusion is not incidental to the meaning of the sentence, as in Irenaeus' claim that "in every Epistle [*epistola*] the apostle plainly testifies, that through the flesh of our Lord, and through His blood, we have been saved" (5.14.3). These findings suggest that the practice of referring to an ἐπιστολή in introductions to apostolic citations may in fact have been quite rare for Irenaeus.

[57] 4.14.2, 4.17.6, 4.18.6, 4.20.11, 4.21.3, 5.28.2, 5.34.2, *frg.* 38 (ANF 37).

[58] 4.32.1. This passage is adduced as evidence that Irenaeus cites the gospels as a written text by Benoit, *Irénée*, 108, though he concedes that Irenaeus exhibits "une certaine hésitation à citer ceux-ci exactement de la même maniére que l'Ancient Testament" (121).

[59] Cf. Blanchard, *Sources*, 153–4.

largely refrains from referring to the apostolic writings as a written collection, and his few textual references are always either accompanied by direct reference to the apostolic author or are references to heretical practice. In neither case do these references indicate that Irenaeus uses the apostolic writings as an *inherently authoritative text*, contrary to Campenhausen's claim that for Irenaeus "the Gospels and Acts as 'canonical books' constitute a new entity."[60]

It was previously argued in Chapter 1 that Irenaeus does not use γραφή as a scriptural title for the apostolic writings, but only occasionally uses the term in reference to the specific *writings* under discussion.[61] In the majority of these passages, γραφή refers to the Jewish scriptures and apostolic writings together as those writings that his opponents misuse,[62] and therefore describes their use of the apostolic writings, rather than Irenaeus' own use. The few remaining passages occur when Irenaeus discusses the teachings of the apostles who put the Gospel into *writing* (3.1.1, 3.2.1, 3.2.2, and 3.4.1), in a section discussing what "John has thus described in the Apocalypse"[63] (5.30.1-2), and once in reference to what the Lord has said (4.41.2). The text of the apostolic writings itself is never the focus or the basis of authority in these passages.

Irenaeus also occasionally refers to a specific "letter" or to the title of an individual apostolic writing. There are six instances where Irenaeus refers to Paul's letters using ἐπιστολή,[64] as he has in his introductions to citations. In each of these instances, Irenaeus refers primarily to the apostolic author and uses the language of ἐπιστολή to describe where his teachings are found, as in his statement that "in every Epistle the apostle plainly testifies [*in omni autem epistola manifeste testificatur Apostolus*]" (5.14.3). Similarly, Irenaeus refers to the Ἀποκάλυψις on five occasions,[65] all but one of which are explicit references to what "John … saw in the Apocalypse [*Johannes … vidit in Apocalypsi*]" (4.30.4). In the final instance John is not directly mentioned: "This tribe is not reckoned in the Apocalypse [*in Apocalypsi*]" (5.30.2). However, this passage occurs within a section discussing John's words in the Apocalypse, which begins, "John has thus described in the Apocalypse" (5.28.2), indicating Irenaeus' concern to exhibit the thought of John. In one further instance Irenaeus mentions "the Acts of the Apostles [*Actibus apostolorum*]," which shows that "the preaching of Paul agrees with and is the same as the testimony of Luke [*Lucae … testificatio*]" (3.13.3). In each of these passages, Irenaeus uses the title of the work in order to state where the apostles' words are found, rather than to describe "what the apocalypse teaches" in an appeal to the authority of the text itself, as he does with the Jewish scriptures.

Irenaeus completely refrains from using "the gospels and apostles" or "the apostles" as titles for the apostolic writings in the way he can speak of the Jewish scriptures as "the law and the prophets" or "the prophets,"[66] despite claims to the

---

[60] McDonald, *Formation*, 191. He believes that "Irenaeus has fashioned a new, solid block of canonical Scriptures" (202).
[61] See Section 1.2B.
[62] 1.8.1, 1.8.2, 1.9.1, 1.9.3, 1.27.4, 2.24.4, 2.27.2, and 3.12.12.
[63] 5.28.2.
[64] 1.27.2, 3.12.9, 3.12.12, 4.41.4, 5.pre, and 5.14.3.
[65] 1.26.3, 4.30.4, 5.26.1, 5.30.2, and 5.35.2.
[66] Noted above p. 55 n. 18.

contrary.⁶⁷ When Irenaeus refers to "the apostles," it is always in reference to their preaching,⁶⁸ their tradition,⁶⁹ or their doctrine or teaching,⁷⁰ which they have handed down.⁷¹ However, "the Gospel" occasionally functions as a title for one or the whole of the apostolic accounts of the Gospel that he accepts, in similar fashion to his introductions to citations. The majority of these occur within a single small section spanning 3.11.7-9, which merits its own discussion (below). Outside of this section, Irenaeus uses the language of εὐαγγέλιον in reference to the text of the apostolic writings on eight occasions,⁷² always in order to assert that his opponents pervert these writings to their own ends.⁷³ Five of these passages also explicitly name the apostolic author of the gospel under discussion,⁷⁴ as observed in the following statement:

> The same things we will allege also against those who do not acknowledge the apostle Paul. Either they will have to reject the rest of the words of the Gospel [*uerbis Euangelii*], namely, those which we know only through Luke, and not use them, or if they receive all of them, they must also accept the testimony that Luke gives concerning Paul. (3.15.1)

Irenaeus is here commenting on his opponents' use of the apostolic writings, and he specifically states that the gospel he names is the testimony of Luke. In all eight passages Irenaeus' use of εὐαγγέλιον as a title solely within descriptions of heretical

---

[67] Irenaeus is occasionally claimed to have used "gospels and apostles" as a title on the basis of 1.3.6 (discussed below p. 75 n. 96) and to use "apostles" as a title on the basis of such formulations as "prophets and apostles" (3.8.1, 3.9.1), "prophets, apostles, and the Lord" (1.8.1, 3.9.1), etc. (2.35.4, 3.19.2). Cf. Denis M. Farkasfalvy, "'Prophets and Apostles:' The Conjunction of the Two Terms before Irenaeus," in *Texts and Testaments: Critical Essays on the Bible and the Early Church Fathers*, ed. W. Eugene March (San Antonio, TX: Trinity University Press, 1980), 109; Farkasfalvy, "Theology," 323 n. 7, 328–9; Ferguson, "Selection and Closure," 306 n. 52; Hoh, *Lehre*, 83–6; etc. However, none of these instances are clearly intended as titles of written works, while many are explicit references to the apostles themselves.

[68] 2.35.4, 3.3.3, 3.12.2, 3.12.7, 3.12.12, 3.15.3, 4.34.4, 4.36.8, 5.12.3, etc.

[69] 2.9.1, 3.2.2, 3.3.1, 3.3.2, 3.3.3, 3.3.4, 3.4.1, 3.4.1, 3.5.1, 3.21.3, 5.20.1, *Dem.* 86, etc.

[70] 3.11.9, 3.12.5, 3.12.11, 3.14.4, 3.15.1, 4.26.4, 4.32.1, 4.32.2, 4.33.8, 4.41.4, 5.pre, *Dem.* 46, etc.

[71] 1.27.2, 2.20.9, 3.1.1, 3.3.3, 3.4.1, 3.11.9, 5.pre, *Dem.* 98, *Dem.* 99, etc.

[72] 1.8.4, 1.20.2, 1.26.2, 1.27.2, 2.22.3, 3.12.12, 3.15.1, and 4.34.1. An additional possible instance occurs in 3.10.2: "By these important testimonies, therefore, the Gospel shows [*monstrat Euangelium*] that the God who spoke to the fathers is the one who made the law through Moses" (3.10.2). It seems most likely that *Euangelium* in this passage is not functioning as a title but as a reference to the Gospel of Jesus Christ. Cf. Reed, "ΕΥΑΓΓΕΛΙΟΝ," who maintains that *Euangelium* in this instance likely "does not here refer to any particular document, but rather to an entire category of revelation" (24). In either case, this passage occurs within a section where Irenaeus is describing Luke's statements concerning the oneness of God, which he begins by saying, "if we are truly their disciples, we must follow their testimonies, which are as follows" (3.9.1). This statement indicates that the authority of Luke's testimony, rather than a written gospel, remains primarily in view in the previous statement, which occurs below it as part of the same argument. Hoh, *Lehre*, notes 2.22.3 and 4.34.1 as evidence that "ev. = Schrift" (5).

[73] Cf. Reed, "ΕΥΑΓΓΕΛΙΟΝ," who notes some of these passages as pointing out "the heretical preference for a single gospel, the heretical rejection of a gospel, and the heretical redaction of a gospel" (20).

[74] 1.26.2, 1.27.2, 3.12.12, 3.15.1, and 4.34.1.

practice indicates that it is the heretics who treat the gospels as written texts—using τό εὐαγγέλιον as a title—rather than Irenaeus himself.[75]

The majority of Irenaeus' references to a written εὐαγγέλιον or εὐαγγέλια occur within a single section from 3.11.7-9,[76] where Irenaeus defends the use of all four and only these four apostolic proclamations of the Gospel against his opponents' additions or subtractions of them. This section therefore merits closer examination.

Irenaeus' Argument for a Fourfold Gospel

Irenaeus' argument in 3.11.7-9 has traditionally been understood as an argument for a four-gospel canon, and taken as evidence that Irenaeus understands these four gospels as part of the canon of scripture alongside the Jewish scriptures. This understanding contains the presupposition that the apostolic writings are used as authoritative *texts* on the basis of scriptural status, and his textual use of εὐαγγέλιον within this section is understood to reinforce this view. As Campenhausen declares on the basis of this passage, "Thanks to Irenaeus [the gospels] had become a single canonical book in the strict sense."[77] Irenaeus begins his argument at 3.11.7 by explaining that many of his opponents accept only a single written account of the Gospel, and briefly describes the errors they fall into as a result, before making his famous claim:

> It is not possible that there be more Gospels in number than these, or fewer [Οὔτε δὲ πλείονα τὸν ἀριθμὸν τούτων οὔτε πάλιν ἐλάττονα ἐνδέχεται εἶναι τὰ εὐαγγέλια]. By way of illustration, since there are four zones in the world in which we live, and four cardinal winds, and since the Church is spread over the whole earth, and since "the pillar and bulwark" of the Church is the Gospel and the Spirit of life [στῦλος δὲ καὶ στήριγμα τῆς ἐκκλησίας τὸ εὐαγγέλιον καὶ Πνεῦμα ζωῆς], consequently she has four pillars, blowing imperishability from all sides and giving life to men. From these things it is manifest that the Word, who is Artificer of all things and "is enthroned upon the Cherubim and holds together all things," and who was manifested to men, gave us the fourfold Gospel [ἔδωκεν ἡμῖν τετράμορφον τὸ εὐαγγέλιον], which is held together by the one Spirit. Just

---

[75] Reed, "ΕΥΑΓΓΕΛΙΟΝ," notes, "these examples may simply reflect common usage, particularly among the groups whose textual preferences Irenaeus here cites" (21). Reed sees parallels between Irenaeus' textual use of εὐαγγέλιον and that of Justin Martyr (16–18). Justin refers to a written εὐαγγέλιον only three times throughout his writings (1 *apol.* 66.3; *Dial.* 10.2; 100.1), preferring instead to refer to the Gospel accounts as "the memoirs of the apostles [τὰ ἀπομνημονεύματα τῶν ἀποστόλων]," often shortened to "the memoirs." His few references to a textual εὐαγγέλιον suggest that they are current naming conventions that he would prefer not to use. In *1 apol.* 66 he writes, "For the apostles, in the memoirs composed by them, which are called Gospels." (ANF 1:185). Similarly, in *Dial.* 10.2 Trypho refers to "the so-called gospel" (ANF 1:199). Commenting on *1 apol.* 66, Otto Piper, "The Nature of the Gospel according to Justin Martyr," *JR* 41:3 (1961), argues that "the very fact that [Justin] uses the neutral expression 'they are called' rather than 'we call them' can be interpreted only as an indication of his unwillingness to adopt such terminology himself" (155).

[76] Εὐαγγέλιον is used to refer directly to a (or multiple) written apostolic Gospel account(s) thirteen times within this section, of which only four occur without direct reference to the apostolic author(s).

[77] McDonald, *Formation*, 201.

as David, when petitioning His coming, said, "You who are enthroned upon the cherubim, shine forth." For the Cherubim, too, had four faces, and their faces are images of the dispensation of the Son of God. For the first one, he says, was like a lion, symbolizing His powerful, sovereign, and kingly nature. The second was like a calf, symbolizing His ministerial and priestly rank. The third animal had a face like a man, which manifestly describes His coming as man. The fourth is like a flying eagle, manifesting the gift of the Spirit hovering over the Church. (3.11.8)

Irenaeus then goes on to describe how each Gospel account represents one of the four animals he has described, and to suggest a parallel between the four Gospel accounts and the four covenants given to humanity. He ends his argument by describing the way in which his various opponents claim to possess either fewer or more Gospel accounts than these four, thereby destroying the form of the Gospel (3.11.9). He concludes,

> For since God arranged and harmonized all things well, it is necessary that also the form of the Gospel be arranged and fitted together well [*oportebat et speciem Euangelii bene compositam et bene compaginatam esse*]. (3.11.9)

Irenaeus' argument in this section occupies a place of prominence within the field of New Testament canon studies, where it has traditionally been understood to be the earliest argument for the canonical status of the four accepted Gospel accounts, and has become a key piece of evidence in establishing the timeline of completion of the New Testament canon. As T. C. Skeat describes, "Every study of the Canon of the Four Gospels begins, and rightly begins, with the famous passage in which Irenaeus, writing about the year 185, seeks to defend the Canon by finding a mystical significance in the number four."[78] This view had previously been influentially put forth by Campenhausen,[79] and has been adopted by a majority of contemporary New Testament canon studies scholars.[80] Thus, on the basis of this passage Metzger maintains, "for

---

[78] T. C. Skeat, "Irenaeus and the Four-Gospel Canon," *NT* 34 (1992): 194.

[79] McDonald, *Formation*, 196–203. He claims, "for Irenaeus the Four-Gospel canon is already an established entity, which he champions as an indisputable and recognized collection against all the deviations of the heretics" (172). He qualifies his statement slightly, as he explains,

> Irenaeus does not proceed simply by putting the new Scripture alongside the old, and then asserting its authority by analogy. He does not start from a general "principle of scripture," which would carry over from the Old Testament to the New. His concern is solely to establish the credibility and value as witnesses of those books from which he intends to give the original teachings of Jesus and the apostles a status so exalted that even the heretics will not be able to gainsay it. (188–9)

Cf. Graham N. Stanton, "The Fourfold Gospel," *NTS* 43 (1997), who comments, "under the influence of Hans von Campenhausen, most scholars have accepted that the fourfold Gospel emerged in the *second half* of the second century and that the Muratorian Fragment and Irenaeus are our primary witnesses" (317). Stanton believes that in his argument at 3.11.7-9, "Irenaeus comments on the origin of the four individual gospels, which he clearly accepts as 'Scripture,' and sets out the earliest defence of the Church's fourfold Gospel" (319; cf. 341–5).

[80] Cf. McDonald, *Formation*, 166–7; Ferguson, "Selection and Closure," 301; Bruce, *Canon*, 174–7; Metzger, *Canon*, 155; Bokedal, *Significance*, 292–3; etc. For a critique of this view, and of the traditional understanding of Irenaeus' intentions in his argument, cf. Allert, *High View*, esp. 119–26, who follows Sundberg, "Revised History," 452–61; and "Canon Muratori," 1–41, in arguing

Irenaeus the Gospel canon is closed and its text is holy," and concludes that the gospels are "joined to the Old Testament as holy Scripture."[81] This influence has been widely felt within Irenaean scholarship as well. Steenberg states, on the basis of this passage, that "Irenaeus provides us with a closed canon of the Gospels ... in this he offers us the first definition of such a closed Gospel canon in the patristic witness."[82] Steenberg is not alone in this contention.[83] However, this view of Irenaeus' understanding of the Gospel accounts as canonical writings distorts his thought by giving disproportionate and uncritical attention to a single section whose discussion of a portion of the apostolic writings as texts differs significantly from the rest of his work, and further, by ignoring the context in which this argument for a fourfold Gospel occurs and his own stated purpose for making it.

Taking place within Book 3, which is built on the foundation of Irenaeus' in-depth defense of the authority of the apostles (3.1-4), this fourfold Gospel argument occurs as the conclusion of a single section spanning 3.9-11. Within this section he examines each Gospel account in turn to demonstrate that they teach one God as both the Creator and the Father of Jesus, and he begins this section with a succinct description of its purpose: speaking of the apostles, he says, "if we are truly their disciples [*si quidem illorum summus discipuli*], we must follow their testimonies [*sequi nos oportet ... testimonia illorum*], which are as follows" (3.9.1). It is the apostles themselves who function as authorities for Irenaeus, and his purpose throughout this section is to demonstrate their teachings of the Gospel message from their written testimonies.

Irenaeus' statement here indicates that the purpose of his argument for a fourfold Gospel in 3.11.7-9 at the conclusion of this section is to safeguard the authority of these testimonies against those who reject them, and to assert the exclusivity of their authority over other non-apostolic gospels proposed by the Valentinians. Irenaeus' many references to these written εὐαγγέλια within this argument are in response to his opponents' rejections of or additions to these four apostolic accounts, both of which represent a rejection of apostolic authority. Speaking of the latter practice in the close of his argument, Irenaeus reaffirms his purpose, explaining that the Valentinians

> give the title "*Gospel of Truth*" ["*ueritatis Euangelium*" *titulent*] to a book which they have but recently composed, and which agrees in no wise with the Gospels of the apostles [*in nihilo conueniens apostolorum Euangeliis*]. (3.11.9)

The primary problem with other gospels is that they do not agree with the testimonies of the apostles, and cannot trace their origins back to them. It is the authority of

---

for a late-fourth-century closing of the New Testament canon, and disagrees with the traditional interpretation of Irenaeus' argument that is used as evidence of a second-century date. Cf. also Reed, "ΕΥΑΓΓΕΛΙΟΝ," 11–46.

[81] Metzger, *Canon*, 155.

[82] Steenberg, "Graphe," 54. However, Steenberg continues by saying, "yet we must be careful not to call Irenaeus a canonist. He does not believe in the authority of a text based simply on its inclusion in an official listing of sacred documents" (54).

[83] General agreement with the conclusions of New Testament canon studies scholars can also be seen in Hitchcock, *Irenaeus*, 215–16; Osborn, *Irenaeus*, 175–6; Lawson, *Biblical Theology*, 35–6 and 43–4; Benoit, *Irénée*, 114–21; et al.

the apostles themselves that is central to Irenaeus' claim that only the four apostolic gospels should be accepted, and that all of them together are of supreme authority and necessary for understanding the Gospel message. Irenaeus concludes this section by saying,

> Now that we have examined ... the doctrine of those who handed the Gospel down to us [*sententia eorum qui nobis tradiderunt Euangelium*], let us go also to the other apostles [*ueniamus et ad reliquos apostolos*] and investigate their doctrine of God. (3.11.9)

The apostles have continued to be Irenaeus' primary focus in his references to τὰ εὐαγγέλια throughout this section.

A similar interpretation of the purpose of Irenaeus' argument for a fourfold Gospel and its effect on the meaning(s) of his use of εὐαγγέλιον is given by Reed in her study "ΕΥΑΓΓΕΛΙΟΝ: Orality, Textuality, and the Christian Truth in Irenaeus' *Adversus Haereses*." In order to better understand the context in which Irenaeus makes his fourfold Gospel argument, Reed undertakes a detailed analysis of all of Irenaeus' 101 uses of εὐαγγέλιον in *Adversus haereses*. On the basis of this study, she cautions against interpreting Irenaeus as demonstrating a shift in meaning of εὐαγγέλιον from its oral meaning to a textualized meaning, marking the beginning of a "canonical consciousness," as is often claimed.[84] She contends instead that his use of the term in relationship to his argument for a fourfold Gospel "reflects his primary concern, not to establish the canonicity of these four gospels, but rather to defend the singular Gospel message against a multiplicity of heretical deviations," and further, to demonstrate that the unified apostolic tradition is attested to in "the apparently multiple but essentially unified testimony of the evangelists." She believes that "Although proper text selection is defended in 3.11.7-9, what is ultimately at stake is the unity of apostolic testimony," which ensures the truth of the apostolic tradition.[85] Similar questions concerning

---

[84] Reed, "ΕΥΑΓΓΕΛΙΟΝ," 18. This is important

> since the two specialized Christian meanings that had been established at his time have profoundly different epistemological ramifications: Paul's Gospel invokes a dynamic, living Christian truth, whose orality stands in essential contrast to writings. However, Marcion's project of compiling one true gospel document tacitly equates the quest for the Christian truth with the isolation of authentically apostolic written records from the distorting accretions of tradition. (19)

[85] Ibid., 41-2. She explains,

> he does not simply contest Marcion's adoption of a canon by articulating an orthodox "counter-canon" rejecting his choice of a gospel and asserting that a four-gospel Canon must instead serve as the written criterion for discerning Christian truth. Rather, the inclusivity of the Pauline sense of εὐαγγέλιον remains determinative, not only in Irenaeus' description of the four gospels as a single "four-formed Gospel," but also in his efforts throughout *Adversus Haereses* to articulate the one Christian message that unifies the multiplicity of authentic apostolic witnesses. (42)

whether Irenaeus' argument should be understood as evidence of a scriptural canon of four gospels have been raised by others.[86]

Irenaeus' style of argument in this section itself provides additional evidence for his purpose. Many who have examined Irenaeus' argument in 3.11.7-9 have commented that it is quite unconvincing, apparently lamenting the fact that an argument relying on numerological speculation would be used to establish such an important point.[87] This in itself is an indication that Irenaeus is not attempting to make an argument for a four-gospel canon. Reed notes how uncharacteristic this argument is for Irenaeus, suggesting on this basis that it should not be interpreted outside the context of the overall meaning of εὐαγγέλιον in his thought.[88] She points out that Irenaeus constantly chides his opponents for the faulty logic of their numerological arguments, in one instance proving explicitly that the exact logic he will later use is meaningless (2.24-25). He describes numerological proofs as

> inconsistent and entirely stupid, because every number occurs in the Scriptures in a variety of ways, so that, if anyone would so wish, he could construct from the Scriptures not only an Ogdoad, a Decad, and a Dodecad, but any number, and assert this to be a type of the error devised by him. (2.24.3)

This statement would seem to call into question either the validity of his own arguments in 3.11.7-9 or else his purpose in making them, and Reed suggests the latter, maintaining that his arguments are not meant to be a "proof" at all. While his arguments would indeed be unconvincing as proof of the exclusive scriptural status of these gospels, they are well suited as descriptions of the fittingness of the fact that four apostolic (and therefore authoritative) accounts of the Gospel exist. As Behr explains,

> The reasons given for this by Irenaeus—that there are only four winds and four corners of the earth—are hardly likely to persuade anyone who does not already accept the fact, but this is itself important: Irenaeus is musing on what is already a given fact, the fixed number of Gospels, rather than himself imposing the limit.[89]

Irenaeus simply has no need at this point to prove the authority of these four Gospel accounts. He has already demonstrated the basis of their authority previously,

---

[86] Cf. William R. Farmer and Denis. M. Farkasfalvy, *The Formation of the New Testament Canon: An Ecumenical Approach* (New York: Paulist Press, 1983), 144–5; Allert, *High View*, 119–26; etc. Allert concludes,
> Irenaeus' primary goal was not to establish the canonicity of the four Gospels. … The point in Irenaeus is that the church safeguards proper doctrine, whether it be written or oral, and that proper interpretation is needed to ensure that it remains pure. He sees these texts, therefore, not as the "literary guarantors of the sacred tradition, [but] merely [as] its special guardians." (126; quoting Reed, "ΕΥΑΓΓΕΛΙΟΝ," 45)

[87] Cf. Zahn, *Neutestamentlichen Kanons* 1:153; Oscar Cullmann, *The Early Church* (London: SCM, 1956), 50–2; McDonald, *Formation*, 167–8; Robert M.Grant, *Irenaeus of Lyons* (London: Routledge, 1997), 33; Hitchcock, *Irenaeus*, 214–19; etc.

[88] Reed, "ΕΥΑΓΓΕΛΙΟΝ," 22.

[89] Behr, *Nicaea*, 113. Cf. Farkasfalvy, "Theology" 329–30; Benoit, *Irénée*, 117; Bruce, *Canon*, 175.

in his description of their origin at the beginning of Book 3 in which he describes the authority of the Gospel accounts solely in terms of constituting the written testimony of the apostles.[90] It is from this perspective that Irenaeus' argument for a fourfold Gospel must be understood: it is not an argument for a closed canon of four gospels, but an argument that only the apostolic accounts of the Gospel have authority, and a description of the fittingness of the fact that the apostles handed down those four accounts.[91] For, "they collectively, and each of them individually, equally possessed the Gospel of God" (3.1.1).

Read within the context of Book 3 and as the conclusion to the section spanning 3.9-11, Irenaeus' fourfold Gospel argument demonstrates that he believes the singular Gospel message is authoritatively preserved by four apostolic written testimonies. Irenaeus is not arguing for the canonicity of the texts themselves but defending the unique authority of the apostolic authors, and therefore his use of εὐαγγέλιον in this section does not indicate that he was in the practice of describing the Gospel accounts as an authoritative *text* without requiring reference to authoritative authors. Closer examination reveals the opposite. These Gospel accounts (and the other apostolic writings) are considered to be identical in content to the preaching of the apostles,[92] and so are used to discover "the mind of the apostles."[93] It is the apostles themselves who are uniquely authoritative for Irenaeus, and the value of these written testimonies lies primarily in the fact that they provide access to these apostles' teachings.

These findings may be added to the analysis of Irenaeus' references to the apostolic writings, leading to the conclusion that his references to them as written texts are exceedingly rare, and never occur without direct reference to their apostolic authors or as a reference to the heretical use of them. Irenaeus gives no indication of using the apostolic writings as an *inherently authoritative text*, as he consistently does with the Jewish scriptures.

C. Irenaeus' Use of the Apostolic Writings in Contrast with the Jewish Scriptures

The distinction between Irenaeus' common use of the Jewish scriptures as an inherently authoritative *text* and his unwavering use of the apostolic writings as the *testimony* of authoritative human authors is also positively indicated in a number of places where Irenaeus directly contrasts the two collections. A few examples from Book 2 illustrate this pattern:

> The Scriptures [*Scripturae*] know only this God, and the Lord acknowledges [*Dominus ... confitetur*] only him as his own Father. (2.28.4)

---

[90] Cf. Benoit, *Irénée*: "Mais Irénée va donner une autre raison d'accepter les quatre évangiles. Il les reçoit à cause de leur origine apostolique ... Ce qui fonde l'autorité des quatre évangiles, c'est donc leur apostolicité" (118).
[91] Cf. Ferguson, "Selection and Closure," 301.
[92] 3.3.1-2.
[93] 3.16.1: "*necesse habemus uniuersam apostolorum de Domino nostro Iesu Christo sententiam adhibere.*"

Neither does any Scripture relate, nor does the Apostle tell us, nor did the Lord teach [*neque Scriptura aliqua retulit neque Apostolus dixit neque Dominus docuit*] what the cause of the nature itself of sinners is. (2.28.7)

All the Scriptures loudly proclaim [*uniuersae clamant Scripturae*] that there are spiritual creatures in heaven. Paul, too, testifies [*et Paulus autem testimonium perhibet*] that these are spiritual beings. (2.30.7)[94]

In all these passages Irenaeus simultaneously refers to the Jewish scriptures as a scriptural text and the apostolic writings as the words of either the Lord or an apostle. This explicit contrast between *text* and *testimony* demonstrates the distinction in his treatment of the two collections. Even when Irenaeus is discussing the text of the Jewish scriptures and comparing it to the apostolic writings, the apostolic writings nonetheless retain their essential character as the testimony of the apostles and witness to the words of the Lord. This contrast is made more explicit in the following statement:

> Such indeed is what they say concerning their pleroma and of the formation of all, doing violence to *things well said* to adapt them to their wicked inventions [ἐφαρμόζειν βιαζόμενοι τὰ καλῶς εἰρημένα τοῖς κακῶς ἐπινενοημένοις ὑπ' αὐτῶν]; and not only from the evangelical and the apostolic [sayings] do they attempt to make proofs [καὶ οὐ μόνον ἐκ τῶν εὐαγγελικῶν καὶ τῶν ἀποστολικῶν πειρῶνται τὰς ἀποδείξεις ποιεῖσθαι], perverting the interpretations and falsifying the explanations; but also from Law and Prophets [ἀλλὰ, καὶ ἐκ νόμου καὶ προφητῶν]. (1.3.6)[95]

Though this passage has been used as evidence that Irenaeus equates the two, treating the apostolic writings as a scriptural text in identical fashion to the Jewish scriptures,[96] his parallel statements illustrate a contrast between that *which has been said by* the apostles (about the Gospel) and the written collection titled "Law and Prophets." This passage encapsulates a central difference between his use of the apostolic writings and the Jewish scriptures.

Irenaeus also demonstrates this difference by his differing methods of defense of the authority of the two written collections. In his defense of the authority of the apostolic writings, their authority is always located in the apostles themselves. This has already

---

[94] Similar examples of citations from the Jewish scriptures contrasted directly with citations from the apostolic writings can be found in 2.2.5, 2.22.2, 4.16.1, 4.40.3, 5.5.2, 5.15.2, etc.

[95] My trans.; emphasis added. Unger translates the relevant section as follows: "Not only from the words of the evangelists and the apostles do they try to make proofs by perverting the interpretations and by falsifying the explanations, but also from the law and the prophets" (ACW 55:29).

[96] Ferguson, "Selection and Closure," follows Roberts–Donaldson's translation of this passage (ANF 2:320), claiming that "Irenaeus could put the 'writings of the Evangelists and the Apostles' alongside 'the Law and the prophets'" (306) in order to demonstrate that Irenaeus uses "gospels and apostles" as a title for the apostolic writings. Metzger, *Canon*, 155, also follows this translation in order to argue that the apostolic writings are here placed "on a par with" the Jewish scriptures. T. F. Torrance, *Divine Meaning: Studies in Patristic Hermeneutics* (Edinburgh: T&T Clark, 1995), opts to translate this passage as "the evangelical and apostolic scriptures" (128). Hoh, *Lehre*, notes this passage as evidence that "ev. = Schrift" (5). Cf. also Farkasfalvy, "Theology," 329–30; Benoit, *Irénée*, 90; Hitchcock, *Irenaeus*, 214; etc.

been observed in his argument for a fourfold Gospel, but it is made most explicit at the beginning of Book 3,[97] where he defends his use of the Gospel accounts:

> 3.pre. For the Lord of all gave the power of the Gospel to His apostles, through whom we too know the truth.
>
> 1.1. For we know the economy of our salvation through no others than those through whom the Gospel has come to us: at one time they certainly proclaimed this Gospel publicly, but afterwards through God's will they handed it down to us in writings [*postea uero per Dei uoluntatem in Scripturis nobis tradiderunt*], ensuring that it would be the foundation and pillar of our faith. ... Accordingly, Matthew produced a writing of the Gospel among the Hebrews in their own language, while Peter and Paul were proclaiming the Gospel in Rome and establishing the Church. But after their departure, Mark, Peter's disciple and interpreter, also himself handed down to us in writing the preaching of Peter. And Luke, Paul's follower, also put down in a book the Gospel preached by him. Then John, the Lord's disciple who had also leaned against his breast, did himself also deliver the Gospel while staying in Ephesus of Asia.
>
> 1.2. And all these have handed down to us [*Et omnes isti ... tradiderunt nobis*] one God the Creator of heaven and earth, announced by the law and the prophets, and one Christ the Son of God. (3.pre-1.2)[98]

In his defense of the apostolic writings, Irenaeus is explicit that their authority is derived from their apostolic origin, describing them straightforwardly as the testimony of the apostles who "handed [the Gospel they had proclaimed] down to us in writings, ensuring that it would be the foundation and pillar of our faith."[99] The teachings of the apostles are Irenaeus' focus, and the apostolic writings serve as the point of access to these teachings.[100] His description in this passage contrasts sharply with his description of the basis of authority of the Jewish scriptures in Book 2:

> We know very well that the Scriptures are perfect, inasmuch as they were given by God's Word and Spirit [*quippe a Verbo Dei et Spiritu eius dictae*]. (2.28.2)

In Irenaeus' description of the authority of the Jewish scriptures the text itself becomes the focus, without the requirement of appeal to the authority of the prophets, for it is the divine source of the text itself that grants the Jewish scriptures their authority.

The contrast evident in Irenaeus' descriptions of the basis of authority of the Jewish scriptures and apostolic writings, alongside a number of statements in which he directly contrasts the two collections as *text* and *testimony*, confirm the conclusions of the above analyses of his use of the apostolic writings.

---

[97] In addition to these, another extended discussion of the authority of Paul and the twelve apostles occurs in 3.13-15.
[98] My trans.
[99] Cf. Lawson, *Biblical Theology*, 35–6.
[100] Alongside and as part of the tradition that is preserved by the church (3.3-4).

Conclusion

Irenaeus is consistent in his distinct use of the apostolic writings as the testimony of authoritative human authors throughout his writings. Both in his method of introducing citations from the apostolic writings and in his references to them Irenaeus almost entirely refrains from describing them as written texts, instead exhibiting a consistent focus on the apostolic authors themselves. These findings demonstrate a definite distinction from his use of the Jewish scriptures. This treatment has thus far been noticed only by John Barton, who remarks, "Christian writers in the first two centuries often retain a sense that the Gospels are not holy texts but the records of living memory ... The vehicle for this testimony is seen as primarily oral in character,"[101] noting that "One of the most striking witnesses to this way of thinking is Irenaeus."[102] Irenaeus' occasional textual use of εὐαγγέλιον comes closest to resembling his descriptions of the Jewish scriptures: a single citation is introduced as "εὐαγγέλιον" without mention of the apostolic author, while a number of references to written εὐαγγέλια without direct apostolic attribution occur within a single section in 3.11.7-9. Yet closer examination reveals that Irenaeus' purpose in his argument for a fourfold Gospel in this section is concerned primarily with the unique authority of apostolic testimony, indicating that even here Irenaeus' use of the apostolic writings does not resemble his use of the Jewish scriptures. The findings of these analyses are confirmed by Irenaeus' repeated references to the apostolic writings alongside the Jewish scriptures that form a contrast between *text* and *testimony*, and by his distinct defense of the authority of the apostolic writings on the basis of apostolic authorship. This leads to the conclusion that Irenaeus' use of the apostolic writings as the testimony of authoritative authors represents a significant distinction from his treatment of the Jewish scriptures as an inherently authoritative text, in opposition to the claim of the traditional interpretation.

2.3. Do Irenaeus' Interpretations Seem Indifferent to the Intentions of the Apostolic Authors?

Having demonstrated in the previous section that Irenaeus' use of the apostolic writings as the testimony of an authoritative author differs significantly from his use of the Jewish scriptures as an authoritative text, the current section investigates a second central aspect of his use of the apostolic writings—his principle of interpretation. It was demonstrated in Section 2.1B that Irenaeus seeks the Word's intended meaning in his interpretation of the Jewish scriptures, without regard for the historical contexts of its prophetic writers. This is seen once again to contrast with his use of the apostolic writings.

---

[101] John Barton, *Holy Writings, Sacred Text: The Canon in Early Christianity* (Louisville, KY: Westminster John Knox Press, 1997), 79. He also maintains that second-century writers including Irenaeus "ascribe authority to the contents of the Gospels, considered as independent of the books in which they appear" (80).
[102] Ibid., 82.

A. Irenaeus' Principle of Interpretation of the Apostolic Writings

According to Irenaeus, interpretations of the apostolic writings must seek the intended message of their apostolic authors. This interpretative principle is prescribed at the end of ch. 12 of Book 3. In this chapter, after having spent the first ten paragraphs demonstrating the apostles' doctrine of God from the witness of Acts, Irenaeus pauses in 3.12.11 to declare that "The entire doctrine of the apostles [*omnem apostolorum doctrinam*] announced one and the same God," which "all who are willing can learn from the very sermons and deeds of the apostles [*ex ipsis sermonibus et actibus apostolorum*]." He continues,

> But if anyone has a "morbid craving for controversies" and imagines what the apostles said about God should be allegorized [*ab apostolis de Deo dicta sunt allegorizanda*], let him examine our previous treatises, in which we have shown that there is one God, the Creator and Maker of all things, and have overthrown and laid bare the assertions of these men; and he will find these [treatises] agreeing with the doctrine of the apostles and containing exactly what they used to teach and that of which they were themselves convinced [*et inueniet consonantes eos apostolorum doctrinae et sic habere quemadmodum docebant et persuadebantur*]. (3.12.11)

Irenaeus denies that the words of the apostles should be allegorized,[103] and contends that his own interpretation is correct because it has been made according to what the apostles intended to teach and were themselves convinced of.[104] Irenaeus' description contrasts with his descriptions of the proper interpretation of the Jewish scriptures, for which allegorical interpretations are expressly affirmed.[105]

In practice, Irenaeus' own interpretations of the apostolic writings are consistent with his description of their proper interpretation. He is concerned to express the intended message of the apostolic authors within their own contexts, as he demonstrates in ch. 7 of Book 3. Here Irenaeus dedicates the entire chapter to engaging in a detailed argument about what Paul actually meant in a certain passage and describing how to properly understand Paul. He explains,

> They maintain that in his second letter to the Corinthians, Paul said openly, "In their case, the God of this world has blinded the minds of unbelievers," and therefore they claim that there is one God "of the world" and another who is above every dominion and principality and power. But we are not at fault if these men, who assert that they know the mysteries which are above God, do not even know

---

[103] The context of Irenaeus' use of *allegorizo* in this passage illustrates that his concern is the improper use of allegory that is contrary to the meaning intended by the apostles. In 5.13.2 (discussed below), he takes issue instead with his opponents' over-literal interpretation of Paul's writings when Paul intended to speak metaphorically.

[104] The same concern is present in Irenaeus' assertion that he will make use of "the entire mind of the apostles [*uniuersam apostolorum ... sententiam*]" (3.16.1) in order to overthrow the teachings of his opponents.

[105] 1.3.6, 2.22.1, 5.26.2, and *Dem.* 56.

how to read Paul [*ne quidem legere Paulum sciunt*]. For, in keeping with Paul's style, which makes use of transpositions [*enim quis secundum Pauli consuetudinem ... hyperbatis eum utentem*] as we have shown elsewhere by many examples, if anyone reads it thus: "In their case, God," and then puts punctuation and a slight pause, and reads the rest together, "of this world has blinded the minds of the unbelievers," he will find the true sense. [The passage] would read thus: "God has blinded the minds of the unbelievers of this world." (3.7.1)

Irenaeus takes issue with his opponents interpreting Paul as saying "the God of this world has blinded the minds of unbelievers,"[106] understood as a reference to the Demiurge, in distinction from the Father of Christ. To combat this interpretation, Irenaeus works hard to explain that they have misunderstood what Paul meant, and that Paul's own distinctive style exhibits transpositions and requires pauses in order to be understood. When this is done properly, the passage instead reads, "God has blinded the minds of the unbelievers of this world."[107] Irenaeus then adduces two other passages in Paul's writings where he exhibits similar stylistic tendencies, in order to validate his exegesis as accurately presenting the intended message of Paul. His method of interpretation in this chapter demonstrates an overriding concern to discover the intention of the apostolic author.[108]

In addition to illustrating Irenaeus' concern for interpreting the apostolic writings according to the intended message of the author, the preceding example also indicates a distinction from his opponents' use of the apostolic writings. Unlike Irenaeus, his opponents are unconcerned with the intended message of the apostolic authors and feel justified in treating the apostolic writings as texts to be mined for deeper spiritual meaning.[109] A number of examples of this method of interpretation are described by Irenaeus in a section of Book 1 spanning 1.8.2-5. Explaining some of the passages they interpret to refer to Achamoth, Irenaeus describes,

And that the Saviour appeared to her when she lay outside of the Pleroma as a kind of abortion, they affirm Paul to have declared in his Epistle to the Corinthians,

---

[106] 2 Cor. 4:4.

[107] It appears that Irenaeus was incorrect in his interpretation of Paul here. The consensus reading of 2 Cor. 4:4 posits that the genitive refers to God (cf. ACW 64:41, nn. 1 and 3). Yet the intention to interpret Paul properly remains, even if it falls short in this instance. His conclusion that Paul is not referring to the Demiurge is certainly accurate: "*Non enim Deum huius saeculi dicit Paulus, quasi super illum alterum aliquem sciens, sed Deum quidem Deum confessus est*" (3.7.1).

[108] Similar instances occur in 3.8.1, 4.6.1-3, 4.8.1, 5.8.1, 5.9.1-4, 5.11.1, etc. There are also a number of instances in which his interpretations of the apostolic writings occur side-by-side with interpretations of the Jewish scriptures, illuminating the distinction between them: 3.8.2, 3.9.1-3, 4.10.1-2, 4.11.3, 4.12.1-5, 4.33.11, 5.8.1-4, 5.12.1-4, 5.24.1, *Dem.* 43, *Dem.* 87, etc.

[109] In 3.1.2 Irenaeus describes his opponents' tendency to use the apostolic writings as divine discourses that are said to come from the various deities within their systems, as he explains, "they maintain that the apostles mixed with the Savior's words matter from the law, and that not only the apostles but the Lord Himself gave discourses derived at times from the Demiurge, at others from the Intermediate Region, and at yet others from the Highest Authority." This description parallels his descriptions of their interpretations of the Jewish scriptures as divine discourses from various deities in 1.30.11 and 4.35.1-4.

"And last of all, He appeared to me also, as to one born out of due time."[110] Again, the coming of the Saviour with His attendants to Achamoth is declared in like manner by him in the same Epistle, when he says, "A woman ought to have a veil upon her head, because of the angels."[111] (1.8.2)[112]

The Valentinian interpretations of the two statements by Paul in this passage ignore the context of his statements, instead transferring his words to their own systems and assigning their own meanings to them. This practice is similarly observed in the following paragraph where Irenaeus describes how the Valentinians interpret Paul to prove the three classes of people:

Paul, too, very plainly set forth the material, animal, and spiritual, saying in one place, "As is the earthy, such are they also that are earthy;"[113] and in another place, "But the animal man receiveth not the thing of the Spirit;"[114] and again: "He that is spiritual judgeth all things."[115] (1.8.3)[116]

Here again the context of Paul's words is lost and his intended message concerning living by the flesh and by the Spirit is ignored in favor of an out-of-context interpretation of his words according to a foreign ὑπόθεσις.

Irenaeus does not mince words describing his assessment of his opponents' interpretative methods. In the following chapter he passes judgment on another of the examples he has described, declaring,

The fallacy, then, of this exposition is manifest ... Thus it is that, wresting from the truth every one of the expressions which have been cited [ἓν ἕκαστον τῶν εἰρημένων ἄραντες ἀπὸ τῆς ἀληθείας], and taking bad advantage of the names, they have transferred them to their own system [καταχρησάμενοι τοῖς ὀνόμασιν, εἰς τὴν ἰδίαν ὑπόθεσιν μετήνεγκαν]; so that, according to them, in all these terms John makes no mention of the Lord Jesus Christ. (1.9.2)[117]

According to Irenaeus, his opponents' interpretations are false because they apply foreign meanings to the apostles' words and remove them from their contexts, deriving meaning instead from the relation of these words—taken in the abstract—to their own ὑπόθεσις. In response to the interpretation he has just criticized, Irenaeus instead contends, "But the Apostle himself made it clear [αὐτῶν ὁ Ἀπόστολος εἴρηκεν] that he did not speak of their conjugal couples" (1.9.2). Their interpretation must be false because they have not heeded John's intended meaning.

---

[110] 1 Cor. 15:8.
[111] 1 Cor. 11:10.
[112] ANF 1:327.
[113] 1 Cor. 15:48.
[114] 1 Cor. 2:14.
[115] 1 Cor. 2:15.
[116] ANF 1:327.
[117] ANF 1:329.

Later, in Book 5, Irenaeus dedicates a number of chapters to explaining the correct interpretation of Paul's claim that "flesh and blood cannot inherit the kingdom of God,"[118] against the Valentinian interpretation of this passage as proof of their claim that matter and spirit are opposed to one another.[119] Beginning in ch. 9, Irenaeus takes five chapters to explain Paul's meaning in this passage in light of his overall understanding of these concepts. His meaning is demonstrated by bringing in dozens of his other statements on the subject and explaining in great detail what he means, proving that Paul himself contradicts the Valentinian interpretation of this passage. As Irenaeus explains,

> In all these passages, therefore, as I have already said, these men must either allege that the apostle expresses opinions contradicting himself [*aut contraria sentientem sibimetipsi Apostolum dicent*], with respect to that statement, "Flesh and blood cannot inherit the kingdom of God;" or, on the other hand, they will be forced to make perverse and crooked interpretations of all the passages, so as to overturn and alter the sense of the words [*malignas et extortas cogentur omnium dictorum facere expositiones ad transvertendam et mutandam sententiam dictorum*]. (5.13.5)

Having completed his demonstration, Irenaeus concludes that his opponents' interpretation of this passage is merely an exercise in

> taking two expressions of Paul's, without having perceived the apostle's meaning, or examined critically the force of the terms [οὔτε τὴν δύναμιν τῶν λεγομένων προερευνήσαντες], but keeping fast hold of the mere expressions by themselves [ψιλῶς δὲ αὐτῷ μόνον τὰς λέξεις κρατοῦντες]. (5.13.2)

Instead of seeking to understand Paul's intentions, they ignore his intended meaning and abstract his words from their original context to fit into their own ὑπόθεσις. This is their exegetical method for all the apostolic writings that they use. Irenaeus, in contrast, is concerned with the intentions of the apostolic authors.

In Irenaeus' evaluation of heretical interpretations of the apostolic writings, which he criticizes for out-of-context interpretations that ignore the intended message of the apostolic author, there is an evident distinction from his evaluation of their interpretations of the Jewish scriptures, which are criticized instead for replacing the rule of truth with a foreign ὑπόθεσις.[120] The examined passages also indicate an

---

[118] 1 Cor. 15:50.

[119] The Valentinian interpretation of this passage is an example of a literal interpretation that goes against the author's intended meaning, as the Valentinians interpreted Paul's words *too literally*, when Paul was speaking metaphorically. Related to this, an example of Irenaeus correctly describing Paul's metaphorical use of "day" is found in 2.22.2.

[120] See the previous discussion in Section 2.1B. There are no instances in *Adversus haereses* in which Irenaeus criticizes his opponents' interpretations of the Jewish scriptures for failing to properly take into account the intended meaning of the human author of the passage. This criticism is leveled exclusively in reference to the apostolic writings. Likewise, his opponents' interpretations of the apostolic writings are never criticized for deviating from the rule of truth, as their interpretations of the Jewish Scriptures are. It is always their failure to perceive the apostles' own meanings that is condemned.

important difference in Irenaeus' understanding between orthodox and heretical conceptions of the apostolic writings: it is the heretics who treat the apostolic writings themselves as *scripture*, as texts to be scoured for divine meaning, in similar fashion to the Jewish scriptures.[121] Irenaeus refuses to make this move and criticizes his opponents for doing so, for he believes that this is an improper use of the apostolic writings.

B. Does Irenaeus Exhibit "Allegorical" Interpretations of the Apostolic Writings?

Contrary to the conclusions reached so far in this section, a number of scholars have suggested that Irenaeus is in fact comfortable interpreting the apostolic writings in the same way as the Jewish scriptures. Osborn, in his description of Irenaeus' "Principles of Interpretation" of scripture (which for him means both the Old and New Testaments), describes a number of principles that disregard the intended meaning of the author that conform to Irenaeus' use of the Jewish Scriptures, alongside the principles of "History" and "Grammar" that seek the intentions of the human author, of which his examples are drawn exclusively from the apostolic writings.[122] This leads him to the conclusion that all seven of these principles apply to all the "Scriptures," and as a result of this conflation the apostolic writings are claimed to be interpreted according to "the rule of truth," "logical coherence and aesthetic fitness," and "fulfillment of prophecy and recapitulation" as the Jewish scriptures are.

Hitchcock has previously engaged in a similar conflation in which Irenaeus' concern for punctuation in his reading of Paul (3.7.2) is understood to be an additional aspect of his nonetheless "mystical principle of interpretation" of the Old and New Testament scriptures.[123] More recently, Lewis Ayres has given accounts of Irenaeus' interpretative methods that involve the assertion that Irenaeus "treats Old and New Testaments as two sections of a unified body of texts, to be read and analyzed by the same close methods."[124] His statement is not intended as a claim that both collections are interpreted by Irenaeus either according to or without regard for the intentions of the human authors,[125] but his account ignores the possibility of such a distinction,

---

[121] For his description of the heretical treatment of the apostolic writings as divine discourses, see 3.1.2, while parallel treatments of the Jewish scriptures are described in 1.30.11 and 4.35.1-4. Irenaeus gives examples of this method of interpretation of the apostolic writings in 1.7.3-4 and of the Jewish scriptures in 4.35.4.
[122] Osborn, *Irenaeus*, 173–4.
[123] Hitchcock, *Irenaeus*, 191.
[124] Ayres, "Reading the Letter," 622; "Irenaeus vs. the Valentinians."
[125] Ayres is concerned to describe the *methods* of interpretation used by Irenaeus rather than commenting on the *principle* described here, and identifies a primary method of interpretation according to the "plain sense" of the text itself (cf. "Irenaeus vs. the Valentinians," 169–80) which is not an assertion (or a denial) of concern for authorial intention. Explaining this distinction in "Theologies of Scripture," Ayres writes, "Early Christian exegesis takes as its point of departure the 'plain' sense of the text. I avoid the term 'literal' here because it is frequently associated in modern discussion with the sense intended by the human author of a text or the sense that a text had for its initial readers" (14).

combining Irenaeus' treatments of the apostolic writings and the Jewish scriptures into a single method of interpretation of the "scriptures,"[126] as Osborn and Hitchcock have.

Other interpreters have adduced specific passages from *Adversus haereses* that are claimed to exhibit "allegorical" interpretations of the apostolic writings.[127] Lawson has argued that Irenaeus occasionally interpreted the Pauline epistles "allegorically," though it is evident that his examples do not substantiate his implicit claim that Irenaeus ignored Paul's intended meaning.[128] Maurice Wiles has also accused Irenaeus of what he calls "spiritual interpretations of the factual details of a historical narrative" for his treatment of John's accounts of Jesus restoring the sight of the man born blind[129] and Mary asking Jesus to miraculously provide wine for the wedding feast,[130] in both

---

[126] In "Reading the Letter," Ayres describes a series of aspects of Irenaeus' interpretative method with corresponding passages from *Adversus Haereses* provided as evidence. In this description, all examples of "prosopological exegesis" concern passages from the Jewish scriptures, while all examples of the importance of "punctuation" and "personal patterns of speech" concern passages from the apostolic writings (620–1 and n. 16). Similarly, in "Irenaeus vs. the Valentinians," Ayres uses Irenaeus' method of interpretation of Paul according to his own intended meaning as determined by attention to the author's style and punctuation in 3.7 in order to demonstrate that in Irenaeus' method of interpretation of "the scriptures," "The 'manifest' meaning of the text is discovered by one who believes that interpretation proceeds in the light of a knowledge of an author's life, and their patterns of expression" (172). In both articles, no distinction is identified between Irenaeus' patterns of interpretation of the Jewish scriptures and the apostolic writings.

[127] This claim is taken to mean that Irenaeus can interpret the apostolic writings without concern for the intended meaning of the apostolic authors, both because this meaning is often implied and because it would be rather redundant to make the claim that Irenaeus interpreted intentional allegorical statements in the apostolic writings as allegories.

[128] Lawson, *Biblical Theology*, claims that nine Pauline texts are "rendered allegorically" by Irenaeus (80), though he does not list them. He explicitly notes 5.10.1, and he has earlier noted 3.13.3, 3.16.9, and 3.18.3 as proof that "Irenaeus approaches allegorism in Pauline exegesis" (47). In 5.10.1, Lawson claims that Rom. 11:17 is "further allegorized to refer to the salvation of the body" (80). In reality, Irenaeus draws on Paul's reference to a wild olive branch grafted into an olive tree in order "to share the fatness of the olive tree" as meaning the engrafting of the Spirit and its results in order to demonstrate that Paul does not preach that "material" people cannot inherit the kingdom of God, as his opponents claim. The metaphor is surely not far from Paul's own, so it is difficult to maintain the charge that Irenaeus' interpretation allegorizes Paul or ignores his own intention, even if Paul's own purpose for using the metaphor is not to disprove these later heretics. Lawson also (47, 67, 81) finds an allegory in Irenaeus' use of Paul's statement "How beautiful are the feet of those who bring good news" (Rom. 10:15) as evidence that Paul believed many people preached the true Gospel, and not just Paul himself as Marcion claimed (3.13.1). Yet Paul is referring to those people who proclaim the Gospel, and his reference to others besides himself doing this is precisely Irenaeus' point. Certainly Paul is not attempting to refute Marcion, but it is clear that his understanding lines up with Irenaeus' description of it. Perhaps Lawson's most striking claim is that Irenaeus' use of Paul in 3.16.9 is allegorical (47, 71), where Irenaeus quotes Paul's reference to "Jesus Christ" (Rom. 5:17) as evidence that Paul did not hold to the heretical conception of Jesus and Christ as two different beings. Though Paul's intention is not to attack this later heretical position, his statement nonetheless demonstrates Irenaeus' point. The same claim is also made by Lawson about Irenaeus' use of Rom. 14:14-15 in 3.18.3 (47, 72). The most that can be said in these passages is that Irenaeus often uses Paul's words to answer questions that Paul was not attempting to answer. But this does not mean that Irenaeus' interpretations do not attempt to understand Paul's meaning, as Lawson suggests. Irenaeus' use of Paul is more accurately characterized by Mark Jeffrey Olson, *Irenaeus, the Valentinian Gnostics, and the Kingdom of God* (Lewiston: Edwin Mellen Press, 1992), as exhibiting occasional *eisegesis* (2).

[129] Maurice M. Wiles, *The Spiritual Gospel: The Interpretation of the Fourth Gospel in the Early Church* (Cambridge: Cambridge University Press, 1960), 37 n. 6; in reference to Irenaeus' use of Jn 9:1-12 in 5.15.2 (cf. 55).

[130] Ibid., 44, in reference to Irenaeus' use of Jn 2:3-4 in 3.16.7.

of which there is no indication that Irenaeus is not seeking to describe John's own purpose in describing the events as he does.[131]

The source most commonly cited as evidence that Irenaeus occasionally interprets the apostolic writings allegorically is R. P. C. Hanson's claim in his 1959 work *Allegory and Event* that "Irenaeus is the first writer to allegorize the New Testament," which Hanson believes occurs because "he is among the first writers to treat the New Testament unreservedly as inspired Scripture."[132] Hanson provides a single example to demonstrate this claim, taken from Irenaeus' reference to the parable of the Good Samaritan in the course of his argument at 3.17.3.[133] Here, in the midst of describing the new way in which the Spirit becomes manifest throughout the world after the resurrection and ascension, Irenaeus gives the following description:

> Wherefore, we have need of God's dew, that we might not be burned up or become unfruitful; and that where we have an Accuser, we would have also the Advocate. And so the Lord entrusted His human nature to the Holy Spirit. It had fallen in with robbers, but He had pity on it and bound its wounds, giving it also two royal denarii [*cui ipse misertus est et ligauit uulnera eius, dans duo denaria regalia ut*],[134] that having received through the Spirit the image and inscription of the Father and the Son, we might make the denarius entrusted to us productive, thereby returning to the Lord the increase in denarii. (3.17.3)

In this passage Irenaeus makes reference to the parable of the Good Samaritan, comparing Christ to the Samaritan and humanity to the half-dead man who is rescued. Hanson's claim is accurate inasmuch as Irenaeus here deviates from Jesus' (and Luke's) observable intended meaning. However, it is misleading to describe this passage as an "interpretation" of the parable. There is no indication that Irenaeus in fact takes this to be the meaning of the parable, and his usage suggests that he is not claiming this

---

[131] Behr, in his recent work *John the Theologian and His Paschal Gospel: A Prologue to Theology* (forthcoming), interprets John's meaning in both passages in the same way Irenaeus has, and credits Irenaeus with having accurately described John's intention (ch. 3, Sects. 3 and 8), casting doubt on Wiles' assertion.

[132] R. P. C. Hanson, *Allegory and Event: A Study of the Sources and Significance of Origen's Interpretation of Scripture* (London: SCM Press, 1959), 112–13. Citation of Hanson as evidence of this assertion is observed in Bruce, *Canon*, 267; Henri de Lubac, *Scripture in the Tradition* (New York: Crossroad, 2001), 195; Torrance, *Divine Meaning*, 105; and Jorgensen, *Treasure Hidden*, 86. Jorgensen points out, in opposition to Hanson's claim, that Irenaeus could be neither the first writer nor the first Christian writer to allegorize the New Testament. "Rather, by Irenaeus' own report, it was his Valentinian opponents who, in the second century, first extended allegorical interpretation of Scripture to the texts that in successive centuries would come to be key components of the New Testament corpus" (86–7).

[133] Ibid., 113, 76 n. 2. Hanson cites 3.18.2, using Harvey's numbering. Harnack also cites this passage as evidence that Irenaeus was "the first to apply the scientific and mystical explanation to the New Testament" (HD 2:252), as does Hoh, *Lehre*, 101. Hanson makes clear that he is using "allegorize" to refer to interpretations that have not sought the writer's (or speaker's) intentions, as he says of Irenaeus' interpretation of this passage, "the suggestion that this interpretation was one intention in our Lord's mind in his producing of the parable of the Good Samaritan I cannot regard as worthy of serious consideration" (76 n. 2).

[134] Lk. 10:30-35.

passage as evidence of an assertion. Irenaeus merely borrows its imagery in order to draw comparisons between Jesus' salvation of humanity and the Samaritan's rescue of the half-dead man. Irenaeus' genuine interpretations of the parables are always immediately recognizable, and exhibit divergent results.[135]

At least four other passages could be added to Hanson's example, in which Irenaeus' use of a passage from the apostolic writings deviates to some degree from the observable intent of its author. In 3.22.4 Irenaeus asserts that Jesus' words in the parable of the Laborers in the Vineyard that "the last will be first and the first will be last"[136] are also applicable in the case of the obedience of Mary counteracting the disobedience of Eve. In another instance, in 4.36.6 Irenaeus describes the wedding garment in Jesus' parable of the Wedding Banquet, without which a guest was thrown into "the outer darkness,"[137] as the Spirit resting upon those who are "adorned with works of righteousness." In the following paragraph the workers in the parable of the Laborers in the Vineyard who arrive at different points of the day[138] are compared to the different generations and dispensations who were called by God, but received the same reward. Later, in 5.26.1 Irenaeus uses Jesus' words in the parable of the Strong Man that "every kingdom divided against itself is laid waste, and no city or house divided against itself will stand,"[139] to refer to the future Babylon that must be destroyed at the second coming.[140]

These four passages share a common theme with Hanson's example: in each case the reference is to one of the parables of Jesus. This pattern is recognized by David Jorgensen, who also notes, in addition to Hanson's example, Irenaeus' use of the parable of the Treasure Hidden in a Field to signify Christ hidden in the scriptures,[141] and his use of the parable of the Lost Sheep in reference to Jesus seeking after lost humanity.[142] Commenting on this pattern, Jorgensen explains,

---

[135] Cf., for example, Irenaeus' interpretation of the parables of the Sheep and the Goats and the Tares and the Wheat in 4.40-1. The differences between this interpretation and his utilization of the parable of the Good Samaritan in 3.17.3 are striking, both in the degree of attention given and in the conclusions reached.

[136] Mt. 20:16.

[137] Mt. 22:13.

[138] Mt. 20:2-6.

[139] Mt. 12:25.

[140] Cf. Rev. 17:12, etc.

[141] Jorgensen, *Treasure Hidden*, 86, in reference to 4.26.1:

> If any one, therefore, reads the Scriptures with attention, he will find in them an account of Christ, and a foreshadowing of the new calling. For Christ is the treasure which was hid in the field [*Mt.* 13:44], that is, in this world (for "the field is the world"); but the treasure hid in the Scriptures is Christ, since He was pointed out by means of types and parables.

> Campenhausen, *Formation*, also cites this passage as evidence that "it is ... the parables, interpreted generally as dogmatic allegories, which are given prominence" in his use of the apostolic writings (92). Brox, "Irenaeus," also cites this passage as evidence that "there is a whole swarm of allegories from the pen of Irenaeus himself" (1:489).

[142] Ibid., 116–17, in reference to 3.19.3:

> Since He had a human generation from Mary, who was of the human race and was herself a human being, He became the Son of Man. For this reason the Lord Himself gave us a sign in the depths below and in the heights above. Man [Ahaz] did not ask for that [sign], because he did not hope that a virgin, as a virgin, could become pregnant, and that she [could] also

Irenaeus does not apply allegorical reading strategies to apostolic texts very often, and in fact his use of them is quite restrictive. The one way in which Irenaeus is willing to apply allegorical meanings to the New Testament texts is to add allegorical interpretation to synoptic parables.[143]

Jorgensen identifies the parables of Jesus as the only elements of the apostolic writings that may be described as having additional meanings not clearly intended by their human author. He overstates Irenaeus' use of these parables, declaring Irenaeus' reference to the parable of the Lost Sheep to be an "allegorical interpretation of this parable in order to utilize it as an important justification for [his theology]."[144] This description does not correspond to Irenaeus' use of this parable or the other parables identified, for in each case he does not attempt to set out an interpretation of the parable, but instead makes oblique reference to its imagery for the sake of drawing comparisons in the course of his own argument.[145] However, Jorgensen has correctly identified that Jesus' parables may function in a way that the apostolic writings themselves do not: they may provide imagery by which to illustrate his points, just as the Jewish scriptures can. Jesus' words are uniquely able to contain additional layers of meaning, above and beyond their observable surface meaning.[146]

Irenaeus' use of Jesus' parables nevertheless differs from both his interpretations of the Jewish scriptures and from his opponents' interpretations of the apostolic writings. As explained in Section 2.1B, Irenaeus consistently provides interpretations of passages from the Jewish scriptures that focus on the Word as author, to the neglect of the historical contexts of their human authors, and uses these interpretations as proof of his assertions. This mirrors the heretical use of the apostolic writings as described in Section 2.3A. The rule established in Section 2.3 that Irenaeus' principle of interpretation of the apostolic writings differs from that of the Jewish scriptures therefore remains in force even in his unique use of Jesus' parables.

---

give birth to a son, and that this child [could] be "God with us," and that He [could] descend into the lower parts of the earth, searching for the sheep that was lost—which really was His own handiwork—and ascend to the heights above there offering and recommending to the Father humanity who was found. (Cf. 5.12.3 and 5.15.3)

[143] Ibid., 86. Cf. Manlio Simonetti, *Profilo Storico dell' Esegesi Patristica*; reproduced in English as *Biblical Interpretation in the Early Church*, trans. John A. Hughes (Edinburgh: T&T Clark, 1994), who similarly contends that we might expect Irenaeus to exhibit "a systematically literalist approach" to the New Testament, and notes that "Such interpretation is indeed predominant, but it is sometimes accompanied by an allegorical reading, especially in the interpretation of the details of the parables, which Irenaeus readily interprets in relation to salvation history" (23). Cf. Brox, "Irenaeus," 1:490–1.

[144] Ibid., 92.

[145] Irenaeus' practice of *interpreting* Jesus parables may be observed in 4.40-41.

[146] This may be seen in some ways as a parallel to his use of the Jewish scriptures, which can be understood to possess additional meanings on the basis of their divine authorship. Similarly, the words and actions of Jesus can at times be seen to possess similar additional meanings not necessarily evident in the descriptions of the apostolic writers who report them. The significance of this is explored further in Chapter 4, where the Word's function as the source of revelation on the basis of his role as Revealer of the Father is considered.

Conclusion

The second central element of Irenaeus' use of the apostolic writings, his principle for determining their correct interpretation, once again differs significantly from his use of the Jewish scriptures. While the Jewish scriptures are consistently interpreted according to the rule of truth in order to discover the meaning intended by the Word, the apostolic writings must be interpreted according to the meanings intended by their apostolic authors within their own contexts. Irenaeus explicitly describes this as the correct method of interpretation, and his own interpretations follow this rule. Irenaeus criticizes his opponents for their divergent interpretations of the apostolic writings, not because they fail to follow the rule of truth but because they ignore the intended meanings of the apostolic authors. Jesus parables may represent something of an exception to this rule, as Irenaeus occasionally references them in such a way as to suggest additional meanings, though this creative use of imagery does not constitute a true "interpretation."

The difference identified in this section between Irenaeus' principles of interpretation of the Jewish scriptures and of the apostolic writings initially appears to suggest that he is unconcerned with the intended meanings of the prophetic authors. However, closer analysis reveals that this distinction is more accurately described as a reflection of Irenaeus' conception of the difference between a prophet and an apostle. Irenaeus conceives of distinct roles for the prophets and apostles in relation to divine revelation, with consequences for how they should be interpreted. The derived authority of the prophets rests in their reception and faithful transmission of the message given to them by the Word, so it is the Word's intention that must be sought in the Jewish scriptures, and this is achieved by interpreting them according to the rule of truth. There is therefore no reason to attempt to determine the meaning intended by the prophets within their own historical contexts apart from this, for they have no message other than that communicated to them by the Word.[147] Their conscious purpose is to record the Word's enigmatic revelation for future generations.

In contrast to this, Irenaeus' treatment of the apostolic writings indicates that their own intended meanings and contexts are Irenaeus' central concern in his interpretations of their writings, and he rejects the interpretations of his opponents because they fail to seek the apostles' own intentions. This indicates that the apostles' words are authoritative in their own right, suggesting that they have received the full deposit of the Gospel and have been given the authority to preach it. This authority appears to provide the basis for the unique revelatory authority of the apostolic writings, and this distinguishes them from the Jewish scriptures, which acquire their authority directly from the Word, who is the true author of their message. A complete account of the distinct relationship between the apostles and divine revelation awaits additional analysis in the following chapters.

---

[147] As Reilly, "L'inspiration," describes, "On attache pourtant très peu d'importance, semble-t-il, à ce rôle du prophète considéré comme homme; dans l'idée de saint Irénée, il est presque exclusivement un intermédiaire par lequel Dieu parle aux chrétiens" (497).

The conclusions reached in this section support the findings of the previous section that Irenaeus uses the apostolic writings as the testimony of authoritative authors. Together, these two elements of Irenaeus' use of the apostolic writings demonstrate a significant difference in use from the Jewish scriptures, contrary to the claim of the traditional interpretation that Irenaeus' use of the apostolic writings is equivalent. Irenaeus' patterns of use of the apostolic writings suggest that they do not possess their unique revelatory authority on the basis of perceived scriptural status as the Jewish scriptures do, but instead on the basis of the derived authority of their apostolic authors.

Excursus: Evaluating a Possible Alternative Conclusion

It is possible to arrive at a different conclusion on the basis of the findings of this section, which proposes that the difference in principles of interpretation identified here arises because the Jewish scriptures were understood to prophesy future events, while the apostolic writings comment on events that have already taken place. For this reason, the apostolic writings would not require an interpretation that disregards the original contexts of their human authors, as the Jewish scriptures do, in order to conform to the rule of truth. There would therefore be no reason to suggest that Irenaeus' differentiated methods of interpretation of the apostolic writings represent an authentic difference in use or indicate that he perceives a difference in basis of authority.[148] Irenaeus' assertion that Christ is "the treasure hid in the [Jewish] Scriptures ... pointed out by types and parables" (4.26.1) would seem to naturally support this position.[149]

Two issues weigh against this conclusion. First, it struggles to explain why Irenaeus never criticizes his opponents' interpretations of the apostolic writings for failing to conform to the rule of truth, just as he never criticizes their interpretations of the Jewish Scriptures for failing to heed the intentions of their authors. A certain overlap in criticism would be expected, given that his opponents' interpretations of the two collections are equivalent. Second, this conclusion is unable to account for important differences between Irenaeus' interpretative methods and those of later interpreters. If the distinction identified between Irenaeus' distinct principles of interpretation for the Jewish scriptures and apostolic writings is understood to be merely a function of their differing roles and relations to the prophesied Incarnation, it should be expected that all later interpreters would share this distinction. However, subsequent interpreters, beginning with Origen, are observed to utilize methods of interpretation that disregard the apostles' intended meanings, analogous to their use

---

[148] Lawson, *Biblical Theology*, reaches a rather different conclusion. He argues that Irenaeus resorts to allegory only when he is faced with objectionable claims he needs to minimize (47), or when he lacks the necessary knowledge of the historical situation required to engage in "more historical treatment" and must therefore resort to allegorical interpretation to make up for his deficiency (85). It is therefore considered by Lawson to be only natural that Irenaeus engaged in allegorical interpretation primarily in his use of the Jewish scriptures.

[149] Robert M.Grant, *A Short History of the Interpretation of the Bible* (London: A&C Black, 1965), finds evidence in this passage for the position described here (53).

of the Jewish scriptures.[150] These two factors indicate that the distinction between Irenaeus' interpretations of the Jewish scriptures and apostolic writings cannot be accounted for by the fact that the apostolic writings are not prophesying future events as the Jewish scriptures do.

Chapter Conclusion

In this chapter I have sought to evaluate the traditional interpretation's second argument for its claim that Irenaeus considers the apostolic writings to be scripture equivalent to the Jewish scriptures—that Irenaeus uses the apostolic writings in the same manner as he uses the Jewish scriptures, as a *scriptural text*. The findings of this chapter have led to the conclusion that two central elements of Irenaeus' use of the apostolic writings—his treatment of them as the testimony of the apostles and his central concern for the intentions of the apostles in his interpretations—differ significantly from his use of the Jewish scriptures as an inherently authoritative scriptural text that is interpreted according to the rule of truth in order to discover the meaning intended by the Word. The traditional interpretation's second argument therefore cannot be substantiated: Irenaeus' use of the apostolic writings does not provide evidence for the claim that Irenaeus considers the apostolic writings to be scripture equivalent to the Jewish scriptures.

The significant differences that have been identified in Irenaeus' patterns of use of the two collections in fact indicate an underlying conceptual distinction.[151] Irenaeus' treatment of the apostolic writings as the testimony of the apostolic authors suggests a conception of the unique revelatory authority of the apostolic writings arising on the basis of the derived authority of the apostles, rather than on the basis of perceived scriptural status, as the Jewish scriptures are conceived. In his use of the apostolic writings Irenaeus is not utilizing an authoritative scriptural text; he is *interpreting the apostles*.[152] As Barton has described, "Irenaeus draws extensively on the New Testament to support his presentation of the faith, but (in this contrasting with his use of the Old Testament) he does *not* treat it as a divinely guaranteed source of supernatural information."[153] The authority of the gospels in Irenaeus' thought is instead predicated on "the authority of the apostles who are supposed to have written them; it is as these men's testimony, not as holy scripture, that the Gospels are to be believed" for Irenaeus, who "does not apply the same methods to the Old Testament, which he treats much more unequivocally as 'Scripture.'"[154] The identification in

---

[150] Cf. Origen, *comm. in Mt.* 10.24; Augustine, *de Gen. ad lit.* 1.1.1; etc.
[151] The logic of this move from identified patterns of use to an underlying conceptual distinction is defended by Ayres, "Theologies of Scripture," who, in reference to early Christian exegetical practices, notes the "close connection between the reading practices that these Christians took to be fundamental and their overall understanding of the purpose and nature of scripture. Almost all methods for reading scripture imply assumptions about the nature of the text" (17).
[152] More specifically: he is interpreting the apostolic preaching of Christ.
[153] John Barton, *People of the Book? The Authority of the Bible in Christianity* (London: SPCK, 1988), 39.
[154] Ibid.

this chapter of Irenaeus' attribution of a different basis of authority for the apostolic writings confirms the existence of the conceptual distinction suggested in the previous chapter between the apostolic writings and the Jewish scriptures, and indicates a possible basis for it.

Conclusion to Part 1

The investigations of the previous two chapters have led to the conclusion that the first two arguments given by the traditional interpretation are unable to substantiate its claim that Irenaeus considers the apostolic writings to be scripture equivalent to the Jewish scriptures. In Chapter 1, the argument that Irenaeus uses γραφή as a scriptural title for the apostolic writings alongside the Jewish scriptures, demonstrating that they possess equivalent scriptural status, was assessed. The investigation of Irenaeus' use of γραφή found that Irenaeus in fact refrains from using the term as a scriptural title in reference to the apostolic writings, instead reserving this title exclusively for the Jewish scriptures. Next, in Chapter 2, the argument that Irenaeus uses the apostolic writings in the same manner as the Jewish scriptures, as a *scriptural text*, was evaluated. The investigation of Irenaeus' patterns of use of the apostolic writings found a significant difference from his use of the Jewish scriptures: while the Jewish scriptures are used straightforwardly as an inherently authoritative scriptural text, the apostolic writings are used instead as a record of the testimony of authoritative human authors.

As a result of these conclusions, the traditional interpretation's central claim therefore relies on its third substantiating argument: the apostolic writings are equally authoritative with the Jewish scriptures in Irenaeus' thought. This argument may be seen, for example, in Steenberg's assertion that Irenaeus' concept of scripture must include the New Testament, because

> When Irenaeus uses the Church's texts polemically or dogmatically, he calls upon those of our New Testament as much as, and in the same manner as, he does those of the Old, whether or not he gives them the proper title "scripture." Functionally they are of equal merit and stature.[1]

Lawson is even more direct: "In actual practice S. Irenaeus quotes the Apostolic writings as equal authority with the Old Testament Scriptures … Thus the Apostolic writings are to Irenaeus fully authoritative Scripture."[2] This method of interpreting Irenaeus' conception of scripture according to demonstration of authoritative status is common.[3] However, while I affirm Irenaeus' belief in the equivalent authority of the

---

[1] Steenberg, "Graphe," 32; cf. 54.
[2] Lawson, *Biblical Theology*, 35; cf. 46.
[3] Benoit, *Irénée*, maintains,

apostolic writings,[4] the subsequent conclusion that this entails his acceptance of their scriptural status has not been established.

Evaluating the Implications of the Traditional Interpretation's Third Argument

As I understand it, the attempt to establish that the equivalent authority of the apostolic writings and Jewish scriptures entails equivalent scriptural status relies on a definition of "scripture" as "uniquely authoritative religious writings." There is precedent for such a definition, which often appears to be in use by scholars attempting to determine the process of New Testament canonization. McDonald, for example, in describing the criteria for "when Christians viewed certain writings as sacred scripture," points to

> the manner in which the New Testament writings are cited in the various communities of faith. When the citations or allusions recognize the authority of the writing to settle issues of faith, mission, and disciplinary matters, or when they are used in worship or in a liturgical setting, we can be assured that they carried a sacred authority not found in other writings of the time.[5]

On this basis, Gamble defines "scripture" in his study of the formation of the New Testament canon as "writings which are taken to be religiously authoritative and are used and valued as such."[6] Similar definitions are not infrequently used to determine where and when the New Testament documents came to be viewed as scripture.[7]

> S'il y a hésitation quant à la terminologie, et si l'on se trouve un peu gêné pour parler d'Écriture à propos des évangiles, il n'y a aucun doute sur le fond: les évangiles sont utilisés de la même manière que l'Ancien Testament et leur autorité est identique. Irénée les cite côte à côte, sans donner l'impression qu'il va d'un plus vers un moins ou inversement. (122; cf. 104, 136–7)

Campenhausen, *Formation*, suggests similar implications when he states that although Irenaeus does not seem to call the New Testament writings "scripture," "The instances in which Irenaeus combines Old and New Testament quotations as proofs of equal value are, however, innumerable" (188 n. 204). Cf. also Hoh, *Lehre*, 75–8; Ferguson, "Selection and Closure," 298; McDonald, *Formation*, 197; Ochagavia, *Visibile*, 176; Hitchcock, *Irenaeus*, 213, 223–4, and 228; etc.

[4] Cf. 1.2.
[5] Lee M. McDonald, "Identifying Scripture and Canon in the Early Church: The Criteria Question," in *The Canon Debate*, ed. Lee M. McDonald and James A. Sanders (Peabody, MA: Hendrickson, 2002), 420. In *Formation*, he also writes, "When the NT writings were placed alongside the scriptures of the OT and were appealed to authoritatively in the life and worship of the early church, they functioned as scripture in the church" (142).
[6] Gamble, *New Testament*, 18.
[7] Ferguson, "Selection and Closure," for example, writes,

> Although second-century Christian authors accepted the Old Testament as scripture, they used the New Testament writings, in relation to their quantity, much more than the Old Testament. Citation as "scripture" appears to be less significant than the overwhelming use and importance attached to the writings that form the core of our New Testament ... In terms of scriptural status, there is no time when Christians did not treat the writings that would become the New Testament as scripture. (298)

However, definitions of scripture of this type are problematic: they are not sufficiently narrow to exclude other writings that have never been considered to be in the category of "scripture." If scripture is defined as "those writings which function authoritatively for the church," "those writings which are used in liturgy," "those writings which are appealed to as a standard of orthodoxy," and so on, then in addition to the Old and New Testaments the canon of Christian scripture would seem to require the inclusion of major creeds, canons, confessions, and statements; hymns, prayer books, and liturgical texts; and perhaps even formative systematic theologies and commentaries. All of these meet the criteria for one or more of the suggested definitions, yet none have been included in any historical or contemporary conception of the contents of scripture.

This problem is illustrated by Steenberg in his treatment of Irenaeus' own writings. Steenberg advocates that the apostolic writings are to be considered as scripture for Irenaeus because the Old and New Testaments "are of equal merit and stature."[8] While this approach to interpreting Irenaeus is not unique to Steenberg, he is among the first to fully comprehend and apply its logical conclusions. For this definition of scripture does not only include the apostolic writings. As he explains,

> It seems clear that perceptions of "scripture" in Irenaeus, beyond the delimited contents of the Septuagint, are more nuanced and fluid than in much later history, and certainly modern scholarship. The canon or rule of right belief, and the authority discovered in a given text to proclaim it, defines "scripture" more readily than could any listing of accepted books ... it is a text's capability to proclaim the Christocentric vision of the cosmos, exemplified in the preaching of the apostles, which stands as the canon that authenticates the truth of scripture, that Irenaeus *sees* as the very heart of a given text's status as γραφή.[9]

When it is defined on the basis of authority, scripture becomes a concept that may be much more widely applied than many interpreters understand or are prepared to admit. Steenberg argues on the basis of this principle that Irenaeus certainly considered the *Shepherd of Hermas*, and presumably also many other early Christian documents, to be scripture alongside both the Jewish scriptures and apostolic writings, though that is not to say that he would have wanted to place them into any sort of canon. According to Steenberg, this would miss the point. He explains,

> Scripture is not, then, to be confined for Irenaeus to a strictly delimited set of texts, save for when he uses the term to refer to the received collection of the Septuagintal Old Testament ... Christological revelation as paradigmatically set forth by the apostles becomes the living tradition of scriptural authority, by which

---

Cf. Metzger, *Canon*, 156, 160, etc.; Campenhausen, *Formation*, 168 and 182; Bruce, *Canon*, 23–4; etc. However, the use or nonuse of γραφή/*scriptura* is still considered to be the chief test of scriptural status by the majority of New Testament canon scholars.

[8] Steenberg, "Graphe," 32.
[9] Ibid., 65–6.

the Old Testament collection is itself given Christian heritage, and by which all new documents may be judged.[10]

Steenberg's definition of "scripture" may theoretically include anything that genuinely expresses the apostolic tradition. This conception arises largely as a result of conflating the concepts of authority and scriptural status. His decision to follow this common definition to its logical conclusions aptly illustrates its inadequacy.

The issues identified here indicate that the traditional interpretation's third substantiating argument for its claim that Irenaeus considers the apostolic writings to be scripture relies on an inadequate definition of scripture, one that is unable to correspond to contemporary or historical conceptions. This requirement necessarily invalidates the argument's conclusions: Irenaeus' recognition of the equivalent authority of the apostolic writings is an insufficient basis for positing scriptural status.

I can think of no plausible alternative basis for drawing this inference, and such an inference in fact appears to be ruled out by Irenaeus. He makes clear that the rule of Truth, deriving also from the apostolic tradition, is equally authoritative to the apostolic writings. Yet even though the rule can be written down, he gives no indication that it should be considered as "scripture," in the same category as the Jewish scriptures. Authority and scriptural status appear to have no equivalence for him.

Conclusion

As the final substantiating argument given for the traditional interpretation is unable to justify its conclusions, the central claim of the traditional interpretation that Irenaeus considers the apostolic writings to be scripture therefore cannot be sustained. Careful examination of its arguments has led instead to the opposite conclusion: Irenaeus clearly and consistently distinguishes between the apostolic writings and "the Scriptures" as separate entities. The apostolic writings are not scripture.

It is worth highlighting that the difference between possessing scriptural status and possessing unique authority equivalent to the Jewish scriptures is slight; unique authority is in many ways arguably more significant than scriptural status. John Barton contends that the New Testament writings originally had greater authority than the Old Testament in early Christianity, and that "the status of the two Testaments approached equality by the end of the third century," once the New Testament came to be considered as scripture.[11] On this basis he maintains that the search for scriptural status fails to answer the important practical question of authority because the most important books were *not* scripture, and in fact were functionally more important than scripture.[12] Yet for precisely this reason, the tendency to conflate the concepts of authority and scriptural status by a number of interpreters of Irenaeus serves to

---

[10] Ibid., 59.
[11] Barton, *Holy Writings*, 65.
[12] Ibid., 67–8.

obscure significant elements of his conception of the apostolic writings and the important distinctions that exist between these and the Jewish scriptures.

While the apostolic writings are equal in authority to the scriptures, the findings of the investigation in Part 1 indicate that they do not possess scriptural status. Irenaeus maintains a significant status distinction between the two collections, on the basis of their distinct bases of authority. On this basis, the second half of this book seeks to construct an alternative account of Irenaeus' conception of the nature and status of the apostolic writings, focusing on his concepts of apostolicity and of the Word as Revealer of the Father. This investigation simultaneously provides increased clarification of the extent of the differences between Irenaeus' understanding of the apostolic writings and the Jewish scriptures, confirming the conclusions reached so far that the apostolic writings are not conceived of as scripture.

Part 2

Constructing an Alternative Interpretation

3

The Apostolic Writings and the Tradition, the Rule of Truth, and the Jewish Scriptures

The evaluation of the traditional interpretation of Irenaeus' view of the apostolic writings undertaken in the first part of this book has led to a rejection of its central claim that Irenaeus considered the apostolic writings to be scripture alongside the Jewish scriptures. The abandonment of the traditional interpretation opens up space for the construction of an alternative interpretation of the nature and status of the apostolic writings in Irenaeus' thought, and this is the central task undertaken in Part 2. To this end, the present chapter builds on the findings of Chapter 2 that Irenaeus treated the apostolic writings as a record of the testimony of authoritative human authors through an investigation of the centrality of the apostolic tradition and the rule of truth for Irenaeus' understanding of the nature of the apostolic writings and the basis of their authority, in order to begin to define the unique status of the apostolic writings. Beginning in the first two sections with detailed discussions of tradition and the rule of truth as they relate to the apostolic writings in Irenaeus' thought, I argue that the apostolic writings, together with the rule of truth, are elements of the apostolic tradition and the primary means of accessing its content. The apostolic writings are therefore best understood as the authoritative written record of the apostolic tradition, and it is by virtue of this status that they derive their unique revelatory authority. That this is the case is because *apostolicity* functions for Irenaeus as the overarching authority for the apostolic writings, the apostolic tradition, the rule of truth, and the church, none of which stand above the other sources or apart from their apostolic connection.[1]

On the basis of this understanding of the apostolic writings as the authoritative record of the tradition of the apostles, the final section of this chapter examines the way in which the apostolic writings relate to the Jewish scriptures. Here I argue, contrary to the traditional interpretation, that Irenaeus views the apostolic writings not as a new set of scriptures to be added to the first but as themselves constituting the

---

[1] The Jewish scriptures are another source of authority for Irenaeus, which do not stand directly under apostolicity. The relation between the Jewish scriptures and the apostolic writings as *apostolic tradition* is discussed in Section 3.3, and their distinct bases of authority are examined in the following chapter.

apostolic *interpretation* of the (Jewish) scriptures in light of the Incarnation, Passion, and Resurrection of Christ.

3.1. The Concept of Tradition in Irenaeus' Thought

This investigation begins with an analysis of Irenaeus' concept of "tradition" and its relation to the apostolic writings. This concept is essential to his overarching notion of revelatory authority, and illuminates the place of the apostolic writings within his theological system. Much ink has been spilled discussing Irenaeus' understanding and use of tradition, and little consensus has been reached. It would appear that the difficulty arises at least in part because of the various additional meanings that the term has taken on over the course of history,[2] and the importance of these concepts within the different ecclesial communities in which they are used.[3] Irenaeus' use of "tradition" has variously been interpreted to refer to unwritten traditions,[4] to the interpretation of "scripture,"[5] or to the teachings of the church;[6] to come from the

---

[2] Everett Ferguson, "Paradosis and Traditio: A Word Study," in *Tradition and the Rule of Faith in the Early Church*, ed. Ronnie J. Rombs and Alexander J. Hwang (Washington, DC: Catholic University of America Press, 2010), 3–29, argues on the basis of his study of the use of παράδοσις/*traditio* in early Christianity that "Actual word usage does not support the modern distinction between Scripture and tradition, nor the identification of tradition with unwritten transmission" (3). This distinction is seen, for example, in the Roman Catholic Church's Dogmatic Constitution on Divine Revelation at the Second Vatican Council, titled *Dei Verbum*, in which scripture and tradition are treated as distinct sources (2.7-10), partially demonstrated by reference to Irenaeus (2.7).

[3] John Friesen, in his PhD dissertation *A Study of the Influence of Confessional Bias on the Interpretations in the Modern Era of Irenaeus of Lyons*, concludes that

> most of the interpretations were strong in the area of asking questions from the perspective of the present, especially from the standpoint of the confessional bias of interpreters … [while being] weak in the matter of placing Irenaeus into his own cultural and intellectual context. Very few studies made a serious attempt to do this … The result of this lack has been a view of Irenaeus which suggests that his concerns were the concerns of today which are of significance to the various confessions. (147)

However, Friesen does not see this as a wholly negative thing. He explains, "scholars from the main line confessions have asked the questions which are important for their confession's self-identity … It follows that scholars from churches with a different self-identity would be able to ask different questions. Such questions could well help reveal a different Irenaeus than has been revealed up to this point" (149).

[4] Lawson, *Biblical Theology*, refers to tradition as "unwritten Scripture" and "the unwritten New Testament" (87), and understands its content to be entirely distinct from the apostolic writings. Hitchcock, *Irenaeus*, understands Irenaeus' use of "tradition" to refer to teachings not found in scripture (196–7), though whether he means oral teachings or non-scriptural writings is left unstated. Bengt Hagglund, *History of Theology*, trans. Gene J. Lund (St. Louis: Concordia Publishing House, 1968), believes that tradition refers to oral teachings from the apostles (45). Other examples include Osborn, *Irenaeus*; Flesseman-van Leer, *Tradition*; D. B. Reynders, "*Paradosis*: Le progrés de l'idée de tradition jusqu'à saint Irénée," *RThAM* 5 (1933): 177.

[5] Andre Benoit, "Écriture et Tradition chez Saint Irenee," *RHPR* 40.1 (1960), maintains that tradition is understood by Irenaeus as a norm and principle for the interpretation of scripture (37).

[6] Van den Eynde, *Normes*, contends that according to Irenaeus, "La tradition est d'abord le dépôt que l'Église universelle a reçu des mains des apôtres et qu'elle garde fidélement. L'expression 'tradition apostolique de l'Église' est synonyme de cette autre: 'prédication' ou 'foi de l'Église' " (159–60). The church transmits this "living" tradition "par la succession des évêques" (163), as "L'autoritee

apostles,[7] or from the church;[8] and to be subordinated to "scripture,"[9] or superior to "scripture,"[10] or equal to "scripture,"[11] or identical in content to "scripture."[12] Occasionally

doctrinale de l'Église se concentre dans la personne des évêques ... qui déjà était impliqueé dans la notion de la tradition" (180).

[7] Hägglund, *History of Theology*; Tomas Bokedal, "The Rule of Faith: Tracing Its Origins," *JTI* 7.2 (2013): 233–55; Flesseman-van Leer, *Tradition*; Behr, *Nicaea*; Ochagavia, *Visibile*; etc.

[8] Hitchcock, *Irenaeus*, interprets Irenaeus' reference to "the Gospel and all the elders" (2.22.5) to be a reference to scripture and tradition (197), illustrating that tradition refers to the teachings of the church. Van den Eynde, *Normes*, while acknowledging the apostles as the source of tradition, nonetheless understands it as the possession of the church that exercises apostolic authority over it (170–80).

[9] Hitchcock, *Irenaeus*, believes that tradition is subordinated to scripture, citing the order of "the Gospel and all the elders" (2.22.5), and concluding, "The Scriptures were then his chief authority and test of truth" (197). Hitchcock believes that tradition is only appealed to by Irenaeus in order to demonstrate the authority of scripture and its correct interpretation when his opponents question it (198). Osborn, *Irenaeus*, believes that "the Bible is the highest source of truth because the prophets were inspired of God" (162), and argues that tradition is not "a saving supplement which rescues the inadequacy of scripture" because Irenaeus refers to scripture much more than tradition, having thousands of scriptural citations, and concludes that "His account of tradition is therefore a second line of defense which points back to the truth of scripture. The scriptures provide the basis, and tradition is appealed to as confirmation of the scripture" (172). Bokedal, *Significance*, argues that although Irenaeus claims that the Rule of Faith is the "criterion of Christian faith, his writings none the less point to the Scriptures as the ultimate canon and criterion" (300–1).

[10] Van den Eynde, *Normes*, understands the church to be the fundamental authority in Irenaeus, so that he can speak of "la subordination des Écritures à la tradition" (280), which preserves and interprets it. He cites 3.4.1 as proof that Irenaeus "peut s'imaginer l'Église sans Écritures, mais pas sans tradition" (261–2). Steenberg, "Graphe," would go so far as to say that Irenaeus in some sense *defines* scripture according to tradition, as he says, "'Scripture' is not, then, to be confined for Irenaeus to a strictly delimited set of texts, save for when he uses the term to refer to the received collection of the Septuagintal Old Testament," because "Christological revelation as paradigmatically set forth by the apostles becomes the living tradition of scriptural authority ... by which all new documents may be judged" (59). Steenberg continues, "It seems clear that perceptions of 'scripture' in Irenaeus, beyond the delimited contents of the Septuagint, are more nuanced and fluid than in much later history, and certainly modern scholarship. The canon or rule of right belief, and the authority discovered in a given text to proclaim it, defines 'scripture' more readily than could any listing of accepted books" (65).

[11] Benoit, "Écriture et Tradition," holds that the church receives its authority from both tradition and scripture in Irenaeus' thought, though scripture remains the priority. Philip Hefner, "Theological Methodology and St. Irenaeus," *JR* 44.4 (1964), understands tradition as a separate source from scripture which is equally subordinated to Irenaeus' overall "hypothesis" (294–309). Lawson, *Biblical Theology*, believes that neither tradition nor scripture are elevated to the primary authority for Irenaeus, but rather that both are different aspects of one and the same apostolic truth that is his primary authority. He maintains, "It is clear from this that the determinative factor for faith is simply the preaching of the Apostles, whether written or unwritten" (87). However, Lawson critiques Irenaeus on this account, denying Irenaeus' argument that the tradition can be faithfully passed on without corruption, and claiming that Irenaeus held it only for polemical necessity. He says,

> Nowhere is the work of Irenaeus more seriously at fault than where he avowedly bases himself upon oral tradition ... That this could be so even in the case of one so relatively near in time to the first days of the Church is a standing warning to any who would lay undue store upon the unwritten tradition of the Church as a source of authentic information. (91)

Lawson also argues that while Irenaeus *claimed* that apostolic truth was his ultimate authority, in reality he operates under the authority of the "Living Voice of the Church," understood as the present doctrines of the church, though he believes Irenaeus would not have recognized that this was in fact the case (94–6).

[12] Hägglund, *History of Theology*, believes that for Irenaeus, oral tradition is comprised of the teachings of the prophets and apostles, being identical to their written teachings in scripture, though he concludes that "Irenaeus therefore derived his theology from the Scriptures" (45). Flesseman-van

two or more contradicting interpretations appear to be operating simultaneously in the minds of commentators, depending on which issues are being discussed. Within these differences of interpretation, however, there are also substantial areas of agreement. There is widespread agreement that according to Irenaeus the tradition originates from the apostles, and the majority of interpreters understand tradition as a separate source from "scripture" that is equal in authority and/or identical in content. The following investigation validates the first of these claims while calling into question the second.

A. What Does Irenaeus Mean by "Tradition"?

A precise understanding of how Irenaeus makes use of the terminology he employs is essential in order to accurately perceive the concepts he intends to communicate. Irenaeus' discussions of and references to tradition center around the noun παράδοσις (usually translated *traditio*) and the related verb παραδίδωμι (usually translated *trado*). Brief analyses of each of these terms (once again treating them as "instruments characterized by their use" within each particular context)[13] lead to the conclusion that "tradition" itself is not an authoritative concept for Irenaeus; rather, the *apostolic* tradition, or the teachings which the apostles have handed down, is the concept Irenaeus' has in mind in his positive uses of the language of παράδοσις and παραδίδωμι.

Irenaeus' Use of παράδοσις

The direct English translation of παράδοσις/*traditio*, both within Irenaeus' writings and throughout Greek (and Latin) literature of the period, is "tradition," the modern connotations of which may serve to obscure Irenaeus' intention if they are not suspended and Irenaeus allowed to supply its meaning for himself. Irenaeus can use παράδοσις both negatively and positively, either in reference to his opponents' teachings (or, in one section, to the "tradition of the elders")[14] or in reference to the

---

Leer, *Tradition*, believes that for Irenaeus tradition and scripture are independent sources, identical in content and authority (128–30). Behr, *Nicaea*, distinguishes between the scriptures and the apostolic writings, and therefore takes only the apostolic writings to be identical in content to the tradition, though these are both intimately related to the scriptures: "The apostolic writings and tradition are not two independent or complementary sources, but two modalities of the Gospel 'according to the Scriptures'" (44). Ochagavia, *Visibile*, insists that the content of the tradition is identical to the scriptures, saying, "Irenaeus never thought for a moment that one part of the *Evangelium Dei* went into the Scriptures, while the other was only orally handed down" (197–8). This is because he believes that Irenaeus' notion of tradition includes within it the scriptures (or at least those written by the apostles), as he explains, "[Irenaeus] finds 'tradition' both in the Scriptures and in the oral preaching of the apostles ... This apostolic teaching was first given orally and only later was put into writing. But in both cases it was the same 'apostolic tradition'" (194).

[13] Cf. pp. 14–15.
[14] Irenaeus only refers to the "traditions" of his opponents on three occasions: 1.21.1, 1.21.5, and 3.2.1. His references to the "tradition of the elders" are equally rare. Three times in Book 4, Irenaeus refers to the "*traditionem seniorum*" (4.9.3, 4.12.1, 4.12.4), quoting Mt. 15:2-4 in order to demonstrate (or at least claim, "*contraria erat legi quae data est per Moysen*" (4.12.1). Cf. the list of occurrences of *traditio* in *Adversus haereses* supplied by Reynders, "*Paradosis*," 180–1.

true faith. Παράδοσις is therefore a neutral term for Irenaeus,[15] designating both the content of what has been passed down and the process of passing it down. When used negatively, παράδοσις is used interchangeably with terms such as πλάσμα/*figmentum* (1.8.1), φαντασία/*phantasia* (1.8.1), ὑπόθεσις/*argumentum* (1.9.3), μῦθος/*fabula* (1.9.5), *doctrina* (1.31.4), *haeresis* (2.pre.1), *regula* (2.pre.2), *malus* (3.pre), *fictio* (3.2.1), πλάνη/*error* (3.2.3), *sententia* (4.pre.3), and so on. When used positively, the content referred to by παράδοσις may equally be referred to as ἀλήθεια/*veritas* (1.9.5), κήτυγμα/*praedicatio* (1.10.2), *euangelium* (3.1.1), πίστις/*fides* (3.3.3), *doctrina* (4.32.2), and so on.[16]

Irenaeus' abundant positive uses of παράδοσις, forming an essential part of his case in *Adversus haereses*, are *always* to the teachings that are handed down by the apostles, and in the majority of instances are called simply *apostolorum traditio*.[17] Therefore he can refer to "the tradition of the apostles that has been manifested in the whole world [*Traditionem itaque apostolorum in toto mundo manifestatam*]" (3.3.1). In the few instances where παράδοσις is used in its positive sense without direct reference to the apostles, its direct connection to the apostles is explicitly stated within the immediate context, almost always within the same paragraph.[18] Thus, when Irenaeus says, "For, though the languages of the world are dissimilar, nevertheless the meaning of the tradition [παραδόσεως] is one and the same" (1.10.2), he has already explained in the previous paragraph: "The Church, indeed, though disseminated throughout the world, even to the ends of the earth, received from the apostles and their disciples the faith in one God" (1.10.1). This leads Blanchard to posit, "In each case, the Tradition is defined always by its relation to the apostles."[19] Irenaeus acknowledges as authoritative no tradition that is not apostolic.

---

[15] It is notable, however, that παράδοσις/*traditio* is only rarely used in its negative sense. Of the thirty-four occurrences of the noun *traditio* throughout his writings, only eleven refer to the teachings of the heretics or the tradition of the Jews. While Reynders is incorrect in his claim that the term has achieved its technical sense in Irenaeus (155), παράδοσις is nonetheless most commonly used by Irenaeus as a term for the Christian Gospel. Cf. Ferguson, "Paradosis and Traditio," 11.

[16] This indicates that παράδοσις and παραδίδωμι are not the only, or even necessarily the primary terms used by Irenaeus to refer to Christian teachings. The κήρυγμα in particular is often associated with παράδοσις and παραδίδωμι (1.10.2, 3.1-3, 5.pre, *Dem.* 98, etc.) and sheds light on its origin and content. Cf. Henri Holstein, "La Tradition des Apôtres chez saint Irénée," *RSR* 36.2 (1949): 242–59; Ochagavia, *Visibile*, 185–90; Tracy Lee Russell, *Authority and Apostolicity in Irenaeus of Lyons* (MATS thesis: Regent College, 2014), 53–61.

[17] Cf. 3.3.2, 3.5.1, 3.21.3, 5.20.1, *Dem.* 86, etc. Irenaeus can also refer to "the tradition of truth" (3.4.1), "the ancient tradition" (3.4.2), or simply "tradition" (3.2.2), but it is always referred back to the apostles as its source. There is a single instance where *traditio* refers positively to a teaching not originating from the apostles. In 2.9.1 Irenaeus refers to the "*a primoplasti traditione*" as the teaching passed down from Adam and guarded by the "*ueteribus*" that God is the Maker of the world. Yet Irenaeus ends this paragraph by saying, "*Ecclesia autem omnis per uniuersum orbem hanc accepit ab apostolis traditionem.*"

[18] 1.10.1-2, 2.9.1, 3.2.2, 3.4.1, and 3.4.2.

[19] Blanchard, *Sources*, 169; my trans. Cf. Reynders, "*Paradosis*," who writes, "La tradition chrétienne enfin,—c'est-à-dire la vérité même, la foi,—c'est sans exception la tradition des apôtres (*traditio ab apostolis*), jamais la tradition du Christ ou de l'Église" (179).

Irenaeus' Use of παραδίδωμι

Irenaeus' use of παραδίδωμι/*trado* follows a similar pattern. Usually rendered "I hand down," "I give over," "I entrust," and so on, παραδίδωμι is even more wide-ranging in meaning than παράδοσις, able to refer to the general process of handing over anything,[20] though it is most commonly used to refer specifically to the transmission of doctrine. Occasionally it is heretical teachings that are being handed down,[21] while the majority of occurrences of the term refer to orthodox teaching.[22] Of those instances where the object of παραδίδωμι is the Christian faith, the apostles are frequently the subject,[23] but the subject may also be God, Christ, Moses, the church, the Gospel, and so on,[24] suggesting the possibility that Irenaeus may be able to conceive of tradition as an authoritative source without reference to the apostles. However, his uses of παραδίδωμι in reference to Christian teaching handed down by others than the apostles exhibit a number of features that make such a conclusion untenable.

In his analysis of these passages, Holstein explains that even in those instances where the apostles are not made the explicit subject of παραδίδωμι, Irenaeus makes clear either immediately or elsewhere in his arguments the direct relationship between these various other subjects and the apostles, concluding, "παραδιδόναι designates the transmission of the message of the apostles."[25] Irenaeus makes the relations between these subjects regarding the transmission of the Christian faith explicit in a number of places, as when he states that it is this one God "whom the Law announces [*lex adnuntiat*], whom the Prophets herald [*prophetae praeconant*], whom Christ reveals [*Christus reuelat*], whom the apostles hand down [*apostoli tradunt*], whom the church believes [*Ecclesiae credit*]" (2.30.9).[26] In addition to this,

---

[20] Cf. 4.36.2, where Irenaeus makes use of παραδίδωμι in his explanation of the parable of the wicked tenants in Mt. 21:33-46, saying that "*tradidit eam* [the vineyard] *Dominus Deus ... aliis colonis*"; as well as 5.3.1, where παραδίδωμι is used in order to say that man is delivered over to his own infirmity: "παρεδόθη τῇ ἑαυτοῦ ἀσθενείᾳ ὁ ἄνθρωπος." In 5.20.1, Irenaeus speaks of "*episcopi, quibus Apostoli tradiderunt Ecclesias*."

[21] *Trado* refers to heretical teachings on nine occasions. However, παραδίδωμι is only confirmed by the Greek text twice (1.21.1 and 1.21.2), while the Greek text demonstrates that *trado* is translating a different term on four occasions (ὑποτίθενται in 1.5.2 and 1.8.4; λέγει in 1.11.1; and ὑπέθετο in 1.14.1), and the Armenian translation suggests the same on one additional occasion (ուսուցանել, rather than աւանդել in 1.27.2). Two remaining instances cannot be verified one way or the other (2.21.2 and 3.2.1). Cf. Reynders, "*Paradosis*," who notes that in the Armenian translations of *Adv. haer.*, աւանդել consistently translates παραδίδωμι, allowing for more precise reconstruction of the original Greek in those places where the Latin translation is inexact (184).

[22] Reynders, "*Paradosis*," catalogues thirty-five occurrences in *Adv. haer.* (181-4), while an additional three occurrences may be found in the *Dem.* (3, 98, 99). Holstein, "Tradition des Apôtres," lists twenty-eight occurrences (238).

[23] Holstein, "Tradition des Apôtres," counts seventeen instances (237). Reynders' list (181-4) seems to give eighteen instances.

[24] Cf. Holstein, "Tradition des Apôtres," 237; Reynders, "*Paradosis*," 181-4.

[25] Holstein, "Tradition des Apôtres," 239; my trans. Cf. Ochagavia, *Visibile*, who concludes, "We can therefore define Christian tradition as Christ's revelation perfectly handed down by the apostles to the Church" (184). Cf. also Russell, *Authority and Apostolicity*, 47-53.

[26] Similarly, in *Dem.* 98 Irenaeus writes, "This, beloved, is the preaching of the truth ... which the prophets announced and Christ confirmed and the apostles handed over (παραδίδωμι) and the Church, in the whole world, hands down (ἐγχειρίζω) to her Children." The Greek terms supplied by Behr in his translation (PPS 17:100) are indicated by the Armenian translation, where the apostles are said "to hand down" (աւանդել) the faith, while the church is said "to supply" (ընծայել) it to her

Reynders recognizes that whenever the apostles are the subject of *trado*, παραδίδωμι is the Greek term being translated, while on a number of occasions where they are not the subject of the Christian faith and the Greek text is extant, *trado* is not in fact a translation of παραδίδωμι but instead translates some other term.[27] These findings further cement the conclusion that the apostles are always the subject of tradition for Irenaeus, leading Holstein to conclude, "This doctrine is that of the apostles, disciples of Christ and founders of the churches, to the point that the verb *tradere* is reserved for them, if not exclusively, at least with a marked preference: *Apostoli tradiderunt*."[28]

While many interpreters have correctly identified the importance of apostolic origin in Irenaeus' concept of tradition, an important distinction must be recognized. Irenaeus does not operate with a general concept of tradition as a source of authority, one that happens to have its source in the apostles. As we have seen, παράδοσις and παραδίδωμι are neutral terms for Irenaeus with a wide range of possible meanings; it is the source of what has been passed down that determines whether he understands a given παράδοσις to be authoritative or not. Only the *traditio apostolorum*, designating the truth of the Christian faith, functions as an overarching authority for Irenaeus. No discussion about Irenaeus' sources of authority can legitimately refer to his concept of tradition as a general category, but only to the *apostolic* tradition, which functions as an authoritative source solely on the basis of its apostolic origin.

---

children. Behr believes (PPS 17:118 n. 228) that Irenaeus' statement here is parallel to the statement made in 5.pre: "*praeconio Ecclesiae, quod prophetae quidem praeconaverunt, quemadmodum demonstravimus, perfecit autem Christus, Apostoli vero tradiderunt, a quibus Ecclesia accipiens per universum mundum sola bene custodiens tradit filiis suis*." Here it is notable that the church is also said to *tradit* the faith, but if Behr is correct, then *Dem*. 98 casts suspicion on the accuracy of the Latin here. In either case Irenaeus clarifies that the church received the preaching from the apostles and preserves it.

[27] Cf. Reynders, "Paradosis." On the basis of his analysis he concludes, "Les apôtres bénéficiaient déjà de la grande majorité des attestations dans la version latine, cette faveur est confirmée par l'original, quand on le possède, et par la version arménienne. Tous les autres: Dieu, le Christ, la Loi, les gnostiques, se voient retirer en tout ou en partie par le grec ou l'arménien ce que leur octroyait la version latine" (184). His findings show that of the instances where *trado* refers to the apostles as its subject, on only one occasion does a verb other than παραδίδωμι appear in the Greek (ἐνεχείρισαν in 3.3.2), as well as one further instance in which the Armenian translation suggests another verb (ոատեոյւ in 1.27.2), while in four instances παραδίδωμι is confirmed by the Greek (1.8.1, 1.25.5, 2.22.5, 3.1.2), and in six additional instances it is suggested by the Armenian (1.27.2, 3.11.9, 4.33.8, 4.37.7, 5.pre, 5.20.1). Of the other possible subjects of παραδίδωμι: the use of *trado* in reference to God finds no confirmation in either the Greek or Armenian, while the Greek twice contradicts it (*trado* is γεγόνασι in 1.10.3 and Θεόσδοτον in 1.13.4) and the Armenian once suggests the same (ողողեյւ rather than աւանդել in 4.9.1); *trado* in reference to the Law finds no confirmation in the Greek or Armenian, while on one occasion the Armenian contradicts it (ուսնյարուեյւ rather than աւանդել in 4.11.3); *trado* in reference to Moses is neither supported nor contradicted; *trado* in reference to Christ is not contradicted and is on two occasions supported by the Armenian (աւանդել in 4.27.4 and 4.36.2); *trado* in reference to Polycarp is not contradicted and is confirmed by the Greek twice (both in 3.3.4); and *trado* in reference to the church is not contradicted and is confirmed on two occasions by the Greek (both in 1.10.2) and is supported once by the Armenian (աւանդել in 5.pre).

[28] Holstein, "Tradition des Apôtres," 240; my trans.

B. Does "Tradition" Refer to Unwritten Teachings?

Having concluded that Irenaeus' use of *traditio* as an authoritative source refers exclusively to the *apostolic* tradition, it remains to determine the content of this tradition. I contend that the common belief that "tradition" for Irenaeus refers exclusively to unwritten teachings is unfounded. Instead, a closer examination of Irenaeus' references to the *traditio apostolorum* reveals that it is largely indifferent in regard to the method of its transmission, and further, that in practice Irenaeus' use of the apostolic tradition is primarily through the medium of the apostolic writings.

The belief that Irenaeus' appeal to tradition is an appeal to oral teachings in contrast to scripture is held by many interpreters of Irenaeus.[29] Evidence for this belief is most commonly found in Irenaeus' statements within 3.1-5 of *Adversus haereses*,[30] a distinct section—dubbed his "little treatise"[31]—in which Irenaeus embarks on a detailed discussion and argument concerning the apostolic tradition. Here, it is argued, Irenaeus differentiates between oral traditions and apostolic "scripture" as distinct, and perhaps even independent sources.[32] This interpretation involves a fundamental misunderstanding of Irenaeus' overall purpose in this section and of his many arguments throughout it. Before embarking on a detailed analysis of this section, it is worth first briefly examining Irenaeus' references to "tradition" throughout the rest of *Adversus haereses*, where his concept of the apostolic tradition remains operative even when it is not his focus.

References to "Tradition" Outside of 3.1-5

Irenaeus occasionally refers specifically to the oral handing down of the apostolic tradition by the apostles, as in his statement that "the path of those belonging to the Church circumscribes the whole world, as possessing the sure tradition from the apostles [*quippe firmam habens ab Apostolis traditionem*]" (5.20.1).[33] However, he also clearly and consistently refers to apostolic teachings that are *handed down* (*traditus*) in writing. In 3.11.9, for example, Irenaeus writes,

> If the Gospel that was composed by them is the Gospel of Truth, but differs from *those handed down* [*tradita sunt*] *to us by the apostles*, anyone who wishes may learn, as is proved from the Scriptures, that *the Gospel handed down* [*traditum est*] *by the apostles* is no longer the Gospel of Truth.[34]

---

[29] Cf. p. 100 n. 4 above. Against this view, see especially Ochagavia, *Visibile*, 191–4.
[30] Cf. Lawson, *Biblical Theology*, 87; van den Eynde, *Normes*, 159; Hitchcock, *Irenaeus*, 198–9.
[31] This phrase was first used by Holstein, "Tradition des Apôtres," 230; and has been subsequently taken up by Ochagavia, *Visibile*, 192–3; and others.
[32] Cf. Reynders, "*Paradosis:*" "It reste donc acquis 1) qu'Irénée, le premier parmi les écrivains orthodoxes, entend par παράδοσις l'enseignement oral en tant que distinct de l'Écriture" (177). Cf. also van den Eynde, *Normes*, 159. Ochagavia, *Visibile*, argues against Reynders that "tradition" for Irenaeus includes both the writings and oral teachings of the apostles (192–4).
[33] There is of course no way to verify that Irenaeus here refers *exclusively* to unwritten teachings, but in the context of this paragraph, where he has already discussed "the bishops to whom the apostles committed the Churches," it seems likely that he is referring primarily to the initial preaching of the apostles. Two similar passages are found in 5.pre and 3.14.2.
[34] Emphasis added.

Irenaeus is explicit here that the apostles *handed down* (*traditus*) their written gospels. There is no doubt, within this passage at least, that written teachings are included in the teachings handed down by the apostles; and this passage is not unique. A few chapters later Irenaeus makes a related claim, as he says,

> Luke, likewise, with envy toward no one, handed down [*tradidit*] to us what he had learned from them, as he himself testifies: "Just as they who from the beginning were eyewitnesses and ministers of the word have handed them down [*tradiderunt*] to us."[35] (3.14.2)

Irenaeus claims that Luke has *handed down* (*tradidit*) the teachings of the apostles, and quotes the Gospel of Luke in demonstration of the content of what Luke has handed down. The same pattern is seen again in the following chapter, where, immediately after quoting the words of Jesus in Matthew and Paul's words in 1 Corinthians, Irenaeus concludes: "both the Lord has taught and the apostle has enjoined [*tradidit*] us the more to love God" (4.37.7). There can be no doubt that Irenaeus believes the apostles παρέδωκαν their teachings in writing.

In addition to his use of the verb παραδίδωμι in this way, Irenaeus also speaks specifically of the apostolic writings as the object of the apostolic παράδοσις. In the course of his argument for the legitimacy of the LXX translation of the scriptures, Irenaeus argues,

> The translation agrees with the tradition of the apostles [*apostolorum traditioni*]. For Peter and John and Matthew and Paul, and the rest after them, and also the followers of these, preached all the prophetical writings, just as they are contained in the translation of the elders. (3.21.3)[36]

Here "*apostolorum traditioni*" refers to the four Gospel accounts (matching his description of their authorship in 3.1.1) in which the apostles' quotations of the Jewish scriptures prove that they considered the LXX to be scripture, and therefore verify the authenticity of its translation. In this comment Irenaeus demonstrates that he considers the Gospel accounts to be part of the *apostolorum traditio*.[37]

---

[35] Lk. 1:2.

[36] See also 2.9.1, where it appears that Paul's epistle to the Romans is the content of "*ab apostolis traditionem*."

[37] Reynders, "*Paradosis*," would prefer to disagree with this conclusion, on the basis that the written gospels are not explicitly mentioned and the LXX translation of "virgin" that Irenaeus is discussing is only mentioned in Matthew's account. Reynders asks, "La tradition apostolique est-elle donc contenue dans les Écritures? Ce n'est pas absolument nécessaire. Les écrits ne sont pas mentionnés: rien ne dit donc que Pierre, Jean et Paul entrent en scéne à titre d'écrivains" (176). He seems to have misunderstood Irenaeus' point here, as Irenaeus is attempting to validate the entire LXX translation—not simply the passage relating to the virgin birth—and would therefore have reason to bring in all four Gospel accounts to witness to its validity because all four quote from it extensively. It is therefore evident from Irenaeus' decision to specifically name Peter, John, Matthew, and Paul here that Irenaeus is referring to the four apostolic gospel accounts, echoing his description of their authorship in 3.1.1. Despite his misunderstanding, however, Reynders admits that the presence of Matthew's name in this section alone is sufficient to illustrate that Irenaeus has written teachings in mind: "Malgré tout, la présence de Matthieu reste embarrassante. Il semblera

On the basis of these passages and others, Ochagavia concludes that outside of the opening chapters of Book 3,

> tradition is totally indifferent regarding the way of its transmission: at times it is oral, other times written. More often than not, it seems to prescind entirely from the way of transmission: it designates the doctrine which is handed down, no special attention being focussed on the way in which it is handed down.[38]

It is evident from these passages that the apostles were understood to have *handed down* the *apostolorum traditio* in writing, contradicting the claim that Irenaeus' conception of the apostolic tradition consists of oral teachings in distinction to the written teachings of "scripture."[39] The remaining passages that demonstrate his understanding of the apostolic tradition, and those that have been traditionally held as evidence that "tradition" represents unwritten teachings, occur within the section spanning 3.1-5.1, to which this investigation now turns.

Irenaeus' Little Treatise on Tradition (3.1-5)

The opening section of Book 3 has been understood to be the primary source of evidence that Irenaeus contrasted oral tradition with written scripture as distinct sources. Careful analysis of this section demonstrates that such a conclusion represents a misunderstanding of what Irenaeus is attempting to accomplish and a flawed interpretation of the arguments he makes to prove his case.

It is first important to grasp that the section spanning 3.1.1-3.4.3 (with a transitional paragraph in 3.5.1) is a distinct unit with its own unique theme and purpose.[40] This is made clear by Irenaeus' description of his intention for Book 3 in the preface. He says, "in this third book we will bring forward demonstrations from the Scriptures [*ex Scripturis inferemus ostensiones*],"[41] yet nowhere in the first four chapters does he attempt his stated task. However, he begins the chapter following this section by writing,

> Therefore, the tradition [*traditione*] which is from the apostles thus being held in the Church and persevering among us, we may return to the [previously-mentioned] demonstration from the Scriptures [*eam quae est ex Scripturis ostensionem*]. (3.5.1)[42]

---

donc sage d'observer une attitude minima et d'admettre que παράδοσις a momentanément perdu la précision qu'elle obtient au début du livre III" (176). The previous passages suggest this is no mere "momentary loss," however. Cf. Ochagavia, *Visibile*, 192; Flesseman-van Leer, *Tradition*, 102–3; and Unger (ACW 64:99 n. 9); all of whom also conclude that the presence of Matthew in this passage requires that Irenaeus has the written gospels in view.

[38] Ochagavia, *Visibile*, 192.
[39] This claim is also opposed by Ochagavia, *Visibile*, 191–200; Russell, *Authority and Apostolicity*, 67–9; and Behr, *Nicaea*, 45.
[40] This is recognized by Ochagavia, *Visibile*, 191–4.
[41] My trans.
[42] My trans.

From this point on the rest of Book 3 does precisely what Irenaeus has promised. The opening section is therefore a discrete unit with a distinct purpose and argument. Far from being a "digression,"[43] however, this section is integral to Irenaeus' entire argument throughout the rest of *Adversus haereses*. It is not an off-the-cuff argument from (oral) tradition;[44] rather, it is a carefully planned first premise that provides the foundation for the whole of Books 3, 4, and 5. Irenaeus intends to use the apostolic "demonstrations from the Scriptures"[45] as his primary source to disprove the claims of his opponents, but because they often reject some of these writings in part or in whole, in order to do this he must first defend their authority. Demonstrating the authority of the apostolic writings (rather than tradition, understood as a separate, oral source) is therefore his primary purpose in this section, and he accomplishes this purpose through a demonstration of their apostolic origin. In order to properly understand this section as it relates to Irenaeus' overall argument, it must be remembered that the arguments he makes here are for this specific purpose, that they are made in reaction to the competing claims of his opponents, and that "tradition" is never described or applied in the same way outside of this section.

Irenaeus' purpose is first stated explicitly at the beginning of Chapter 1, at which point the equivalence between the apostolic writings and the apostolic tradition is also demonstrated. Here is the passage in full (including the final sentence of the preface):

> For the Lord of all gave the power of the Gospel to His apostles, through whom we too know the Truth, which is the teaching of the Son of God; to whom also the Lord said, "Whoever hears you hears me; and whoever despises you despises me and Him who sent me."[46]
>
> 1.1 For we know the economy of our salvation through no others than those through whom the Gospel has come to us [*eos per quos Euangelium peruenit ad nos*]: at one time they certainly proclaimed this Gospel publicly, but afterwards through God's will they handed it down to us in writings [*in Scripturis nobis tradiderunt*], ensuring that it would be the "foundation and pillar of our faith." And it is not right to say that they preached before they possessed complete knowledge, as some dare to say, boasting of being correctors of the apostles. For, after our Lord rose from the dead, and they "were clothed with power from on high"[47] when the Holy Spirit came upon them, they were filled and possessed complete knowledge. They went forth "to the ends of the earth,"[48] preaching the good news about the blessings from God to us and announcing heavenly peace to

---

[43] Reynders, "*Paradosis*," 189; repeated by Holstein, "Tradition des Apôtres," 230; Benoit, "Écriture et Tradition," 37; Ochagavia, *Visibile*, 193; and Ferguson, "Paradosis and Traditio," 12.
[44] This has become a common claim, seen in Reynders, "*Paradosis*," 189–90; Ochagavia, *Visibile*, 193; etc.
[45] Recall the discussion on the meaning of the phrase *ostensiones ex Scripturis* in Section 1.2A, where it was concluded that this phrase refers to the apostolic writings, which are themselves "demonstrations" from the Jewish scriptures.
[46] Lk. 10:16.
[47] Lk. 24:49.
[48] Acts 1:8.

humanity; who assuredly also all equally—and each of them individually—possess the Gospel of God.

Accordingly, Matthew produced a writing of the Gospel among the Hebrews in their own language, while Peter and Paul were proclaiming the Gospel in Rome and establishing the Church. But after their departure, Mark, Peter's disciple and interpreter, also himself handed down to us in writing the preaching of Peter [ἐγγράφως ἡμῖν παραδέδωκεν]. And Luke, Paul's follower, also put down in a book the Gospel preached by him. Then John, the Lord's disciple who had also leaned against his breast, did himself also deliver the Gospel while staying in Ephesus of Asia. (3.pre-1.1)[49]

Immediately after having stated his purpose in Book 3 (to provide "demonstrations from the Scriptures"), Irenaeus now begins a detailed defense of the supreme authority of the apostles, and by extension, of the Gospel accounts they wrote down, clarifying his purpose in this section to demonstrate the authority of the apostolic writings that he will use for the rest of *Adversus haereses*. In the course of this defense he twice states that the Gospel has been handed down (παραδέδοται) by the apostles in written form, further indicating that the apostolic writings are part of the apostolic tradition. It is also implied that there cannot be additional traditions outside of the apostolic writings, because the same Gospel they first proclaimed orally, they afterward "handed it down to us in writings."

It is within this context that he makes his widely misunderstood statements in Chapter 2. Here, after asserting that his opponents reject the tradition that the apostles *tradiderunt* in their Gospel accounts (3.1.2), Irenaeus continues,

Indeed, when they are exposed by writings, they turn around to accuse the writings themselves, as if these are not correct or are not of authority, and that various [things] are stated [in them], and that the truth can not be found from them by those who do not know the tradition [*et quia non possit ex his inueniri ueritas ab his qui nesciant traditionem*]. For [they declare that] this [truth] was not handed down through letters but by a living voice [*Non enim per litteras traditam illam sed per uiuam uocem*], for which reason Paul said, "Yet among the perfected [*perfectos*] do we speak wisdom, but not the wisdom of this world."[50] And each one of them declares this wisdom to be what he has invented for himself ...

2.2 But when we direct them again to the tradition which is from the apostles [*traditionem quae est ab apostolis*], which through the succession of the presbyters is guarded in the Churches, they are opposed to the tradition [*aduersantur traditioni*], calling themselves wiser not only than the presbyters but even than the apostles, having found the pure truth. For they maintain that the apostles mixed the words of the law with the words of the Savior ... It has therefore come to pass that they no longer agree with either the writings or the tradition [*Euenit itaque neque Scripturis iam neque traditioni consentire eos*]. (3.2.1-2)[51]

---

[49] My trans.
[50] 1 Cor. 2:6.
[51] My trans.

The separation of oral and written teachings into distinct sources in this chapter is commonly understood to reflect Irenaeus' own understanding and use of these concepts, demonstrating that Irenaeus uses the language of *traditio* to refer to the apostles' oral teachings, and the language of *scriptura* to refer to their written teachings.[52] However, upon closer examination, this does not appear to be the case.

In this chapter Irenaeus explains that when his opponents are shown from the apostolic writings "that there is one God, the Creator of heaven and earth, who had been announced by the Law and the Prophets; and one Christ, God's Son" (3.1.2), their first response is to claim that the apostolic writings are incorrect and inauthentic, and that only those who know the secret teachings from the "living voice" of the apostles— which they apparently reserved only for their "perfect" members[53]—can be properly understood to possess the true apostolic tradition. It is Irenaeus' opponents who open up this distinction between oral and written traditions, and in fact the more essential distinction they seek to make is between public and secret teachings.[54] After describing this practice, Irenaeus continues in 3.2.2 by explaining that when he disproves their theory by pointing to the tradition that the churches received from the apostles, which is proved to be identical to their written teachings, their second response is to go a step further and reject the authority of the apostles themselves. Irenaeus is referring to these two responses when he makes his statement that "they no longer agree with either the writings or the tradition" (3.2.2). By this he means that they first reject the apostolic writings in favor of a secret tradition, and then, when it is demonstrated that their true tradition is contained in their writings, they reject the apostles themselves.

Irenaeus' purpose throughout this chapter has not been to open up a distinction between oral and written teachings as separate sources but to respond to the distinction introduced by his opponents, and his response is to declare the distinction invalid. He continues to refute their distinction by demonstrating throughout the rest of this section that the apostolic writings *are* the apostolic tradition preserved in the churches. After explaining the two responses of his opponents in Chapter 2, Irenaeus first briefly answers their second response (that they are wiser even than the apostles) by virtually throwing his hands in the air and declaring them to be nothing but "slippery serpents who try to escape on all sides" (3.2.3), before stepping back in the final two chapters of this section to deal with their first response (that the apostles handed down their true teachings in secret) in great detail.[55] Irenaeus' answer to this charge throughout the rest of this section of Book 3 is an exercise in fighting his opponents on their own ground, allowing their distinction between the apostles' writings and their secret oral teachings for the sake of argument, in order to prove that no such distinction actually exists.

---

[52] Cf. Hitchcock, *Irenaeus*, 198–9; Flesseman-van Leer, *Tradition*, 102; van den Eynde, *Normes*, 159.
[53] Cf. Irenaeus' other descriptions of this claim in 3.3.1, 3.5.1, and 3.12.6.
[54] This distinction is also described and rebuked more fully in 3.14.1-2, in Irenaeus' defense of Luke's account of the Gospel as representing the true teachings of Paul.
[55] Irenaeus apparently did not think that his opponents' second response was worth arguing against (cf. 3.2.3), or else he believed that simply exposing such claims was in itself a sufficient refutation of them. In either case, he never does set forth a refutation of their claim that the apostles themselves did not know the full truth (and that even Christ himself did not know their hidden mystery), though he will bring it up again (3.12.7).

Beginning in Chapter 3, Irenaeus demonstrates that the church contains the genuine apostolic tradition by showing that every church can trace its successions of bishops back to the apostles themselves—using the succession lists of the church of Rome, which was founded by Peter and Paul, and with whom all the other churches agree, as an example (3.3.2-4)—and arguing that "if the apostles had known of any hidden mysteries that they taught to the 'perfect' separately and privately from the rest, they would most certainly have handed them down to those to whom they entrusted the Churches themselves" (3.3.1).[56] In the midst of his succession list, Irenaeus mentions Clement of Rome, who "both saw the blessed apostles themselves and conversed with them, and still had the preaching of the apostles ringing in his ears and their *tradition before his eyes* [καὶ ἔτι ἔναυλον τὸ κήρυγμα τῶν ἀποστόλων καὶ τὴν παράδοσιν πρὸ ὀφθαλμῶν ἔχων]" (3.3.3),[57] suggesting that the "tradition" he refers to is the apostolic writings themselves.

By demonstrating in Chapter 3 that the church has preserved the authentic apostolic tradition, Irenaeus can successfully counter his opponents' claim that the apostolic writings are not the true apostolic tradition (3.2.1), in order to accomplish his overall purpose in this section of legitimizing his use of the apostolic writings as the authoritative statement of the apostolic tradition for the rest of *Adversus haereses*. It is within this context, as an argument for the equivalence of the apostles' writings with their teachings, that Irenaeus rhetorically asks in the following chapter:

> What if the apostles had not left us writings; would it not be necessary to follow the order of the tradition [*traditionis*] which they have handed down [*tradiderunt*] to those to whom they entrusted the Churches? (3.4.1)[58]

He answers his rhetorical question in the affirmative, describing "barbarian" Christians who preserve the "ancient tradition of the apostles [*ueterem apostolorum traditionem*]" without possessing their writings.

Because Irenaeus once again opens up a distinction between the oral and written teachings of the apostles, a number of interpreters have also taken this passage as evidence that Irenaeus envisions a distinction between them as separate sources.[59] However, this interpretation fails to take the context of his argument into account and so misses his intent. Irenaeus is still in the midst of his demonstration that the apostolic writings are equivalent to their teachings. As part of this argument, he suggests in this passage that if the apostles had not left their writings the church could simply follow the apostolic tradition, *because the two are identical*. Having shown how his opponents have opened up this artificial distinction between the apostolic writings and the secret oral teachings of the apostles, Irenaeus now emphatically closes it, asserting that the

---

[56] On this basis he concludes at the beginning of 3.4.1: "Since there are, then, such great proofs, it does not behoove to seek further among others for the truth, which can be obtained easily from the Church; for the apostles most abundantly placed in her, as in a rich receptacle, every thing that belongs to the truth."
[57] Emphasis added.
[58] My trans.
[59] Cf. Lawson, *Biblical Theology*, 87; Hitchcock, *Irenaeus*, 198–9; etc.

apostolic writings are themselves the content of the apostolic tradition. On this basis he may conclude in 3.5.1:

> Therefore, the tradition which is from the apostles [*Traditione ... ab apostolis*] thus being held in the Church and persevering among us, we may return to the [previously-mentioned] demonstration from the Scriptures [*ex Scripturis ostensionem*], which is from those of the apostles who have put the Gospel into writing [*eorum qui Euangelium conscripserunt apostolorum*].[60]

Now that he has demonstrated that the apostolic writings are in fact the true apostolic tradition, Irenaeus may finally begin his stated intention in Book 3 to make use of the apostolic writings as the authoritative "demonstrations from the Scriptures" by which to disprove the false ὑπόθεσις of the heretics.[61]

When viewed from the perspective of his overall purpose in this section, Irenaeus' references to a distinction between oral and written teachings may be properly understood as a description of the false claims of his opponents by which they reject the apostolic writings, and a distinction that is made use of for rhetorical effect, only within this section, in order to combat the claim that there exists a secret apostolic tradition opposed to the apostolic writings.[62] These findings overturn the common claim that the opening section of Book 3 of *Adversus haereses* demonstrates that Irenaeus made use of oral traditions and written "scripture" as separate sources.

On the basis of the analysis in this section it may be concluded that παράδοσις does not consist of distinct oral teachings independent from the apostolic writings. Oral teachings are not a separate category for Irenaeus, and he does not appear to conceive of the possibility of additional unwritten apostolic traditions that are not also found in the apostolic writings.[63] Oral and written apostolic traditions can be conceived of

---

[60] My trans.

[61] Behr, *Nicaea*, also maintains that tradition and the apostolic writings are identical in content, and that Irenaeus turns to the apostolic writings to determine what the apostolic tradition is (44–5), though he nonetheless maintains that tradition and apostolic writings remain distinct sources for Irenaeus.

[62] As Behr, *Identifying*, concludes, "Irenaeus' point [in 3.2-4] is that the content of this apostolic tradition is identical to that handed down by the apostles in writing" (125–6). Cf. the similar conclusions reached by Ochagavia, *Visibile*, 193–4.

[63] It is occasionally asserted that Irenaeus relies on unwritten traditions not found in the apostolic writings in the course of his own arguments, and that this demonstrates that he does in fact conceive of tradition as a distinct oral source (Cf. Lawson, *Biblical Theology*, 90–1; Hitchcock, *Irenaeus*, 196–7; Osborn, *Irenaeus*, 172). This assertion is made on the basis of a passage in 2.22 in which Irenaeus appears to call upon an oral teaching that Jesus lived to be almost fifty years old (2.22.4), which he states was handed down (*traditus*) by John (2.22.5), yet does not appear in the apostolic writings. However, Irenaeus in fact claims the gospels as the basis of this view, and only mentions the claims of "the presbyters" as a witness to it. He states, "Witnesses of this are the Gospels and all the presbyters" (2.22.5). It is impossible that a teaching that was passed down orally would not agree with the apostolic tradition as seen in the Gospel accounts, and Irenaeus here brings forward the testimony of "the presbyters" specifically in order to support the testimony of the gospels. Irenaeus understands the Gospel accounts to witness to this teaching on the basis of the claim that Jesus taught for multiple years (2.22.3; Jn 2:1-11, 5:1, etc.), that he began to teach after thirty years old (2.22.5; Lk. 3:23), and that the Jews said to Jesus "you are not yet fifty years old" (2.22.6; Jn 8:56-7), indicating that he must have been over forty years old at that time. Irenaeus therefore does not view himself as bringing forth an oral tradition distinct from the apostolic writings but rather

as distinct in the sense that there was a time where the apostolic tradition existed in the absence of any writings, just as there are places where the apostolic tradition exists in the absence of writings. However, from Irenaeus' perspective, on the far side of the process of the apostolic writings having been handed down to the church, there can be no distinction between the two. Irenaeus is unconcerned with whether the apostles' teachings are found in oral or written forms, and in practice his references to the apostolic tradition are always to the apostolic writings themselves. Whenever Irenaeus discusses the apostolic writings he is discussing the apostolic tradition, and whenever he discusses apostolic tradition he does so through the medium of the apostolic writings.

Conclusion

The conclusions reached in this section concerning Irenaeus' conception of the apostolic tradition serve to clarify the nature of the apostolic writings in his thought. As the authoritative written record of the apostolic tradition, the apostolic writings are the primary means of accessing the content of their tradition. Whenever Irenaeus wishes to demonstrate what their tradition teaches, he turns to the apostolic writings, and his defense of the tradition of the church is in fact a defense of the apostolic writings as being equivalent to this tradition. As the authoritative record of the content of the apostolic tradition, the apostolic writings possess the status of unique revelatory authority, and this status is derived on the basis of their apostolic origin. Apostolicity functions as an overarching criterion of authority for Irenaeus, and this authority is materially accessed through the apostolic writings, as the record of the apostolic tradition. This conclusion is supported by the findings of Part 1: the supreme importance of the apostolic writings for Irenaeus is not based on any notion of their scriptural status, in the way that the Jewish scriptures derive their authority, but rather on the basis of the authority of the apostles and as the written record of the tradition they handed down to the church.

In the following section, Irenaeus' concept of the rule of truth is investigated in order to discern how it fits within his understanding of apostolic tradition and relates to the apostolic writings.

---

believes that the apostolic writings can be shown to be true by those who talked to the apostles. In Book 3 Irenaeus specifically refutes the idea that there could be extra apostolic teachings outside the apostolic writings. He states, "we consider it necessary to make use of the entire doctrine of the apostles [*uniuersam apostolorum ... sententiam*] concerning our Lord Jesus Christ" (3.16.1), and then proceeds to exhaustively present the "entire doctrine of the apostles" for the remainder of this section of Book 3 exclusively by presenting their statements in the apostolic writings (3.16-24). Ochagavia, *Visibile*, notes this passage as evidence that "Irenaeus was convinced that the New Testament writings contain the whole teaching of the apostles about the Christian faith" (198 n. 154).

3.2. The Rule of Truth in Irenaeus' Thought

Irenaeus' concept of the rule of truth (*regula veritatis*), or canon of truth [κανών τῆς ἀληθείας], is also of central importance, both for his primary arguments throughout *Adversus haereses* and for ascertaining his sources of authority. As with his understanding of tradition, much has been written on the subject, resulting in many competing theories of the meaning and significance of the rule of truth in his thought.

Because of the similarity of his statements of the rule of truth to creedal statements, the *regula veritatis* was first understood to be a baptismal creed. This theory was originally proposed by Zahn,[64] and subsequently taken up in revised form and popularized by Harnack.[65] Harnack argued that preexisting baptismal confessions would eventually come to be used as the "rule of truth" to safeguard the faith, maintaining that this move was first made by Irenaeus, who "proclaimed the baptismal confession, definitely interpreted and expressed in an Antignostic form, to be the apostolic rule of truth."[66] Irenaeus is thought to write with "a rigidly formulated creed before him," so that the rule of truth is straightforwardly "the old baptismal confession well known to the communities for which he immediately writes."[67] Harnack's thesis would remain influential among interpreters of Irenaeus[68] until it was challenged by J. N. D. Kelly in 1950.[69] Kelly argued that Irenaeus' conception of the rule of truth neither has a set formulation nor shows any evidence of having an underlying creed in mind, so it could not be directly related to a fixed baptismal confession. He explains, "If [Irenaeus'] summaries of it have a concrete outline and distinctive note, that is because they are giving expression to a common body of doctrine."[70] In the aftermath of Kelly's critique, the rule of truth has no longer been viewed as a creed or confessional statement, though it continues to be understood primarily as a summary statement of the content of the faith.[71]

Prior to Kelly, the primary counterpoint to Harnack's view was first put forward by Valdemar Ammundsen,[72] who contended that for Irenaeus the rule of truth refers not to a creedal statement but to "the main, unambiguous content of the Scriptures."[73] This view would also prove to be very influential, especially after Harnack's view was challenged by Kelly. Ochagavia would adopt essentially the same view as Ammundsen in 1964, contending that "practically every time the expression *regula veritatis* appears,

---

[64] Theodor Zahn, "Glaubensregel und Taufbekenntnis in der alten Kirche," in *Skizzen aus dem leben der alten Kirche* (Leipzig: Deichert, 1908), esp. 245–6; Zahn, "Glaubensregel," in *Realencyklopadie fur protestantische Theologie und Kirche*, ed. Albert Hauck (Leipzig: J.C. Hinrichs, 1899), 6:685.
[65] Adolf von Harnack, *Lehrbuch der Dogmengeschichte*, vol. 2 (Freiburg: Mohr, 1888).
[66] HD 2:26.
[67] Ibid., 27–8.
[68] Cf. Hitchcock, *Irenaeus*, 66–7; Lawson, *Biblical Theology*, 95–6.
[69] J. N. D.Kelly, *Early Christian Creeds*, 3rd ed. (New York: Longman, 1983). 1st ed. published in 1950.
[70] Ibid., 96.
[71] Osborn, *Irenaeus*, 143–9; "Reason and the Rule of Faith in the Second Century AD," in *The Making of Orthodoxy: Essays in Honour of Henry Chadwick*, ed. Rowan Williams (Cambridge: University Press, 1989), 40–51; Bokedal, "The Rule of Faith," 233–51; *Significance*, 166–71; Behr, *Nicaea*, 35–7.
[72] Valdemar Ammundsen, "The Rule of Truth in Irenaeus," *JTS* 13 (1912): 574–80.
[73] Ibid., 576.

it refers either explicitly or implicitly to the Scriptures,"[74] and concluding, "the 'rule of truth' is not limited to the four or five points expressly mentioned therein, but it embraces all the Scriptures."[75]

A number of commentators sought to combine these two views, presenting the rule of truth as both a summary of scripture and confession of faith. The first and most influential of these accounts was put forward by Ellen Flesseman-Van Leer in 1954.[76] She describes the rule of truth as an all-embracing concept for Irenaeus encompassing both the notion of formal confession of faith and summary of scripture, yet surpassing both. She believes it refers to the Truth itself, "the real purport of Scripture … it is not a formal principle for exegesis, brought to the Bible from the outside, but the real teaching of the Bible, that is, the revelation as embedded in scripture."[77] Materially, its content is identical to revelation, but formally, the rule of truth is distinct from the Truth itself because it is revelation as mediated through the apostles. It is therefore also materially identical to the apostolic tradition, though formally distinct, for Flesseman-van Leer understands the tradition to be the same revelation as it is continually passed on by the church. Therefore, "Truth, tradition, faith, *regula veritatis*, these terms express the same reality. The difference is merely that each one views this reality from a particular point."[78]

Bengt Hägglund would adopt a similar approach, further emphasizing Flesseman-van Leer's contention that the rule of truth refers neither to a fixed formula nor to the scriptures, but rather "revealed truth" itself, the Truth that was revealed to the apostles and transmitted both in scripture and the tradition of the church. The rule of truth functions as an authoritative summary of these teachings. Hägglund takes this as evidence that "Scripture" is therefore Irenaeus' primary source, concluding on this basis that "Irenaeus therefore derived his theology from the Scriptures."[79] Around the same time, André Benoit would argue that tradition and scripture—which are for Irenaeus two sides of the same coin—meet in the "Creed," which summarizes their content.[80]

The various aspects of these accounts of Irenaeus' conception of the rule of truth have exerted a great deal of influence, providing the basis for the majority of subsequent accounts. Among all these more recent accounts the notion is repeatedly found that the rule of truth refers to the Truth itself,[81] that it provides the content of the faith,[82] that it is a summary of scripture,[83] and/or that it is equivalent to

---

[74] Ochagavia, *Visibile*, 203.
[75] Ibid., 203. However, Ochagavia also maintains that the rule of truth is a synonym for the preaching of the church, and can therefore state that "the 'rule of truth' embraces the whole Christian faith as found in the Scriptures and in the preaching of the Church" (204).
[76] Flesseman-Van Leer, *Tradition*, esp. 125–8.
[77] Ibid., 127.
[78] Ibid., 128.
[79] Hägglund, *History of Theology*, 45.
[80] Benoit, "Écriture et Tradition," 32–44.
[81] Osborn, *Irenaeus*, 143–9; "Reason," 40–51; Bokedal, "The Rule of Faith," 233–51; *Significance*, 166–71.
[82] Osborn, *Irenaeus*, 143–9; "Reason," 40–51; Bokedal, "The Rule of Faith," 233–51; *Significance*, 166–71; Behr, *Nicaea*, 35–7.
[83] Bokedal, "The Rule of Faith," 233–51; *Significance*, 166–71, 281–308.

tradition.[84] It is also claimed to function as the standard of orthodoxy,[85] as an interpretative principle,[86] and/or as the ὑπόθεσις of faith.[87] Each of these perspectives illuminates an aspect of the rule of truth and its function in Irenaeus' thought, but they must be carefully combined and properly nuanced in order to accurately describe this elusive concept.

In order to fully comprehend the rule of truth, it is necessary to determine what it *is*— that is, what the phrase "rule of truth" refers to—as well as what its function is and what purpose it serves for Irenaeus. The following two sections provide careful analyses of these aspects of Irenaeus' conception of the rule of truth.

A. Defining the Rule of Truth

Although Irenaeus does not articulate his conception of the rule of truth in any systematic or comprehensive manner, his numerous references to it provide insight into the nature of this concept. He makes explicit reference to the *regula veritatis* (τὸν κανόνα τῆς ἀληθείας), the *regula fidei* (qfiшιωιnnιɢ ρωɢnιɢ), or simply the *regula* on fourteen occasions in his writings.[88] In these passages the content of the rule of truth is displayed, and its connection to the apostolic tradition is demonstrated. The content of the rule of truth is expressed in detail by Irenaeus in three passages in particular. First, at 1.22.1, Irenaeus states,

> The rule of truth [*regulam veritatis*] which we hold is, that there is one God Almighty, who made all things by His Word, and fashioned and formed, out of that which had no existence, all things which exist … but the Father made all things by Him, where visible or invisible … He who, by His Word and Spirit, makes, and disposes, and governs all things, and commands all things into existence,—He who formed the world (for the world is of all),—He who fashioned man … He is the Father of our Lord Jesus Christ, as we shall prove. Holding, therefore, this rule [*regulam*], we shall easily show … that these men have deviated from the truth.[89]

This passage contains Irenaeus' clearest assertion that he is describing the content of the *regula veritatis*, though perhaps not his clearest description of it. His second reference

---

[84] Young, *Biblical Exegesis*, 18–21; Donovan, *Reading*, 11–17; Russell, *Authority and Apostolicity*, 70–96; van den Eynde, *Normes*, 286–7.
[85] Osborn, *Irenaeus*, 143–9; "Reason," 40–51.
[86] Young, *Biblical Exegesis*, 18–21; Donovan, *Reading*, 11–17; Bokedal, "The Rule of Faith," 249–50.
[87] Behr, *Nicaea*, 35–7; *Identifying*, 113–17; Young, *Biblical Exegesis*, 18–21; Hefner, "Theological Methodology"; Norris, "Theology and Language," 285–95; van den Eynde, *Normes*, 289; Russell, *Authority and Apostolicity*, 70–96; Vallée, "Theological Motives," 178; Einar Thomassen, *The Spiritual Seed: The Church of the Valentinians* (Leiden: Brill, 2008), 13–17.
[88] The phrase "rule of truth" occurs almost exclusively in those sections of Irenaeus' writings for which the Greek text is lost; for this reason the Latin form is primarily referred to in this section. *Regula veritatis* is found in 1.9.4, 1.22.1, 2.27.1, 2.28.1, 3.2.1, 3.11.1, 3.12.6, 3.15.1, and 4.35.4; *regula fidei* is found in *Dem.* 3 (additionally, in *Dem.* 6 a statement of the rule of faith is introduced as "the order [τάξις] of our faith"; cf. SC 406:90); and *regula* is used in 1.22.1, 2.25.1 (twice), and 2.25.2.
[89] ANF 1:347. Cf. ACW 55:80.

to "this Rule" at the end of the passage demarcates the end of his description.⁹⁰ This statement occurs in the midst of his argument against the heretical separation of the Father of Christ from the Creator of the world, and Irenaeus' description here indicates its purpose. When this statement is compared with another similar statement from twelve chapters earlier, a number of interesting features arise, which aid in determining the content of the rule of truth.

In 1.10.1 Irenaeus writes,

> The Church, though dispersed throughout the whole world, even to the ends of the earth, has received from the apostles and their disciples this faith: in one God, the Father Almighty, Maker of heaven, and earth, and the sea, and all things that are in them; and in one Christ Jesus, the Son of God, who became incarnate for our salvation; and in the Holy Spirit, who proclaimed through the prophets the dispensations of God, and the advents, and the birth from a virgin, and the passion, and the resurrections from the dead, and the ascension in to heaven in the flesh of the beloved Christ Jesus, out Lord, and His manifestation from heaven in the glory of the Father "to gather all things in one."⁹¹

This description of the faith is not explicitly declared to be a description of the rule of truth by Irenaeus, but both its similarities to the previous passage and other explicit statements of the rule of truth, as well as Irenaeus' reference to τὸν κανόνα τῆς ἀληθείας in the previous paragraph which the current passage is expanding on, make it evident that Irenaeus is giving this passage as a statement of the rule of truth. The immediately apparent variations from the previous statement indicate that the rule of truth is fluid in its formulation, and confirm that Irenaeus feels free to tailor it to meet his current needs. While the previous statement focused primarily on God the Father and only parenthetically mentioned God's Word and Spirit as the agents of God's creative activity in order to demonstrate that the God who created all things is the same Father of Jesus Christ, the second statement provides a more balanced description of the roles of the Father, Son, and Spirit, and includes more than their roles in the process of creation.

A third description of the rule of truth, this time from his less polemical *Demonstration*, is different again:

> And this is the order [τάξις] of our faith, the foundation of [the] edifice and the support of our conduct: God, the Father, uncreated, uncontainable, invisible, one God, the Creator of all: this is the first article of our faith. And the second article: the Word of God, the Son of God, Christ Jesus our Lord, who was revealed by the prophets according to the nature of the economies of the Father, by whom all things were made, and who, in the last times, to recapitulate all things, became a

---

⁹⁰ This can be observed more clearly in the Latin translation. The entire passage as quoted is a single conditional sentence that begins, "*cum teneamus*" and finally ends, "*facile eos deuiasse a ueritate arguimus.*" Cf. ACW 55:80, n. 1.
⁹¹ ANF 1:330; citing Eph. 1:10. Cf. ACW 55:48-9.

man amongst men, visible and palpable, in order to abolish death, to demonstrate life, and to effect communion between God and man. And the third article: the Holy Spirit, through whom the prophets prophesied and the patriarchs learnt the things of God and the righteous were led in the path of righteousness, and who, in the last times, was poured out in a new fashion upon the human race renewing man, throughout the world, to God. (*Dem.* 6)

Here again Irenaeus does not introduce his description as the rule of truth—though he has urged his reader to "keep the rule of faith" three paragraphs previously—but its similarity to the above two statements illustrates its equivalence. In this passage, where Irenaeus is dedicated to expounding the apostolic tradition rather than disproving the claims of his opponents, he makes explicit that the rule of faith contains three articles, describing the role of the Father, the Son, and the Spirit.

In each of these passages (as well as a number of other, smaller descriptions of the rule of truth[92]), to varying degrees, we find the same themes: the one uncreated, infinite God the Father who created all things through God's Word and Spirit; Jesus Christ, the Son of God and Word of God, through whom God created all things, who was revealed by the prophets, and who has become man, died, rose, ascended, and will return for the purpose of salvation; and the Holy Spirit, through whom God created all things, who prophesied the Incarnation of Christ through the prophets and who in the last days has been poured out for all humanity. This is the content of the rule of truth.

The Rule of Truth and "Scripture"

The argument has been made that the content of the rule of truth for Irenaeus is in fact "scripture" itself, and consequently that Irenaeus' statements of the rule of truth must be only summaries of its content.[93] Ochagavia finds evidence for this view primarily from two passages. He first cites 4.35.4, where Irenaeus writes,

> But as we follow for our teacher the one and only true God, and possess his words as the rule of truth [*Nos autem unum et solum verum Dominum doctorem sequentes et regulam veritatis habentes ejus sermones*], we do all speak alike with regard to the same things, knowing that one God [*Deum*].

On the basis of this passage, Ochagavia concludes that "the truth is found in God's words as recorded in the Scriptures."[94] The reference to the *sermones* of *Dominum* in this passage, though translated by Roberts–Donaldson as the "words" of "God,"[95] is a phrase used by Irenaeus' Latin translator throughout *Adversus haereses* specifically in

---

[92] 3.1.2, 3.4.2, 3.11.1, 4.33.7, 4.35.4, 2.30.9, 5.20.1, etc.
[93] Cf. Ammundsen, "Rule of Truth," 574–80; Ochagavia, *Visibile*, 201–5; Bokedal, "Rule of Faith," 250–1; *Significance*, 300–1; ACW 55:48 n. 23.
[94] Ochagavia, *Visibile*, 203. Ochagavia may have gotten this evidence from Ammundsen, "Rule of Truth," who made a similar claim on the basis of this passage fifty years prior: "In this clearest of all passages *the rule of truth* is the words of God contained in Scripture" (578).
[95] Rousseau et al. translate "paroles" of "le Seigneur" (SC 100:875).

reference to the discourses of Jesus in the gospels.⁹⁶ This indicates that the apostolic writings are related to the rule of truth in some way; however, it requires a leap on Ochagavia's part to arrive at the conclusion that the content of the rule of truth is simply "scripture" itself (here understood to encompass both the Jewish scriptures and apostolic writings). From this passage alone, such a leap does not find justification. The relation between the words of Jesus and the apostolic writings is evident, yet it has already been demonstrated that Irenaeus does not simply treat them as identical, nor does he treat the apostolic writings simply as scripture. However, Ochagavia believes his interpretation is confirmed by another passage.⁹⁷

In Irenaeus' reference to the κανών τῆς ἀληθείας in 1.9.4, in the midst of comparing the interpretations of the Valentinians to the act of rearranging the lines in the poems of Homer to create an entirely different poem, Irenaeus says,

> In the same way, anyone who keeps unchangeable in himself the Rule of the Truth [τον κανόνα τῆς ἀληθείας] received through baptism will recognize the names and sayings and parables from the Scriptures, but this blasphemous theme of theirs he will not recognize.

Ochagavia argues on the basis of this passage that the content of the rule of truth must be greater than any of his descriptions of it, because Irenaeus has clearly stated that whoever holds the rule of truth "will recognize the names and sayings and parables from the Scriptures," yet none of Irenaeus' statements of the rule of truth include these details. Thus, Ochagavia concludes, "This affirmation comes to saying that the knowledge of the rule of truth is equivalent to the knowledge of the Scriptures."⁹⁸

However, this interpretation ignores the purpose of Irenaeus' argument, which relies on the notion that Christians who know the scriptures are the ones being taken in by heretical teachings because these teachings use the language of scripture. Therefore those who keep the rule of truth, while they also recognize the familiar language, will not recognize the blasphemous ὑπόθεσις of these heretics. Irenaeus' point is that the rule of truth proves the error of his opponents' ὑπόθεσις; he is not suggesting that the rule of truth is required to recognize that they have made use of the scriptures. If his argument required that only those who possessed the rule of truth knew the scriptures, it would cease to make sense. It is only because Christians are familiar with the scriptures that they are deceived by the heretics who "speak the same language that we do, but intend different meanings" (1.pre.2). Irenaeus' argument in this passage demonstrates, counter to Ochagavia's thesis, that the content of the rule of truth must be something other than simply the "Scriptures," and is used to provide their correct ὑπόθεσις.

---

⁹⁶ 3.5.3, 3.11.9, 3.25.7, 4.pre, 4.41.4, etc. Cf. the discussion of Irenaeus' use of the phrase *Domini sermones* in Section 1.2A, p. 29 nn. 81–2.
⁹⁷ In addition to 1.9.4 (described presently), Ochagavia also indicates that 3.11.1, 3.15.1, and 2.25.1-2 provide evidence for his thesis (203). I have presented only his most convincing arguments.
⁹⁸ Ochagavia, *Visibile*, 203. This argument also had previously been made by Ammundsen, "Rule of Truth," 576.

The Rule of Truth and the Baptismal Formula

Ochagavia's argument also fails to account for Irenaeus' statement in 1.9.4 that the rule of truth has been "received through baptism [*quem per baptismum accepit*]." This statement must refer to the three articles of the faith into which Christians were baptized, and therefore equates the content of the rule of truth with baptismal formulas. The similarity between preserved early baptismal formulas and Irenaeus' descriptions of the rule of truth is evident,[99] leading inevitably to the conclusion, on the basis of his claim that the rule of truth is received through baptism, that his descriptions of the rule of truth do not merely provide a summary of its content but give a full presentation of it.[100]

The similarity of content between the rule of truth and baptismal formulas is also made evident by Irenaeus in the *Demonstration*. Here Irenaeus states,

> We have received baptism for the remission of sins, in the name of the Father, and in the name of Jesus Christ, the Son of God, [who was] incarnate, and died, and was raised, and in the Holy Spirit of God. (*Dem.* 3)

This statement unmistakably alludes to a baptismal formula, and echoes his other statements of the rule of truth. Three paragraphs later, immediately following his comparable—albeit more detailed—statement of the rule of truth (*Dem.* 6, presented above), articulated as three articles, Irenaeus concludes with this statement: "For this reason the baptism of our regeneration takes place through these three articles" (*Dem.* 7). In both of these instances Irenaeus' descriptions of the rule of truth are explicitly tied to baptismal confessions, demonstrating their content.

Irenaeus' declarations that the rule of truth corresponds to baptismal formulas here and in 1.9.4 leave no doubt that the content of the rule of truth is comparable to that of early three-article baptismal formulas. Contrary to the arguments of Ochagavia and others who contend that the content of the rule of truth is scripture itself, and therefore that Irenaeus' statements of the rule of truth are only summaries of its content, for Irenaeus the rule of truth is itself composed of a short, fluid, summary statement of the essential points of the faith. These conclusions similarly contradict the view that the rule of truth is equivalent to the tradition, though the two are intimately related.

The Rule of Truth and the Apostolic Tradition

A number of Irenaeus' statements of or references to the rule of truth illustrate its relationship to the apostolic tradition. One of Irenaeus' clearest and most detailed statements of the rule of truth occurs in 1.10.1. He begins his description by saying: "The Church, indeed, though disseminated throughout the world, even to the ends of the

---

[99] Cf. *Didache* 7; Hippolytus, *Ap. Trad.* 21; Justin Martyr, *1 apol.* 61; as well as Kelly, *Creeds*, ch. 3.
[100] At the same time, the fluidity of his expressions of the rule of truth within their various polemical contexts demonstrates that it cannot simply be equated with a baptismal confession or creed, as had previously been argued by Zahn, Harnack, Hitchcock, Lawson, etc.

earth, received from the apostles and their disciples the faith in one God." Then, upon finishing his statement of the rule of truth, he concludes,

> The Church ... carefully guards this preaching and this faith which she has received ... For, though the languages of the world are dissimilar, nevertheless the meaning of the tradition [ἡ δύναμις τῆς παραδόσεως] is one and the same. (1.10.2)

Irenaeus' introductory and concluding statements indicate that his statement of the rule of truth is a description of the "preaching" and "faith" received from the apostles, and that the church preserves this "tradition." The apostolic origin of this faith, as well as Irenaeus' use of παραδόσεως in reference to it, demonstrates that the rule of truth describes the apostolic tradition. The relationship between the apostolic tradition and the rule of truth is described more fully in two passages at the beginning of Book 3.

In Chapter 3, Irenaeus states that Clement's letter to the Roman church proclaimed

> the tradition which it had but recently received from the apostles [νεωστὶ ἀπὸ τῶν ἀποστόλων παράδοσιν εἰλήφει]. This tradition proclaims one God almighty, the Creator of heaven and earth, the Fashioner of man, who brought on the flood and called Abraham, who led the people out of the land of Egypt, who conversed with Moses, who gave the law and sent the prophets ... this Father of our Lord Jesus Christ is announced by the Churches. (3.3.3)

Irenaeus' description of the chief points of the apostolic tradition (as it relates to his present polemical purpose) takes the form of a statement of the rule of truth. Similarly, in the following chapter Irenaeus mentions the "barbarian" Christians who possess the apostolic tradition in the absence of writings,

> guarding carefully the ancient tradition [*ueterem traditionem diligenter custodientes*]; believing in one God the Creator of heaven and earth and all things which are in them, and Christ Jesus the Son of God, who on account of his surpassing love toward his creation underwent the birth from the Virgin, uniting man to God through Himself, and having suffered under Pontius Pilate, and rising and returning in splendor, to come in glory as the Savior of those who are saved. (3.4.2)[101]

Once more Irenaeus' description of the essential points of the tradition which the "barbarian" Christians preserve takes the form of a statement of the rule of truth.[102]

In each of these passages a statement of the rule of truth explicitly describes the apostolic tradition, confirming the direct relation of these two concepts. All three passages indicate that the rule of truth is not *identical* to the apostolic tradition but is

---

[101] My trans.
[102] These three passages from Book 3 have also been noted by Russell, *Authority and Apostolicity*, 91–3, though she concludes that these passages demonstrate "that the Rule is itself the content of the apostolic Tradition" (93), rather than an expression of its primary elements.

rather a sort of summary statement, a description of its primary elements. This same conclusion concerning the relation of the rule of truth to the apostolic tradition is reached by Behr, who explains, "The key elements of the faith delivered by the apostles are crystallized in the canon of truth. This canon expresses the basic elements of the one Gospel, maintained and preached in the Church, in an ever-changing context."[103]

The Rule of Truth and the Apostolic Writings

As a fluid expression of the primary elements of the apostolic tradition, the rule of truth is also intimately related to the apostolic writings. This is evident both from the status of the apostolic writings as the authoritative written record of the apostolic tradition (Section 3.1) and from a few of Irenaeus' statements in *Adversus haereses*. One passage has already pointed out by Ochagavia (4.35.4), indicating that the rule of truth is in some way identified with the discourses of the Lord as contained in the apostolic writings. A related passage suggests that it is not only the Lord's discourses but the apostolic writings themselves to which the rule of truth relates:

> The Disciple of the Lord therefore wishing to invalidate all such [errors], and to establish the rule of truth in the Church [*et regulam ueritatis constituere in Ecclesia*] that there is one almighty God who made all things both visible and invisible through His Word ... thus began in his teaching according to the Gospel [*sic inchoauit in ea quae est secundum Euangelium doctrina*]: "In the beginning the Word was, and the Word was with God, and God was the Word."[104] (3.11.1)[105]

Here it is John whose written testimony is considered to be the method by which the rule of truth is established in the church. It is evident that this is not because John has in any sense composed the rule of truth but rather that the content of the rule of truth is described by what John has written concerning the Word and his relationship to God.

Irenaeus does not state his view of the relation of the rule of truth to the apostolic writings more precisely than this, but it is safe to conclude from his few brief references that the relation between the rule of truth and the apostolic writings is similar or equivalent to its relation to the apostolic tradition. The content of the rule of truth is not the apostolic writings themselves, but Irenaeus can affirm that its content summarizes the central teachings of the apostolic writings.

The foregoing analysis leads to the conclusion that the rule of truth does not provide the content of either "scripture" or the apostolic tradition but rather that it is a brief summary of the essential points of the apostolic tradition (and therefore also of the apostolic writings as the record of this tradition). Its content is roughly synonymous with that of the three-article baptismal confessions with which Irenaeus is familiar; however, it is not simply identical to these confessions. The rule of truth is much more

---

[103] Behr, *Nicaea*, 37.
[104] Jn 1:1.
[105] My trans.

fluid in form. It is able to be tailored to suit his particular polemical purposes, being expanded or contracted as the situation requires. The rule of truth may therefore be defined as *a fluid expression of the primary elements of the faith as delivered by the apostolic tradition.*

B. The Function and Purpose of the Rule of Truth

Now that the rule of truth has been defined, it remains to describe how it functions for Irenaeus, as well as the primary purpose it serves within his overall theological vision. Irenaeus' choice of terminology for this concept may suggest an answer.

The Rule of Truth Functions as the Standard of the Truth

In only one of Irenaeus' references to the rule of truth is the original Greek text preserved (1.9.4), providing the sole source for identifying κανών as the term that is translated *"regula"* in each other instance.[106] The definition of κανών as a measuring rod, and its common connotation prior to Irenaeus as a standard against which an idea can be tested for veracity,[107] offers a clue to the function of Irenaeus' κανών τῆς ἀληθείας. Given this context, one might expect the rule of truth to act as a standard by which one measures the correspondence of a claim, teaching, interpretation, etc. to "the Truth." When Irenaeus' references to the κανών τῆς ἀληθείας are analyzed, this is precisely what is found.

Upon finishing his description of the rule of truth in 1.22.1, Irenaeus concludes,

> If, therefore, we hold fast this Rule, we shall easily prove that they have strayed from the Truth, even though their statements are quite varied and numerous [*hanc ergo tenentes regulam, licet ualde uaria et multa dicant, facile eos deuiasse a ueritate arguimus*].

The rule of truth that Irenaeus has just described functions as the standard or criterion of "the Truth," by which deviations from it may be clearly seen. The correspondence of this rule to the Truth is made even more explicit in 2.28.1:

> In this manner, keeping the Truth itself as our rule [*Habentes itaque regulam ipsam ueritatem*] and the testimony about God set down openly before us, we are obligated not to reject the firm and true knowledge of God, by turning away to seek numerous questions and diverse solutions.[108]

---

[106] The lack of available evidence allows this conclusion only tentative support, especially as there is at least one occasion (1.20.3) in which *regula* (though not as part of the phrase *regula veritatis*) is a translation of ὑπόθεσις, rather than κανών. However, the direct correspondence in meaning between *regula* and κανών, as well as the evidence provided by the context of 1.9.4, strengthens this conclusion considerably.

[107] Cf. Aristotle, *On the Soul* 1.5; Epicurus' *Canon*, in Diogenes Laertius, *Lives of Eminent Philosophers* 10.31; Behr, *Identifying*, 112–13.

[108] My trans. Roberts–Donaldson similarly preserve the meaning of the Latin text for the relevant phrase: "Having therefore the truth itself as our rule" (ANF 1:399), while Unger translates this

Irenaeus' rule, as an expression of the apostolic tradition revealed by Christ,[109] is the rule of the Truth itself. Irenaeus does not merely possess a "true rule" but rather possesses the Truth itself as his rule; for this is the only way the rule could act as the standard or criterion of the Truth.

The correspondence of the rule of truth to "the Truth" itself was first expressed by van den Eynde,[110] and repeated and clarified by Flesseman-van Leer,[111] before being described most fully by Hägglund.[112] In his description the rule of truth refers to objective Truth itself, the very revelation of God, which is preserved by the church. This Truth is reflected in the apostolic tradition, through baptismal confession, scriptures, and the preaching of the church. The rule of truth therefore corresponds to Truth itself, which the apostolic tradition has delivered. Only because it is "the rule of the Truth" (1.9.4; 1.22.1) can it therefore also be the "rule of our faith" (*Dem.* 3; 1.10.1-2). As an expression of the primary elements of the apostolic tradition, it functions as the criterion of the Truth, providing the standard by which all other claims can be tested for conformity to it.

As the Standard of the Truth, the Rule of Truth Serves Three Purposes

On the basis of its function as the standard of the Truth, the rule of truth serves a number of purposes for Irenaeus. The relationship between the rule of truth and the baptismal confession has already been noted. As the standard of the Truth, the rule provides a helpful shorthand for expressing the faith (which corresponds to the Truth) for the purpose of catechesis and profession of faith.[113] This illustrates why the rule of truth cannot be reduced to a baptismal confession, for serving as a baptismal confession is merely one of its purposes (1.9.4).

A second purpose of the rule of truth is to test the orthodoxy of other teachers or teachings. This has already been seen in 1.22.1, where Irenaeus declares that the errors of his opponents' teachings are easily demonstrated by holding fast to the rule

---

phrase instead as, "Since, then, we possess the Rule of Truth itself" (ACW 65:87). Rousseau-Doutreleau explain that the Latin as it stands can only be translated "Ayant donc pour règle la vérité elle-même," but contend that this translation does not fit the present context, and opt to adjust the Latin phrase "*regulam ... ueritatem*" to "*regulam ... ueritatis*," thereby arriving at the translation: "Ainsi donc, puisque nouse possédons la règle même de la vérité" (SC 293:313–14). Unger's translation is the result of adopting Rousseau-Doutreleau's emendation (Cf. ACW 65:154 n. 1). However, I do not find Rousseau-Doutreleau's arguments convincing and see no reason why the original Latin phrase as it stands is not entirely appropriate for its context.

[109] Cf. 3.12.6, according to which if Christ had not spoken the Truth to his apostles, then the rule of truth could be with no one.
[110] van den Eynde, *Normes*, 282–5.
[111] Flesseman-van Leer, *Tradition*, 125–8.
[112] Bengt Hägglund, "Die Bedeutung der 'regula fidei' als Grundlage theologischer Aussagen," *StTh* 12 (1958): 4–19; Hägglund, *History of Theology*, 45.
[113] Historically speaking, the baptismal confession predates Irenaeus' formulation of the concept of the rule of truth. However, he is merely describing and giving a title to a concept that he believes was an essential part of the faith from its beginnings. The same preexisting rule can function as an expression of the essential elements of the faith for the purposes of catechesis and profession of faith as well as acting as a standard against which all other claims may be tested for conformity to the Truth.

of truth.[114] On this basis the rule of truth guards against heretical teachings, as can be seen in his claim that John wrote his account of the Gospel because he wished "to invalidate all such [errors], and to establish the rule of truth in the Church" (3.11.1).[115] A similar declaration is made in the *Demonstration*, where he states that the "evil and twisted" teachings of his opponents are a poison to those who receive them (*Dem.* 2), and advises, "Therefore, lest we suffer any such thing, we must keep the rule of faith" (*Dem.* 3).[116] Because the rule of truth functions as the standard of the Truth, it can be used to test the orthodoxy of other teachings by their conformity to it, and thereby guard against any teachings that fail this test. In this way the rule of truth preserves the apostolic tradition in the church.

The final purpose is a subset of the second purpose and is the central purpose of the rule of truth for Irenaeus throughout *Adversus haereses*. The rule of truth is primarily used to protect the correct interpretation of the Jewish scriptures and to guard against false interpretations. The primary passage in which Irenaeus explains this purpose occurs in Book 1. He begins in Chapter 8 by explaining that the false ὑπόθεσις of the Valentinians (which he has spent the previous seven chapters describing) was not handed down by the prophets, the Lord, or the apostles but is only artificially adapted to their words by the Valentinians in order to deceive the faithful. Irenaeus explains that this is done by transferring and rearranging passages in such a way as to make them express this foreign ὑπόθεσις, and uses the example of a mosaic of a king being rearranged into the likeness of a fox to illustrate their use of the scriptures. Then, in the following chapter he makes use of a similar illustration of taking verses from various places in the works of Homer and rearranging them into a new poem with a different meaning. Commenting on this practice, he says,

> What simple-minded person would not be misled by these verses and believe that Homer composed them in that manner for that very theme? One who is well-versed in Homeric themes [ὑποθέσεως] will recognize the verses, but he will not recognize the theme [ὑπόθεσιν], since he knows that some of them were spoken of Ulysses, others of Hercules himself, others of Priam, others of Menelaus and Agamemnon. However, if he takes them and puts each one back into its own [theme] [ἄρας δὲ αὐτὰ καὶ ἕκαστον ἀποδοὺς τῇ ἰδίᾳ],[117] he will make their fabricated theme [ὑπόθεσιν] disappear. In the same way, anyone who keeps unchangeable in himself the Rule of the Truth [τὸν κανόνα τῆς ἀληθείας] received through baptism will recognize the names and sayings and parables from the Scriptures, but this blasphemous theme [ὑπόθεσιν] of theirs he will not recognize.

---

[114] The text of 1.22.1 is presented above, p. 117.
[115] My trans.
[116] Cf. 3.2.1 and 4.35.4.
[117] Unger's decision to supply "theme" at the end of this clause (which in the Greek lacks a noun for ἰδίᾳ) suggests that Irenaeus means to refer back to ὑπόθεσις (Unger explains his decision in ACW 55:182 n. 22). Roberts–Donaldson instead supply "proper position" (ANF 1:330), while Rousseau-Doutreleau's translation supplies "livre," following the Latin (SC 264:150-1). Given the following clause, ὑπόθεσις would be an awkward antecedent for ἰδίᾳ, suggesting that "proper position" and "book" are closer to Irenaeus' intended meaning.

For even if he recognizes the jewels, he will not accept the fox for the image of the king. He will restore each one of the passages to its proper order and, having fit it into the body of the Truth [τῆς ἀληθείας σωματίῳ], he will lay bare their fabrication and show that it is without support. (1.9.4)

Just as familiarity with the Homeric ὑπόθεσεις allows one to see that the supposedly Homeric poem has been fabricated, so also possessing the rule of truth allows one to see that the Valentinians have rearranged passages so as to fit them into their own foreign ὑπόθεσις. This is Irenaeus' primary purpose for utilizing the rule of truth throughout *Adversus haereses*; by exposing heretical interpretations as corrupt, the rule of truth safeguards the true interpretation of the (Jewish) scriptures.

However, this is not to say that the rule of truth is used as a formal principle for interpretation.[118] The content of the rule of truth itself offers little in the way of exegetical instruction. It supplies the boundary that cannot be transgressed, in much the same way that the rules of a game ensure that it is played properly. In neither case do the rules themselves instruct the participants in proper methods and strategies.[119] The rule of truth safeguards interpretation, which it accomplishes by articulating the central message of the scriptures. As Young describes, it provides "the extra-canonical framework or 'overarching story' by which the scriptures were to be read and interpreted."[120] It is the key that provides the internal coherence of the text.[121] Irenaeus explains that all the various passages of the scriptures proclaim the same message, just as the various notes on a harp form a single melody; therefore, interpretation "should never change the rule [*regulam*], or stray from the Artist, or reject the faith in one God" (2.25.2). The rule of truth expresses the "system of truth [*ueritatis argumento*]" that all interpretations should be adapted to (2.25.1), and by possessing it, "we do all speak alike with regard to the same things, knowing but one God" (4.35.4). Without the rule of truth, "as many interpreters of the parables as there would be, just so many truths would be seen at war with each other and setting up contradictory opinions" (2.27.1), and so it has been established "to put an end to all such tenets" (3.11.1).

As the standard of the Truth, the rule of truth demonstrates that these competing interpretations destroy the Jewish scriptures' own ὑπόθεσις. The rule of truth therefore is not an external criterion that is brought to the scriptures but rather expresses their own ὑπόθεσις, the knowledge of which makes the error of any competing ὑπόθεσις

---

[118] Such an understanding is suggested by Donovan, *Reading*, 11; and Bokedal, "The Rule of Faith," 249–50; and rejected by van den Eynde, *Normes*, 286; Flesseman-van Leer, *Tradition*, 127; and Young, *Biblical Exegesis*, 18–21.

[119] I am indebted to Fr. John Behr for this analogy, who in turn received it from Paul Saieg.

[120] Young, *Biblical Exegesis*, 18.

[121] However, the rule of truth should not be understood as a *narrative summary* of the scriptures. It does not summarize the storyline but expresses the central presuppositions that allow them to be read correctly. The notion of the rule of truth as a narrative summary of the scriptures or of the history of salvation is most fully articulated by Paul M. Blowers, "The *Regula Fidei* and the Narrative Character of Early Christian Faith," *ProEccl* 6 (1997): 199–228; and is refuted by Nathan McDonald, "Israel and the Old Testament Story in Irenaeus' Presentation of the Rule of Faith," *JTI* 3.2 (2009): 281–98. Cf. Young, *The Art of Performance: Towards a Theology of Holy Scripture* (London: Darton, Longman, and Todd, 1990), 48–53; Behr, *Nicaea*, 35–6 n. 52.

immediately evident.¹²² Irenaeus states that the one who keeps the rule of truth is able to "restore each one of the passages to its proper order" (1.9.4), because he believes that the ὑπόθεσις of the scriptures is plainly evident when their "order and connection" is not disregarded (1.8.1).¹²³

However, the relationship between the rule of truth and the ὑπόθεσις of the scriptures is not one of direct equivalence.¹²⁴ Κανών refers to the rule or standard that expresses the central elements of the Truth, while ὑπόθεσις refers to a fuller system describing its theme or subject matter. This relationship is most accurately described by the following formula: the rule of truth—as an expression of the central elements of the apostolic tradition—stemming from its function as the standard of the Truth against which all other claims may be measured, and as part of its purpose to safeguard the correct interpretation of the scriptures and to guard against false interpretations, *expresses* in summary form scripture's own ὑπόθεσις,¹²⁵ or overall argument or theme. This relationship is recognized by Behr, who describes the rule of truth as "an articulation of the hypothesis [of scripture] in a particular situation, outlining the presupposition needed for seeing in Scripture the image of the king, the Christ revealed in and through the Gospel."¹²⁶ The rule of truth, τῆς ἀληθείας ὑποθέσει (1.10.3), the *ueritatis traditionem* (3.4.1)—all of these express the Truth itself, each in a unique way.

Conclusion

The rule of truth performs a key role within Irenaeus' overall theological framework, and in his arguments against his opponents throughout *Adversus haereses*. It presents the central tenets of the apostolic tradition, and therefore its content is equivalent to the three-article baptismal confession. However, the rule of truth is much more fluid in form, able to be expanded or contracted to suit his particular polemical purposes. It corresponds to the Truth itself, which has been delivered by the apostolic tradition. For this reason the rule of truth functions as the rule or criterion of the Truth, providing the standard by which all other claims can be tested for conformity to it. On the basis of this function, the rule of truth serves a number of purposes for Irenaeus. In addition to providing a helpful shorthand for expressing the faith for the purpose of catechesis and profession of faith, and acting as a test of orthodoxy for other teachings by their level of conformity to it, the central purpose of the rule of truth for Irenaeus is to protect

---

[122] Cf. van den Eynde, *Normes*, 286; Flesseman-van Leer, *Tradition*, 127.
[123] Cf. 2.27.1-2, 2.28.3, etc.; though this ὑπόθεσις only becomes clear when it is read in light of Christ (4.26.1). Cf. also Christopher R. Seitz, *The Character of Christian Scripture: The Significance of a Two-Testament Bible* (Grand Rapids, MI: Baker Academic, 2011), who describes the purpose of the rule of truth as "ruling out alternatives that have failed to see the order and coherence of the Scriptures, in their totality, as speaking of Christ" (198).
[124] The distinction between these two concepts is slight, but it is visible in 1.9.4 and 2.25.1. Van den Eynde, *Normes*, 84, contends against this that for Irenaeus κανών and ὑπόθεσις are synonymous.
[125] This is the same as saying it expresses the ὑπόθεσις τῆς ἀληθείας, for the (Jewish) scriptures, given by the Word, share this ὑπόθεσις.
[126] Behr, *Identifying*, 113. Cf. Behr, *Nicaea*, 35-7. Seitz, *Christian Scripture*, states that the rule of truth "is not an effort at a precise statement of the 'hypothesis' of Scripture but rather *is based upon* a proper identification and apprehension of this, as over against alternatives" (195; cf. 198, 202).

the correct interpretation of the scriptures and to guard against false interpretations. It accomplishes this purpose by articulating scripture's own ὑπόθεσις. The rule of truth may therefore be defined as a fluid expression of the primary elements of the true faith as delivered by the apostolic tradition, which functions as the criterion or standard of the Truth itself against which claims may be tested for veracity by conformity to it, the primary purpose of which is to safeguard the correct interpretation of the scriptures by expressing their own ὑπόθεσις.

As an expression of the content of the apostolic tradition, the rule of truth is also intimately related to the apostolic writings. The rule of truth and the apostolic writings are twin elements of the apostolic tradition,[127] and together are the primary means of accessing its content. The apostolic tradition, the rule of truth, and the apostolic writings are united by apostolicity as the overarching authoritative source from which they derive their unique revelatory authority. While the apostolic writings are the authoritative written record of the apostolic tradition, the rule of truth guards the apostolic interpretation of the Jewish scriptures. Thus, the relationship between the apostolic writings and the Jewish scriptures finds its expression in the rule of truth. The nature of this relationship and its implications for Irenaeus' understanding of the nature of revelation is the focus of the final section of this chapter.

3.3. The Relationship between the Apostolic Writings and the Jewish Scriptures

It has become evident that the apostolic writings relate to the Jewish scriptures on a different basis than that of the traditional understanding of them as a new set of scriptures to be added to the first. This is not to say, however, that the apostolic writings are less directly related to the Jewish scriptures than has been believed. In reality, the opposite is the case. Not only does the apostolic tradition hold the key (the rule of truth) for correctly interpreting the Jewish scriptures, but further, the apostolic writings—as the authoritative record of the apostolic tradition—are themselves understood by Irenaeus as the apostolic *interpretation* of the Jewish scriptures in light of Christ.

A. The Apostolic Writings as the Apostolic Interpretation of the Jewish Scriptures

This thesis was first articulated by Behr,[128] who describes the Gospel in Irenaeus' thought as "the evangelical rereading of Scripture."[129] He identifies two central passages in *Adversus haereses* that demonstrate Irenaeus' understanding. The first of these occurs in 3.5.1:

---

[127] This is recognized by Bokedal, *Significance*, 167–71; who mentions "the Scriptures and the Rule, both of which are considered to be authentic expressions of the apostolic tradition" (167–8).
[128] Behr, *Identifying*, 124–40; *Nicaea*, 116–24.
[129] Behr, *Nicaea*, 122.

Therefore, the tradition which is from the apostles thus being held in the Church and persevering among us, we may return to the [previously-mentioned][130] demonstration from the Scriptures which is from those of the apostles who have put the Gospel into writing [*reuertamur ad eam quae est ex Scripturis ostensionem eorum qui Euangelium conscripserunt apostolorum*].[131]

The phrase "*ex Scripturis ostensionem*" in this passage has already been discussed in Chapter 1, where it was concluded that the apostolic writings are not themselves being called *Scripturis* but a *demonstration* from the scriptures.[132] In this passage Irenaeus describes the Gospel as a demonstration from the (Jewish) scriptures, indicating that he understands the apostolic tradition, and therefore the apostolic writings,[133] not merely as historical accounts of the life and teachings of Christ but as the exposition of the scriptures in the light of this new reality. As Behr explains, "The Gospel, in other words, is not simply a liberating message independently proclaimed on its own terms; rather, the very shape and terms in which it is proclaimed by the apostles … are drawn from the Scriptures."[134] This makes the Gospel itself "the apostolic demonstration from the Scriptures."[135]

As a demonstration from the Jewish scriptures, illustrating how Christ was preached in them, the apostolic writings represent the apostolic interpretation of the scriptures according to the rule of truth. This is their true interpretation, undertaken on the basis of their own newly revealed ὑπόθεσις. Though not fully understood prior to the Incarnation,[136] Christ has always been the subject of the scriptures, now openly revealed on the far side of his Incarnation. Irenaeus describes this understanding throughout Book 4, perhaps most explicitly in 4.26.1, the second passage identified by Behr:

> If any one, therefore, reads the Scriptures with attention, he will find in them an account of Christ, and a foreshadowing of the new calling. For Christ is the treasure which was hid in the field,[137] that is, in this world (for "the field is the world"[138]); but the treasure hid in the Scriptures is Christ, since He was pointed out by means of types and parables. Hence His human nature could not be understood, prior to the consummation of those things which had been predicted, that is, the advent of

---

[130] Referring back to 3.pre; recall the discussion in Section 3.1B.
[131] My trans.
[132] Section 1.2A. The phrase is found in 3.pre, 3.5.1, and 5.14.4; and the related phrase "*ex Scripturis diuinis probationes*" occurs in 2.34.5.
[133] I take the referent of "demonstrations from the Scriptures" to be the apostolic writings as a whole, rather than only the four Gospel accounts, on the basis of the fact that Irenaeus understands the entire apostolic tradition, which encompasses all of the apostolic writings, to be an account of the Gospel, even if the four writings titled "Gospel" hold this status most directly.
[134] Behr, *Identifying*, 126.
[135] Ibid. Cf. Behr, *Nicaea*, 121: "the apostolic preaching of the Gospel is, from the beginning, 'according to the Scriptures,' exegeting Scripture to interpret Christ."
[136] Or, more precisely, prior to Jesus' post-resurrection teaching on the road to Emmaus (Lk. 24:13-32, 44-7).
[137] Mt. 13:44.
[138] Mt. 13:38.

Christ. And therefore it was said to Daniel the prophet: "Shut up the words, and seal the book even to the time of consummation, until many learn, and knowledge be completed. For at that time, when the dispersion shall be accomplished, they shall know all these things."[139] But Jeremiah also says, "In the last days they shall understand these things."[140] For every prophecy, before its fulfillment, is to men [full of] enigmas and ambiguities. But when the time has arrived, and the prediction has come to pass, then the prophecies have a clear and certain exposition. And for this reason, indeed, when at this present time the law is read to the Jews, it is like a fable; for they do not possess the explanation of all things pertaining to the advent of the Son of God, which took place in human nature; but when it is read by the Christians, it is a treasure, hid indeed in a field, but brought to light by the cross of Christ, and explained, both enriching the understanding of men, and showing forth the wisdom of God and declaring His dispensations with regard to man, and forming the kingdom of Christ beforehand, and preaching by anticipation the inheritance of the holy Jerusalem, and proclaiming beforehand that the man who loves God shall arrive at such excellency as even to see God, and hear His word, and from the hearing of His discourse be glorified to such an extent, that others cannot behold the glory of his countenance. (4.26.1)

In this lengthy passage, Irenaeus affirms that Christ is the "treasure hid in the Scriptures"[141] and explains that this meaning was hidden before its fulfillment. Christ is not merely *read into* the Jewish scriptures but is their own true ὑπόθεσις.

Christopher Seitz, in his recent study on the Old Testament as Christian scripture, echoes this thesis. He explains, "Jesus Christ is known not because all that can be said about him exists in clear apostolic form independently from an account of what God was doing in the material witness of the OT," but rather "the canon [of the Jewish scriptures] exists as a given and in this material form it speaks of Christ."[142] However, Seitz has only half the picture, for he further contends that the Christological interpretation of the Jewish scriptures, according to the rule of faith, originates from the Jewish scriptures themselves. According to Seitz, the rule of faith "arises on the basis of a stable, anterior witness (the OT)," and the Jewish scriptures "provide the very canon of truth operative in the period in question."[143] According to Irenaeus however, this cannot be the case, for as he has explained in 4.26.1, the true Christological meaning of the Jewish scriptures remains hidden until it is "brought to light by the cross of

---

[139] Dan. 12:4-7.
[140] Jer. 23:20.
[141] Elsewhere, Christ is "sown in the Scriptures": "*inseminatus est ubique in Scripturis eius Filius Dei*" (4.10.1). This sowing was done by the prophets, that the church would reap it (4.23.1, 4.25.3). Cf. Behr, *Identifying*, 127.
[142] Seitz, *Christian Scripture*, 196–7. Cf. 4.34.1: "read with earnest care that Gospel which has been conveyed to us by the apostles, and read with earnest care the prophets, and you will find that the whole conduct, and all the doctrine, and all the sufferings of our Lord, were predicted through them." Cf. also 4.9-11.
[143] Ibid., 200–1.

Christ."[144] This is why when "the law is read to the Jews, it is like a fable." The rule of truth does not come *from* the Jewish scriptures but comes *to* them from the Gospel of Christ and illuminates their previously enigmatic and ambiguous prophecies. As Behr explains, "They could not be known, Irenaeus claims, as in fact they were not, prior to their consummation."[145] It is only in the *rereading* in light of Christ that the true meaning of the Jewish scriptures can be discovered. The Incarnation "provides the catalyst for the veil to be removed and the books to be opened, and itself now becomes the subject of interpretation."[146]

Following 4.26.1, Irenaeus spends the remainder of the chapter explaining that for this reason "it is incumbent to obey the presbyters who are in the Church—those who, as I have shown, possess the succession from the apostles" (4.26.2), which he clarifies as meaning those who "do hold the doctrine of the apostles [*Apostolorum ... doctrinam custodiunt*]" (4.26.4), because by holding this apostolic tradition the presbyters of the church are able to "expound the Scriptures to us without danger [*Scripturas sine periculo nobis exponunt*], neither blaspheming God, nor dishonoring the patriarchs, nor despising the prophets" (4.26.5). The apostolic tradition, in material form as the apostolic writings, is what allows the presbyters to expound the scriptures without danger, because it is the apostolic interpretation of the Jewish scriptures in the light of the Incarnation of Christ. For this reason Irenaeus urges his readers "to take refuge in the Church, and to be brought up in her bosom, and to be nourished with the dominical Scriptures [*dominicis Scripturis*]" (5.20.2).[147]

B. The Apostolic Writings as a Recapitulation of the Scriptures

This relationship between the apostolic writings and the Jewish scriptures is directly related to Irenaeus' theme of "recapitulation" (ἀνακεφαλαίωσις; *recapitulatio*).[148] As the correct interpretation of the scriptures in light of their now visible ὑπόθεσις, the apostolic preaching of the Gospel (recorded in the apostolic writings) is itself a recapitulation or summing up of the scriptures. Though often underemphasized in the secondary literature, this literary aspect of recapitulation in Irenaeus' thought comes

---

[144] Seitz does not explicitly claim to be stating Irenaeus' own position, but his argument occurs within a section describing the relationship between the rule of faith and the Jewish scriptures in the early church, and his description is given exclusively in reference to Irenaeus.
[145] Behr, *Identifying*, 128.
[146] Ibid., 131.
[147] My trans. Recall the discussion in Section 1.2A which concluded that "*Scripturis dominicis*" and related phrases refer not to the gospels but to the dominical prophecies in the Jewish scriptures.
[148] Holsinger-Friesen, *Irenaeus and Genesis*, sets out a useful critique of the tendency among Irenaean scholars to treat recapitulation as a "master-concept" for Irenaeus (25–30). He describes "a modern tendency to first isolate then inflate a concept of recapitulation. As a result, its contextual roots are obscured and this concept acquires disproportionate independent significance" (27). Explaining the problem with this move, he maintains, "To trumpet recapitulation as a master-concept is to loosen it from its roots in biblical interpretation amid efforts to construe it as the key to Irenaeus' thought" (28). Holsinger-Friesen argues instead for the subordination of its role within Irenaeus' "broader hermeneutical endeavor" to illustrate "how texts may be appropriately read and *used* as Christian Scripture" (26).

into focus when the evident Pauline influence of his theology of recapitulation[149] is investigated with reference to his use of Romans 13,[150] rather than the more common examinations of his use of Ephesians 1.[151] Irenaeus' use of Romans 13 demonstrates an additional dynamic at play in Irenaeus' understanding, leading Behr to the conclusion that the grounding of Irenaeus' theory of recapitulation lies "in the relationship between the Scriptures and the Gospel which is that of a literary 'recapitulation.'"[152] The relevant passage in Romans states,

> The commandments, "You shall not commit adultery; You shall not murder; You shall not steal; You shall not covet;" and any other commandment, are summed up [ἀνακεφαλαιοῦται] in this word, "Love your neighbor as yourself." Love does no wrong to a neighbor; therefore, love is the fulfilling [πλήρωμα] of the law. (Rom. 13:9-10; NRSV)

Unlike the passage in Ephesians, which refers to "the summing up [ἀνακεφαλαιώσασθαι] of all things in Christ," in this passage the recapitulation described is primarily literary, emphasizing the commands from the scriptures that are summed up in the words of Christ. The same fundamental idea of Christ recapitulating what has come before is present, but here the emphasis is on the Gospel as the summing up and fulfillment of the scriptures. This is a fitting use of the concept of recapitulation, for as Behr explains, the term has its roots in literary or rhetorical theory,[153] where it functions as a summary or restatement of the whole case.[154]

This literary emphasis may be observed in Irenaeus' use of Romans 13 to explain the theme of recapitulation:

> And that, not by the prolixity of the Law, but according to the brevity of faith and love, men were going to be saved, Isaias, in this fashion, says, "He will complete and cut short [His] Word in righteousness; for God will make a concise Word in all the world."[155] And therefore the Apostle Paul says, "Love is the fulfilment of the Law,"[156] for he who loves God has fulfilled the Law. Moreover the Lord also, when

---

[149] Paul uses the language of ἀνακεφαλαίωσις in Eph. 1:9-10 (cited in 1.3.4, 1.10.1, 3.16.6, and 5.20.2) and Rom. 13:9-10 (cited in 4.12.2 and *Dem.* 87). It has also been argued that Irenaeus received the language (and therefore theology) of "recapitulation" from Justin. Cf. Gustaf Wingren, *Man and the Incarnation: A Study in the Biblical Theology of Irenaeus*, trans. Ross MacKenzie (London: Oliver and Boyd, 1959), 80–1; Minns, *Irenaeus*, 108.

[150] As is done by Behr, *Identifying*, 136–40; *Nicaea*, 123–4.

[151] Seen in Lawson, *Biblical Theology*, 143; Minns, *Irenaeus*, 108; etc.

[152] Behr, *Identifying*, 136–7 n. 22.

[153] Ibid., 136–7.

[154] Quintilian, *Institutio Oratoria*, writes,

> The repetition and grouping of the facts, which the Greeks call ἀνακεφαλαίωσις and some of our own writers call the enumeration, serves both to refresh the memory of the judge and to place the whole of the case before his eyes, and, even although the facts may have made little impression on him in detail, their cumulative effect is considerable. (6.1.1).

English trans. by John Watson, *Quintilian's Institutes of Oratory* (London: H.G. Bonn, 1856).

[155] Isa. 10:22-3; cf. Rom. 9:28.

[156] Rom. 13:10.

He was asked, which is the first commandment, said, "You shall love the Lord your God with [your] whole heart and [your] whole strength; and the second is like it, you shall love your neighbour as yourself. On these two commandments," He says, "depend all the Law and the Prophets."[157] ... therefore He made "a concise word in the world." (*Dem.* 87)

In this passage, extending Paul's point that the commandments are recapitulated by Christ's single commandment to love one's neighbor, Irenaeus uses Romans 13 alongside Isaiah to demonstrate that the Gospel of Christ has summed up the scriptures in a "concise word," since "not by the prolixity of the Law, but according to the brevity of faith and love, men were going to be saved."[158] Understood in this way, the Gospel does not present anything not previously present in the scriptures; nor does it extend, limit, or critique them. Rather it summarizes and clarifies the original (obscure and enigmatic) message of the scriptures themselves, and in this way fulfills them. As Behr describes in his comments on this passage, "The Gospel, as the recapitulation of Scripture in a 'concise word,' is its fulfilment."[159]

C. The Sufficiency of the Jewish Scriptures, Observed in the Demonstration

The literary understanding of recapitulation as the concise summing up and fulfilling of the Jewish scriptures in the Gospel identified above emphasizes an important aspect of the relationship between the Jewish scriptures and the apostolic writings in Irenaeus' thought: the Jewish scriptures are themselves fully sufficient to function as the sole scriptures of the Christian faith, requiring only that their interpretation is guided by the rule of truth that expresses the cardinal points of that Gospel that has recapitulated these scriptures. The apostolic writings exist not as a new set of scriptures necessary for the new Christian faith but as the apostolic record of this Gospel, and therefore as a description of the proper interpretation of the scriptures according to the rule of truth. The unique place of the apostolic writings in Irenaeus' thought only further emphasizes the supreme importance of the Jewish scriptures, necessary to demonstrate their proper interpretation in his arguments against the many heretics who corrupt it.

This relationship is particularly evident in the logic of the *Demonstration*. Its full title indicates with unmistakable clarity that Irenaeus intends to demonstrate (in the dual sense of expositing and proving[160]) the content of the Gospel preached by the apostles. However, his demonstration of the apostolic tradition is undertaken with hardly any mention or citation of the apostles themselves,[161] instead relying fully on the Jewish scriptures to describe and prove the truth of the Gospel in great detail

---

[157] Mt. 22:37-40.
[158] A similar sentiment is expressed when he cites the same Romans passage in 4.12.2.
[159] Behr, *Identifying*, 138.
[160] Cf. Behr's introduction to his translation, PPS 17:17.
[161] Outside the introduction and conclusion the apostles are mentioned four times (*Dem.* 41, 46, 47, 86) and cited four times (*Dem.* 8, 43, 87, 94). Behr, *Nicaea*, comments on Irenaeus' methods in the *Demonstration*, "Although Irenaeus clearly knows the apostolic writings, the substance of his exposition is drawn exclusively from Scripture" (30).

throughout the whole of the work. This strategy entails that Irenaeus is operating with the belief that the entire Gospel that is preached by the apostles has already been prophesied by the scriptures.[162] As Behr concludes on the basis of his reading of the *Demonstration*, "The whole content of the apostolic preaching is derived, for Irenaeus, from the Old Testament."[163] In the *Demonstration* the Jewish scriptures are Irenaeus' primary source for demonstrating the truth of the Gospel, and it is by its adherence to the prophecies of the scriptures that the Gospel is validated, as their recapitulation. The truth of the Christian faith is understood and explained most fundamentally through the Christian reading of the Jewish scriptures.[164] This sentiment is made explicit by Irenaeus in a number of places. Most notably, in *Dem.* 52 Irenaeus explains that the Gospel (that Christ is the Son of God and Savior of all who believe) is

> demonstrated by such [previously indicated] Scriptures. Since it is not possible to draw up an ordered account of all the Scriptures, from these you can also understand the others, which speak in a similar manner, believing Christ and seeking wisdom and understanding from God, in order to understand what was said by the prophets.

All the Jewish scriptures are to be read in this way, and this reading of the scriptures *is* the Gospel, the apostolic tradition recorded in the apostolic writings.

The underlying structure of the *Demonstration* further expresses Irenaeus' purpose. In order to accomplish the task of demonstrating the apostolic preaching of the Gospel from the scriptures, the *Demonstration* is ordered into three sections, dealing with the subjects of the Father, the Son, and the Spirit.[165] By this Irenaeus establishes

---

[162] Irenaeus repeatedly expresses this sentiment within the *Demonstration*. As he introduces the second section, on the Son of God, Irenaeus writes that the prophets "were made heralds of the revelation of our Lord Jesus Christ" (*Dem.* 30). Then, as he transitions into the third section, on the Spirit and prophecy, he explains:

> That all those things would thus come to pass was foretold by the Spirit of God through the prophets, that the faith of those who truly worship God might be certain in these things, for whatever was impossible for our nature, and because of this would bring disbelief to mankind, these things God made known beforehand by the prophets, that, by foretelling them a long time beforehand, when they were fully accomplished in this way, just as they were foretold, we might know that it was God who previously proclaimed to us our salvation. (*Dem.* 42b; echoing Justin, *1 apol.* 33)

Finally, in the conclusion he writes, "This, beloved, is the preaching of the truth, and this is the character of our salvation, and this is the way of life, which the prophets announced and Christ confirmed and the apostles handed over" (*Dem.* 98).

[163] PPS 17:8. Cf. Seitz, *Christian Scripture*, 191–203.

[164] As Seitz describes, "The Scriptures of Israel are viewed as fully sufficient to preach Christ, prophesy Christ, adumbrate Christ, demonstrate Christ and the Holy Spirit both as active and functioning from beginning to end, through the various economies of the Scriptures' long story" (194). Rousseau goes so far as to argue that it is the polemical nature of *Adversus haereses* centering on the fundamental disagreement concerning the meaning of the apostolic preaching that caused Irenaeus to make such extensive use of the apostolic writings, while the *Demonstration* illustrates that in general it is the Jewish scriptures that form the basis of Christian arguments and explanations (SC 406:50-2).

[165] This structure was first suggested by James B. Wiegel, "The Trinitarian Structure of Irenaeus' *Demonstration of the Apostolic Preaching*," *SVTQ* 58.2 (2014): 113–39; correcting the proposals of Joseph Smith. *St. Irenaeus: Proof of the Apostolic Preaching*, ACW 16 (Westminster: Newman

that the scriptures are to be interpreted through the lens of the rule of truth, and, by extension, that the apostolic preaching is straightforwardly the interpretation of the Jewish scriptures according to the rule of truth. Irenaeus illustrates his purpose in the introduction, urging that "we must keep the rule of faith unswervingly" and stating its three articles (*Dem.* 3), and then providing a fuller statement of the rule of truth according to these three articles (*Dem.* 6), in order to set the stage for his three-part demonstration.[166] It is evident that the rule of truth controls his reading of the Jewish scriptures, a reading that is intended to both explain and demonstrate the truth of the apostolic preaching.

By its focus on the extensive and exclusive use of the Jewish scriptures to "demonstrate" the Gospel that is preached by the apostles, the whole of the *Demonstration* indicates that the Gospel is a description of the true interpretation of the Jewish scriptures according to the rule of truth, which summarizes their own newly revealed ὑπόθεσις. Read in this way, the Jewish scriptures are fully sufficient to serve as the scriptures for the Christian faith.[167] This relationship between the Gospel and the scriptures underlying the *Demonstration* supports and extends Irenaeus' use of Romans 13 in discussions of recapitulation,[168] and his comments on the relationship between the apostolic writings and the Jewish scriptures throughout *Adversus haereses*. The Gospel is handed down in the apostolic writings as the record of the apostolic

---

Press, 1952), 15–19; Ferguson, "Irenaeus' Proof of the Apostolic Preaching and Early Catechetical Instruction," *SP* 18.3 (1989): 119–35; Rousseau, *Démonstration* (SC 406), 50–78; Behr, *On the Apostolic Preaching* (PPS 17); and Susan Graham, "Structure and Purpose of Irenaeus' *Epideixis*," *SP* 36 (2001): 210–21; all of whom presented a two-part structure comprised of an opening section on the history of salvation and a second section detailing the scriptural prophecies that predicted the advent of Christ. The chief factor hindering the discovery of the Trinitarian structure of the *Demonstration* seems to have been that the third section, on the Spirit, is predominantly composed of scriptural prophecies of Christ and his advent, similar to the subject matter of the second section, leading Ferguson (126–9) and Graham (214–15) to reject a Trinitarian outline governing the primary structure of the *Demonstration* (cf. Wiegel, "Trinitarian Structure," 124). However, Wiegel has been able to demonstrate that because the Spirit is primarily identified with prophecy, Irenaeus organizes the events of Christ's life under the section on the Spirit who prophesied them, making reference to Irenaeus' statement of the rule of truth in 1.10.1 where the events of Jesus' life are also included under the third article (125–30). This explanation, alongside a detailed analysis of the introduction, conclusion, and major transition statements in the *Demonstration* (121–4), and fruitful comparisons to parallel structures present in *Adversus haereses* (130–5), has convincingly demonstrated the existence of a clear Trinitarian structure to the *Demonstration*. Wiegel's arguments have convinced Behr, and his next edition of *On the Apostolic Preaching* (PPS 17) set to be structured according to Wiegel's proposal and begin with an introductory explanation by him.

[166] Cf. Wiegel, "Trinitarian Structure," 124.

[167] This point is also made by Barton, *Holy Writings*, who argues that for early Christians the Old Testament "is virtually a New Testament itself, once it is read through properly enlightened, that is, Christian eyes" (76).

[168] On the basis of his reading of the *Demonstration* according to its Trinitarian structure, Wiegel is able to interpret one of Irenaeus' themes to be Christ as "the *recapitulation* and *fulfillment* of the Scriptures" (128). He is able to come to this conclusion because his realization that *Dem.* 8-30 concerns the work of the Father and *Dem.* 31-42a concerns the Incarnation of the Son (rather than the traditional interpretation of *Dem.* 8-42a as a description of the history of salvation) indicates that "The concern in section one, then, is not history as we think of it but rhetorical-narrative continuity between the scriptures and the apostolic kerygma" (128).

tradition, and in this form it acts as a recapitulation of the scriptures, clarifying and preserving their true interpretation according to their now visible ὑπόθεσις.

Chapter Conclusion

The purpose of this chapter has been to identify the underlying conceptual distinction motivating the differences in Irenaeus' understanding of the apostolic writings and the Jewish scriptures identified in the previous two chapters, in the hope of discovering the basis of the unique revelatory authority of the apostolic writings. The examination of his concept of tradition led to the conclusion that the only authoritative tradition for Irenaeus is the apostolic tradition, and that this tradition is accessed primarily through the apostolic writings. The apostolic writings are therefore to be understood as the authoritative written record of the apostolic tradition, and to derive their unique revelatory authority by virtue of this status, on the basis of their apostolic origin. Next, an analysis of Irenaeus' concept of the rule of truth led to the conclusion that this concept constitutes an additional aspect of the apostolic tradition alongside the apostolic writings, as an expression of the central elements of the true faith as delivered by the apostolic tradition, primarily for the purpose of safeguarding the true (apostolic) interpretation of the Jewish scriptures by articulating their own ὑπόθεσις. This purpose indicates its direct relationship with the apostolic writings, and illuminates the intimate relationship between the apostolic writings and the Jewish scriptures, which became the object of analysis in the following section. Here it was determined that the apostolic writings, by virtue of being the authoritative written record of the Gospel proclaimed by the apostolic tradition, relate to the Jewish scriptures as the record of the apostolic interpretation of the scriptures. The Gospel itself is not merely a description of the life and teachings of Christ but is the new reading of the scriptures in light of the Incarnation. Viewed from this perspective, the apostolic writings may be understood as the rule of truth put into practice: they are the record of the apostolic interpretation of the scriptures in light of the revelation of the incarnate Christ. Likewise, the rule of truth is a distillation of the content of the apostolic tradition, providing the blueprints for Christians to interpret the Jewish scriptures as the apostles have: according to Christ, their true ὑπόθεσις.

The view of the place of the apostolic writings within Irenaeus' theological system advanced in this chapter indicates the nature of the departure from the traditional interpretation that is being advanced in this book. According to this proposal, the apostolic writings relate to the Jewish scriptures not as a new set of scriptures to be added to them but as the apostolic record of their true interpretation. For Irenaeus the Jewish scriptures are themselves fully sufficient to remain the sole scriptures of the new Christian faith, so long as their proper interpretation is clarified and preserved, and so do not require a supplementary set of scriptures. As the authoritative record of the apostolic tradition, the unique authority of the apostolic writings therefore arises not on the basis of scriptural status but because of their perceived apostolicity— Irenaeus' second locus of revelatory authority. The conceptual distinction observed but yet to be identified in Part 1 is now at least partially visible. The reason apostolicity operates for Irenaeus as a second category of unique revelatory authority, as well as the difference in relationship to the divine between the Jewish scriptures and the apostolic writings, remains to be determined in order to fully answer the question of the nature and status of the apostolic writings. These questions make up the subject of the final chapter.

4

The Question of Inspiration

This chapter builds upon the conclusions of the previous chapter that apostolicity is the basis of the unique revelatory authority of the apostolic writings, in order to arrive at a determination of the nature and status of the apostolic writings in Irenaeus' thought. Two central questions remain unanswered in this investigation. First, the underlying basis of the unique status of *apostolicity* as a category of revelatory authority has yet to be identified. Second, the differences in the nature of the relationship to the divine between the Jewish scriptures and the apostolic writings, first observed in Chapter 2, still await precise classification. In order to answer these questions, the present chapter examines the implications of Irenaeus' understanding of the concept of divine inspiration and its relationship to authorship, hinted at in Chapter 2 but left largely unexamined, in order to determine the nature and extent of its role regarding the unique revelatory authority of the apostolic writings. This investigation therefore also involves an assessment of the traditional interpretation's corollary claim that the apostolic writings acquire their scriptural status on the basis of their inspiration by the Spirit.

This investigation begins with an analysis of the concept of inspiration and its relation to divine authority and resulting scriptural status, in order to determine the parameters of the investigation (Section 4.1). I contend, against the traditional interpretation, that divine *inspiration* and *authorship* are distinct concepts in Irenaeus' thought, which do not equally confer authority. Irenaeus' perception of the apostles as having been inspired by the Spirit therefore does not lead automatically to a view of their writings as having been *authored* by the Spirit or granted their authority on this basis. This distinction sets the stage for an examination of Irenaeus' patterns of reference to the divine in relation to the composition of the Jewish scriptures (Section 4.2), in order to determine what is said about their authorship and so to provide a baseline against which his references to the inspiration of the apostles and their writings are subsequently compared (Section 4.3). I argue on the basis of this comparative analysis that Irenaeus' references to the Jewish scriptures and apostolic writings and his discussions of divine inspiration and authorship indicate a clear and consistent claim of the divine authorship of the Jewish scriptures and of their scriptural authority on this basis, contrasted with a notable lack of emphasis on the inspiration of the apostolic writings and virtually no account of their divine authorship, supporting the conclusion that their unique revelatory authority is not directly related to their inspiration.

Finally, on the basis of these findings and the conclusions of the previous chapters, I attempt to construct Irenaeus' conception of the nature and status of the apostolic writings on the foundation of his doctrine of the Word (Section 4.4). Here I contend that the difference in relationship to the divine between the Jewish scriptures and apostolic writings exists as a result of the Word's differing functions in his role as Revealer of the Father. The Incarnation represents the culmination of the Word's revelatory role, and for this reason apostolicity operates as a distinct category of unique revelatory authority on the basis of the apostles' unparalleled relationship to the incarnate Word. This grants the apostolic writings the status of authoritative written record of the divinely sanctioned mediation of the Word's consummate revelation to humanity.

4.1. The Relationship between Inspiration and Authority

A number of interpreters of Irenaeus have, either explicitly or implicitly, attributed his supposed advocacy for the scriptural status of the apostolic writings to his belief that they are inspired by the Spirit. Among studies of the formation of the New Testament canon, in addition to maintaining that Irenaeus considered the apostolic writings to constitute a new set of scriptures, a number of treatments have identified his belief in their inspiration as the basis for his acceptance of their scriptural status. This view has received perhaps its most vigorous defense in R. Laird Harris's 1957 study *Inspiration and the Canonicity of the Bible*. One of Harris's central theses in this work is that "the test of canonicity is inspiration. The Early Church put into its canon, and we receive, those books which were regarded as inspired, and no others,"[1] and his interpretation of Irenaeus forms a significant part of his demonstration. In his chapter "Verbal inspiration in Church History," Harris writes, "When we come to the great authors of the late second century where witness abounds, we also find full testimony to belief in a doctrine of inspiration [of scripture, here specifically the New Testament] that must be described as verbal," and seeks to demonstrate this claim by a series of citations from Irenaeus.[2] In a later section on Irenaeus, his primary contention is that "The Scriptures are true, according to Irenaeus, because they are apostolic and therefore inspired. … This apostolic authority is the result of their enduement with the Holy Spirit."[3]

Harris's study represents an extreme view of the formation of the New Testament canon, yet similar understandings of Irenaeus' conception of the apostolic writings may be observed in many subsequent studies on the subject. F. F. Bruce's 1988 study *The Canon of Scripture* provides another example. Within his section on Irenaeus, in order to demonstrate his claim that Irenaeus considered the four gospels to be scripture, Bruce states, "All four were inspired by the same Spirit as spoke through the prophets. This inspiration extended to the choice of one word rather than another."[4] More

---

[1] 200.
[2] Ibid., 79–80; argued on the basis of his readings of 3.2.1, 3.14.4, 3.16.2, 3.1.1, and 2.28.2.
[3] Ibid., 147–8. Harris similarly contends that if a writing is apostolic, "it is true and will agree with previous revelation, for it is spoken by the same Spirit and prearranged by the same Christ" (249).
[4] 175–6.

recently, Tomas Bokedal has argued within his work *The Formation and Significance of the Christian Biblical Canon* that the formation of the New Testament canon is a process of "deliberate and conscious selection, preservation and interpretation closely tied up with the notion of inspiration,"[5] and points to Irenaeus as evidence of the importance of inspiration in this process. He believes that the scriptures—specifically "the prophets, the Lord and the apostles"—are shown to be perfect by Irenaeus and argues that according to him, "Another feature ascribed to 'all the Scriptures' is their character as inspired text."[6] Bokedal's interpretation of Irenaeus leads him to conclude, "Thus, when considering second-century canon reception, the question of inspiration is crucial."[7]

In opposition to this view, there are a number of studies of the formation of the New Testament canon that question the significance of inspiration for the scriptural status of the apostolic writings,[8] and Hans von Campenhausen, in his influential study *Die Entstehung der christlichen Bibel*, does so specifically in reference to Irenaeus. While he believes that Irenaeus was the first theologian to elevate the New Testament writings to the status of scripture,[9] he maintains that "Irenaeus does not yet think in terms of a specific 'inspiration' of the New Testament writers."[10]

Among Irenaean scholars there is more of a consensus, with the vast majority of treatments of Irenaeus' thought arguing in favor of the importance of inspiration for the authority and scriptural status of the apostolic writings. This view can be traced at least as far back as Harnack,[11] who claims that Irenaeus and Tertullian operate with

> the assumption that the apostolic writings were inspired, that is, in the full and only intelligible sense attached to the word by the ancients. By this assumption the Apostles, viewed as *prophets*, received a significance quite equal to that of the Old Testament writers.[12]

The inspiration of the apostolic writings is identified as the basis of their equivalence to the Old Testament scriptures. Similar conclusions would subsequently be reached by many of the major interpreters of Irenaeus.

Two examples may illustrate this trend. According to Flesseman-van Leer, "The Spirit of God who assumes the form of the prophets and speaks through them ... also speaks through the writers of the New Testament books," and this leads her to

---

[5] 6.
[6] Ibid., 295.
[7] Ibid. Bokedal further contends, "Bruce Metzger's remark, that 'inspiration' should *not* be taken into account when discussing the issue of canonization, therefore needs reconsideration" (295), here referring to Metzger's comments in *Canon*, 254–7.
[8] Cf. Metzger, *Canon*, 254–7; Gamble, *New Testament*, 71–2; McDonald, *Formation*, 239–46; "Identifying Scripture," 435–9; Allert, *High View*.
[9] 186–8, 202–3.
[10] Ibid., 205. Cf. n. 290. Cf. McDonald, "Identifying Scripture," who contends, "Irenaeus makes it clear that the scriptures [in this context the New Testament] even when they were not clearly understood, 'were spoken by the Word of God and by His Spirit'" (435–6), but questions whether inspiration played a significant role in the eventual canonization of the New Testament.
[11] Adolf von Harnack, *Lehrbuch der Dogmengeschichte*, vol. 2 (Leipzig: Mohr, 1888).
[12] HD 2:54.

conclude, "Scripture being in this sense 'inspired' (a term not used by Irenaeus), it is a matter of course that it has the same divine authority as revelation."[13] In a similar vein, Anthony Briggman states that "Irenaeus views the Spirit as the source of the oral and written message of the Apostles,"[14] and on this basis he describes Irenaeus as "founding the unity and authority of the oral and written traditions on the work of the Spirit" and "basing the transmission of every message of the gospel on the work of the same Spirit."[15] In these and other cases,[16] the inspiration of the apostles is identified as *a* or *the* primary motivating factor in Irenaeus' acceptance of their status as scripture.

The suggested link between inspiration and scriptural status in these accounts rests on the (often unstated) belief that the divine inspiring agent is ultimately in some sense the author of the document it inspires. This tacitly understood equivalence between *inspiration* and *authorship*, in which inspiration is directly linked to divine authority and resulting scriptural status, anachronistically applies modern concepts to Irenaeus' thought that, I contend, misconstrue his intentions.

A. Differentiating between *auctoritas* and *inspiratio*

It is difficult to determine the precise nature of inspiration and its relationship to divine (and therefore scriptural) authority in Irenaeus' thought. He very rarely uses the terminology of "inspiration," "inspired," and so on,[17] and even more rarely applies it to

---

[13] Flesseman-van Leer, *Tradition*, 130.
[14] Briggman, *Holy Spirit*, 48.
[15] Ibid., 50. He also contends, "according to Irenaeus, the veracity, reliability, and numerical perfection of the Gospel accounts depend upon the activity of the Spirit" (53).
[16] Hitchcock, *Irenaeus*, 192–3; Benoit, *Irénée*, 137–9; Minns, *Irenaeus*, 137; Osborn, *Irenaeus*, 177–8; Hill, "Patristic Period," 55, 80; Hanson, *Allegory and Event*, 112–13; Robert M. Grant, *The Letter and the Spirit* (London: Macmillan, 1957), 75, 81–4. Lawson, *Biblical Theology*, provides a more nuanced view (26–35). He contends that according to Irenaeus,

> every part of the Bible was inspired by one and the same God. We must, however, be cautious in drawing from the statements of S. Irenaeus the consequence that he regarded the New Testament writings as inspired and canonical equally with the Old Testament. When he argues the point he always has in mind those who would detract from the authority of the Hebrew Scriptures. The position of the Apostolic writings is thus in effect left open. (26)

He maintains that "the doctrine [of inspiration] typical of and general to Irenaeus is not that of a Spirit who comes to dwell in an individual prophet and inspired him to declare new truth, but of a Spirit who indwells and lifts to perfection those who faithfully adhere to the established tradition of truth" (29). However, Lawson also claims, "The divine inspiration of the Evangelists clearly extends to the choice of particular words and phrases" (32; citing 3.16.2), and concludes on this basis, "We may therefore agree that Beuzart is correct in stating that had S. Irenaeus lived in later times he would probably have been an upholder of the doctrine of literal inspiration" (32), referencing Beuzart, *Théologie d'Irénée*, 138. Lawson defines canonicity as "that which grows out of inspiration by virtue of the passage of time" (32) and states, "To [Irenaeus] it is an article of faith that the Apostles, as inspired by God, are an organ of supreme and unquestioned authority" (35).

[17] The only eleven instances of this are found in 1.15.6, where Irenaeus describes an unknown non-scriptural writer as "divinely inspired [*divinae aspirationis*/θεῖος]"; 1.23.3, where Irenaeus reports that the heretics claim the prophets were "inspired [*inspiratos*/ἐμπνευσθέντας]" by angels, rather than God; 2.14.4, where Irenaeus reports that the heretics claim ancient philosophers were "inspired [*inspirati*]" by their Mother; 2.22.6, where Irenaeus reports that the heretics claim that Homer was "inspired [*inspiratus*]" by their Mother; 2.31.3, where Irenaeus claims that the heretics are full of rebellious "inspiration [*adinspiratione*]"; 3.21.2 (twice), where Irenaeus claims that the LXX was translated through the inspiration of God (*aspirationem*/ἐπίπνοιαν; and *inspirauit*/ἐπέπνευσεν);

the process of writing either the Jewish scriptures or apostolic writings. The only two instances of Irenaeus using the term "inspiration" (*inspiratio*, etc.; ἐμπνευστός, etc.[18]) in any way relating to this process occur when he reports that Simon Magus claimed that the prophets gave prophecies under the inspiration (*inspiratos*/ἐμπνευσθέντας) of angels, rather than God (1.23.3), and again when he denies his opponents' claim that the prophets "received prophetical inspiration [*propheticam inspirationem*] from another God" (4.34.3).[19] In neither instance does Irenaeus make use of the term to positively describe his own view, nor does he use it in reference to the apostles or their writings. This is not to say that Irenaeus does not make use of the concept of inspiration to describe the composition of either the Jewish scriptures or the apostolic writings, even if he opts not to use the language of *inspiratio*/ἐμπνεθστός. However, it illustrates that his understanding does not necessarily correspond to modern conceptions, and suggests that determining his understanding may be more complicated than is often acknowledged.

Within modern theological discourse, "inspiration" is an underdefined concept encompassing a number of different possible forms of divine interaction with humanity, ranging from divine possession of a human agent to be used as the instrument by which to convey the divine message,[20] to the gentle suggestion of some previously unformed

---

3.24.1, where Irenaeus claims that the Spirit (or the faith; cf. ACW 64:212 n. 7 and SC 211:473 n. 2) is "the life-breath [*aspiratio*] to the first-fashioned"; 4.34.3, where Irenaeus denies that the prophets received "prophetical inspiration [*propheticam inspirationem*]" from another god; 5.1.3, where Irenaeus states that the "breath of life [*aspiratio vitae*]" from God animated Adam; and 5.8.2, where Irenaeus states that whoever rejects the Spirit's counsel does not have the inspiration (aspirationem/ἐπίπνοιαν) of the Divine Spirit (cf. SC 153:99). In addition, there are six places where Irenaeus uses a form of *spiro/spiratio* not referring to inspiration (1.15.4, 1.30.4, 2.26.1, 2.33.4, 2.35.3, 3.7.2), such as Irenaeus warning that, when reading Paul's letters, "if one would not pay attention to the reading and indicate the breathing [*aspirationis*] pause in that which is read," then Paul's meaning would be lost (3.7.2).

[18] The few surviving fragments that preserve the original Greek behind *inspiro*, *inspiratio*, and their cognates in the Latin translation indicate that they consistently translate forms of the verb πνέω or the noun πνοή, usually with the prefixes ἐν or ἐπί. The possible exception in 1.15.6 (θεῖος) is discussed in Section 4.1C, where it is concluded that θεόπνευστος is likely the original Greek term.

[19] Irenaeus also uses the term in reference to the LXX translation of the scriptures twice in 3.21.2. This passage has been excluded because *inspiratio* is used in reference to the process of *translating* and *restoring*, rather than *composing* the scriptures: "κατ' ἐπίνοιαν [*aspirationem*] τοῦ Θεοῦ εἰσιν ἡρμηνευμέναι αἱ γραφαί ... [Θεος] ἐνέπνευσεν [*inspirauit*]"Ἔσδρα τῷ ἱερεῖ ἐκ τῆς φυλῆς Λευὶ τοὺς τῶν προγεγονότων προφητῶν πάντας ἀνατάξασθαι λόγους καὶ ἀποκαταστῆσαι τῷ λαῷ τὴν διὰ Μωϋσέως νομοθεσίαν." Cf. Kalin, *Inspiration*, 12-5. However, Reilly, "L'inspiration," argues against this understanding, contending, "Ce que notre auteur dit des LXX montre qu'il en regardait chaque mot [of the Jewish scriptures] comme l'oeuvre de Dieu" (498).

[20] As seen in Philo, *Questions and Answers on Genesis* 3.9; *de specialibus legibus* 1.65, 4.49, etc.; Athenagoras, *Legatio pro Christianis* 9. The contemporary approach most closely resembling this is represented in fullest measure by Benjamin B. Warfield, *The Inspiration and Authority of the Bible* (Philadelphia, PA: Presbyterian and Reformed, 1970). Warfield does not advocate a strict mechanical or "possession" view of inspiration (421) but contends that the inspiration of the scriptures entails that "God is their author" (111), because he has "such complete control of the human agents that the product is truly God's work" (151). This process occurs as the Spirit is "spontaneously producing under Divine directions the writings appointed to [the apostles]" (158), in which, "while their humanity was not superseded, it was yet so dominated that their words became at the same time the words of God" (422).

idea.²¹ In order to overcome this ambiguity, in this chapter I distinguish between the notions of divine "authorship" (*auctoritas*) and "in-breathing" (*inspiratio*) within the broader concept of inspiration (though they necessarily contain significant overlap), in order to avoid possible misrepresentations of Irenaeus' intentions. According to this rubric, *auctoritas* describes any direct form of inspiration in which God himself composes the message that is written down (whether or not the human writer is active in—or conscious of—the process). On the other hand, *inspiratio* describes less direct forms of inspiration in which the Spirit non-coercively guides a human agent, leads him or her to truth, and sanctifies (for example) the writing process: without composing, determining, or guaranteeing the content of the message. The important distinction being made by the use of these concepts is therefore between *divine authorship* of a message that is written by a human agent, and *human authorship* of a message that is guided or sanctified by a divine agent.

My contention is that the *auctoritas* form of inspiration provides Irenaeus with a basis for the divine scriptural authority of the resulting written work, while the *inspiratio* form does not. I am not claiming that Irenaeus operates under the rubric outlined here (he does not); nor, on the other hand, do I accept that he possesses a singular concept of inspiration according to which all divine acts and communication must conform. These categories are intended as a way of sorting his wide variety of descriptions of divine communication into those that are meant to provide the basis for the authority of the resulting product under the status of divine revelation and those that are not. This contention—that not all forms of inspiration are sufficient to provide a basis for divine or scriptural authority—finds evidence from the fact that Irenaeus and other Christian thinkers of his time, though they grant the apostles and their writings unique authoritative status on par with the Jewish scriptures, do not limit inspiration to the apostles and their writings.

B. Inspiration Is Not a Unique Property of the Apostles

There is abundant evidence that Irenaeus considers the apostles to be divinely inspired. In one of his most detailed descriptions, he states,

> We are not permitted to say that [the apostles] preached before they had received "perfect knowledge" [*perfectam agnitionem*], as some dare to state, boasting that they are correctors of the apostles. For, after our Lord had risen from the dead, and "they were clothed with power [*uirtutem*] from on high when the Spirit came upon them,"²² they had full assurance concerning all things [*de omnibus adimpleti sunt*], and had "perfect knowledge" [*perfectam agnitionem*]. (3.1.1)

The apostles are filled with the Spirit, just as Luke-Acts describes, and the Spirit ensures that they possess "perfect knowledge." The Spirit also gives the apostles

---

[21] Clement of Alexandria, *Stromata* 6.17.157.4; Schleiermacher, *Der Christliche Glaube* §130.1-2; C. S. Lewis, *Reflections on the Psalms* (London: Fount Paperbacks, 1998), 94–103.

[22] Lk. 24:49; Acts 1:8; Acts 2:4.

spiritual foresight or discernment, illustrated in Irenaeus' claim that the apostles "did also preach to us to shun these [Valentinian] doctrines, foreseeing by the Spirit [*Spiritu providentes*] those weak-minded persons who should be led astray" (4.pre.3).[23] The Spirit's inspiration extends also to their writings, as the apostles handed down (*tradiderunt*) their preaching in written form "by the will of God" (3.1.1), and their accounts of the Gospel are "held together by one Spirit" (3.11.8).

Yet the inspiration described in these passages is not considered to be unique to the apostles but is often described as the possession of the whole church. This conviction is discernible in Irenaeus as well as the other early Christian thinkers whose writings are available.

Inspiration and Non-Canonicity

In his 1967 doctoral thesis, Everett R. Kalin investigated the writings of the major church fathers up to 400 AD (including Irenaeus) and found that inspiration was never claimed to be a unique property of the New Testament, nor was any orthodox non-canonical writing ever claimed to be non-inspired.[24] Instead, he found that the same inspiration that was claimed of the apostles and their writings was also claimed by many early patristic writers for themselves and others. These findings led him to the conclusion that "these writers see the inspiring activity of God in the scriptures, but they do not see it confined to the scriptures. Their concept of inspiration is wider than their concept of canonicity."[25]

A brief sample of statements from early church fathers may illustrate his point. Prior to Irenaeus, Clement of Rome could write that Paul "was truly inspired [ἀληθείας πνευματικῶς] when he wrote to you regarding himself and Cephas and Apollos" (*1 Clem.* 47.3)[26] and also claim, "You certainly will give us the keenest pleasure if you prove obedient to what we have written through the Holy Spirit [γεγραμμένοις διὰ

---

[23] Similar implications are suggested in 3.16.1.
[24] Everett R. Kalin, *Argument from Inspiration in the Canonization of the New Testament* (ThD Diss., Harvard University, 1967); summarized in "The Inspired Community: A Glance at Canon History," *CTM* 42 (1971): 541–9. Kalin's thesis was first articulated by his doctoral supervisor Krister Stendahl in "The Apocalypse of John and the Epistles of Paul in the Muratorian Fragment," in *Current Issues in New Testament Interpretation: Essays in honor of Otto A. Piper*, ed. William Klassen and Graydon F. Snyder (New York: Harper & Row, 1962), 239–45; though Kalin would be the first to comprehensively demonstrate it. The same conclusions would be reached independently by Albert C. Jr.Sundberg, "The Making of the New Testament Canon," in *The Interpreter's One-Volume Commentary on the Bible*, ed. Charles M. Laymon (Nashville, TN: Abingdon Press, 1971), 1217, 1224; and "The Bible Canon and the Christian Doctrine of Inspiration," *Int* 29 (1975): 352–71, esp. 364–5. Sundberg and Kalin's conclusions have subsequently been widely adopted by New Testament canon scholars, including Gamble, *New Testament*; Metzger, *Canon*; McDonald, *Formation*; "Identifying Scripture"; Bruce, *Canon*; Allert, *High View*, etc.
[25] Kalin, *Inspiration*, 230. Cf. "Inspired Community," 542: "The Scriptures were for the fathers inspired, but the inspiration of the Scriptures was not that which distinguished them from all other Christian writing and speaking."
[26] Trans. by James A. Kleist, ed., *The Epistles of Clement of Rome and St. Ignatius of Antioch*, ACW 1 (Westminster: Newman Bookshop, 1946), 38; Greek edition by Annie Jaubert, ed., *Clément de Rome: Épître aux Corinthiens*, SC 167 (Paris: du Cerf, 1971), 178.

τοῦ ἁγίου πνεύματος]" (*1 Clem.* 63.2).²⁷ He affirms both the unique authority and the divine inspiration of the apostles, yet he sees no issue with affirming the same inspiration for himself. This sentiment is made more explicit in the writings of Ignatius. In his *Epistle to the Romans*, Ignatius explicitly sets the apostles apart from himself, saying, "Not like Peter and Paul do I issue any orders to you [Οὐκ ὡς Πέτρος καὶ Παῦλος διατάσσομαι ὑμῖν]. They were apostles, I am a convict; they were free, I am a slave [Ἐκεῖνοι ἀπόστολοι ἐγὼ κατάκριτος· ἐκεῖνοι ἐλεύθεροι, ἐγὼ δὲ μέχρι νῦν δοῦλος]" (4.3).²⁸ Yet later in the same letter, he writes, "I did not write to you according to the flesh, but according to the will of God [Οὐ κατὰ σάρκα ὑμῖν ἔγραψα, ἀλλὰ κατὰ γνώμην Θεοῦ]" (8.3),²⁹ and then, in his *Epistle to the Philadelphians*, he claims, "I had not learned it from any human source [ἀπὸ σαρκὸς ἀνθρωπίνης οὐκ ἔγνων]. No, it was the Spirit who kept preaching in these words [Τὸ δὲ πνεῦμα ἐκήρυσσεν λέγον τάδε]" (7.1-2).³⁰

This pattern would also continue after Irenaeus. Clement of Alexandria, in his *Exhortation to the Greeks*, writes, "For the knowledge of God, these utterances, written by those we have mentioned through the inspiration of God [Θεοῦ πρὸς αὐτῶν μὲν ἀναγεγραμμένα], and selected by us, may suffice even for the man that has but small power to examine into truth" (6.72.5).³¹ Similarly, in his *Stromata* he makes the claim that "the thoughts of virtuous men are produced through the inspiration of God [κατὰ ἐπίπνοιαν Θείαν]" (6.17.157.4).³² Cyprian is able to make a similar claim about his own treatise, stating at the beginning of his *Exhortation to Martyrdom* that he writes "instructed by the aid of divine inspiration [*divinae inspirationis*]" (pre.1).³³ Eusebius also begins his *Life of Constantine* by asking, "may the inspiring aid of the heavenly Word be with me [οὐράνιός τε συνεργὸς ἡμῖν ἐμπείτω λόγος] while I commence my history from the earliest period of his life" (1.11.2).³⁴ These examples could be

---

²⁷ ACW 1:48; SC 167:202. Cf. 59.1: "But should any disobey what has been said by Him [Christ] though us [Ἐὰν δέ τινες ἀπειθήσωσιν τοῖς ὑπ'αὐτοῦ δι'ἡμῶν εἰρημένοις], let them understand that they will entangle themselves in transgression and no small danger" (ACW 1:44; SC 167:194).
²⁸ ACW 1:82; P. Th. Camelot, ed., *Ignace d'Antioche, Polycarpe de Smyrne: Letters, Martyre de Polycarpe*, SC 10 (Paris: du Cerf, 1969), 112.
²⁹ My trans.; SC 10:116. Kleist's translation of this passage departs from the Greek. It reads, "What I write to you does not please the appetites of the flesh, but it pleases the mind of God" (ACW 1:84).
³⁰ ACW 1:88; SC 10:126. Many other similar claims exist from this period. The author of the *Shepherd of Hermas* unquestionably believes himself to be inspired (cf. *Vis.* 1.1-3, 2.1.1, 5.5). The author of *2 Clement* introduces a citation from *1 Clement* 11.2 with the words, "For the prophetic word also declares [Λέγει γὰρ καὶ ὁ προ[φη]τικὸς λόγος]" (ANF 9:254; PG 1:34). In *Dialogue with Trypho* 82, Justin explains, "For the prophetical gifts remain with us, even to the present time. And hence you ought to understand that [the gifts] formerly among your nation have been transferred to us" (ANF 1:240). Cf. also *dial.* 87.
³¹ ANF 2:192; J. P. Migne, ed., *Clementis Alexandrini*, vol. 1, PG 8 (Paris: Imprimerie Catholique, 1857), 180.
³² ANF 2:517; Migne, *Clementis Alexandrini*, vol. 2, PG 9:389.
³³ ANF 5:496; J. P. Migne, ed., *Cypriani: Episcopi Carthaginensis et Martyris*, PL (Paris: Imprimerie Catholique, 1844), 4:652.
³⁴ Philip Schaff and Henry Wace, *Eusebius Pamphilus: Church History, Life of Constantine, Oration in Praise of Constantine*, NPNF 2.1 (Edinburgh: T&T Clark, 1890), 485; F. Winkelmann, Luce Pietri, and Marie-Joseph Rondeau, eds. *Eusébe de Césarée: Vie de Constantin*, SC 559 (Paris: du Cerf, 2013), 195. Cf. 3.26.6; *De laudibus Constantini* 11.3; and *Historia ecclesiastica* 6.29.3.

multiplied.[35]

The unanimous teaching of the patristic writers before and after Irenaeus is that the apostles are uniquely authoritative, yet the same inspiration that they receive is available to the entire church. As Kalin concludes, "the early church saw the inspiration of the Scriptures as one aspect of a much broader activity of inspiration in the church."[36] When Irenaeus' own writings are examined, it becomes clear that he is in agreement with this consensus.

The Breadth of Irenaeus' Concept of Inspiration

As previously shown, Irenaeus considered the apostles and their writings to be unique in their authoritative status alongside the Jewish scriptures.[37] Yet, in addition to affirming the inspiration of the apostles, Irenaeus extends the inspiring work of the Spirit to many other non-apostolic figures. He speaks extensively of the work of the Spirit in the church, and maintains that Peter

> would not have gone to [the Gentiles] unless he had been ordered. Nor, perhaps, would he so easily have given them baptism unless the Holy Spirit had rested upon them [τοῦ Πνεύματος τοῦ ἁγίου ἐπαναπαέντος οὐτοῖς] and he had heard them prophesying. And so he said, "Can any one forbid water for baptizing these people, who have received the Holy Spirit [τὸ Πνεῦμα τὸ ἅγιον ἔλαβον] just as we have?"[38] At the same time he convinced those who were with him. He also pointed out that if the Holy Spirit had not rested upon them [τὸ Πνεῦμα τὸ ἅγιον ἐπ' αὐτοὺς ἀναπέπαυτο], someone might have hindered them from being baptized. (3.12.15)

Irenaeus affirms alongside Peter that it is not only the apostles who are inspired by the Spirit, but rather the Spirit is available to all.[39] The same sentiment is observed in his statement:

> We do also hear many brethren in the Church, who possess prophetic gifts [προφητικὰ χαρίσματα], and who through the Spirit [διὰ τοῦ Πνεύματος] speak all kinds of languages, and bring to light for the general benefit the hidden things of men, and declare the mysteries of God [τὰ μυστήρια τοῦ Θεοῦ ἐκδιηγουμένων]. (5.6.1)[40]

---

[35] Gregory of Nyssa, *Apologia in hexameron* (PG 44:61); Gregory of Nazianzus, *Orationes* 21.33; etc. Cf. Kalin's non-exhaustive list, *Inspiration*, 171–83.
[36] Kalin, "Inspired Community," 547.
[37] 1.2.
[38] Acts 10:47.
[39] Kalin, *Inspiration*, agrees, stating that "Irenaeus' use of inspiration terminology centers in the idea that in the last days (the entire time from the advent of Christ to Irenaeus' own time) the Spirit has been poured out and that his inspiring activity manifests itself in the church—with prophecies, healings, in fact, in every phase of the church's life—right up to Irenaeus' day" (232).
[40] Cf. 2.32.4, 3.11.8, 3.11.9.

Irenaeus envisions the distinction between inspired/non-inspired to correspond not to apostle/non-apostle or scripture/non-scripture but to acceptance/rejection of the Spirit. In one of the few passages in which he uses the terminology of *inspiratio*, Irenaeus states on the basis of Paul's distinction between flesh and spirit (Rom. 8:9) that "the Spirit of God dwells in [*Spiritus Dei habitat in*]" those who "are subject to the Spirit," while "those who cast away the Spirit's counsel, and are enslaved to the pleasures of the flesh" are the only ones "not having the inspiration of the Divine Spirit [*nullum habentes aspirationem divini Spiritus*]" (5.8.2).[41] All, therefore, who live according to the Spirit have the "inspiration of the Divine Spirit."[42]

In addition to these examples, Irenaeus also specifically describes a number of non-apostles receiving inspiration from the Spirit. He writes of "Simeon—he to whom it had been revealed by the Holy Spirit [*responsum acceperat a Spiritu sancto*] that he should not see death until he had seen Christ Jesus."[43] (3.16.4). A few chapters later his claim is more striking:

> Elizabeth, "filled with the Holy Spirit [*impleta Spiritu sancto*],"[44] bore witness [to this] when she said to Mary, "Blessed are you among women, and blessed is the fruit of your womb." By this the Holy Spirit pointed out [*significante Spiritu sancto*], to all who wished to hear, that the promise that God had made, namely, that He would raise up the King "from the fruit of the womb," was fulfilled in the birth-giving of the Virgin, that is, of Mary. (3.21.5)

In this passage Irenaeus makes one of his most explicit statements of the inspiration of a non-apostle, demonstrating that inspiration is not confined to the apostles or their writings.

On one occasion Irenaeus explicitly describes a non-apostolic figure as "divinely inspired." This occurs in Book 1, where Irenaeus cites a passage from an unknown writing that he introduces with the words, "the divinely inspired [*divinae adspirationis*; θεῖος] elder and preacher of the Truth burst forth against [Marcus] in the following

---

[41] My trans. Roberts–Donaldson have translated the clause "*nullum habentes aspirationem divini Spiritus*" instead as "having no longing after the divine Spirit" (ANF 1:534), which has contributed to the neglect of this passage in discussions of inspiration. Their translation ignores the Latin text in favor of a Greek fragment of this passage preserved in Basil, *Liber de Spiritu sancto*, 29.72, which reads, "μηδεμίαν ἔχοντας ἐπιθυμίαν Θείου Πνεύματος" (PG 32:201). However, the Armenian translation is in agreement with the Latin text against this fragment, leading Rousseau et al. to adjust ἐπιθυμίαν to ἐπίπνοιαν in their Greek retroversion, and to translate this passage, "n'ont aucune inspiration du divin Esprit" (SC 153:98-9).

[42] Kalin, *Inspiration*, draws similar conclusions. He states on the basis of his investigation of Irenaeus that Irenaeus makes use of the distinction inspired/noninspired only

> in a contrast between the heretics, who are destitute of the Spirit and his gifts, and the church, which possesses the Spirit's gifts in the fullest measure. Irenaeus makes no explicit contrast—inspiration/non-inspiration or any other—between the apostolic scriptures and the writings of men like Polycarp and Clement. There is no indication that Irenaeus regards the apostolic period to be endowed with a measure of the Spirit his age does not possess. (234–5)

[43] Cf. Lk. 2:25-8.
[44] Lk. 1:41.

poetic lines" (1.15.6). If the Latin translation is accurate,⁴⁵ this passage takes on special significance. Irenaeus implies that the writings of this unknown elder are "inspired," while even the apostolic writings are never declared by him to be *inspiratus*, and he almost entirely refrains from using the term in reference to the Jewish scriptures.⁴⁶

Conclusion

Irenaeus' repeated statements throughout *Adversus haereses* demonstrate that he believes inspiration is not unique to the apostles but is also routinely recognized in other non-apostolic figures and non-apostolic and unscriptural writings; yet the authority of the apostles and their writings is consistently distinguished from all others. These findings indicate that "inspiration" broadly defined cannot be considered the basis of the unique revelatory authority of the apostolic writings. It is necessary for this reason to differentiate between the proposed *auctoritas* and *inspiratio* categories of inspiration in Irenaeus' thought, for if inspiration does indeed play a crucial role in the unique revelatory authority of the apostolic writings, the apostles must receive some sort of unique or "special" inspiration, above what is available to the whole church. Such a claim has in fact been made.⁴⁷ The "special" inspiration required would fall under the category of *auctoritas* inspiration, according to which the divine inspiring agent in some sense *authors* or composes the message that is written down in the apostolic writings. It is therefore necessary to determine, not whether Irenaeus considers the apostles and their writings to be inspired *in any sense,* but whether he considers them to be the product of divine *auctoritas*, in a manner similar to the Jewish scriptures. It is the presence or absence of this *auctoritas* alone that can answer the question of whether the unique revelatory authority of the apostolic writings is based on their inspiration.

---

⁴⁵ Roberts–Donaldson (ANF 1:340) translate the clause as "divine elder" on the basis of θεῖος in the Greek fragment of Epiphanius (*Panarion* 34.11.10). Both Unger (ACW 55:68) and Rousseau-Doutreleau (SC 264:251) translate "divinely inspired elder" ("*vieillard divinement inspiré*") on the basis of the rendering of this clause in the Latin translation as *divinae adspirationis*, considering it to be more accurate to the original in this instance. Unger notes (ACW 55:214 n. 29) that the Latin translation supposes θεόπνευστος as the Greek original, and Harvey is in agreement (1:155). The overly literal translation style of the Latin text (in all other instances of *spiro/spiratio* and its cognates where the Greek is preserved, a form of πνέω/πνοή is being translated) suggests that θεόπνευστος is original, and that Epiphanius, writing two hundred years later, has altered his text slightly to θεῖος. It is notable that Frank Williams, ed., *The Panarion of Epiphanius of Salamis: Book 1 (Sects 1-46)* (Leiden: Brill, 2009), translates this clause in Epiphanius as "divinely-inspired elder" (240; 34.11.10).
⁴⁶ The inspiration of the composition of the Jewish scriptures is indirectly alluded to in 4.34.3, and the *translation* of the Jewish scriptures is said to be inspired in 3.21.2. Refer to the discussion in Section 4.1B.
⁴⁷ Harnack suggests that the apostles were understood to possess some sort of unique inspiration by Irenaeus and Tertullian: "The Apostles alone possessed the Spirit of God completely and without measure. They only, therefore, are the media of revelation" (HD 2:54; cf. 55 n. 2). Similarly, Hill, "Patristic Period," states that the "plenary nature" of the inspiration of scripture "separated Scripture from other forms of inspired speech," (80) and cites 2.28.2 as proof. Kalin, *Inspiration*, rejects this theory and argues specifically on the basis of his analysis of Irenaeus' understanding of inspiration that "There is no indication that Irenaeus regards the apostolic period to be endowed with a measure of the Spirit his age does not possess" (235).

Having determined the parameters of the investigation, the examination of this chapter begins in the following section with an examination of Irenaeus' use of the concept of inspiration in relation to the Jewish scriptures, in order to provide a baseline against which the apostolic writings can be compared in the following section.

4.2. Examining the Nature of the Inspiration of the Jewish Scriptures

It was shown in Chapter 2 that Irenaeus interprets the Jewish scriptures according to the rule of truth rather than focusing on the intentions of the prophetic writers, and concluded that the reason for this is that he considers the Word to be their true author and the basis of their revelatory authority as scripture. These conclusions indicate that Irenaeus affirms an *auctoritas* understanding of the inspiration of the Jewish scriptures. In this section, an in-depth analysis of his comments relating to their inspiration is used to determine to what extent Irenaeus describes the divine *auctoritas* of the Jewish scriptures. This analysis serves the dual purpose of identifying his exact understanding of the nature and extent of their inspiration, and illustrating how he discusses the inspiration of writings that he considers to be the product of *auctoritas*. This investigation consists of a brief analysis of Irenaeus' references to divine inspiration in his introductions to citations from the Jewish scriptures, followed by an examination of Irenaeus' discussions of inspiration as they relate to the composition of these scriptures.

A. References to Inspiration in Introductions to Citations from the Jewish Scriptures

Irenaeus often gives an indication of his understanding of the inspiration of the Jewish scriptures in his introductions to citations from them. Of his approximately 500 citations from the Jewish scriptures,[48] Irenaeus introduces a citation as the words of God eighty-eight times. For present purposes, these eighty-eight occurrences can be further subdivided into those passages in which God is said to speak *by* or *through* the human writer of the book that is being cited,[49] and those passages in which God is said to speak to a character within the narrative recorded by the scriptural writer.[50] The

---

[48] Blanchard, *Sources*, counts 450 direct citations (and 820 total references) to the Old Testament in *Adversus haereses* from the SC indexes (122–3); and Benoit, "Écriture et Tradition," counts 100 citations or allusions to the Old Testament in the *Demonstration* (33). Werner, *Paulinismus*, had previously listed 629 Old Testament allusions or citations in *Adversus haereses* on the basis of Harvey's index (7).

[49] For example, Irenaeus writes, "God says through the prophet Ezekiel, 'And I will give them another heart, and I will put a new Spirit in them'" (*Dem.* 93).

[50] For example, Irenaeus writes that "God appeared to [Abraham] in a dream and said, 'I will give you this land, and to your seed after you for an eternal possession'" (*Dem.* 24). These passages are found in *Dem.* 2, *Dem.* 24 (three times), *Dem.* 29, *Dem.* 46, 2.34.4, 3.6.2 (twice), 3.6.5, 4.pre.4, 4.7.4, 4.12.4, 4.15.1, 4.16.1, 4.18.3, 4.20.1, 4.20.9, 4.20.10, 4.29.2, 5.1.3, 5.14.1 (three times), 5.15.4, 5.20.2, 5.21.1, and 5.32.2 (three times).

latter group of citations, though they illustrate that Irenaeus believes the cited work contains the recorded words of God, do not infer anything about the *authorship* of the work in question. The former group of citations, on the other hand, indicate that Irenaeus considers God to be the true *author* of the scriptural work being cited. Of the eighty-eight citations from the Jewish scriptures introduced as the words of God, fifty-eight belong to the former group and have relevance for the present question.

Irenaeus introduces citations from the Jewish scriptures as having been spoken by the Word (or Christ[51]) on sixteen occasions,[52] as in his statement that "the Word says through Isaias, 'The Spirit of … God is upon me'" (3.18.3). Each of these citations is from Isaiah, Jeremiah, the Psalms, or Proverbs. Citations from the Jewish scriptures are also introduced as the words of the Spirit on nineteen occasions,[53] as is illustrated when he says, "the Holy Spirit says through David, 'Blessed is the man who …'" (*Dem.* 2). Seventeen of these citations are from the same prophetic books, while the remaining two are from the Pentateuch.[54] Irenaeus may also introduce citations from the Jewish scriptures as having been spoken by "God" or "the Father," as in his statement that "God says through the prophet Ezekiel, 'And I will give them another heart'" (*Dem.* 93). This occurs twenty-three times, all of which are citations from Amos,[55] Ezekiel,[56] Hosea,[57] Isaiah,[58] Jeremiah,[59] Malachi,[60] or the Psalms.[61]

These passages confirm that at least parts of the Jewish scriptures are consistently claimed to have been authored by God—conforming to the proposed category of *auctoritas* inspiration. They indicate that Irenaeus may equally designate the Word, the Spirit, or God/the Father as the one who speaks through the prophets, without any discernible pattern. The possibility is also suggested that, while all of the Jewish scriptures contain records of divine communication, Irenaeus only declares God to

---

[51] In *Dem.* 50, "Christ" is said to have spoken through David.
[52] *Dem.* 34, *Dem.* 45, *Dem.* 50 (twice), *Dem.* 53, *Dem.* 68, *Dem.* 92, 3.6.1 (twice), 3.18.3, 3.19.1, 4.31.2 (twice), 4.34.4, 5.15.3, and 5.24.1.
[53] *Dem.* 2, *Dem.* 24, *Dem.* 67, *Dem.* 73, 2.34.3 (twice), 3.6.1 (five times), 3.6.5, 3.10.3, 3.21.4 (twice), 4.2.4, 4.20.3 (three times), 5.20.2, and 5.34.3.
[54] *Dem.* 24 and 3.6.1; both citing Genesis. *Dem.* 24 constitutes a clear violation of the pattern. However, it is debatable whether Irenaeus is actually claiming that the Spirit has spoken the passage from Genesis in 3.6.1, or Irenaeus has simply brought in a scripture in support of a number of passages from the Psalms which he certainly does claim to have been spoken by the Spirit. The passage reads: "*merito Spiritus sanctus Domini appelatione signauit eos. Et iterum in euersione Sodomitarum Scriptura ait: 'Et pluit Dominus super Sodomam et Gomorram ignem et sulfur a Domino de caelo'* [Gen. 19:24]. *Filium enim hic significat*" It is unclear in this passage whether the subject of *significat* is *Scriptura* or *Spiritus*. Unger believes the Spirit is the subject, and therefore the one who is said to make the claim recorded in Genesis (ACW 64:38), as he correctly points out that "Irenaeus is continuing his exposition of the Spirit revealing both the Father and the Son as 'Lord,'" and continues to do so throughout the remainder of the paragraph. However, while this point makes Unger's translation plausible, it does not demonstrate that it is any more likely than the alternative, to which Rousseau–Doutreleau (SC 211:67) and Roberts–Donaldson (ANF 1:418) subscribe.
[55] *Dem.* 38.
[56] *Dem.* 93.
[57] 1.10.3, 4.17.4, and 4.20.6.
[58] 1.10.3, 4.18.3, and 4.41.2.
[59] 3.21.9, 4.17.2 (twice), 4.17.3 (twice), 4.19.2, and 4.36.5 (twice).
[60] 4.21.2.
[61] 2.28.7, 4.17.1 (twice), 4.21.3, 4.38.4, and 4.41.2.

be the *author* of the prophetic books, the Psalms, and Proverbs. However, at least one exception casts doubt on this conclusion.[62] The results of this brief survey of Irenaeus' patterns of introducing citations from the Jewish scriptures are confirmed, clarified, and extended by examining a number of Irenaeus' discussions of inspiration as they relate to the composition of these scriptures.

B. Discussions of the Inspiration of the Jewish Scriptures

Irenaeus discusses the inspiration of the Jewish scriptures at a number of places in his writings. His discussions of inspiration can be divided into two categories, corresponding to the questions left unanswered by the analysis of his introductions to citations. His comments indicate his understanding of the *agency* of divine communication, as well as his understanding of the *nature and extent* of the inspiration of the Jewish scriptures.

The Agency of Divine Communication

Attempts to determine Irenaeus' rationale for determining which divine agent is said to be responsible for divine communication initially appear thwarted by seemingly arbitrary or contradictory statements, first attributing prophecy to the Spirit,[63] then to the Word,[64] sometimes one after the other.[65] However, there are a few places where Irenaeus explains his understanding of the divine agency behind inspiration more fully, clarifying the meaning of his other statements. Irenaeus' statement that the scriptures "were given by God's Word and Spirit [*a Verbo Dei et Spiritu eius dictae*]" (2.28.2) communicates that both are active in this process, though without providing any information of the method by which this occurs. His position is articulated further in Book 4 where he mentions the "Word of God who did both visit them through the prophetic Spirit [*per propheticum Spiritum*]" (4.36.8). It may be inferred from this passage that Irenaeus conceives of specific and differing roles for the Word and the Spirit in this process. It is the Word who has spoken prophecies to or through the prophets, and has done so through the agency of the Spirit.

Irenaeus confirms and extends this understanding in the *Demonstration*, asserting that "the Spirit of God ... spoke in the prophets, producing words sometimes from Christ and other times from the Father" (*Dem.* 49). The "words from the Father" mentioned here refer to those passages from the Jewish scriptures that are understood to present the words of the Father to the Word, such as his statement that "we should leave such knowledge ... to God and His Word, to whom alone He said, 'Sit at my right hand until I make Thine enemies Thy footstool'" (2.28.7; citing Ps. 109:2).[66] The

---

[62] Genesis is said to have been spoken by the Spirit once in *Dem.* 24, and possibly a second time in 3.6.1; cf. p. 151 n. 54.
[63] 3.9.3, 3.21.9, 4.20.5, 4.20.8, *Dem.* 30, *Dem.* 42, etc.
[64] 4.10.1, 4.20.4, 4.20.7, 4.20.9.
[65] In 4.11.1 Irenaeus mentions the prophets "seeing through the Holy Spirit [the Word's] advent," before asking in the same paragraph, "how do the Scriptures testify of Him, unless all things had ever been revealed and shown to believers by one and the same God through the Word?" Cf. 4.20.4-8.
[66] Cf. 4.21.3.

passage above from *Dem.* 49 is not an affirmation that Irenaeus believes prophecies were spoken by the Father as well as the Son, as he has explained a few paragraphs prior:

> It is not the Father of all, who is not seen by the world, the Creator of all, who said, "Heaven is my throne and the earth is my footstool ..."[67] and who holds the dry land in His hand and the heavens in his palm, [it is not] this One who, standing in a very small space, talked with Abraham, but the Word of God, who was always with mankind and who foretold things of the future, which were to come to pass, and taught men the things of God. (*Dem.* 45)

In light of this passage, the "words of the Father" mentioned in *Dem.* 49 and occasionally used to introduce citations refer primarily to messianic statements in which the Spirit has presented the words of the Father to the Son in order to foreshadow the Incarnation, rather than referring to prophecies *given by* the Father, for that is not how prophecy functions.[68] As Irenaeus explains, "since the Father is invisible, the Son who is in His bosom declares Him to all. On this account, those to whom the Son revealed Him, know Him" (3.11.6). Ochagavia identifies these two passages as evidence that "the Word is the necessary mediator in imparting to man the knowledge of God"[69] and sees an explanation of this process in Irenaeus' formula: "unto the Father, through His Son, by the Holy Spirit" (*Dem.* 7).

Irenaeus' statements in these passages confirm that depending on the subject at hand, Irenaeus can refer to the Jewish scriptures as having been spoken by the Word, the Spirit, the Father, or "God," in each case referring to the same process of the Father speaking through his Word, by his Spirit. The Father is the ground of all forms of revelation, as the Word speaks the Father's message by the agency of the Spirit. This provides the framework for interpreting Irenaeus' statements of divine agency when introducing citations from the Jewish scriptures and in his comments concerning their inspiration. Which divine agent is mentioned in any specific instance depends on his present purpose. When he wishes to emphasize the process of divine communication he speaks of the Spirit speaking through the prophets, when he wants to emphasize the author of prophecy he speaks of the Word speaking to the prophets, and when he wants to emphasize the will of the Father or refer to those passages that present the words of the Father to the Son in order to foreshadow the Incarnation, he speaks of the

---

[67] Isa. 40:12.
[68] This receives further confirmation from Justin Martyr, *1 apol.* 36–9, whose comments Irenaeus' statement in *Dem.* 49 is undoubtedly based on. Justin states,

> But when you hear the utterances of the prophets spoken as it were personally, you must not suppose that they are spoken by the inspired themselves, but by the Divine Word who moves them. For sometimes He declares things that are to come to pass, in the manner of one who foretells the future; sometimes He speaks as from the person of God the Lord and Father of all; sometimes as from the person of Christ. (ANF 1:175)

For a detailed treatment of Justin Martyr's use of the Jewish Scriptures, as well as a description of Irenaeus' dependence on Justin Martyr, see Oskar Skarsaune, *The Proof from Prophecy: A Study in Justin Martyr's Proof-Text Tradition* (Leiden: Brill, 1987).
[69] Ochagavia, *Visibile*, 61 (59–62).

Father speaking to the prophets or to the Son. In all cases Irenaeus envisions the same thoroughly Trinitarian process of divine communication.

The Nature and Extent of Inspiration

In addition to clarifying Irenaeus' understanding of the agency of divine communication as it relates to the formation of the Jewish scriptures, his comments concerning their inspiration also clarify the nature and extent of the inspiration involved. It has already been demonstrated in Chapter 2 that Irenaeus believes the prophets, guided by the Spirit, intentionally leave the messages spoken to them by the Word scattered throughout their writings, even when they do not claim to be doing so, or appear to be discussing the same subject.[70] Irenaeus' patterns of introducing citations have confirmed that he believes that at least parts of the Jewish scriptures have been authored by God, and suggested the possibility that this *auctoritas* may not extend to the entirety of the Jewish scriptures, while offering little indication of the character of the inspiration involved. A number of his comments about inspiration shed further light on these questions, and when these are viewed as a whole, a clearer picture emerges.

Irenaeus' understanding of the method of inspiration of the Jewish scriptures is stated most explicitly in the *Demonstration*. Here, after adducing Psalm 2:7-8 as an example of a messianic prophecy in which the Father addresses the Son: "The Lord said to me, 'You are my Son, <today> have I begotten you; ask me and I will give you the nations for your inheritance and the ends of the earth as a possession'" (*Dem.* 49), he goes on to explain,

> Since David says, "the Lord says to me," it is necessary to affirm that it is not David nor any other one of the prophets, who speaks from himself—for it is not man who utters prophecies—but [that] the Spirit of God, conforming Himself to the person [ηհմագն; πρόσωπον][71] concerned, spoke in the prophets, producing words sometimes from Christ and at other times from the Father. (*Dem.* 49)

All of the prophecies were spoken by the Spirit; none were the work of human reasoning. The phrase "the Spirit of God, conforming Himself to the person concerned" is not a description of the interaction taking place between the Spirit and the human prophet, but describes the Spirit adopting the *persona* or perspective of either the Son or (as in Irenaeus' example) the Father when making prophetic statements.[72] Rousseau contends that this passage demonstrates that Irenaeus believes the prophet is merely an instrument through whom the Spirit speaks prophecies. However, it is not clear that this passage provides warrant for such a conclusion.[73]

---

[70] Section 2.1B; Conclusion to Section 2.3.
[71] Rousseau believes that ηհմագն is a translation of πρόσωπον, and provides *personae* as the Latin translation (SC 406:156). ηհմակ is translated into English as "facet," "face," or "mask" by Bedrossian, *Armenian-English*, 144.
[72] This is seen more clearly in Justin's *1 apol.* 36–9, which this passage is based on. Cf. p. 153 n. 68 above.
[73] Rousseau claims, "le prophet est un instrument: lorsqu'il parle, c'est un autre qui parle en lui et à travers lui, à savoir l'*Esprit Saint*" (SC 406:308). His reading disregards the context of this chapter, in

The Question of Inspiration 155

In any case, *Dem.* 49 confirms an *auctoritas* understanding of inspiration, in which the message recorded has been divinely authored, and which is understood to extend to all the prophets. Given that Irenaeus considers Moses, David, and Solomon to be among the prophets, it may be presumed that Irenaeus here refers to the entirety of the Jewish scriptures.[74] This is supported by an equivalent sentiment in *Adversus haereses*: "we know very well that the Scriptures are perfect [*perfectae sunt*], inasmuch as they were given [*dictae*] by God's Word and Spirit" (2.28.2). All the (Jewish) scriptures were authored by God, and this provides the basis for their authority. In one final passage, after quoting the words of Jesus in John 5:46-7 that "If ye had believed Moses, ye would have believed me: for he wrote of me," Irenaeus continues,

> He thus indicates in the clearest manner that the writings of Moses are His words [*Moysi litteras suos esse sermones*]. If, then, [this be the case with regard] to Moses, so also, beyond a doubt, the words of the other prophets are His [*prophetarum sermones ipsius sunt*], as I have pointed out. (4.2.3)

Here most explicitly, Irenaeus explains that the entirety of the Jewish scriptures has been authored by the Word.

Conclusion

Examinations of Irenaeus' patterns of introducing citations to the Jewish scriptures and of his comments on inspiration relating to the composition of the Jewish scriptures combine to create a clear picture of a number of aspects of his understanding of the inspiration of the Jewish scriptures and the relation of inspiration to their authoritative scriptural status. Irenaeus consistently states that the whole of the Jewish scriptures is authored by God. His comments indicate that he does not support a *possessio* view of inspiration in which human agency is negated, nor does he affirm only a soft *inspiratio* view. Rather, he clearly and consistently describes an *auctoritas* form of inspiration in which the Word is sent from the Father to transmit a message to (and therefore *through*) the prophets by the agency of the Spirit.[75] The authority of the Jewish

---

which Irenaeus' present intention is to explain that when the prophets give a messianic prophecy in the first person, they are not referring to themselves but to the Son or the Father, whose perspective is assumed by the Spirit who gives the prophecy. It is not necessary to extrapolate that David's agency is denied in this passage, nor is there evidence elsewhere in Irenaeus' writings to support a strong "*possessio*" view of inspiration. Irenaeus often refers to the human agency involved in prophecy, as in 4.2.3, 4.20.4, 4.20.8, 4.27.1, etc. He also appears to indicate a distain for ecstatic prophecy in 1.13.2-5 (cf. Lawson, *Biblical Theology*, 29). However, as Reilly, "L'inspiration," notes, "Saint Irénée ne donne pas beaucoup de détails sur la nature précise de l'inspiration prophétique ou de l'état psychologique du prophète pendant qu'il reçoit ou communique son message, ni par conséquent sur la nature précise de l'inspiration biblique" (496).

[74] Irenaeus declares David to be a prophet in *Dem.* 49; he cites Solomon as a prophet in 4.20.3 and 5.24.1; and he declares Moses to be among the prophets in 2.2.5, 2.30.6, 4.20.9-10, and *Dem.* 43. In addition, Joshua, Samuel, and Ezra are called prophets in 1.30.11, theoretically allowing Irenaeus to account for the books of Joshua, 1 and 2 Samuel, 1 and 2 Chronicles, and Ezra, leaving only a few minor works with no explicit claim to prophetic connection.

[75] Reilly, "L'inspiration," seems to suggest something similar to the proposed category of *auctoritas* when he describes Irenaeus' view of the Jewish scriptures: "On l'interprète comme si vraiment Dieu

scriptures is consistently tied directly to their perceived divine *auctoritas* by Irenaeus, supporting the conclusions reached in Chapter 2 that the basis of the authority of the Jewish scriptures is found in its authorship by the Word.

In the following section, these findings are compared with Irenaeus' comments concerning the role of inspiration in the composition of the apostolic writings, in order to determine what similarities and differences arise, and what these indicate about his understanding of the nature and basis of authority of the apostolic writings.

4.3. Evaluating the Evidence for the Divine *Auctoritas* of the Apostolic Writings

It has been shown above that Irenaeus affirms the inspiration of the apostles and their writings.[76] The type of inspiration identified in the passages described there falls into the proposed *inspiratio* category of revelation, establishing divine interaction with human agents without indicating divine authorship of the messages they preach and put into writing. This element of the Spirit's activity, at least, does not provide a basis for the unique revelatory authority of the apostles' writings. In order to affirm the possibility of inspiration providing the foundation for their unique revelatory authority it is therefore necessary to locate, in addition to inspiration of the *inspiratio* type, evidence that Irenaeus also acknowledges *auctoritas* inspiration for the apostolic writings. The investigation in this section therefore seeks to determine whether and to what extent Irenaeus describes an *auctoritas* form of inspiration for the apostolic writings, using his comments on the inspiration of the Jewish scriptures as a point of comparison.

A. References to Inspiration in Introductions to Citations from the Apostolic Writings

When Irenaeus' introductions to his citations from the apostolic writings throughout his works are surveyed, he is found to introduce fourteen passages as having been spoken by God, the Word, or the Son.[77] In one case it is the audible words of the Father to Christ within the narrative of Luke 2:14 that are being cited (3.10.6), while in every other instance Irenaeus is citing the recorded words of Christ, rather than claiming that the Word spoke *through* an apostle. In addition to these, Irenaeus introduces two passages from the apostolic writings as having been spoken by the Spirit. These are the only two passages that represent possible claims of divine *auctoritas* of the apostolic writings.

---

avait dicté à son prophète. La distinction entre révélation et inspiration dans l'A.T. est inconnue aux auteurs du deuxième siècle" (506).

[76] Cf. 4.1.
[77] These are found in 1.26.3, 3.10.6, 3.18.5, 3.19.1, 3.22.1, 4.2.5, 4.9.2, 4.13.4, 4.14.1, 4.20.11, 4.36.8, 5.17.1, 5.22.1, and 5.24.4. All of these are citations from the gospels or Revelation (1.26.3 and 4.20.11).

The first passage takes place in 4.8.1. Here, in the midst of demonstrating that there is only one Father, who is known through the Son, Irenaeus states,

> Vain, too is [the effort of] Marcion and his followers when they [seek to] exclude Abraham from the inheritance, to whom the Spirit through many men, and now by Paul, bears witness [*cui Spiritus per multos, jam autem et per Paulum, testimonium reddit*], that "he believed God, and it was imputed unto him for righteousness." (4.8.1)

In this passage Irenaeus unequivocally states that the Spirit has given testimony through Paul, citing his words in either Romans 4:3 or Galatians 3:6. This echoes his introductions to citations from the Jewish scriptures as the words of the Spirit, suggesting an *auctoritas* form of inspiration for Paul's writings. As Benoit states, "Paul appears here, in the same manner of the figures of the Old Testament, as the instrument of the Holy Spirit."[78] However, the cited passage is in fact Paul's citation of Genesis 15:6. Irenaeus' comment is a description of the fact that the Spirit spoke through Moses, and the Spirit's testimony concerning Abraham is now given through Paul's citation of it. Paul's citation is the medium through which the words of the Spirit (through Moses) are heard again. Paul is inspired by the Spirit, but it was the Spirit's *auctoritas* inspiration of Moses that is responsible for the composition of the message quoted by Paul. This passage therefore is further evidence of the divine *auctoritas* of the Jewish scriptures, rather than the apostolic writings.

This leaves one possible instance of Irenaeus introducing a citation from the apostolic writings as the words of God. It occurs in 3.16.2, and is perhaps the most commonly cited passage as evidence of the inspiration (and resulting scriptural status) of the apostolic writings.[79] After stating in the previous paragraph that "through the Holy Spirit [the apostles] even pointed out the ones who would in the future teach [heretical doctrines]" (3.16.1), Irenaeus explains the proper interpretation of Matthew 1:18-23, saying,

> Thus [Matthew] clearly indicates that the promise that had been made to the fathers was fulfilled, namely, that the Son of God was born of the Virgin, and that this one is Himself the Savior Christ whom the prophets foretold. It is not, as these heretics assert, that Jesus indeed is the one who was born of Mary, but that Christ is the one who descended from on high. In that case, Matthew would have said, "the generation of *Jesus* was in this wise." But since the Holy Spirit foresaw the perverters, He fortified against their fraud beforehand by saying through Matthew [*sed prouidens Spiritus sanctus deprauatores et praemuniens contra fraudulentiam eorum, per Matthaeum ait*], "The generation of Christ was in this wise;" and also

---

[78] Benoit, *Irénée*, 138; my trans. Cf. Flesseman-van Leer, *Tradition*, 130; Farkasfalvy, "Theology," 331; Hoh, *Lehre*, 90; Werner, *Paulinismus*, 30.

[79] Cf. Bruce, *Canon*, 175–6; Lawson, *Biblical Theology*, 31–2; Benoit, *Irénée*, 138 n. 1; Campenhausen, *Formation*, 205 n. 290; Hoh, *Lehre*, 90; Hitchcock, *Irenaeus*, 194; Harris, *Inspiration and Canonicity*, 79–80, 247–8; Flesseman-van Leer, *Tradition*, 130; Briggman, *Holy Spirit*, 50 n. 17; Werner, *Paulinismus*, 30; etc.

that this one is "Emmanuel," so that we would not consider Him merely a man. (3.16.2)

This passage once again mirrors the numerous instances in which Irenaeus has declared a passage from the Jewish scriptures to have been spoken by the Spirit, through the human writer. It therefore appears to suggest that inspiration of the *auctoritas* type extends also to the apostolic writings, at least in certain instances. According to Bruce, this passage demonstrates that Irenaeus believes "inspiration extended to the choice of one word rather than another."[80]

The use of this passage as evidence of *auctoritas* inspiration is hindered by the fact that Irenaeus makes a similar claim for a non-apostolic figure just a few chapters later, when he states,

> Elizabeth, "filled with the Holy Spirit [*impleta Spiritu sancto*],"[81] bore witness [to this] when she said to Mary, "Blessed are you among women, and blessed is the fruit of your womb." By this the Holy Spirit pointed out [*significante Spiritu sancto*], to all who wished to hear, that the promise that God had made. (3.21.5)

Irenaeus' equivalent claim for the inspiration of Elizabeth in this passage suggests that his claim in 3.16.2 above is not intended to communicate that Matthew is the recipient of any sort of unique *auctoritas* inspiration, but is something of a figure of speech by which to highlight the Spirit's inspiring role. Whatever the form of Matthew's inspiration in 3.16.2 entails, Irenaeus does not hesitate to apply it equally to non-apostolic figures.

It is much more common for Irenaeus to claim that the Spirit grants insight to the apostles, rather than using them as instruments. This is illustrated a few paragraphs after 3.16.2, when Irenaeus makes a similar claim about Paul, repeating his familiar contention that the apostles foresaw things through the Spirit. He says, "Indeed, foreknowing through the Spirit [*Praeuidens enim et ipse per Spiritum*] the subdivisions of these evil teachers, and wishing to cut off from them every occasion for contention, [Paul] expressed what has been mentioned" (3.16.9). Here Irenaeus has returned to his standard practice of placing the emphasis of agency on the human writer,[82] indicating an *inspiratio* understanding seemingly contradicting the possible *auctoritas* implications of 3.16.2 (and 3.21.5).[83]

The results of this remarkably brief survey indicate that when Irenaeus' introductions to citations from the Jewish scriptures and the apostolic writings are compared, the most significant finding is the stark contrast evident in references to inspiration. Irenaeus almost entirely refrains from introducing passages from the apostolic writings

---

[80] Bruce, *Canon*, 176.
[81] Lk. 1:41.
[82] Cf. 3.16.1, 4.pre.3.
[83] Hoh, *Lehre*, contends based on the seeming contradiction between 3.16.2 and 3.16.9 that Irenaeus "schient auf eine solche Unterscheidung kein Gewicht gelegt zu haben" between "*spiritus ait per*" and "*apostolus praevidens per spiritum*" (94). For him divine *auctoritas* is entailed by all such passages. A similar conclusion is reached by Werner, *Paulinismus*, 30.

as having been spoken by God: of his approximately 1,000 citations from the apostolic writings,[84] only one possible instance of Irenaeus suggesting that a passage from the apostolic writings has been authored by God is discovered.[85] This represents a massive discrepancy from his introductions to citations from the Jewish scriptures, in which fifty-eight of only approximately 500 citations are introduced as the words of God. A discrepancy of this magnitude limits the possibility of further points of comparison, but this alone suggests a significant distinction in Irenaeus' conception of the nature and extent of the inspiration of the Jewish scriptures and apostolic writings. It is also notable that passages from the apostolic writings are never introduced as having been spoken by the Word or God/the Father, as is routinely claimed of the Jewish scriptures. Instead, the sole possible instance of divine *auctoritas* is attributed to the Spirit, just as his statements exhibiting an *inspiratio* form of inspiration for the apostolic writings were observed to be.

B. Discussions of the Inspiration of the Apostolic Writings

Outside of his introductions to citations, there are a few additional passages within *Adversus haereses* that have traditionally been interpreted as affirmations of the (*auctoritas*) inspiration of the apostolic writings and their resulting scriptural status.[86] Two of the most prominent are found in 2.28.2-3: "the Scriptures are perfect, inasmuch as they were given by God's Word and Spirit" (2.28.2), and "all the Scriptures are spiritual" (2.28.3).[87] Bokedal, for example, cites 2.28.3 as evidence that an "important feature ascribed to '*all* the Scriptures' is their character as inspired text."[88] It has been concluded in Chapter 1 that the title αἱ γραφαί is reserved for the Jewish scriptures, and that in these passages αἱ γραφαί is used for this purpose. It may therefore be equally concluded that these passages give no indication of Irenaeus' understanding of the nature and extent of the inspiration of the apostolic writings. Hans von Campenhausen comes to the same conclusion, maintaining in reference to the use of 2.28.2 to establish the New Testament as the

---

[84] Blanchard, *Sources*, counts 950 New Testament citations (and 1,800 total references) from the indexes of the SC editions for *Adversus haereses* alone (122–3). Hoh, *Lehre*, catalogues 1,122 New Testament citations (out of 1,778 total references) across all of Irenaeus' works (198; cf. 189–99).
[85] Campenhausen, *Formation*, similarly notes that 3.16.2 is "the only text which could possibly be adduced in support of [this] thesis" (205 n. 290).
[86] For example, Hoh, *Lehre*, provides a brief examination of Irenaeus' view of the inspiration of the apostolic writings (90–4), which identifies a conception of the relationship between God and the apostolic writers that can only be classified as divine *auctoritas* (94–5). He concludes that although Irenaeus is not concerned to answer the question, "Seine Prinzipien drängen zur Annahme der Verbalinspiration" (95).
[87] Cf. McDonald, "Identifying Scripture," 435; *Formation*, 240; Blanchard, *Sources*, 126–7; Hitchcock, *Irenaeus*, 194; Hoh, *Lehre*, 92; Osborn, *Irenaeus*, 162; Flesseman-van Leer, *Tradition*, 130; Minns, *Irenaeus*, 137. Hill, "Patristic Period," 55; Grant, *Letter and Spirit*, 81; Harris, *Inspiration and Canonicity*, 79–80.
[88] Bokedal, *Significance*, 295. Inspiration is understood by Bokedal to be central to the formation of the New Testament canon: "Thus, when considering second-century canon reception, the question of inspiration is crucial."

inspired Word of God that such a view "overlooks the fact that here only the O.T. Scriptures can be meant."[89]

Another passage that has been understood to indicate the scriptural status of the apostolic writings on the basis of inspiration occurs in 3.1.1, where Irenaeus defends the apostles' knowledge of the Gospel against his opponents' claim that the apostles were ignorant of certain aspects. In response to this charge, Irenaeus claims,

> We are not permitted to say that [the apostles] preached before they had received "perfect knowledge" [*perfectam agnitionem*], as some dare to state, boasting that they are correctors of the apostles. For, after our Lord had risen from the dead, and "they were clothed with power [*uirtutem*] from on high when the Spirit came upon them,"[90] they had full assurance concerning all things [*de omnibus adimpleti sunt*], and had "perfect knowledge" [*perfectam agnitionem*]. (3.1.1)[91]

The apostles are filled with the Spirit, just as Luke-Acts describes, and the Spirit ensures that the apostles possess "perfect knowledge." Harris, who claims that "The Scriptures are true, according to Irenaeus, because they are apostolic and therefore inspired," finds in 3.1.1 proof that "This apostolic authority is the result of their induement with the Holy Spirit."[92] The inspiration described by Irenaeus here is intended to demonstrate that, by the aid of the Spirit, the apostles possess the full understanding of the Gospel message. Irenaeus does not, however, intend to convey that their "perfect knowledge" consists in having received the message that they preached and wrote down directly from the Spirit, as the divine basis of its unique revelatory authority. Irenaeus clarifies this point and explains what he means by "perfect knowledge" later in Book 3. After repeating that the apostles "were made perfect by the Spirit [διὰ τοῦ Πνεύματος τελειωθέντων[93]]" (3.12.5), he goes on to ask:

> Or did Peter then not yet possess the perfect knowledge [*perfectam cognitionem*] that these [heretics] discovered later? As such, according to them, Peter was imperfect [*imperfectus*], and the rest of the apostles were imperfect [*imperfecti*]. (3.12.7)

---

[89] Campenhausen, *Formation*, 205 n. 290. This conclusion is also reached by Farkasfalvy, "Theology," 326.

[90] Lk. 24:49; Acts 1:8; Acts 2:4.

[91] Unger's translation illustrates the common interpretation of this passage. Cf. my translation of this passage in Section 3.1B, where *perfectam agnitionem* is rendered as "complete knowledge."

[92] Harris, *Inspiration and Canonicity*, 247–8. He also uses this passage to defend his claim that "When we come to the great authors of the late second century where the witness abounds, we also find full testimony to belief in a doctrine of inspiration that must be described as verbal" (79–80). Briggman, *Holy Spirit*, claims on the basis of 3.1.1 that "Irenaeus views the Spirit as the source of the oral and written message of the Apostles" (48). He further describes Irenaeus as "founding the unity and authority of the oral and written traditions on the work of the Spirit" and "basing the transmission of every message of the gospel on the work of the same Spirit" (50). Cf. Hoh, *Lehre*, 90.

[93] This phrase is rendered in the Latin translation as "*per Spiritum et perfecti exstiterunt*," suggesting that the Latin *perficio*/*perfectus* always translates τελειόω/τέλειος in this context, as in 3.1.1 above where the Greek text has been lost. Rousseau-Doutreleau's Greek retroversion of 3.1.1 agrees (SC 211:21).

Both here and in 3.1.1 above, Irenaeus calls the apostles "perfect" (τέλειος) in response to the Valentinian claim that the apostles did not know the full truth (3.2.2). Irenaeus is not contending that the apostles or their message have somehow been divinized or made "perfect" bearers of the Gospel, but that the apostles have received the *complete* truth, as τέλειος implies.[94] The apostles' endowment with the Spirit assures us that they are not deficient in their knowledge of the Gospel, or ignorant of some special knowledge that Irenaeus' opponents claim to possess.[95]

Irenaeus continues to explain what he means by "perfect knowledge" a few paragraphs later. After detailing some of the ways in which the Marcionites and Valentinians corrupt "the doctrine of the Gospel" (3.12.12), he explains that "both the apostles and their disciples thought exactly as the Church preaches, and were by this teaching made perfect and were called to perfection [*et sic docentes perfecti fuerunt, propter quod et euocabantur ad perfectum*]" (3.12.13). He continues, labeling the church's teaching "the perfect doctrine [*perfectam doctrinam*]" and explaining, "In this manner those were perfect [*perfecti*] who recognized one and the same God as assisting the human race from the beginning to the end by the various economies" (3.12.13). Perfection, according to Irenaeus, consists in holding the true teaching of the Gospel, and it is the possession of this "perfect doctrine" that makes one perfect. Irenaeus makes clear that being made perfect is not an exclusive property of the apostles but extends to their disciples and anyone who keeps the teaching of the church.

In light of Irenaeus' extensive comments on "perfect knowledge" and being made "perfect," his comments in 3.1.1 are clarified. Absent is any claim of the Spirit divinely authoring the message of the apostles, as the Word had previously done for the prophets. The "perfect knowledge" possessed by the apostles is the complete knowledge of the Gospel,[96] possessed also by all others in the church who similarly have the Spirit and are thus equally inspired.

Another passage commonly cited as evidence of the inspiration and resulting scriptural status of the apostolic writings occurs within Irenaeus' arguments concerning the proper interpretation of Paul's words in ch. 7 of Book 3. After arguing for his interpretation of 2 Corinthians 4:4, Irenaeus states,

> From many other examples we can discover that the apostle frequently uses a transposed order of words because of the speed of his speech and the impulse of the Spirit that is in him [*et propter impetum qui in ipso est Spiritus*]. (3.7.2)

---

[94] Rousseau–Doutreleau provide τέλειος as the Greek term behind *perfectus* in their Greek retroversion of 3.12.7 (SC 211:213). Ἀτελής, Rousseau–Doutreleau's retroversion of *imperfectus* (supported by the Greek text preserving 3.12.5), indicates that the opposite of "perfect" is "incomplete" or "unfinished," signaling the intended meaning of Irenaeus' phrase *perfectus cognitio*.

[95] Cf. Campenhausen, *Formation*, 189–90.

[96] This point has also been made by Lawson, *Biblical Theology*, who states,

> The doctrine typical of and general to Irenaeus is not that of a Spirit who comes to dwell in an individual prophet and inspires him to declare a new truth, but of a Spirit who indwells and lifts to perfection those who faithfully adhere to the established tradition of truth. ... when Irenaeus is seeking to establish the authority of the four Evangelists, he is content to do so upon the natural ground of human knowledge, and has nothing to say about ecstasy or other unusual phenomena. (29–30)

Benoit interprets this passage as a claim by Irenaeus that "when Paul writes, it is the Spirit who speaks,"[97] though if this were the case, Irenaeus would then be attributing Paul's mistakes to the Spirit, rather than granting him divine authority on this basis. However, Irenaeus here only affirms what he has already declared in 3.1.1, that the apostles have received the Spirit. Irenaeus presumably wishes to lay the blame for Paul's numerous grammatical mistakes on his passion to proclaim the Gospel at the urging of the Spirit within him, a desire that Irenaeus makes evident throughout 3.7.1-2. There is no basis to uphold Benoit's interpretation of this passage as evidence of the divine *auctoritas* of the apostolic writings. The same conclusion is reached by Johannes Werner, who finds in this passage proof that Irenaeus conceives of a distinction between the inspiration of the Jewish scriptures (and the gospels) and that of the Pauline epistles:

> For it must obviously be another concept of the holiness of the text and of inspiration, which allows one to accuse Paul of arbitrary obscurity in his texts and to explain his *hyperbata* themselves, as Irenaeus has done (III, 7, 1 ff). Nor would he in this way, as he strives to dismantle—he calls it *exponere*—the contents of the Pauline letters, have spoken of the necessity of a clarification of the meaning of the other writings.[98]

One final passage is often adduced as evidence of the inspiration and resulting scriptural status of the apostolic writings. In his defense of the reliability of the Septuagint translation, Irenaeus argues that the translation agrees with the tradition of the apostles, who "are much earlier than all of these [heretics]" (3.21.3), and then concludes,

> For one and the same Spirit of God, who indeed in the prophets foretold how and in what manner the Lord would come, and in the elders translated well what had been prophesied well, Himself also in the apostles announced [*ipse et in apostolis adnuntiauit*] that the fullness of the times of the adoption had come, and that "the kingdom of the heavens was near," and that it dwells within the people who believe in Emmanuel who was born from the Virgin. As they themselves testify. (3.21.4)[99]

---

[97] Benoit, *Irénée*, 138; my trans. That Irenaeus does not make this claim more directly is due to the fact that "Pour ce qui est de Paul, Irénée est bien obligé de tenir compte du facteur humain, qu'il avait négligé chez les prophètes de l'Ancien Testament. Il remarque que le style paulinien est difficile et prête à cause de la rapidité de ses paroles et de l'impétuosité de l'Esprit qui est en lui," referencing 3.7.2. Cf. also Hitchcock, *Irenaeus*, 195; Lawson, *Biblical Theology*, 31; Hoh, *Lehre*, 90; Harris, *Inspiration and Canonicity*, 247–8; Briggman, *Holy Spirit*, 50 n. 17; Farkasfalvy, "Theology," 327 and 331.

[98] Werner, *Paulinismus*, 34; my trans.

[99] My trans. Unger renders the relevant clause "preached in turn through the apostles" (ACW 64:99); Roberts–Donaldson translate it "He did Himself, by the apostles, announce" (ANF 1:452); Rousseau-Doutreleau suggest "c'est encore lui qui, chez les apôtres, a annoncé" (SC 211:411). The Latin *in* is almost certainly a translation of the Greek ἐν.

Here Irenaeus appears to attribute the same work of the Spirit in authoring the message of the Jewish scriptures and inspiring the Septuagint translation (3.21.2) also to the preaching of the apostles, leading Benoit to the conclusion that the apostolic writings are therefore inspired in identical fashion to the Jewish scriptures.[100] Benoit's interpretation of this passage as a claim that "the Spirit who has spoken by the prophets speaks also by the apostles" is not unreasonable; yet this passage displays a level of ambiguity regarding the role of the Spirit in relation to those it inspires, resisting definitive conclusions. Irenaeus' purpose in this section is to defend the virgin birth of Christ by demonstrating the harmony between the Septuagint translation and the tradition of the apostles, which he does primarily by showing that the apostles support and make use of the Septuagint translation (3.21.3). In light of this, it would be reasonable to interpret his claim here as an affirmation that the Spirit has ensured this harmony between the two, rather than as a claim that the Spirit spoke through the apostles as through the prophets, as Benoit suggests. This passage also occurs immediately before Irenaeus describes the same type of inspiration by the Spirit for Elizabeth (3.21.5), further impeding Benoit's interpretation. Nonetheless, this passage remains the most likely candidate for evidence of an affirmation of the *auctoritas* inspiration of the apostolic writings.

Taken as a whole, Irenaeus' discussions of the inspiration of the apostolic writings lead to conclusions similar to those of his introductions to citations. Once again there is a single instance of possible divine *auctoritas* of the apostolic writings. This contrasts sharply with Irenaeus' dozens of explicit claims of the divine *auctoritas* of the Jewish scriptures, including his unparalleled claim that "it is not David nor any other one of the prophets, who speaks from himself—for it is not man who utters prophecies—but the Spirit of God ... spoke in the prophets" (*Dem.* 49), for which the apostles and their writings have no equivalent. Irenaeus is also found once again to mention the inspiration of the apostolic writings only in relation to the Spirit, mirroring those statements that exhibit only an *inspiratio* form of inspiration for the apostolic writings, and contrasting with his comments on the inspiration of the Jewish scriptures.

This survey of Irenaeus' introductions to citations from and discussions of inspiration in relation to the apostolic writings has identified two passages (3.16.2 and 3.21.4)[101] that could indicate the existence of *auctoritas* inspiration of the apostolic writings. This contrasts with nearly a hundred unambiguous statements of the divine *auctoritas* of the Jewish scriptures. Neither passage occurs in the context of Irenaeus setting out to describe the inspiration or basis of authority of the apostolic writings, and both passages have other plausible interpretations that do not entail divine

---

[100] Benoit, *Irénée*, asks, "La même doctrine de l'inspiration [as the Jewish scriptures] est-elle appliquée par Irénée aux lettres de Paul?" and answers, on the basis of 3.21.4, "Ce que l'on peut d'abord constater, c'est que l'Esprit qui a parlé par les prophétes, parle aussi par les Apôtres et par Paul" (138). Cf. Werner, *Paulinismus*, 29; Unger, ACW 55:8; Farkasfalvy, "Theology," 331; Blanchard, *Sources*, 144; Osborn, *Irenaeus*, 177.

[101] Campenhausen, *Formation*, believes that 3.16.2 is in fact the only possible passage that could support the thesis that the New Testament was considered by Irenaeus to be the "inspired Word of God," and doubts that even this passage is meant to communicate such a view (205 n. 290).

auctoritas. Irenaeus' description of inspiration by the Spirit in both passages mirrors his numerous descriptions of the *inspiratio* inspiration of the apostles and the rest of the church, rather than that of the Jewish Scriptures. These findings combine to demonstrate an evident contrast between the inspiration of the apostolic writings and the Jewish scriptures, suggesting the conclusion that only the Jewish scriptures are understood by Irenaeus to be the product of divine *auctoritas*.

C. Statements That Oppose Divine *auctoritas* for the Apostolic Writings

In addition to the conclusions reached in the previous section, Irenaeus also makes a number of statements that oppose the divine *auctoritas* of the apostolic writings. These statements fall into three categories: (1) divine authorship is claimed for the Jewish scriptures to the exclusion of the apostolic writings; (2) the authority of the apostolic writings is defended on the basis of proximity to Christ, rather than inspiration; and (3) Irenaeus presents a pneumatology that rules out divine *auctoritas* for the apostolic writings.

Divine Authorship Is Claimed for the Jewish Scriptures to the Exclusion of the Apostolic Writings

It is common for Irenaeus to directly equate the Jewish scriptures with the Spirit while simultaneously drawing a distinction between the Spirit and the apostles, indicating a distinction in his understanding of the inspiration of the two written collections and the bases of their authority. This practice can be observed in ch. 5 of Book 3. Here Irenaeus attempts to demonstrate that the apostles did not lie or accommodate their teachings to the views of their audience (as the Valentinians claim), in the course of which he refers to the categories of "the Lord's discourses," "the prophets," and "the apostles" (3.5.3), before concluding in the following paragraph,

> Therefore neither the Lord, nor the Holy Spirit, nor the apostles would precisely and absolutely ever have named "God" one who was not God, unless He was truly God. (3.6.1)

Irenaeus has replaced "the prophets" with "the Holy Spirit" in the second passage, indicating his view of the agency behind the composition of the Jewish scriptures without extending the same divine agency to the apostolic writings. Throughout the rest of 3.6.1, seven passages from Genesis and the Psalms are cited in quick succession as having been spoken by the Spirit, confirming that "Holy Spirit" is intended as a reference to the Jewish scriptures. In this way the Jewish scriptures are set apart from the apostolic writings as the words of the Spirit. Three chapters later Irenaeus returns once again to the original formula, "neither the prophets nor the apostles nor Christ the Lord in His own name acknowledged any other as Lord or God but the one who is preeminently God and Lord" (3.9.1), confirming the interchangeability of the Spirit with the prophets, to the exclusion of the apostolic writings.

Irenaeus follows a similar pattern in Book 4, where he states,

> There is none other called God by the Scriptures [*appellari a Scripturis*] except the Father of all, and the Son, and those who possess the adoption.[102] [4.1.1] Since, therefore, this is sure and steadfast, that no other God was announced by the Spirit [*a Spiritu praedicatum*], except Him who, as God, rules over all, together with His Word, and those who received the Spirit of adoption, that is, those who believe in the one and true God, and in Jesus Christ the Son of God; and likewise that the apostles did of themselves term no one else as God [*similiter et Apostolos neminem alium a semetipsis Deum appellasse*]. (4.pre.4-1.1)

Here Irenaeus uses "Scripture" and "the Spirit" interchangeably in consecutive sentences, and once again sets the apostles apart as distinct from the Spirit/scriptures. This decision is difficult to account for if Irenaeus is held to take the apostolic writings to be equally authored by the Spirit.[103]

A number of Irenaeus' statements elsewhere suggest similar implications.[104] Taken as a whole, these passages demonstrate a pattern of attributing divine *auctoritas* to the Jewish scriptures alone, to the explicit exclusion of the apostolic writings, contradicting his supposed claims in 3.16.2 and 3.21.4.

The Authority of the Apostolic Writings Is Defended on the Basis of Proximity to Christ, Rather Than Inspiration

A number of Irenaeus' discussions of the apostolic writings also resist the conclusion that their authority is based on their (*auctoritas*) inspiration. When Irenaeus defends the authority of the apostles, he does not do so on the basis of their inspiration, as he consistently does with the Jewish scriptures. The gospels of Mark and Luke (as well as Acts), for example, are argued at great lengths by Irenaeus to be equally as authoritative as anything written by an apostle, yet without recourse to claims of equivalent inspiration. Instead, Irenaeus argues solely on the basis of the writers' direct relationship to the apostles. Mark is held up as "Peter's translator and follower" (3.10.6),[105] while Luke is called "the follower and disciple of the apostles" (3.10.1), and "Paul's inseparable companion and his fellow worker in the Gospel" (3.14.1).[106] Defending Luke's narrative in Acts, Irenaeus writes,

> Since Luke was present for all these events, he wrote them down carefully and so cannot be reproved as a liar or one who is puffed up, because all these things make

---

[102] A reference to Ps. 81:6 (LXX), discussed in 3.6.1.
[103] Kalin, *Inspiration*, also identifies 3.6.1 and 4.1.1 as evidence that "'the Sprit' in these passages is a designation for the Old Testament prophetic witness," which he explains "is clear both from the context and from the parallel expression Irenaeus uses several times elsewhere to designate the same trio of witnesses" (18). Cf. Sesboüé, "Preuve," who similarly concludes on the basis of 3.6.1 that "the Spirit" is synonymous with "the Old Testament" for Irenaeus (881-2).
[104] 1.10.1, 4.6.6, 4.20.5, *Dem.* 6, etc.
[105] Cf. 3.1.1.
[106] Cf. 3.1.1.

it clear that he is older than all those who now teach something different, and that he was not ignorant of the truth. That he was not merely a follower of the apostles but also a fellow worker, especially of Paul, Paul himself declared in his letters. (3.14.1)[107]

If Irenaeus considered inspiration to be the basis of Luke's authority, one would expect this argument to come into play. Instead, his authority is defended solely on the basis of his status as an eyewitness and his direct relationship to Paul.

The same is true of the apostles themselves, who also are not defended as authoritative on the basis of their inspiration. In ch. 5 of Book 3, Irenaeus is concerned to demonstrate the authority of the writings of the apostles against those who claim that they were dishonest or lacked full knowledge. In his defense of the apostles as being "beyond all falsehood" (3.5.1)[108] he makes no claim to inspiration, as one would expect if he understood the inspiration of their writings to be the source or guarantee of their authority.[109] Instead he argues that they were "sent to search out these who had gone astray," and addressed their hearers "according to the manifestation of the truth [*ueritatis manifestationem*]" (3.5.2). It is clear what "manifestation of the truth" refers to "The Word ... who was manifested to men [φανερωθεὶς τοῖς ἀνθρώποις],[110] gave us the fourfold Gospel" (3.11.8). The incarnate Christ is the "manifestation of the truth" from whom the apostles receive their teaching and their authority, as Irenaeus confirms a few sentences further in 3.5.2: "the Lord brought knowledge to his disciples, by which he both cured the ailing and forced sinners away from sin." Instead of appealing to inspiration, Irenaeus maintains that the source of the apostles' authority is the incarnate Christ.

Irenaeus repeats this claim on numerous occasions:

> For the Lord of all things gave to His apostles the power of the Gospel [*Etenim Dominus omnium dedit apostolis sui potestatem Euangelii*], and through them we, too, know the truth, that is, the doctrine of God's Son. To them the Lord also said, "He who hears you hears me; and he who despises you, despises me and Him who sent me" (3.pre).
>
> Thus the apostles, whom the Lord made witnesses of all His acts and His doctrine—as a matter of fact, Peter and James and John were always found present with him ... (3.12.15)

---

[107] Cf. Flesseman-van Leer, *Tradition*, 131.
[108] My trans.
[109] This is especially the case in light of the fact that in his description of the false claims of the heretics against the apostles in 3.2.2, Irenaeus points out that his opponents claimed "not only the apostles but the Lord Himself gave discourses derived at times from the Demiurge, at others from the Intermediate Region, and at yet others from the Highest Authority." One would expect that such an account of the imperfect inspiration of the apostles would be answered with a counterclaim of inspiration by the Spirit as the basis of their authority.
[110] Φανερωθεὶς appears in Latin as *declaratus* here, but previously in the same sentence, *manifestum est* translates φανερὸν, indicating that *manifestus/manifestatio* are translations of forms of φανερός/φανέρωσις where they occur without Greek attestation, as in 3.5.2 above. Rousseau-Doutreleau agree in their Greek retroversion of 3.5.2 (SC 211:59).

Thus did the apostles, with simplicity and with envy toward no one, hand down [*tradebant*] to all whatever they had learned from the Lord. (3.14.2)

The ideas of the apostles have been set forth ... who from the beginning were eye-witnesses and ministers of the word of truth [*Verbi veritatis*]. (4.pre.3)[111]

Irenaeus consistently maintains that while the Spirit inspires and "perfects" their knowledge (3.1.1), it is Christ, the incarnate Word, who has given the apostles their teachings and is the basis of their authority. These statements stand in contradiction to the view that Irenaeus believes the apostles or their writings possess their unique revelatory authority on the basis of their (*auctoritas*) inspiration.

Irenaeus' Pneumatology Rules Out Divine auctoritas *for the Apostolic Writings*

A third factor opposing the *auctoritas* inspiration of the apostolic writings arises from Irenaeus' pneumatology. The only two passages that might suggest divine *auctoritas* concern the work of the Spirit (3.16.2 and 3.21.4), yet Irenaeus presents a pneumatology that rules out the possibility that the Spirit could be the agent behind the *auctoritas* of the apostolic writings. The first reason for this is that in Irenaeus' conception the Spirit who had previously inspired the prophets now performs a different role within the divine economy after the Incarnation.[112] While previously the prophets were endowed with a unique charism of inspiration, after Pentecost the Spirit was poured out in a new way upon the whole church.[113] Irenaeus describes these differing roles when he writes of

---

[111] Cf. 3.21.3, in which Irenaeus bases the authority of the apostles on the fact that they were earlier than his opponents; as well as 3.4.3, in which his opponents are denied authority because they were later than the apostles. The implication of these passages is that proximity to Christ is a central mark of authority. Even Paul, who was not an eyewitness, has his authority traced to a vision from Christ prior to his preaching (3.12.9), rather than on the basis of the inspiration of his words or writings by the Spirit. Cf. Flesseman-van Leer, *Tradition*, who also points to 1.9.2, 3.1.1, and 3.3.4 as examples of Irenaeus founding John's authority on his direct relationship to Christ, the point being that "these books contain that which the apostles had heard from Jesus Christ" (131 n. 5).

[112] This point has been raised by Kalin with reference to Irenaeus and a number of other patristic figures, particularly in relation to reactions to the Montanist movement. He challenges the notion that the early church responded to the Montanist claim of special inspiration by asserting that the inspiration of the Spirit was confined to the apostles just as it had been to the prophets, and contends against this that they affirmed instead that the Spirit had been poured out on the whole church. Cf. *Inspiration*, 1–4, 26–9, and 38–43; "Inspired Community," 543–5. Kalin writes,

> The idea that the Spirit had ceased in Israel with the last of the prophets was mentioned by several early Christian authors, among them Justin, Irenaeus, and Origen. But in every case the idea that the Spirit had ceased among the Jews with the last of the prophets was accompanied not by the idea that he had ceased among the Christians with the last of the apostles, but instead by the idea that the Holy Spirit, having ended his presence among the Jews, had been poured out in all His fullness and with all His gifts on the Christians, among whom He continued to abide and act. (544)

[113] Briggman, *Holy Spirit*, though he acknowledges the significance of Luke's account of Pentecost and the new outpouring of the Spirit upon the church for Irenaeus' thought (46–51, 78, 86–9), nevertheless appears to ignore the differing roles of the Spirit prior to and after Pentecost, and imply instead that the Spirit was uniquely poured out on the apostles in the same fashion as the prophets and is the basis of their special authority. He contends that "Irenaeus views the Spirit as

the Holy Spirit, through whom the prophets prophesied and the patriarchs learnt the things of God and the righteous were led in the path of righteousness, and who, in the last times, was poured out in a new fashion upon the human race renewing man, throughout the world, to God. (*Dem.* 6)

No specific relationship to the apostles or their writings is noted by Irenaeus in his description of the various roles of the Spirit, who is described instead as having been poured out upon humanity. This change in the Spirit's role is understood by Irenaeus to have been prophesied beforehand, as he explains that Isaiah had prophesied that Israel

> would no longer possess the Holy Spirit from God, as Isaias said, "I will also command the clouds they rain no rain upon it,"[114] and that, on the contrary, on the entire earth there would be dew, which is the Spirit of God, who descended on the Lord ... The Lord Himself in turn gave Him to the Church, when He sent upon the entire earth the Paraclete from heaven [*in omnem terram mittens de caelis Paraclitum*]. (3.17.3)[115]

This Paraclete is "the one whom He promised through the prophets, to pour out even upon menservants and maidservants in those days, that they might prophesy [*hunc enim promisit per prophetas effundere se in nouissimis temporibus super seruos et ancillas ut prophetent*]" (3.17.1).[116]

The Spirit is now available to all,[117] and Irenaeus believes that all who believe are endowed with the Spirit in the same manner as the apostles, even citing Peter's words to this effect:

> Men, brethren, you know that in the early days God made a choice among you, that through my mouth the Gentiles should hear the word of the Gospel and believe. And God who knows the heart bore witness to them, giving them the Holy Spirit just as He did to us [*dans eis Spiritum sanctum sicut et nobis*]; and He made no distinction between us and them [*et nihil discreuit inter nos et ipsos*], but cleansed their hearts by faith. (3.12.14; citing Acts 15:7-11)[118]

---

the source of the oral and written message of the Apostles" (48), and similarly describes Irenaeus as "founding the unity and authority of the oral and written traditions on the work of the Spirit" and "basing the transmission of every message of the gospel on the work of the same Spirit" (50). This demonstrates the Spirit's direct role in the "guidance of the composition of Scripture" (50 n. 17).

[114] Isa. 5:6.

[115] This passage provides the basis of Kalin's assertion that "the idea that prophecy ceased among the Jews finds an echo in Irenaeus not in an analogous idea that also among the Christians there was a prophetic period that is now past, but in another idea. The Spirit that is no longer active among the Jews has now been poured out upon the Church" (*Inspiration*, 38). Cf. 3.12.1, 3.12.15, 3.17.2, 5.18.2, etc.

[116] Cf. *Dem.* 89: "He promised, by the prophets, to pour forth the Spirit upon the face of the earth in the last days."

[117] "For where the Church is, there is the Spirit of God; and where God's Spirit is, there is the Church" (3.24.1). Cf. 5.18.2, 4.36.6, *Dem.* 42.

[118] Cf. 3.24.1, *Dem.* 41.

While formerly the prophets were unique in their inspiration by the Spirit for the purpose of recording the prophecies given by the Word, the Spirit is now available for all who believe, without any unique charism of inspiration for the apostles.

The Spirit's new role and availability for all who believe entails that the *auctoritas* inspiration of the prophets that formed the basis of the divine scriptural status of the Jewish scriptures is not mirrored in the apostles to form the basis for the unique revelatory authority of the apostolic writings. The apostles' inspiration by the Spirit is not that which grants them their unique authority, for the Spirit is the possession of the entire church.

This relates to the second reason why the Spirit cannot provide the divine *auctoritas* of the apostolic writings according to Irenaeus' pneumatology. As the description of the Trinitarian process of *auctoritas* inspiration of the Jewish scriptures in Section 4.2B has demonstrated, this process takes place as the Word, sent from the Father, delivers a message to the prophets by the agency of the Spirit.[119] The Spirit's role in this process is not to provide the content of revelation but to "nourish and increase" that which has been made (4.38.3).[120] The Spirit performs the same role in the church after the Incarnation. As Ochagavia notes, Irenaeus' discussions of the Spirit's role in the church, "rather than suggesting the activity of imparting new contents of knowledge, seem to stress the notion that the Spirit preserves the faith transmitted by Christ."[121] The Spirit plays a guiding role in divine economy, first by inspiring the prophets to hear the Word, then by guiding, inspiring, and "perfecting" the whole church who has received the Gospel of Christ.[122]

---

[119] Briggman, *Holy Spirit*, demonstrates that one of the most important distinctions between Irenaeus' understanding of the roles of the Word and Spirit and the understanding held by Justin and others is that Irenaeus maintains a consistent distinction between their activities. He explains, "Christian thinkers of this period often utilized Jewish traditions of the Spirit in such a way that weakened the distinction between the identity and activity of the Spirit and that of the Word. This effect contrasts with Irenaeus' utilization of Jewish traditions, which strengthens the distinction of the identity and activity of the Spirit, reinforcing his Trinitarian account" (2).

[120] Briggman, *Holy Spirit*, similarly speaks of the Spirit's role as establishing unity and productivity (78). He explains that unity is established as "The Spirit unites the bodies and souls of the individual with the incorruptible and immortal One, and in the process unites each of those individuals into the one body of Christ" (83), and productivity is established as "the Spirit renders Christians productive, as dry trees that receive water are able to bring forth fruit" (85). Briggman also contends that Irenaeus' understanding of the role of the Spirit evolves throughout his career (cf. 32–3), such that the Spirit has no role in creation in the opening books (cf. 1.22.1, 3.8.3) but comes to be described as part of the process of creation in the *Demonstration* (cf. *Dem.* 5), which is argued to have been written after all five books of *Adversus haereses* (against this hypothesis, see Behr, *Identifying*, 68–9, who argues that the *Demonstration* was written between Books 2 and 3 of *Adversus haereses*). However, Briggman's argument ignores the substantial agreement over the Spirit's role throughout Irenaeus' writings (*Dem.* 5, 3.24.1, 5.8.1, etc. which do not oppose 1.22.1, e.g.). The differences that Briggman identifies are more easily explained by the differing purposes and contexts of each book.

[121] Ochagavia, *Visibile*, 133.

[122] Cf. 5.8.1, 3.17.2, 4.38.1-3, 5.20.2. The Spirit first descended on Christ in order to become accustomed to dwell in humanity:

> And for that purpose He [the Spirit] descended on the Son of God, when He had been made the Son of man, becoming accustomed with Him [Christ] to dwell in the human race, and to rest among human beings, and to dwell in God's handiwork, thus fulfilling the Father's will in them, and renewing them from their old selves for the newness of Christ. (3.17.1)

Irenaeus' descriptions of the role of the Spirit preclude the possibility of *auctoritas* inspiration of the apostles and their writings *by the Spirit*, for this is not the Spirit's role. As the following section demonstrates, divine *auctoritas* resides principally with the Word who creates.

Conclusion

The three considerations identified in this section—that Irenaeus consistently claims divine authorship for the Jewish scriptures to the exclusion of the apostolic writings, that the authority of the apostolic writings is not defended on the basis of their inspiration but rather on the basis of the apostles' proximity to Christ, and that Irenaeus presents a pneumatology that rules out the Spirit's *auctoritas* inspiration of the apostles—all stand together in opposition to the two passages identified in the previous sections, which could be interpreted as indicating an *auctoritas* form of inspiration of the apostles. The evidence supplied by these considerations necessitates a reinterpretation of 3.16.2 and 3.21.4 as descriptions of an *inspiratio*—rather than *auctoritas*—form of inspiration. These conclusions coincide with the stark contrast between Irenaeus' clear and consistent references to the inspiration of the Jewish scriptures and the notable lack of emphasis on the inspiration of the apostolic writings, indicating a perceived difference in origin and basis of authority of the two written collections. The findings of this investigation therefore lead to the conclusion that the apostolic writings are not understood by Irenaeus to have been the product of divine *auctoritas*.

If the two central theses of this chapter are accepted—that divine *auctoritas* is the only form of inspiration sufficient to confer revelatory authority, and that Irenaeus does not advocate the *auctoritas* inspiration of the apostolic writings—the conclusion follows that Irenaeus does not attribute the unique revelatory authority of the apostolic writings to the inspiration of the apostles, as the traditional interpretation holds. These findings agree with the conclusions of the previous chapters in support of the thesis that the revelatory authority of the apostolic writings is founded directly on their understood apostolicity, not on a notion of scriptural status derived on the basis of divine authorship. In the final section, an analysis of the implications of Irenaeus' doctrine of the Word is used to identify the reason for the unique authority attributed to apostolicity, and by this to fully determine the nature and status of the apostolic writings in Irenaeus' thought.

4.4. Constructing Irenaeus' Conception of the Status of the Apostolic Writings on His Doctrine of the Word

This book has arrived at the conclusion that according to Irenaeus apostolicity is the basis of the unique revelatory authority of the apostolic writings, and that inspiration

---

Cf. Briggman, *Holy Spirit*, 78. Irenaeus discusses the concept of becoming the "image and likeness" of God further in 3.18.1, 4.38.1-3, 5.1.3, 5.6.1, 5.8.1, 5.10.1, *Dem* 5, *Dem*. 32f. Cf. also Briggman's detailed discussion on the meaning of "the image and likeness of God," 173–81.

is not a primary factor in the unique status of apostolicity as a category of revelatory authority. This chapter began by noting two questions that remained to be answered in order to determine Irenaeus' conception of the nature and status of the apostolic writings. The second of these is now able to be answered: the investigation in this chapter has led to the conclusion that the difference in relationship to the divine between the Jewish scriptures and the apostolic writings in Irenaeus' thought can be described as a difference in type of inspiration. The Jewish scriptures are divinely inspired throughout in the *auctoritas* sense, as they are understood by Irenaeus to have been *authored* by God as the Word transmitted messages to the prophets by the Spirit, and this forms the basis of their divine scriptural status. In contrast, the apostolic writings are inspired, but are not understood to be the product of divine *auctoritas* which results in scriptural status. They acquire their unique revelatory authority on the basis of their apostolicity without requirement of divine *auctoritas*. This leads back to the first unanswered question: why does apostolicity operate for Irenaeus as a second category of unique revelatory authority, equal yet distinct from the *auctoritas* inspiration of the prophets? The answer has already been hinted at. Apostolic authority is based on direct relation to the incarnate Word. A closer analysis of Irenaeus' understanding of the Word's role within the divine economy in this section will determine in greater detail the link between apostolicity and the incarnate Word, and its implications for his understanding of revelation and of the nature and status of the apostolic writings.[123]

A. The Word's Functions within the Divine Economy

Irenaeus' account of the Word as *Revealer of the Father* is central to his entire theological task, and is the key to his understanding of the process of revelation. As the Father's *Logos* and one of his two hands,[124] the functions of the Word within the divine economy can be usefully (if simplistically) classified according to three categories in Irenaeus' thought. (1.) The Word is the agent of creation, "by whom all things were made." (2.) The Word spoke to the prophets, prophesying his future coming. (3.) The Word became incarnate as Jesus Christ in order to save humanity.[125] In each of these functions, the Word reveals the Father.

---

[123] Some of the material contained in this section has been previously published in Kenneth R. Laing, "The *Logos* and the Authority of Scripture: A Proposal Motivated by Irenaeus' Trinitarian Account of Revelation," *International Journal of Systematic Theology* 20.4 (2018): 455–71.

[124] Cf. 3.21.10, 4.pre.4, 4.7.4, 4.20.1, 5.1.3, 5.5.1, 5.6.1, and 5.28.4; Briggman, *Holy Spirit*, 104–26.

[125] This simplistic classification ignores other aspects of Irenaeus' understanding of the Word's actions within the divine economy. His Second Coming, for example, is omitted. Additionally, Ochagavia, *Visibile*, 44–59, demonstrates that Irenaeus believed it was the Word who spoke to and visited with Adam and Eve in the Garden of Eden (*Dem.* 12); who warned Cain (4.18.3); who gave Noah the measurements of the Ark (4.10.1) and sent the Flood (4.36.3); who spoke to Abraham (*Dem.* 24) and appeared before him as a man (*Dem.* 44, 4.7.3); who spoke to Moses (4.20.9, *Dem.* 2); and who "took part in [all] the theophanies and typological events of the Old Testament" (4.21.3). Oskar Skarsaune, *Proof from Prophecy*, argues that Justin Martyr originated the practice of taking biblical theophanies to be appearances of the Word, rather than the Father (409–24), though such a view seems already to be discernible in Jn 12:41. Skarsaune also provides an appendix in which he argues that Irenaeus indicates a dependence on Justin in his writings (435–53).

The Word Is the Agent of Creation, "by Whom All Things Were Made"

Irenaeus repeatedly declares that all creation occurs by the Word, often citing Psalm 32:6 and John 1:3 as evidence. In one of his first statements of the rule of truth, he writes:

> There is one God Almighty, who made all things by His Word [*qui omnia condidit per Verbum suum*], and fashioned and formed, out of that which had no existence, all things which exist. Thus saith the Scripture, to that effect: "By the Word of the Lord [*Verbo enim Domini*] were the heavens established, and all the might of them, by the spirit of His mouth."[126] And again, "All things were made by Him, and without Him was nothing made"[127] ... for God needs none of all these things, but is He who, by His Word and Spirit, makes, and disposes, and governs all things, and commands all things into existence [*per Verbum et Spiritum suum omnia faciens et disponens et gubernans et omnibus esse praestans*]. (1.22.1)[128]

The Father creates through his Word, and this means by implication that "the Creator of the world is truly the Word of God" (5.18.3). The mechanism by which creation occurs is described more precisely by Irenaeus when he speaks of

> the Father planning everything well and giving His commands, the Son carrying these into execution and performing the work of creating [*Filio vero ministrante et formante*[129]], and the Spirit nourishing and increasing [what is made][τοῦ δὲ Πνεύματος τρέφοντος]. (4.38.3)

The Word and the Spirit are both active in creation, as the two hands of God. Within this process it is only the Word who properly *creates*. This is illustrated in another of Irenaeus' descriptions of their roles:

> Thus, since the Word "establishes," that is, works bodily and confers existence, while the Spirit arranges and forms the various "powers," so rightly is the Son called Word and the Spirit the Wisdom of God. (*Dem.* 5)[130]

---

[126] Ps. 32:6 (LXX). Cf. Irenaeus' use of this verse to make similar claims in 3.8.3 and *Dem.* 5. In 3.8.3 Irenaeus also cites Ps. 148:1-5 and 32:9 (LXX) to the same effect.

[127] Jn 1:3. Cf. Irenaeus' use of this verse to make similar claims in 3.8.3, 3.11.1, 3.11.3, 3.18.1, 3.21.10, 4.32.1, *Dem.* 43. Irenaeus also routinely refers to the Word "by whom all things were made" (*Dem.* 6, *Dem.* 43, 1.9.2, 3.8.2, 3.11.2), in an allusion to Jn 1:3.

[128] ANF 1: 347. Cf. ACW 55:80. A similar claim is made in the *Demonstration*: "as God is verbal (λογικός), therefore He made created things by the Word; and God is Spirit, so that He adorned all things by the Spirit, as the prophet also says, 'By the Word of the Lord were the heavens established, and all their power by His Spirit'" (*Dem.* 5; citing Ps. 32:6). Cf. 1.9.2, 2.30.9, 4.20.1, 4.20.2, 4.20.4.

[129] The Greek fragment reads, "τοῦ δὲ Υἱοῦ ὑπουργοῦντος καὶ πράσσοντος." Rousseau et al. believe it is corrupt, and amend πράσσοντος to read πλάσσοντος (SC 100:955), on the basis of the Latin and Armenian translations.

[130] Cf. 3.24.2: the Father "by His Word establishes [*confirmans*] all things and by His Wisdom harmoniously unites [*compingens*] them." Cf. also 4.20.4.

The Word is responsible for producing the *content* of creation, while the Spirit "nourishes and increases," "arranges and forms" what the Word creates. Irenaeus also describes the Word as the "Artificer [Τεχνίτης; *Artifex*] of all things" (3.11.8).[131]

The difference between the creative functions of the Word and Spirit may be understood to be in parallel with the Word's *auctoritas* and the Spirit's *inspiratio*. This parallel is no coincidence, for the initial creative function of the Word is itself significant for Irenaeus' understanding of revelation: "by means of the creation itself, the Word reveals [ἀποκαλύπτει] God the Creator" (4.6.6).[132] The Word's function as the creator of all things is an aspect of his revelation of the Father.

The Word Spoke to the Prophets, Prophesying His Future Coming

The second category of the Word's function within the divine economy has been discussed obliquely in Section 4.2B, where it was demonstrated that Irenaeus consistently affirms that the Jewish scriptures are the product of divine *auctoritas*, as the Word delivered the Father's message to the prophets by the Spirit. Irenaeus demonstrates that the Word spoke through the prophets by appealing to Christ's own words:

> But since the writings of Moses are the words of Christ [*Moysi litterae verba sunt Christi*], He does Himself say to the Jews, as John has recorded in the Gospel, "If ye had believed Moses, ye would have believed Me: For he wrote of Me ..."[133] He thus indicates in the clearest manner that the writings of Moses are His words [*manifestissime signifcans Moysi litteras suos esse sermones*]. If, then, [this be the case with regard] to Moses, so also, beyond a doubt, the words of the other prophets are His [words] [*reliquorum ... prophetarum sermones ipsius sunt*], as I have pointed out (4.2.3).[134]

The words of all the prophets come about as a result of the direct *authorship* of the Word who spoke to them.

This second function also relates to the Word's revelation of the Father, for the message that is delivered by the Word originates from the Father. The Word reveals the Father's message to humanity, and by doing so reveals the Father himself. Just as through creation the Word revealed the Father, so also does he do so through the prophets: "by the law and the prophets [*per Legem et Prophetas*] did the Word preach both Himself and the Father alike [*similiter Verbum et semetipsum et Patrem praedicabat*]" (4.6.6). This understanding is similarly expressed when Irenaeus explains that the Father is invisible, so it was not he who spoke to the prophets, "but the Word

---

[131] The same term is used as a descriptor for the Word in 4.6.6 and 5.15.2. The Word also "governs and arranges [*gubernans et disponens*] all things" (5.18.3), and it is by the Word that "everything is administered" (*Dem.* 34).
[132] Cf. 2.9.1.
[133] Jn 5:46-47.
[134] Irenaeus also mentions the Word speaking to Moses in 4.5.2 and 4.20.9. Cf. 2.28.2, 4.20.7, and 4.36.8.

of God, who was always with mankind and who foretold things of the future, which were to come to pass, and taught men things of God" (*Dem.* 45).[135] The Spirit is also active in this process, as Irenaeus describes when he mentions the "Word of God who did both visit them through the prophetic Spirit [*per propheticum Spiritum*]." (4.36.8). Just as in the process of creation, the Word produces the *content* of revelation, while the Spirit inspires the prophets to receive it, corresponding to the *auctoritas* and *inspiratio* forms of inspiration.

The Word Became Incarnate as Jesus Christ in Order to Save Humanity

The third category of the Word's functions within the divine economy is his Incarnation as the man Jesus Christ. In Book 1 of *Adversus haereses* Irenaeus states the second article of the rule of truth with the words, "Jesus Christ, the Son of God, who was enfleshed for our salvation [Χριςὸν Ἰησοῦν τὸν Υἱὸν τοῦ Θεοῦ τὸν σαρκωθέντα ὑπὲρ τῆς ἡμετέρας σωτηρίας]" (1.10.1). Similarly, in his description of the rule of truth in the *Demonstration* he describes,

> the Word of God, Son of God, Jesus Christ our Lord ... who, in the last times, to recapitulate all things, became a man amongst men, visible and palpable, in order to abolish death, to demonstrate life, and to effect communion between God and man. (*Dem.* 6)[136]

The Incarnation is the culmination of the Word's functions within the divine economy, by which he brings about the salvation of humanity. By his birth, life, death, and resurrection, the Word recapitulates all things in himself in order to defeat death and restore the true purpose of humanity to be the image and likeness of God, which had been lost:

> When He became incarnate and was made man, He recapitulated [*recapitulauit*] in Himself the long unfolding of humankind, granting salvation by way of compendium, that in Christ Jesus we might receive what we had lost in Adam, namely, to be according to the image and likeness of God [*secundum imaginem et similitudinem esse Dei*] ... it was not possible for the human race, which had fallen under sin, to receive salvation. And so the Son, Word of God that He is, accomplished [this], by coming down from the Father and becoming incarnate, and descending even to death, and bringing the economy of our salvation to completion [*dispensationem consummans salutis nostrae*]. (3.18.1-2)[137]

The image and likeness of God was restored to humanity by the Word through his Incarnation, through which, by "uniting man with God [*hominem adunans Deo*]" (3.4.2), he would "accustom humankind to receive God [*adsuesceret hominem*

---

[135] Cf. 4.20.7.
[136] Cf. 3.4.2, 5.18.3, etc.
[137] Cf. 3.16.6, 3.19.1-3.20.3, 4.20.4, 5.18.3, 5.21.2, *Dem.* 37–8, etc.

percipere Deum], and accustom God to dwell in humanity [*adsuesceret Deum habitare in homine*] according to the Father's good pleasure" (3.20.2).

As an aspect of the Word's accomplishment of salvation for humanity, the Incarnation is also the culmination of the Word's revelation of the Father. In the Incarnation, the Word both accomplishes the Father's divine plan of salvation and reveals it to humanity, revealing by his advent both himself and the Father. As Irenaeus explains,

> For in no other way could we have learned the things of God, unless our Master, existing as the Word, had become man [εἰ μὴ ὁ διδάσκαλος ἡμῶν, Λόγος ὤν, ἄνθρωπος ἐγένετο]. For no other being had the power of revealing to us the things of the Father, except His own proper Word [εἰ μὴ ὁ ἴδιος[138] αὐτοῦ Λόγος]. (5.1.1)[139]

The Incarnation was the necessary means by which the invisible Father could be revealed to humanity.[140] Irenaeus believes that "the manifestation of the Son *is* the knowledge of the Father [*Agnitio enim Patris est Filii manifestatio*]; for all things are manifested through the Word [*omnia enim per Verbum manifestantur*]" (4.6.3),[141] because "without the Son one is not able to approach the Father" (*Dem.* 7). As he further explains,

> For this purpose did the Father reveal the Son, that through His instrumentality He might be manifested to all … The Father therefore has revealed Himself to all, by making His Word visible to all [*Omnibus igitur revelavit se Pater, omnibus Verbum suum visibilem faciens*]; and, conversely, the Word has declared to all the Father and the Son, since He has become visible to all. (4.6.5)

The Incarnation is the climax of the Word's revelation, through which the Father is most fully revealed, for "the Son [is] the visible of the Father [*visibile autem Patris Filius*]" (4.6.6). In this way the Word is once again responsible for the content of revelation (*auctoritas*), while the Spirit plays a supporting role in this process (*inspiratio*). It is the Spirit of God who

> descended on the Son of God, when He had been made the Son of Man [*unde et in Filium Dei Filium hominis factum descendit*], becoming accustomed with Him [Christ] to dwell in the human race [*cum ipso adsuescens habitare in genere humano*], and to rest among human beings, and to dwell in God's handiwork, thus fulfilling the Father's will in them. (3.17.1)

---

[138] The Greek fragment (*Florilegium Achridense*) gives ἀΐδιος, but Rousseau et al. render it ἴδιος on the basis of both the Latin and Armenian translations (SC 153:16-7).
[139] Cf. 4.6.5, 5.16.2, etc.
[140] *Dem.* 47: "since the Father of all is invisible and inaccessible to creatures, it is necessary for those who are going to approach God to have access to the Father through the Son."
[141] Emphasis added.

After this, "The Lord Himself in turn gave Him to the Church, when He sent upon the entire earth the Paraclete from heaven" (3.18.3).[142] In this way the Spirit inspires the church and so "perfects" their understanding of the Word's revelation; this is true of the apostles (3.1.1) just as of all others who receive the Spirit (3.12.13, 5.6.1). This description of the Spirit's work indicates that "although the functions of the Son and the Spirit in the process of revelation are intimately related, nonetheless they are different. The basic function of revealing and manifesting the Father belongs to the Son."[143]

B. The Word's Role as Revealer of the Father

In all three of the Word's successive functions within the divine economy, he acts according to his overarching role as the *Revealer of the Father*. This is the key to Irenaeus' understanding of revelation, as he describes in the following passage:

> Through his Word, who is his Son, [the Father] is revealed and manifested to all to whom he is revealed; for those know him to whom the Son has made the revelation. But the Son, always coexisting with the Father, of old and from the beginning always reveals the Father [*Semper autem coexistens Filius Patri olim et ab initio semper reuelat Patrem*]. (2.30.9)

The Word's role as Revealer of the Father entails that all revelation necessarily takes place through the Word, who produces its content, with the help of the Spirit, who "nourishes and increases what is made."

This process of revelation occurs because the Father is utterly transcendent, unobservable and incomprehensible by humanity. Irenaeus cites Exodus 33:20 as proof of the Father's incomprehensibility, saying, "in respect to His greatness, and His wonderful glory, 'no man shall see God and live,' for the Father is incomprehensible [*incapabilis*]" (4.20.5). In another place he explains, "His Word knows that His Father is, as far as regards us, invisible and infinite [*invisibilem et indeterminabilem*]; and since He cannot be declared [*et cum sit inenarrabilis*], He does Himself declare Him to us" (4.6.3).[144]

The transcendence of the Father means that he cannot be known by humanity unless revealed by a mediator, and this is the task of his Word: "since it was impossible, without God, to come to a knowledge of God, He teaches men, through His Word, to know God" (4.5.1). Ochagavia, in his study of Irenaeus' understanding of revelation, argues on this basis that "the absolute transcendence of God the Father regarding human knowledge and the Word's universal mediation concerning revelation ... are the two pillars upon which the Irenaean teaching on revelation rests."[145] Ochagavia identifies Matthew 11:27 as the fundamental verse influencing Irenaeus' understanding

---

[142] Cf. 3.17.1-18.4, 5.18.2, etc.
[143] Ochagavia, *Visibile*, 62.
[144] Ochagavia, *Visibile*, lists all the instances in which Irenaeus describes the Father as *immensurabilis, incapabilis, incomprehensibilis, indeterminabilis, inenarrabilis, inexcogitabilis, investigabilis, invisibilis, non transibilis, ingenitus,* and *ignotus* (22–3).
[145] Ibid., 1.

of revelation, claiming, "It became for [Irenaeus] the scriptural corner-stone of his doctrine on revelation."[146] This is somewhat overstated; the majority of Irenaeus' nine citations of this verse occur as descriptions of his opponents' corrupt interpretations of it[147]—he states that it is "the crown of their system" (1.20.3)—and all of his positive uses of it occur within a single chapter as a response to and correction of its heretical misuse.[148] However, within 4.6.1-7, Matthew 11:27 is the centerpiece of his argument, and this section is one of Irenaeus' most extensive descriptions of the revelatory role of the Word.

The Use of Matthew 11:27 in 4.6.1-7

Irenaeus begins in 4.6.1 by citing Jesus' words in Matthew 11:27: "No man knoweth [*cognoscit*] the Son, but the Father; neither knoweth [*cognoscit*] any man the Father, save the Son, and he to whom the Son has willed to reveal [Him]," followed by his opponents' altered citation of the same verse, in which he says they find proof that "the true God [was] known to none prior to our Lord's advent; and that God who was announced by the prophets, they allege not to be the Father of Christ." As Ochagavia points out, the change in tense from *cognoscit* to *cognovit* and its implications is the central difference in their interpretations.[149] After briefly describing the foolishness of his opponents' interpretation, Irenaeus counters by describing the correct interpretation:

> For no one can know the Father, unless through the Word of God, that is, unless by the Son revealing [Him]; neither can he have knowledge of the Son, unless through the good pleasure of the Father ... And His Word knows that His Father is, as far as regards us, invisible and infinite; and since He cannot be declared [by any one else], He does Himself declare Him to us; and, on the other hand, it is the Father alone who knows His own Word. And both these truths has our Lord declared. Wherefore the Son reveals the knowledge of the Father through His own manifestation. For the manifestation of the Son is the knowledge of the Father; for all things are manifested through the Word. In order, therefore, that we might know that the Son who came is He who imparts to those believing on Him a knowledge of the Father, He said to His disciples: "No man knoweth [*cognoscit*] the Son but the Father, nor the Father but the Son, and those to whomsoever the Son shall reveal Him;"[150] thus setting Himself forth and the Father as He [really] is, that we may not receive any other Father, except Him who is revealed by the Son. (4.6.3)

---

[146] Ibid., 30.
[147] 1.20.3, 2.6.1, 2.14.7, 4.6.1, and 4.7.4. Ochagavia acknowledges that the heretical use of this passage served as an impetus for Irenaeus' own use of it: "Since the Gnostics make use of this text as if it were the crown of their doctrine ... Irenaeus accepts their challenge, going into a long exposition of the way the Church understands it" (62).
[148] 4.6.1, 4.6.3, and 4.6.7 (twice).
[149] Ochagavia, *Visibile*, 63.
[150] Mt. 11:27.

Jesus' words illustrate that he had come to fully reveal the Father to all, not that the Father was unknown prior to his Incarnation. Irenaeus does not dispute his opponents' position that the Father is transcendent and unknowable,[151] but counters that the Father nonetheless desired to reveal himself to his creation, and has done so through his Word:

> For the Lord taught us that no man is capable of knowing God, unless he be taught of God; that is, God cannot be known without God: but that this is the express will of the Father, that God should be known. For they shall know Him to whomsoever the Son has revealed Him. And for this purpose did the Father reveal the Son, that through His instrumentality He might be manifested to all ... The Father therefore has revealed Himself to all, by making the Word visible to all [*Omnibus igitur revelavit se Pater, omnibus Verbum suum visibilem faciens*]. (4.6.4-5)

As Ochagavia explains, "The Father's infinity makes Him ungraspable to creatures, but His love impels Him to manifest Himself to them. This manifestation takes place through the Word, Our Lord Jesus Christ."[152] However, the Word did not only begin to reveal the Father at the Incarnation, as Irenaeus' opponents claim. The Father could not have been unknown prior to the coming of Christ, for the Word has eternally revealed the Father. As Irenaeus explains,

> For by means of the creation [*conditionem*] itself, the Word reveals [ἀποκαλύπτει] God the Creator [*Conditorem*] ... that Father who begat the Son ... But by the law and the prophets [*Legem et Prophetas*] did the Word preach both Himself and the Father alike ... And through the Word Himself who had been made visible and palpable [*ipsum Verbum visibilem et palpabilem*], was the Father shown forth, although all did not equally believe in Him; but all saw the Father in the Son: for the Father is the invisible of the Son, but the Son the visible of the Father [*invisibile etinem Filii Pater, visibile autem Patris Filius*]. (4.6.6)[153]

By the creation of the universe, by speaking to the prophets, and finally by his Incarnation, the Word has always revealed the one Father of all:

> But the Son, administering all things for the Father, works from the beginning even to the end, and without Him no man can attain the knowledge of God. For the Son is the knowledge of the Father ... the Son, being present with His own handiwork from the beginning [*Ab initio enim assistens Filius suo plasmati*], reveals the Father to all. (4.6.7)

---

[151] Ochagavia explains that Irenaeus and his opponents agree that "the supreme God is invisible and incomprehensible in this life ... [and] remains unknowable and unapproachable to His creatures," and therefore, "The gap between God and the world must be filled in by a mediator whose task will be to impart unto men the knowledge of the ungraspable Father" (21).
[152] Ibid., 1.
[153] As Behr, *Identifying*, notes, a similar claim is made when Irenaeus states that the Son is the "measure" of the "unmeasurable" Father (140; 4.4.2).

Throughout this chapter Irenaeus makes clear that while the Father is utterly transcendent, he has nonetheless resolved to reveal himself to humanity throughout all times, and this he has done through his Word. As Ochagavia concludes, "Irenaeus holds that from the very beginning of creation, and all through the different ages of human history, God made Himself known to creatures through His Son. And this brings us to the core of the Irenaean theology of revelation."[154] The Word's central role within the divine economy is to be the Revealer of the Father.

In addition to Matthew 11:27, John 1:18 is another central text controlling Irenaeus' theology of revelation,[155] and it too appears primarily in a single chapter in which Irenaeus sets forth his concept of revelation.[156]

The Use of John 1:18 in 4.20.1-12

In ch. 20 of Book 4, after demonstrating that the Father had no need of any others except his own Word and Spirit, who had always been with him (4.20.1-3), Irenaeus explains that the Father has always been revealed by his Word:

> There is therefore one God ... who, as regards His greatness is indeed unknown to all ... but as regards His love, He is always known through Him by whose means He ordained all things. Now this is His Word, our Lord Jesus Christ, who in the last times was made a man among men, that He might join the end to the beginning, that is, man to God [*qui in novissimis temporibus homo in hominibus factus est, ut finem conjungeret principio, hoc est hominem Deo*]. Wherefore the prophets, receiving the prophetic gift from the same Word, announced His advent according to the flesh, by which the blending and communion of God and man took place according to the good pleasure of the Father, the Word of God foretelling from the beginning that God should be seen by men. (4.20.4)

Irenaeus is explicit: the Father is always known through his Word. Here he also indicates that the Word's ultimate *revelatory* purpose in the Incarnation is the salvation of humanity, by joining "man to God."

Irenaeus goes on to explain that the prophets had "indicated beforehand that God should be seen by men," in spite of the fact that because of "His greatness, and His wonderful glory, 'no man shall see God and live'"[157] (4.20.5). As Ochagavia describes this paradox, "The Father's transcendence forbids Him to appear directly to man; but His goodness impels Him to do it in His own Word."[158] This is proved for Irenaeus by John 1:18, for the Father

---

[154] Ochagavia, *Visibile*, 44.
[155] In spite of his preference for Mt. 11:27, Ochagavia acknowledges Jn 1:18 as "Another text that played an important role in the Gnostic controversy" (31), alongside Exod. 33:20 (29; 1.19.2 and 4.20.5) and Eph. 1:21 (31; 4.24.2 and 4.19.2).
[156] Outside of 4.20.1-12, Irenaeus cites this verse only once (3.11.6).
[157] Exod. 33:20.
[158] Ochagavia, *Visibile*, 67.

is by no means unknown: for all things learn through His Word that there is one God the Father, who contains all things, and who grants existence to all, as is written in the Gospel: 'No man hath seen God at any time, except the only-begotten Son, who is in the bosom of the Father; He has declared [Him].'[159] (4.20.6)

John 1:18 demonstrates for Irenaeus that the Father can only be seen through the Son. As Behr explains, "it is only in the Son, as preached in the Gospel, that the invisible and immeasurable God becomes visible and comprehensible, as Irenaeus repeatedly insists."[160] Irenaeus once again clarifies that the Word's revelation of the Father does not begin only at the Incarnation, as he continues,

> Therefore the Son of the Father declares [Him] from the beginning [*ab initio*], inasmuch as He was with the Father from the beginning [*qui ab initio est cum Patre*], who did also show the human race prophetic visions, and diversities of gifts, and His own ministrations, and the glory of the Father, in regular order and connection, at the fitting time for the benefit [of mankind] … And for this reason did the Word become the dispenser of the paternal grace for the benefit of men, for whom He made such great dispensations, revealing God indeed to men, but presenting man to God, and preserving at the same time the invisibility of the Father … but, on the other hand, revealing God to men through many dispensations [*hominibus per multas dispositiones ostendens Deum*], lest man, failing away from God altogether, should cease to exist. For the glory of God is a living man; and the life of man consists in beholding God. For if the manifestation of God which is made by means of the creation, affords life to all living in the earth, much more does that revelation of the Father which comes through the Word, give life to those who see God. (4.20.7)

The Word's revelation of the Father does not begin only at the Incarnation; yet this is where it reaches its culmination, in which the incarnate Word's revelation of the Father "give[s] life to those who see God." As Irenaeus had said just previously, "Now this is His Word, our Lord Jesus Christ, who in the last times was made a man among men, that He might join the end to the beginning, that is, man to God" (4.20.4). The Word's final revelation of the Father in the Incarnation is central to his accomplishment of the salvation of humanity: "Men therefore shall see God, that they may live, being made immortal [*immortales*] by that sight, and attaining even unto God [*pertingentes usque in Deum*]" (4.20.6).

Throughout the whole of the Father's economy of salvation, the Word reveals the Father in order to accomplish the salvation of humanity, and this revelatory

---

[159] Jn 1:18. Irenaeus cites the verse again in 4.20.11:

> It is manifest that the Father is indeed invisible, of whom also the Lord said, "No man hath seen God at any time." But His Word, as He Himself willed it, and for the benefit of those who beheld, did show the Father's brightness, and explained His purposes (as also the Lord said: "The only-begotten God, which is in the bosom of the Father, He hath declared [Him]."

[160] Behr, "Word of God," 166.

role culminates in the Incarnation, where the Word becomes "the visibility of the Father: *visibile Patris Filius*."[161] This understanding of the process of revelation profoundly influences the conceptual distinction Irenaeus draws between the Jewish scriptures and the apostolic writings as it affects their relationship to revelation.

C. The Revelatory Role of the Word and the Unique Status of the Apostolic Writings

Irenaeus' theology of the Word as Revealer of the Father is the key to his view of the unique status of the apostolic writings, illuminating the relationship between apostolicity as a source of authority and the Word who certifies its revelatory status. The Word's role as Revealer of the Father entails that he is the source of all forms of revelatory authority, including both the scriptures and the apostolic writings. The Spirit is intimately involved in the composition of both, but it is the Word who produces the content of revelation and so ensures its divine authority. As Ochagavia notes,

> A reflection on Irenaeus' theology of the Trinity dissuades us from asserting that the Spirit contributes positively in developing the contents of our faith. His role is not so much to give "form" to creatures (this task belongs to the Word), but to animate and put into action creatures already "shaped" and "formed" by the Word.[162]

In this way Irenaeus emphasizes the vital role of the Word as the foundation of the unique revelatory authority of both the Jewish scriptures and the apostolic writings. Yet within this process, the distinct successive functions of the Word within his revelatory role entail that there is a significant difference in the ways in which the scriptures and the apostolic writings relate to the Word as source of authority. This difference is the basis of the unique status of the apostolic writings.

Within the Word's second revelatory function, the Jewish scriptures were themselves the medium of the Word's revelation as he delivered the Father's message through the prophets: "by the law and the prophets did the Word preach both Himself and the Father alike [to all]" (4.6.6). Irenaeus does not believe that the Word's revelation rests in the fact that he spoke to the prophets, but rather in the fact that what the Word spoke was to be written down as scripture in order to reveal the Father's plan of salvation to humanity.[163] The scriptures are not understood by Irenaeus as merely the written record of what the Word had revealed, but are themselves the instrument of the Word's revelation, and for precisely this reason they possess scriptural status derived from their direct divine authorship by the Word. This sums up Irenaeus' understanding of the nature and status of the Jewish scriptures.[164]

---

[161] Ochagavia, *Visibile*, 1; citing 4.6.6.
[162] Ibid., 133.
[163] Cf. 3.10.2: "Christ Jesus our Lord, 'the Son of God the Most High, who through the Law and the Prophets promised that He would make His salvation visible to all mankind.'" Cf. also 2.11.1, 3.1.2, 3.10.3, 4.5.1, etc.
[164] This may be more succinctly described by stating that the Jewish scriptures are a collection of writings composed through the *auctoritas* inspiration of the Word to be the instrument through

In contrast to this, the subsequent culmination of the Word's revelation was found not in a new set of scriptures, but in his own Incarnation: "through the Word Himself who had been made visible and palpable, was the Father shown forth" (4.6.6). Having previously spoken to humanity indirectly via the Jewish scriptures, the Word at last entered humanity as a man to address his creation directly;[165] the Word of God speaking to humanity face-to-face, manifesting both himself and the Father, and accomplishing the divine plan of salvation. The apostolic writings relate to this consummate revelatory event more indirectly, as the apostolic *record* of this new revelation and of the true interpretation of the Jewish scriptures in light of it. Within his final revelatory function, the Word's *auctoritas* does not reside directly in the production of the apostolic writings, but is located in the Incarnation itself, for it is here that the Father has been truly revealed to humanity and Jesus Christ has become the *auctor* of salvation.

The apostolic writings themselves are not the primary purpose of the Word's ultimate revelatory function, yet they are nevertheless considered by Irenaeus to possess a unique authoritative status equaling that of the scriptures themselves. Like the scriptures, the key to the revelatory authority of the apostolic writings is found in their direct relationship to the Word as the Revealer of the Father, though in this case not through the direct *auctoritas* of their message by the Word. Because the revelation of the Word in the Incarnation occurs directly in the person of Christ, the essential link between the Word and the apostolic writings is found in their *apostolicity*, on the basis of the unique relationship between Jesus Christ and his apostles. This unparalleled relationship is the foundation of the unique status of apostolicity as a category of revelatory authority, and therefore of the unique revelatory authority of the apostolic writings, as Christ's incarnational revelation of himself and the Father is preserved and mediated to the church by the apostles.[166]

This unparalleled relationship and the resulting unique status of apostolicity occurred as the pinnacle of the Word's revelation—the Incarnation itself—was entrusted to the apostles by Christ. Irenaeus explains that Christ chose these apostles to be his followers and disciples, to learn his teachings directly, and to be the primary witnesses of the events of his life: these apostles "whom the Lord made witnesses of all His acts and His doctrine" (3.12.15), and who "from the beginning were eye-witnesses and ministers of the word of truth [*Verbi veritatis*]" (4.pre.3).[167] By this "the Lord of all

---

which the Word revealed the Father and prophesied his own future Incarnation, and which possess scriptural status for the Christian faith on this basis.

[165] Cf. 4.34.3-5, 4.20.4, etc.

[166] Torrance, *Divine Meaning*, provides an apt description of Irenaeus' position:

> Christ himself in his risen power and self-evidencing reality continues to be present in the witness and teaching of the Apostles. This does not mean that Christ the Word was resolved into the apostolic word, but it does mean that after the foundation of his Church upon the Apostles we have access to the self-proclamation and self-communication of Christ only in the form which, under the creative impact of the risen Lord and his Spirit, it has assumed once for all in the apostolic witness and tradition. (59)

[167] The importance of the apostles' role as witness of Christ for Irenaeus has been discussed in Section 4.3C.

gave His apostles the authority of the Gospel [*potestatem Euangelii*]" (3.pre).[168] Having taught them and revealed to them his plan of salvation, Christ also commissioned the apostles (3.5.2) and "sent His apostles into the world to proclaim with accuracy" (4.35.2) all that he had revealed: "Thus did the apostles, with simplicity and with envy toward no one, hand down to all whatever they had learned from the Lord" (3.14.2), sending them with the declaration, "He who hears you hears me" (3.pre; Lk. 10:16). It is for this reason that Irenaeus distinguishes between the roles of prophets and apostles, only the latter being conceived of as authors in the full sense.[169] The apostles' unprecedented relationship to the Word of God which Christ has instituted, and through which he has ensured the preservation and transmission of the culmination of his revelation, grants apostolic tradition the status of *divinely sanctioned mediation of the Word's consummate revelation to humanity*. This is the answer to the question, first raised in the previous chapter and which has formed the subject of this final section, as to why apostolicity operates for Irenaeus as a second category of unique revelatory authority alongside the Jewish scriptures.

This account of the apostolic tradition, with its direct link to the culmination of the Word's revelatory function, in turn forms the basis of the unique nature and status of the apostolic writings, themselves one of the central elements of the apostolic tradition and the primary means of accessing and preserving the apostolic preaching of the Gospel.[170] On this basis, the apostolic writings are understood by Irenaeus to be *the authoritative written record of the divinely sanctioned apostolic mediation of the consummate revelation of the Word to humanity*. This is Irenaeus' understanding of the unique status of the apostolic writings, and the basis of his distinct methods of use of the apostolic writings throughout *Adversus haereses* and the *Demonstration*. This understanding of the status of the apostolic writings indicates the reason Irenaeus held them to possess such paramount importance, equivalent to the revelatory authority of the Jewish scriptures, despite their distinct nature and status.

Chapter Conclusion

This chapter set out to investigate the implications of Irenaeus' understanding of the concept of divine inspiration for his view of the foundation of the unique revelatory authority of the apostolic writings. Its conclusions support the findings of the previous

---

[168] My trans. *Potestatem* is almost certainly a rendering of ἐξουσία, as Rousseau–Doutreleau indicate (SC 211:21).

[169] Discussed in the conclusion to Section 2.3.

[170] The apostles are also inspired by the Spirit, and this is an essential aspect of the nature and basis of authority of the apostolic writings (3.1.1). However, the fundamental difference between the apostles and the rest of the church is not located in their inspiration by the Spirit but in their direct access and unique relationship to the incarnate Word. The Word is therefore the primary basis of the unique authority of the apostolic writings through the Incarnation itself and through his institution of the apostles as the heralds of this message. Within this process, the Spirit does not create the content of the message, nor does the Spirit guarantee its infallibility, for this is not the Spirit's role. The Spirit non-coercively guides and equips, "nourishes and increases" all aspects of the life of the church.

chapters that the revelatory authority of the apostolic writings is founded directly on their perceived apostolic origin, not on a notion of scriptural status derived on the basis of divine authorship. The basis of the unique status of apostolicity as a category of revelatory authority is located in the unparalleled relationship between the apostles and the incarnate Word of God, in the consummation of his role as Revealer of the Father.

These conclusions were reached in four successive stages. An initial analysis of the relationship between inspiration and divine authority in Section 4.1 found that, while the traditional interpretation of Irenaeus identifies the inspiration of the apostles or their writings as a primary motivating factor in his acceptance of their status as scripture—on the basis of a belief that divine inspiration entails divine authorship and resulting scriptural status—closer examination indicated that while Irenaeus affirmed the inspiration of the Spirit on the apostles and their writings, both he and many other patristic writers before and after him also affirmed inspiration for all other aspects of the church's life, indicating that inspiration broadly conceived could not form the basis for the unique revelatory authority (or perceived scriptural status) of the apostolic writings. This led to the initial conclusion that the possibility of inspiration playing a central role in the unique revelatory authority of the apostolic writings requires that the apostles and their writings be considered to be endowed with a "special" form of inspiration, falling under the proposed category of *auctoritas* inspiration that entails divine authorship and resulting scriptural status.

In order to determine whether this could in fact be the case, Irenaeus' patterns of reference to the divine in relation to the composition of the Jewish scriptures were next examined in Section 4.2, in order to determine how Irenaeus discusses writings that receive divine *auctoritas* and resulting scriptural status, and by this to set a baseline against which his references to the apostolic writings could subsequently be compared in Section 4.3. Here it was determined that in his comments on the Jewish scriptures, Irenaeus clearly and consistently describes an *auctoritas* form of inspiration, repeatedly states that the whole of the Jewish scriptures are authored by God, and often ties their authority directly to their divine *auctoritas*. In comparison, a detailed analysis of Irenaeus' statements concerning the inspiration of the apostolic writings found that these exhibit no equivalence to his abundance of affirmations of the *auctoritas* inspiration of the Jewish scriptures. The analysis revealed only two possible instances of claimed divine *auctoritas* for the apostolic writings, each of which exhibits other equally plausible interpretations that do not indicate *auctoritas*. In addition, it was determined that Irenaeus makes three consistent claims that in fact rule out the possibility of *auctoritas* inspiration of the apostolic writings: he repeatedly claims divine authorship for the Jewish scriptures to the explicit exclusion of the apostolic writings; he consistently defends the authority of the apostolic writings on the basis of the apostles' proximity to Christ, rather than inspiration; and he presents a pneumatology that rules out the possibility of divine *auctoritas* by the Spirit for the apostolic writings.

Taken as a whole, these considerations confirm that inspiration cannot form the basis of the unique revelatory authority of the apostolic writings, indicating that a difference in types of inspiration is the cause of the conceptual distinction that had previously been observed between the Jewish scriptures and the apostolic writings. The divine *auctoritas* of the Jewish scriptures forms the basis of their divine scriptural status, while the apostolic writings—though they are endowed with *inspiratio*—acquire their unique revelatory authority on the basis of their apostolic origin, as the previous chapter described.

In the final section, the reason why apostolicity operates for Irenaeus as a second category of revelatory authority was explored in relation to his theology of the Word. Here it was determined that all of the Word's functions within the divine economy—the creation of all things, speaking to the prophets and prophesying his future coming, and becoming incarnate as Jesus Christ for the salvation of humanity—are aspects of his overarching role as Revealer of the Father. According to Irenaeus, the transcendence and invisibility of the Father means that he cannot be known by humanity unless revealed by a mediator, and because the Father has resolved to reveal himself to humanity, he does so through his Word. Throughout the whole of the Father's economy of salvation, the Word reveals the Father in order to accomplish the salvation of humanity, and this revelatory role culminates in the Incarnation, where the Word becomes "*visibile Patris Filius.*"

On the basis of this understanding of the process of revelation, the central difference between the scriptures and the apostolic writings was determined: the scriptures had been the instrument through which the Word first revealed himself to the prophets, while the subsequent culmination of the Word's revelation of the Father did not occur through a new set of scriptures, but through the Incarnation. The apostolic writings therefore constitute the authoritative record of the Word's consummate revelation, rather than that revelation itself. The apostolic origin of the apostolic writings grants them revelatory authority on the basis of the unparalleled relationship between the apostles and the incarnate Word, as Jesus Christ chose the apostles to be the primary witnesses of his life, taught them and revealed himself and the Father to them, and commissioned and sent the apostles to proclaim his revelation to humanity. On this basis, it was determined that the apostolic tradition possesses the status of divinely sanctioned mediation of the Word's consummate revelation to humanity, and the apostolic writings, as one of the central elements of the apostolic tradition and the primary means of accessing and preserving the apostolic preaching of the Gospel, are the authoritative written record of this divinely sanctioned mediation.

These findings confirm and extend the conclusions reached in the previous chapters, and complete the demonstration of the central thesis of this project: the apostolic writings are not, as the traditional interpretation holds, understood by Irenaeus to be a new set of scriptures whose scriptural status is derived on the basis of its divine inspiration. Instead, the apostolic writings are held to be a record of the testimony of the apostles, composed by the apostles themselves, of the consummate revelation of the Word of God to humanity and of the true interpretation of the scriptures in light of this revelation, unparalleled in their authority on the basis of the unique relationship between the apostles and the incarnate Word who is the only Revealer of the Father.

Conclusion

In this book I have advanced a two-part argument for a revised account of Irenaeus' conception of the nature and status of the apostolic writings. Briefly summarized: an initial critical assessment of the traditional interpretation of Irenaeus as one who holds the apostolic writings to be scripture equivalent to the Jewish scriptures was undertaken in Part 1, leading to the conclusion that the traditional interpretation's three supporting arguments are unable to substantiate its claim. Careful analysis instead revealed the existence of a conceptual distinction between the apostolic writings and the scriptures. This was followed in Part 2 by the construction of an alternative interpretation of Irenaeus' understanding of the apostolic writings as the authoritative record of the apostolic tradition, which possesses its unique revelatory authority on the basis of its apostolic origin, rather than its inspiration. The unique status of apostolicity as a distinct category of revelatory authority was found to arise through the apostles' unparalleled relationship to the Word of God and their proximity to his consummate revelation of the Father in the Incarnation of Jesus Christ. On this basis it was concluded that the apostolic writings are conceived as the authoritative written record of the divinely sanctioned mediation of the Word's consummate revelation to humanity.

On the basis of the account advanced here, it is possible to construct a diagram illustrating Irenaeus' conception of revelatory authority (see Figure 1).

All revelation comes from the Word who is the only Revealer of the invisible Father. The Word reveals the truth, first by delivering his Father's message to the prophets and prophesying his future coming, and then at last through his own Incarnation.[1] The apostles—as the primary witnesses of the Incarnation, who are taught by Christ and commissioned by him to proclaim his revelation—preach the Gospel of Jesus Christ as the true interpretation of the Jewish scriptures in light of the final revelation of the Word. Their teaching is the apostolic tradition: the divinely sanctioned mediation of the Word's final revelation to humanity. The apostolic tradition is materially accessed through the apostolic writings (the authoritative record of the apostolic tradition) and the rule of truth (a fluid expression of the central elements of this tradition). The apostolic writings are therefore the record of the apostolic interpretation of

---

[1] The diagram omits the first category of the Word's revelatory functions, his creation of all things visible and invisible. This diagram is concerned only with tracing those elements that function practically for Irenaeus as sources of authority within his writings.

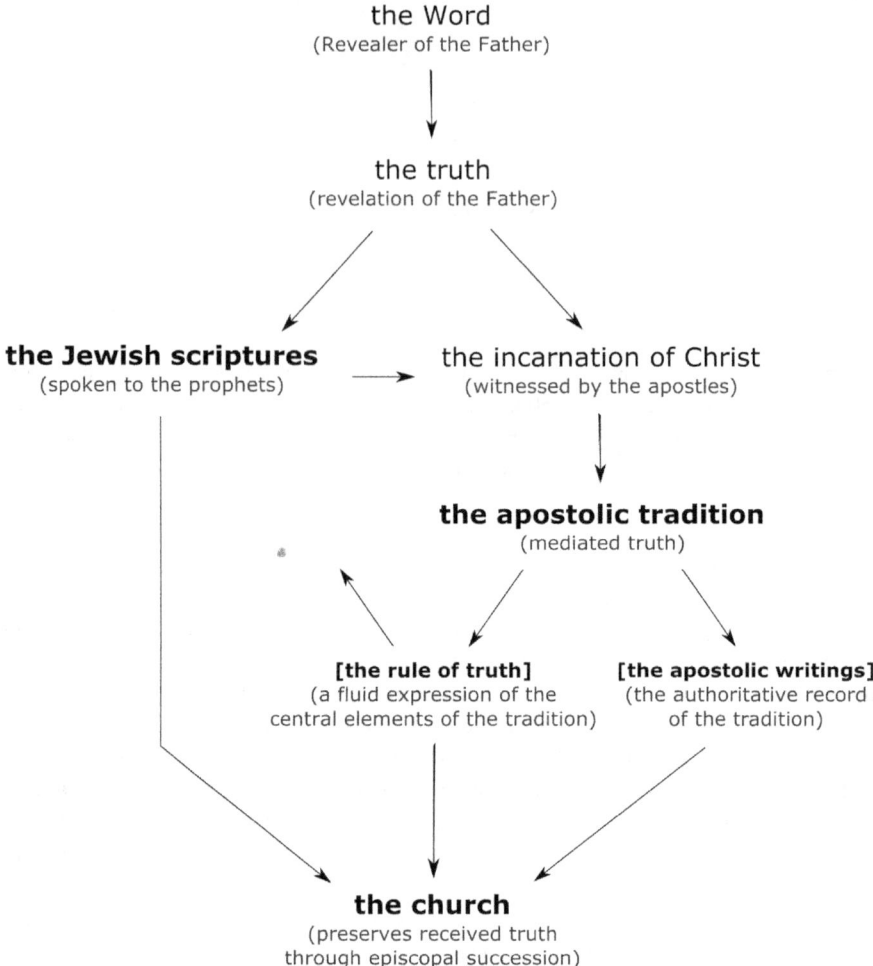

Figure 1 Diagram of Authority.

the scriptures, while the rule of truth is the description of the rules for interpreting the scriptures properly. The church receives the Jewish scriptures and the apostolic tradition (in concrete form as the apostolic writings, and in summary as the rule of truth), as well as the Spirit of God who guides and perfects it, and it is the church's duty to preserve and pass on the truth that it has received by divine revelation. The preservation of the apostolic teaching is ensured by (and is the purpose of) episcopal succession, which can be traced back to the apostles themselves. The Spirit does not appear on this diagram, for the Spirit pervades every aspect, superintending the entire process.

As this diagram indicates, Irenaeus does not conceive of multiple sources of authority that may be pitted against each other or ranked in comparison to one another. The only source of authority is the Word of the Father, who reveals the Truth. This Truth is accessed by the church through the apostolic reading of the scriptures in light of the Incarnation, the record of which is the apostolic writings.

Potential Implications

The account of Irenaeus' understanding of the process of divine revelation and his resulting conception of the status of the apostolic writings advanced in this book potentially has significant implications beyond clarifying how Irenaeus himself should be interpreted on these themes. Implications arise in particular for how the process of New Testament canon formation is conceived, and for contemporary theological formulations of the doctrine of scripture.

Implications for the Process of New Testament Canon Formation

Irenaeus' importance for the question of how and when the New Testament canon was formed is a central motivating factor for this study, as the field of New Testament canon formation scholarship relies heavily on the evidence he provides. He is the first witness to the extensive use of almost all the New Testament writings, he is widely considered to provide the earliest evidence of the acceptance of the scriptural status of the New Testament writings, and he is often held to be the first to advocate a closed gospel canon. A major consequence of the argument of this book is its effect on these significant historical claims.

This significance is particularly felt in relation to the consensus view that all or most of the New Testament documents had attained scriptural status in the early church by the end of the second century. The two primary pieces of evidence used to demonstrate this claim have been the witness of the Muratorian fragment and the testimony of Irenaeus,[2] and since at least 1992 the traditional dating of the Muratorian fragment to the late second century has been widely called into question in the aftermath of Geoffrey Hahneman's influential study *The Muratorian Fragment and the Development of the Canon*, in which he argued instead for a late-fourth-century date.[3] Irenaeus' testimony has therefore been left as the primary piece of evidence substantiating the consensus view, which has nonetheless continued to receive universal acceptance.

---

[2] Campenhausen, *Formation*, has been influential in identifying Irenaeus (182–209) and the Muratorian fragment (243–63) as the earliest conclusive evidence for the scriptural status of the New Testament writings.

[3] Geoffrey M. Hahneman, *The Muratorian Fragment and the Development of the Canon* (Oxford: Clarendon Press, 1992). A. C. Sundberg had previously made the same argument in 1973: "Canon Muratori: A Fourth-Century List," *HTR* 66 (1973): 1–41. However, his conclusions did not receive wide acceptance until Hahneman expanded his argument. His argument has since been accepted by Barton, *Holy Writings*, 10; McDonald, *Formation*, 209–20; "Identifying Scripture," 431; Harry Y. Gamble, "Canon, New Testament," in *The Anchor Bible Dictionary*, ed. David Freedman (Garden City, NY: Doubleday, 1992), 1:856; etc. Helmut Koester, *Ancient Christian Gospels: Their History and Development* (London: SCM Press, 1990), 243, had already accepted Sundberg's arguments previously.

Because of this, if the account of Irenaeus' conception of the status of the apostolic writings presented in this book is accepted, it has the effect of invalidating the claim that the New Testament writings had attained the status of scripture by the end of the second century.

John Barton has argued, against virtually all sides in the debate about the formation of the New Testament canon, that the end of the second century is actually of little importance within this process.[4] The writings that would become the New Testament already possessed as high esteem and authority as they would ever have within the church almost a century earlier, while determinations about the limits of the New Testament, and the conception of scripture this entails, were not in place prior to the end of the fourth century. Barton's claim is supported by the conclusions reached in this book, for Irenaeus demonstrates an extremely high view of the unique revelatory authority of the apostolic writings that he argues has been the case since they were first written down, while simultaneously indicating that the attainment of scriptural (and canonical) status for the apostolic writings must have occurred sometime after him. No important change in the status of the New Testament writings appears to have occurred at the end of the second century.

The implication that the consensus claim of recognition of scriptural status for the New Testament writings by the end of the second century is invalidated by this account indicates that similar reevaluations of other patristic writers following Irenaeus should be conducted, in order to determine whether the same methods of interpretation of Irenaeus have also been applied to other figures of this period. Such reevaluations could lead to a new determination of the point at which the apostolic writings came to attain the status of scripture. Careful studies of the understanding of the nature and basis of authority of the apostolic writings held by Clement of Alexandria, Tertullian, Hippolytus, Origen, Cyprian, Eusebius, Hilary, Athanasius, and so on become necessary in light of the conclusions of this book in order to retrace the development of the scriptural status of the New Testament writings.

Implications for Contemporary Theological Formulations of the Doctrine of Scripture

If the implications of the argument advanced in this book for the process of New Testament canonization were to be confirmed by subsequent studies on other relevant early church figures, additional implications could emerge for how the doctrine of scripture is conceived within accounts that consider the conceptions of those patristic figures who were responsible for the canonization of the New Testament[5] to hold authority for how scripture is to be conceived theologically.[6]

---

[4] Barton, *Holy Writings*, ch. 1, esp. 30–1.
[5] By this I mean those figures who first recognized that the apostolic writings merited scriptural status, and who exerted influence on the process of determining precisely which documents did and did not merit inclusion.
[6] It seems to me that any doctrine of scripture that relies on the conclusions of these influential patristic figures (i.e., the New Testament canon) should also accept the criteria they used to come to these conclusions. If other important thinkers were to be found to hold similar views to Irenaeus on the New Testament writings—that is, if apostolicity rather than inspiration were to be determined

When Irenaeus' conception of the status of the apostolic writings as described in this book is incorporated into contemporary formulations of the doctrine of scripture, it becomes evident that it is misleading and unhelpful to define the New Testament straightforwardly as "scripture" in the modern understanding of the concept, according to which the Old and New Testaments are often treated as a unified whole with the same origin, purpose, and methods of interpretation and application. This does not mean that incorporating Irenaeus' conception requires a denial of the scriptural status of the New Testament. Instead, a revised conception of scripture may be required, which is able to incorporate both the Old and New Testaments in such a way that it remains faithful to their essential characters and distinct relationships to the revelation of the Word. A singular doctrine of scripture that attempts to describe both forms of revelation as a single entity is unable to preserve this distinction, for the Old and New Testaments relate to the revelation of the Word in vitally distinct ways that cannot simply be harmonized into a single system. Any formulation of scripture resulting from Irenaeus' insights should therefore be twofold, describing the direct revelation of the Word delivered to and recorded by the prophets alongside the revelation of the Word in the Incarnation mediated by the apostles, united by a single underlying doctrine of revelation according to which the Word reveals the Father by the agency of the Spirit.

Such a twofold formulation would have practical implications for how scripture is treated. The recognition that the New Testament writings relate to the fullest revelation of the Word, yet relate to this revelation in a less direct way than the Old Testament (characterized by apostolic mediation rather than *auctoritas* inspiration) leads to the requirement of distinct methods of interpretation for each collection. The direct divine authorship of the Old Testament writings imbues them with a level of divine meaning above what may be perceived by seeking only the meaning they had within their original historical context, so other interpretative methods become necessary in order to interpret the meanings intended by the Word as author. In contrast, the direct apostolic authorship of the New Testament writings indicates that the apostolic authors' intentions within their own historical context are paramount, and methods of interpretation should then reflect this concern. At the same time, because the Incarnation represents the Word's fullest revelation of the Father, the apostolic tradition (through the rule of truth and the New Testament) controls the interpretation of the Old Testament.

A twofold formulation of scripture also gives rise to differences in how these interpretations are applied. The *inspiratio* (rather than *auctoritas*) inspiration of the apostles would entail that their words are not as immediate in their relationship to the Word as the words of the prophets, and therefore particular apostolic words would not all automatically and equally command the same direct divine authority as the prophetic words of the Old Testament as the Word of God. If the Word has not directly

---

to be the essential criterion for determining scriptural status—then perhaps any theological account of scripture that is intended to be applied to their listing of scriptures should reflect this conception. Cf. Kenneth R. Laing, "The *Logos* and the Authority of Scripture: A Proposal Motivated by Irenaeus' Trinitarian Account of Revelation," *International Journal of Systematic Theology* 20.4 (2018): 455–71.

composed the words written by the apostles (nor has the Spirit), these apostolic words would not possess the divine status necessary to be treated as inerrant or infallible. The apostles are viewed as reliable witnesses that can be trusted with the truth, and so would not require these divine attributes in order to be treated as authoritative for Christian faith and practice. Yet this also means that specific passages from the New Testament could not simply be abstracted from their contexts and claimed to make definitive judgments about contemporary issues, as if spoken by God for the present situation. In their application, as in their interpretation, the apostolic writings are to be treated as a record of the apostolic mediation of the Gospel of Jesus Christ to his church.

Bibliography

Primary Sources for Irenaeus' Works

Adversus Haereses

Texts

Harvey, W. Wigan, ed. *Sancti Irenaei Episcopi Lugdunensis: Libros quinque adversus haereses*. 2 vols. Cambridge: Typis Academicis, 1857.
Massuet, R., ed. *Sancti Irenaei episcopi Lugdunensis et martyris detectionis et eversionis falso cognominatae agnitionis libri quinque*. Paris: Typis Joannis Baptistae Coignard, 1710. Reprinted in *Sancti Irenaei: Episcopi Lugdunensis et Martyris*. PG 7. Edited by J. P. Migne. Paris: Imprimerie Catholique, 1857.
Renoux, C. *Nouveaux fragments armeniens de l' "Adversus Haereses" et de l' "Epideixis."* PO 39.1. Turnhout: Brepols, 1978.
Richard, M., and B. Hemmerdinger. "Trois nouveaux fragments grecs de l'Adversus haereses de saint Irenée." *Zeitschrift für die Neutestamentliche Wissenschaft* 53 (1962): 252–5.
Rousseau, Adelin, Bertrand Hemmerdinger, and Louis Doutreleau, eds. *Irénée de Lyon: Contre les hérésies: Livre 1*. Sources Chrétiennes 263–4. Paris: du Cerf, 1979.
Rousseau, Adelin, Bertrand Hemmerdinger, and Louis Doutreleau, eds. *Irénée de Lyon: Contre les hérésies: Livre 2*. Sources Chrétiennes 293–4. Paris: du Cerf, 1982.
Rousseau, Adelin, Bertrand Hemmerdinger, and Louis Doutreleau, eds. *Irénée de Lyon: Contre les hérésies: Livre 3*. Sources Chrétiennes 210–11. Paris: du Cerf, 1974.
Rousseau, Adelin, Bertrand Hemmerdinger, Louis Doutreleau, and Charles Mercier, eds. *Irénée de Lyon: Contre les hérésies: Livre 4*. 2 vols. SC 100. Paris: du Cerf, 1965.
Rousseau, Adelin, Bertrand Hemmerdinger, Louis Doutreleau, and Charles Mercier, eds. *Irénée de Lyon: Contre les hérésies: Livre 5*. SC 151–2. Paris: du Cerf, 1969.
Sagnard, F., ed. *Irénée de Lyon: Contre Les Hérésies: Livre 3*. SC 34. Paris: du Cerf, 1952.
Ter-Mekerttschian, Karapet, and E. Ter-Minassiantz, eds. *Irenäus, Gegen die Häretiker* [Ελεγχος καὶ ἀνατροπὴ τῆς ψευδωνύμου γνώσεως], *Buch IV u. V in armenischer Version*. Texte und Untersuchungen 35.2. Leipzig: Hinrichs, 1910.

Translations

Grant, Robert M. *Irenaeus of Lyons*. London: Routledge, 1997.
Roberts, Alexander, and James Donaldson, eds. *The Apostolic Fathers, Justin Martyr, Irenaeus*. ANF Vol. 1. Edinburgh: T&T Clark, 1989.
Rousseau, Adelin, Bertrand Hemmerdinger, Louis Doutreleau, and Charles Mercier, eds. *Irénée de Lyon: Contre les hérésies*. Books 1–5. Paris: du Cerf, 1965–82.

Unger, Dominic J., ed. *St. Irenaeus of Lyons: Against the Heresies (Book 1).* Ancient Christian Writers 55. New York: Paulist Press, 1992.

Unger, Dominic J., ed. *St. Irenaeus of Lyons: Against the Heresies (Book 2).* ACW 65. New York: Paulist Press, 2012.

Unger, Dominic J., ed. *St. Irenaeus of Lyons: Against the Heresies (Book 3).* ACW 64. New York: Paulist Press, 2012.

The Demonstration of the Apostolic Preaching

Texts

Renoux, C. *Nouveaux fragments armeniens de l' "Adversus Haereses" et de l'"Epideixis."* PO 39.1. Turnhout: Brepols, 1978.

Ter Mékérttschian, Karapet, and S. G. Wilson, eds. *Saint Irénée*: Εις Ειδειξιν του Αποστολικου Κηρυγματος; *The Proof of the Apostolic Preaching, with Seven Fragments.* PO 12.5. Turnhout: Editions Brepols, 1989.

Translations

Behr, John., ed. *St Irenaeus of Lyons: On the Apostolic Preaching.* Popular Patristics Series 17. Crestwood, KY: SVS, 1997.

Froidevaux. L. M., ed. *Irénée de Lyon: Démonstration de la Prédication Apostolique.* SC 62. Paris: du Cerf, 1959.

Robinson, J. Armitage, ed. *The Demonstration of the Apostolic Preaching.* London: SPCK, 1920. Reprinted in *Irenaeus's Demonstration of the Apostolic Preaching: A Theological Commentary and Translation.* By Iain M. Mackenzie. Burlington: Ashgate, 2002.

Rousseau, Adelin., ed. *Irénée de Lyon: Démonstration de la Prédiction Apostolique.* SC 406. Paris: du Cerf, 1995.

Smith, Joseph P., ed. *Proof of the Apostolic Preaching.* ACW 16. Westminster: Newman, 1952.

Fragments of Lost Writings

Texts

Eusebius. *Historia Ecclesiastica.* Edited by Eduard Schwartz. Berlin: GCS, 1952.

Harvey, W. Wigan, ed. *Sancti Irenaei Episcopi Lugdunensis: Libros quinque adversus haereses.* Vol. 2. Cambridge: Typis Academicis, 1857.

Holl, K., ed. *Fragmente vornicänischer Kirchenväter aus den Sacra Parallela.* Texteund Untersuchungen 20.2. Leipzig: Hinrich, 1899.

Translations

Maier, Paul L., ed. *Eusebius: The Church History.* Grand Rapids, MI: Kregel, 2007.

Roberts, Alexander and James Donaldson, eds. *The Apostolic Fathers with Justin Martyr and Irenaeus*. ANF Vol. 1. Edinburgh: T&T Clark, 1989.

Reference Works

Reynders, B. *Lexique Comparé du Texte Grec et des Versions Latine, Arménienne et Syriaque de l'"Adversus Haereses" de saint Irénée*. 2 vols. Louvain: Peeters, 1954.
Reynders, B. *Vocabulaire de la "Démonstration" et des fragments de S. Irénée*. Louvain: Éditions de Chevetogne, 1958.
Sanday, W., and C. H. Turner. *Novum Testamentum Sancti Irenaei*. Oxford: Clarendon Press, 1923.

Secondary Sources Cited

Abbott-Smith, G. *A Manual Greek Lexicon of the New Testament*. Edinburgh: T&T Clark, 1922.
Aichele, George. *Biblical Meaning: Canon as Semiotic Mechanism*. Harrisburg: Trinity Press International, 2001.
Allen, P. S., and H. M. Allen, eds. *Opus Epistolarum Des. Erasmi Roterdami, Vol. 6: 1525–1527*. Oxford: Clarendon Press, 1926.
Allert, Craig. *A High View of Scripture?* Grand Rapids, MI: Baker Academic, 2007.
Ammundsen, Valdemar. "The Rule of Truth in Irenaeus." *Journal of Theological Studies* 13 (1912): 574–80.
Ayres, Lewis. "Irenaeus vs. the Valentinians: Toward a Rethinking of Patristic Exegetical Origins." *Journal of Early Christian Studies* 23.2 (2015): 153–87.
Ayres, Lewis. "Patristic and Medieval Theologies of Scripture: An Introduction." In *Christian Theologies of Scripture: A Comparative Introduction*, 11–20. Edited by Justin S. Holcomb. New York: New York University Press, 2006.
Ayres, Lewis. "'There's Fire in That Rain:' On Reading the Letter and Reading Allegorically." *Modern Theology* 28.4 (2012): 616–34.
Bacq, Philip. *De l'ancienne a la nouvelle alliance selon S. Irenee: Unite du livre IV de l'Adversus haereses*. Paris: Lethielleux, 1978.
Barton, John. *Holy Writings, Sacred Text: The Canon in Early Christianity*. Louisville, KY: Westminster John Knox Press, 1997.
Barton, John. *People of the Book? The Authority of the Bible in Christianity*. London: SPCK, 1988.
Bauer, Walter. *Rechtglaubigkeit und Ketzerei im altesten Christentum*. Tubingen: Mohr, 1934. Reproduced in English from the 2nd ed. (1964, ed. G. Strecker) as *Orthodoxy and Heresy in Earliest Christianity*. Translated by R. Kraft and G. Krodel. Philadelphia, PA: Fortress Press, 1971.
Bedrossian, Matthias. *New Dictionary: Armenian-English*. Venice: S. Lazarus Armenian Academy, 1875-9.
Behr, John. *Asceticism and Anthropology in Irenaeus and Clement*. Oxford: Oxford University Press, 2000.
Behr, John. *Irenaeus of Lyons: Identifying Christianity*. Oxford: Oxford University Press, 2013.
Behr, John. "Irenaeus on the Word of God." *Studia Patristica* 36 (2001): 163–7.

Behr, John. *John the Theologian and his Paschal Gospel: A Prologue to Theology.* Forthcoming.
Behr, John. "Scripture, the Gospel, and Orthodoxy." *St. Vladimir's Theological Quarterly* 43.3–4 (1999): 223–48.
Behr, John. *The Way to Nicaea: Formation of Christian Theology Volume 1.* Crestwood, NY: SVS Press, 2001.
Benoit, André. "Ecriture et Tradition chez Saint Irenee." *Revue d'Histoire de Philosophie Religieuses* 40.1 (1960): 32–44.
Benoit, André. *Saint Irénée: Introduction a l'Étude de sa Théologie.* Paris: Presses Universitaires de France, 1960.
Beuzart, Paul. *Essai sur la Theologie d'Irenee.* Paris: Ernest Leroux, 1908.
Bingham, D. Jeffrey. "The Bishop in the Mirror: Scripture and Irenaeus's Self-understanding in *Adversus haereses* Book One." In *Tradition and the Rule of Faith in the Early Church,* 48–67. Edited by Ronnie J. Rombs and Alexander J. Hwang. Washington, DC: Catholic University of America Press, 2010.
Bingham, D. Jeffrey. *Irenaeus's Use of Matthew's Gospel in* Adversus haereses. Louvain: Peeters, 1998.
Blanchard, Yves-Marie. *Aux Sources du Canon, le Témoignage d'Irénée.* Paris: du Cerf, 1993.
Blowers, Paul M. "The *Regula Fidei* and the Narrative Character of Early Christian Faith." *Pro Ecclesia* 6 (1997): 199–228.
Bokedal, Tomas. *The Formation and Significance of the Christian Biblical Canon: A Study in Text, Ritual, and Interpretation.* London: Bloomsbury, 2014.
Bokedal, Tomas. "The Rule of Faith: Tracing Its Origins." *Journal of Theological Interpretation* 7.2 (2013): 233–55.
Bousset, Wilhelm. *Judisch-christlicher Schulbetried in Alexandria und Rom: Literarische Untersuchungen zu Philo und Clemens von Alexandria, Justin und Irenaus.* Gottingen: Vandenhoeck & Ruprecht, 1915.
Brakke, David. *The Gnostics: Myth, Ritual, and Diversity in Early Christianity.* Cambridge, MA: Harvard University Press, 2010.
Briggman, Anthony. *Irenaeus of Lyons and the Theology of the Holy Spirit.* Oxford: Oxford University Press, 2012.
Brox, Norbert. "Irenaeus and the Bible." In *Handbook of Patristic Exegesis: The Bible in Ancient Christianity,* 1:483–506. By Charles Kannengiesser. Leiden: Brill, 2004.
Bruce, F. F. *The Canon of Scripture.* Downers Grove, IL: InterVarsity Press, 1988.
Camelot, P. Th., ed. *Ignace d'Antioche, Polycarpe de Smyrne: Letters, Martyre de Polycarpe.* SC 10. Paris: du Cerf, 1969.
Campenhausen, Hans von. *Die Entstehung der christlichen Bibel.* Tübingen: Mohr, 1968. Reproduced in English as *The Formation of the Christian Bible.* Translated by J. A. Baker. Mifflintown: Sigler Press, 1997.
Cullmann, Oscar. *The Early Church.* Edited by A. J. B. Higgins. London: SCM, 1956.
Dempster, Stephen G. "Torah, Torah, Torah: The Emergence of the Tripartite Canon." In *Exploring the Origins of the Bible: Canon Formation in Historical, Literary, and Theological Perspective,* 87–127. Edited by Craig A. Evans and Emanuel Tov. Grand Rapids, MI: Baker Academic, 2008.
Donovan, Mary Ann. *One Right Reading? A Guide to Irenaeus.* Collegeville, MN: Liturgical Press, 1997.
Ehrman, Bart D. *Lost Christianities: The Battles for Scripture and the Faiths we Never Knew.* Oxford: Oxford University Press, 2003.

Ellis, E. Earle. *The Old Testament in Early Christianity: Canon and Interpretation in the Light of Modern Research*. Grand Rapids, MI: Baker Academic, 1992.
Eynde, Damien van den. *Les Normes de l'Enseignement Chretien dans la littérature patristique des trois premiers siècles*. Paris: Gabalda & Fils, 1933.
Fantino, Jacques. *La Théologie d'Irénée: Lecture des Écritures en réponse à l'exégèse gnostique: Une approche trinitaire*. Paris: du Cerf, 1994.
Farkasfalvy, Denis M. "'Prophets and Apostles:' The Conjunction of the Two Terms Before Irenaeus." In *Texts and Testaments: Critical Essays on the Bible and the Early Church Fathers*, 109–34. Edited by W. Eugene March. San Antonio: Trinity University Press, 1980.
Farkasfalvy, Denis M. "Theology of Scripture in St. Irenaeus." *Revue Bénédictine* 78 (1968): 319–33.
Farmer, William R., and Denis. M. Farkasfalvy. *The Formation of the New Testament Canon: An Ecumenical Approach*. New York: Paulist Press, 1983.
Ferguson, Everett. "Factors Leading to the Selection and Closure of the New Testament Canon: A Survey of Some Recent Studies." In *The Canon Debate*, 295–320. Edited by Lee Martin McDonald and James A. Sanders. Peabody, MA: Hendrickson, 2002.
Ferguson, Everett. "Irenaeus' Proof of the Apostolic Preaching and Early Catechetical Instruction." *Studia Patristica* 18.3 (1989): 119–40.
Ferguson, Everett. "Paradosis and Traditio: A Word Study." In *Tradition and the Rule of Faith in the Early Church*, 3–29. Edited by Ronnie J. Rombs and Alexander J. Hwang. Washington, DC: Catholic University of America Press, 2010.
Flesseman-van Leer, Ellen. *Tradition and Scripture in the Early Church*. Assen: Van Gorcum, 1954.
Friesen, John. *A Study of the Influence of Confessional Bias on the Interpretations in the Modern Era of Irenaeus of Lyons*. Ann Arbor, MI: University Microfilms International, 1977.
Gamble, Harry Y. "Canon, New Testament." In *The Anchor Bible Dictionary*. Edited by David Freedman. Garden City, NY: Doubleday, 1992.
Gamble, Harry Y. *The New Testament Canon: Its Making and Meaning*. Philadelphia, PA: Fortress Press, 1985.
Graham, Susan. "Structure and Purpose of Irenaeus' *Epideixis*." *Studia Patristica* 36 (2001): 210–21.
Grant, Robert M. *The Formation of the New Testament*. New York: Harper & Row, 1965.
Grant, Robert M. *Irenaeus of Lyons*. London: Routledge, 1997.
Grant, Robert M. *The Letter and the Spirit*. London: Macmillan, 1957.
Grant, Robert M. *A Short History of the Interpretation of the Bible*. London: A&C Black, 1965.
Greer, Rowan. "The Dog and the Mushrooms: Irenaeus's View of the Valentinians assessed." In *The Rediscovery of Christian Gnosticism: Proceedings of the International Conference on Gnosticism at Yale*, 1:146–75. Edited and translated by Bentley Layton. Leiden: Brill, 1980–1.
Gundry, Robert H. "ΕΥΑΓΓΕΛΙΟΝ: How Soon a Book?" *Journal of Biblical Literature* 115 (1996): 321–5.
Hägglund, Bengt. "Die Bedeutung der 'regula fidei' als Grundlage theologischer Aussagen." *Studia Theologica* 12 (1958): 4–19.
Hägglund, Bengt. *Teologins historia: En dogmhistorisk översikt*. Lund: CWK Gleerups Förlag, 1956. Reproduced in English as *History of Theology*. Translated by Gene J. Lund. St. Louis: Concordia Publishing House, 1968.

Hahneman. Geoffrey M. *The Muratorian Fragment and the Development of the Canon.* Oxford: Clarendon Press, 1992.
Hanson, R. P. C. *Allegory and Event: A Study of the Sources and Significance of Origen's Interpretation of Scripture.* London: SCM Press, 1959.
Harnack, Adolf von. *Das Neue Testament um das Jahr 200.* Freiburg: Mohr, 1889.
Harnack, Adolf von. "Der Presbyter-Prediger des Irenaus (IV,27,1-32,1)." In *Philotesia: Paul Kleinert zum 70. Geburtstag dargebracht,* 1–37. Edited by Adolf von Harnack. Berlin: Trowzisch, 1907.
Harnack, Adolf von. *Lehrbuch der Dogmengeschichte.* Vol. 2. Freiburg: Mohr, 1888. Reproduced in English from the 3rd ed. as *History of Dogma.* Vol. 2. Translated by Neil Buchanan. Boston, MA: Roberts Brothers, 1897.
Harris, R. Laird. *The Inspiration and Canonicity of the Bible: An Historical and Exegetical Study.* Grand Rapids, MI: Zondervan Publishing House, 1969.
Hefner, Philip. "Theological Methodology and St. Irenaeus." *Journal of Religion* 44.4 (1964): 294–309.
Hengel, Martin. *The Septuagint as Christian Scripture: Its Prehistory and the problem of Its Canon.* Translated by Mark E. Biddle. Edinburgh: T&T Clark, 2002.
Hill, Charles. "The Truth above All Demonstration: Scripture in the Patristic Period to Augustine." In *The Enduring Authority of the Christian Scriptures,* 43–88. Edited by D. A. Carson. Grand Rapids, MI: Eerdmans, 2016.
Hitchcock, F. R. Montgomery. *Irenaeus of Lugdunum: A Study of His Teaching.* Cambridge: Cambridge University Press, 1914.
Hitchcock, F. R. Montgomery. "Loofs' Asiatic Source (IQA) and the Ps-Justin De Resurrectione." *Zeitschrift für ntl. Wissenschaft* 36 (1937): 35–60.
Hitchcock, F. R. Montgomery. "Loofs' Theory of Theophilus of Antioch as a Source of Irenaeus." *Journal of Theological Studies* 38 (1937): 130-9, 255–66.
Hoh, Josef. *Die Lehre des hl. Irenäus über das Neue Testament.* Münster: Aschendorff, 1919.
Holsinger-Friesen, Thomas. *Irenaeus and Genesis: A Study of Competition in Early Christian Hermeneutics.* Winona Lake, IN: Eisenbrauns, 2009.
Holstein, Henri. "La Tradition des Apôtres chez saint Irénée." *Recherches de science religieuse* 36.2 (1949): 229–70.
Jaubert, Annie, ed. *Clément de Rome: Épître aux Corinthiens.* SC 167. Paris: du Cerf, 1971.
Jorgensen, David W. *Treasure Hidden in a Field: Early Christian Reception of the Gospel of Matthew.* Berlin: De Gruyter, 2016.
Kalin, Everett R. *Argument from Inspiration in the Canonization of the New Testament.* ThD Diss., Harvard University, 1967.
Kalin, Everett R. "The Inspired Community: A Glance at Canon History." *Concordia Theological Monthly* 42 (1971): 541-9.
Kannengiesser, Charles. "The 'Speaking' God and Irenaeus's Interpretative Pattern: The Reception of Genesis." *Annali di storia dell' esegesi* 15.2 (1998): 337–52.
Kelly, J. N. D. *Early Christian Creeds.* 3rd ed. New York: Longman, 1983.
King, Karen. *What Is Gnosticism?* Cambridge: Belknap Press, 2003.
King, Karen. "Which Early Christianity?" In *The Oxford Handbook of Early Christian Studies,* 66–84. Edited by Susan Ashbrook Harvey and David G. Hunters. Oxford: Oxford University Press, 2008.
Kleist, James A., ed. *The Epistles of Clement of Rome and St. Ignatius of Antioch.* ACW 1. Westminster: Newman Bookshop, 1946.
Koch, H. "Zur Lehre vom Urstand und von der Erlösung bei Irenäus." *Theologische Studien und Kritiken* 96-7 (1925): 183–214.

Koester, Helmut. *Ancient Christian Gospels: Their History and Development*. London: SCM Press, 1990.
Lampe, G. W. H., ed. *A Patristic Greek Lexicon*. Oxford: Oxford University Press, 1961.
Lawson, John. *The Biblical Theology of Saint Irenaeus*. London: Epworth Press, 1948.
Lewis, Charlton T., and Charles Short. *A Latin Dictionary*. Revised ed. Oxford: Clarendon Press, 1962.
Lewis, C. S. *Reflections On The Psalms*. London: Fount Paperbacks, 1998.
Liddell, Henry George, and Robert Scott. *A Greek-English Lexicon*. 9th ed. Oxford: Clarendon Press, 1983.
Loofs, Friedrich. *Theophilus von Antiochien Adversus Marcionem, und die anderen theologischen Quellen bei Irenaeus*. TU 46.2. Leipzig: J. C. Hinrichs, 1930.
Lubac, Henri de. *Scripture in the Tradition*. New York: Crossroad, 2001.
McDonald, Lee M. *The Formation of the Christian Biblical Canon*. Revised ed. Peabody, MA: Hendrickson, 1995.
McDonald, Lee M. "Identifying Scripture and Canon in the Early Church: The Criteria Question." In *The Canon Debate*, 416–39. Edited by Lee M. McDonald and James A. Sanders. Peabody, MA: Hendrickson, 2002.
McDonald, Nathan. "Israel and the Old Testament Story in Irenaeus' Presentation of the Rule of Faith." *Journal of Theological Interpretation* 3.2 (2009): 281–98.
Metzger, Bruce M. *The Canon of the New Testament*. Oxford: Clarendon Press, 1987.
Migne, J. P., ed. *Clementis Alexandrini*. 2 vols. PG 8-9. Paris: Imprimerie Catholique, 1857.
Migne, J. P., ed. *Cypriani: Episcopi Carthaginensis et Martyris*. PL 4. Paris: Imprimerie Catholique, 1844.
Minns, Dennis. *Irenaeus: An Introduction*. London: T&T Clark International, 2010.
Noormann, Rolf. *Irenäus als Paulusinterpret: zur Rezeption und Wirkung der paulinischen und deuteropaulinischen Briefe im Werk des Irenäus von Lyon*. Tubingen: J. C. B. Mohr, 1994.
Norris, Richard. "Theology and Language in Irenaeus of Lyon." *Anglican Theological Review* 76.3 (1994): 285–95.
Ochagavia, Juan. *Visibile Patris Filius: A Study of Irenaeus' Teaching on Revelation and Tradition*. Rome: Typis Pontificiae Universitatis Gregorianae, 1964.
Olson, Mark Jeffrey. *Irenaeus, The Valentinian Gnostics, and the Kingdom of God*. Lewiston: Edwin Mellen Press, 1992.
Osborn, Eric. *Irenaeus of Lyons*. Cambridge: Cambridge University Press, 2001.
Osborn, Eric. "Reason and the Rule of Faith in the Second Century AD." In *The Making of Orthodoxy: Essays in Honour of Henry Chadwick*, 40–61. Edited by Rowan Williams. Cambridge: Cambridge University Press, 1989.
Pagels, Elaine. "Conflicting Versions of Valentinian Eschatology: Irenaeus' Treatise vs. the Excerpts from Theodotus." *Harvard Theological Review* 67 (1974): 35–53.
Pagels, Elaine. *The Gnostic Gospels*. London: Penguin, 1980.
Parvis, Paul. "Packaging Irenaeus: Adversus Haereses and its Editors." In *Irenaeus: Life, Scripture, Legacy*, 183–98. Edited by Sara Parvis and Paul Foster. Minneapolis, MN: Fortress Press, 2012.
Piper, Otto. "The Nature of the Gospel According to Justin Martyr." *Journal of Religion* 41:3 (1961): 155–68.
Reed, Annette Yoshiko. "ΕΥΑΓΓΕΛΙΟΝ: Orality, Textuality, and the Christian Truth in Irenaeus' *Adversus haereses*." *Vigiliae Christianae* 56 (2002): 11–46.
Reilly, W. S. "L'inspiration de l'A.T. chez Saint Irénée." *Revue biblique* 14 (1917): 489–507.

Rescher, Nicholas. *Interpreting Philosophy: The Elements of Philosophical Hermeneutics.* Frankfurt: Ontos Verlag, 2007.
Reynders, D. B. "*Paradosis*: Le progrés de l'idée de tradition jusqu'à saint Irénée." *Recherches de théologie ancienne et médiévale* 5 (1933): 155–91.
Reynders, D. B. "La polemique de Saint Irenee. Methode et principes." *Recherches de Théologie Ancienne et Médiévale* 7 (1935): 5–27.
Russell, Tracy Lee. "Authority and Apostolicity in Irenaeus of Lyons." MATS thesis, Regent College, 2014.
Schaff, Philip and Henry Wace, eds. *Eusebius Pamphilus: Church History, Life of Constantine, Oration in Praise of Constantine.* Nicene and Post-Nicene Fathers Ser. 2. Vol. 1. Edinburgh: T&T Clark, 1890.
Schleiermacher, Friedrich. *Der Christliche Glaube: nach den Grundsätzen der evangelischen Kirche.* Berlin: Reimer, 1821–31.
Second Vatican Council. "*Dei Verbum*: Dogmatic Constitution on Divine Revelation." In *Vatican II: The Essential Texts*, 79–99. Edited by Norman Tanner. New York: Image Books, 2012.
Seitz, Christopher R. *The Character of Christian Scripture: The Significance of a Two-Testament Bible.* Grand Rapids, MI: Baker Academic, 2011.
Sesboüé, Bernard. "La Preuve par les Ecritures chez S. Irenee: A propos d'un texte difficile du livre III de l'*Adversus haereses*." *Nouvelle revue théologique* 103 (1981): 872–87.
Simonetti, Manlio. *Profilo Storico dell' Esegesi Patristica.* Rome: Institutum Patristicum Augustinianum, 1981. Reproduced in English as *Biblical Interpretation in the Early Church.* Translated by John A. Hughes. Edinburgh: T&T Clark, 1994.
Skarsaune, Oskar. *The Proof from Prophecy: A Study in Justin Martyr's Proof-Text Tradition: Text-type, Provenance, Theological Profile.* Leiden: Brill, 1987.
Skeat, T. C. "Irenaeus and the Four-Gospel Canon." *Novum Testamentum* 34 (1992): 194–9.
Sophocles, E. A. *Greek Lexicon of the Roman and Byzantine Periods.* Cambridge, MA: Harvard University Press, 1914.
Stanton, Graham N. "The Fourfold Gospel." *New Testament Studies* 43 (1997): 317–46.
Steenberg, M. C. *Irenaeus on Creation: The Cosmic Christ and the Saga of Redemption.* Leiden: Brill, 2008.
Steenberg, M. C. "Irenaeus on Scripture, Graphe, and the Status of Hermas." *St. Vladimir's Theological Quarterly* 53.1 (2009): 29–66.
Stendahl, Krister. "The Apocalypse of John and the Epistles of Paul in the Muratorian Fragment." In *Current Issues in New Testament Interpretation: Essays in honor of Otto A. Piper*, 239–45. Edited by William Klassen and Graydon F. Snyder. New York: Harper & Row, 1962.
Sundberg, Albert C. Jr. "The Bible Canon and the Christian Doctrine of Inspiration." *Interpretation* 29 (1975): 352–71.
Sundberg, Albert C. Jr. "Canon Muratori: A Fourth Century List." *Harvard Theological Review* 66 (1973): 1–41.
Sundberg, Albert C. Jr. "Canon of the NT." In *The Interpreter's Dictionary of the Bible.* Suppl. vol. Nashville, TN: Abingdon Press, 1976.
Sundberg, Albert C. Jr. "The Making of the New Testament Canon." In *The Interpreter's One-Volume Commentary on the Bible*, 1216–20. Edited by Charles M. Laymon. Nashville, TN: Abingdon Press, 1971.
Sundberg, Albert C. Jr. *The Old Testament of the Early Church.* Cambridge, MA: Harvard University Press, 1964.

Sundberg, Albert C. Jr. "Towards a Revised History of the New Testament Canon." *Studia evangelica* 4.1 (1968): 452–61.
Thiselton, Anthony. *Thiselton on Hermeneutics: Collected Works with New Essays*. Grand Rapids, MI: Eerdmans, 2006.
Thomassen, Einar. *The Spiritual Seed: The Church of the Valentinians*. Leiden: Brill, 2008.
Thomson, Robert W. *An Introduction to Classical Armenian*. Delmar: Caravan Books, 1975.
Torrance, T. F. *Divine Meaning: Studies in Patristic Hermeneutics*. Edinburgh: T&T Clark, 1995.
Trigg, Joseph. "The Apostolic Fathers and the Apologists." In *A History of Biblical Interpretation*, 1:304–33. Edited by Alan Hauser and Duane Watson. Grand Rapids, MI: Eerdmans, 2003.
Vallée, Gérard. "Theological and Non-Theological Motives in Irenaeus' Refutation of the Gnostics." In *Jewish and Christian Self-Definition, Volume One: The Shaping of Christianity in the Second and Third Centuries*, 174–85. Edited by E. P. Sanders. London: SCM Press, 1980.
Warfield, Benjamin B. *The Canon of the New Testament: How and When Formed*. Philadelphia, PA: American Sunday-School Union, 1892.
Warfield, Benjamin B. *The Inspiration and Authority of the Bible*. Philadelphia, PA: Presbyterian and Reformed, 1970.
Watson, John, ed. *Quintilian's Institutes of Oratory*. London: H.G. Bonn, 1856.
Wendt, H. H. *Die christliche Lehre von der menschlichen Vollkommenheit*. Gottingen: Vandenhoeck & Ruprecht, 1882.
Werner, Johannes. *Der Paulinismus des Irenaus: Eine Kirchen- und Dogmengeschtliche Untersuchung uber das Verhaltnis des Irenaus zur Paulinischen Briefsammlung und Theologie*. Leipzig: J. C. Hinrichs'sche Buchhandlung, 1889.
Wiegel, James B. "The Trinitarian Structure of Irenaeus' *Demonstration of the Apostolic Preaching*." *Saint Vladimir's Theological Quarterly* 58:2 (2014): 113–39.
Wiles, Maurice M. *The Spiritual Gospel: The Interpretation of the Fourth Gospel in the Early Church*. Cambridge: Cambridge University Press, 1960.
Williams, Frank, ed. *The Panarion of Epiphanius of Salamis: Book 1 (Sects 1-46)*. 2nd ed. Leiden: Brill, 2009.
Wingren, Gustaf. *Människan och Inkarnationen enligt Irenaeus*. Lund: C.W.K Gleerup, 1947. Reproduced in English as *Man and the Incarnation: A Study in the Biblical Theology of Irenaeus*. Translated by Ross MacKenzie. London: Oliver and Boyd, 1959.
Winkelmann, F., L. Pietri, and M.-J. Rondeau, eds. *Eusébe de Césarée: Vie de Constantin*. SC 559. Paris: du Cerf, 2013.
Wittgenstein, Ludwig. *The Blue and Brown Books: Preliminary Studies for the "Philosophical Investigations."* Oxford: Basil Blackwell, 1969.
Wittgenstein, Ludwig. *Philosophical Investigations*. Oxford: Basil Blackwell, 1967.
Young, Frances. *The Art of Performance: Towards a Theology of Holy Scripture*. London: Darton, Longman, and Todd, 1990.
Young, Frances. *Biblical Exegesis and the Formation of Christian Culture*. Cambridge: Cambridge University Press, 1997.
Zahn, Theodor. *Geschichte des neutestamentlichen Kanons*. Erlangen: Andreas Deichert, 1888.
Zahn, Theodor. "Glaubensregel." In *Realencyklopädie für protestantische Theologie und Kirche*, 6:685. Edited by Albert Hauck. Leipzig: J.C. Hinrichs, 1899.
Zahn, Theodor. "Glaubensregel und Taufbekenntnis in der alten Kirche." In *Skizzen aus dem leben der alten Kirche*, 238–70. Leipzig: Deichert, 1908.

Index

advent 4, 19, 57, 62, 118, 130–1, 136, 147, 152, 175, 177, 179
Adversus haereses 9, 15–18, 20, 28, 45, 51, 53–4, 59, 72, 83, 103, 106, 109–10, 112–13, 115, 119, 123, 126–9, 135–6, 149, 155, 159, 169, 174, 183
αἱ γραφαὶ 16, 20–2, 35, 44–9, 55, 143, 159
allegorical interpretation 56, 78, 82–84, 86, 88
allegory 59, 78, 83–5, 88
Allert, Craig 2, 70, 73, 141, 145
Apocalypse 66–7, 145
apocryphal writings 31, 46–7
apostolicity 5–7, 95, 99, 129, 137, 139–40, 170–1, 181–5, 187, 190
apostolic interpretation 3, 6, 100, 129–30, 132, 137, 187
apostolic preaching 6, 10, 23, 37, 40, 89, 130, 132, 135–6, 183, 185
apostolic tradition 3, 5–6, 16, 36–37, 40, 72, 94, 99, 102, 105–6, 108–114, 116–17, 119, 121–6, 128–30, 132, 134–5, 137, 183, 185, 187–8, 191
Armenian 9–10, 15, 29–31, 65–6, 104–5, 148, 154, 172, 175
auctoritas 142, 144, 149–51, 154–9, 162–5, 167, 169–71, 173–5, 181–2, 184–5, 191
authorial intent 52, 56, 62, 82
authoritative author 51–3, 55, 74, 77, 88
authoritative text 52–4, 63–4, 66–7, 74, 77
authorship 31, 52–5, 65, 77, 86, 107, 139, 142, 144, 151, 156, 164, 170, 173, 181, 184, 191
Ayres, Lewis 53, 56, 82–3, 89

baptism 35, 61, 120–1, 126, 147
baptismal confession/creed 115, 121, 123, 125, 128

barbarian 39–40, 112, 122
Barton, John 4, 77, 89, 94, 127, 136, 189–90
Behr, John 3, 7–10, 25, 27–9, 35, 37–9, 61, 73, 84, 101–2, 104–5, 108, 113, 115–17, 123–4, 127–36, 169, 178, 180
Benoit, André 2, 4, 8, 21–24, 30–1, 37, 41–2, 48, 51, 66, 71, 73–5, 91, 101, 109, 116, 142, 150, 157, 162–3
bishops 37, 39, 106, 112
Blanchard, Yves-Marie 2, 4, 21, 24, 28, 30, 32, 34, 37, 39, 42, 48, 64–6, 103, 150, 159, 163
Bokedal, Tomas 2, 37–9, 41, 70, 101, 115–17, 119, 127, 129, 141, 159
Briggman, Anthony 7–8, 38, 142, 157, 160, 162, 167, 169–71

Campenhausen, Hans von 1, 4, 13, 22–4, 26–8, 37, 39, 41, 51, 67, 69–70, 85, 92–3, 141, 157, 159–61, 163, 189
canon, canonicity, canonization 1–4, 16, 61, 69–74, 92–3, 101, 115, 123, 131, 140–2, 145, 159, 189–90
Clement 30, 37, 40, 112, 122, 144–6, 148, 190
confession 3, 93, 100, 115–16, 121, 123, 125, 128
corrupt, corruption 42, 101, 127, 134, 161, 172, 177
creed 93, 115–16, 121

delimited use 16–19, 27, 30, 32, 34, 36, 43, 93, 101
Demiurge 34, 39, 47, 79, 166
Demonstration, the 9–10, 18–19, 31, 54, 57, 121, 126, 134–6, 150, 152, 154, 169, 172, 174, 183
disciples 22, 35, 68, 71, 103, 105, 118, 122, 161, 166, 177, 182

dominical oracles 27–9, 35, 60, 132

economy 37–8, 56, 76, 109, 118, 135, 161, 167, 169, 171, 173–4, 176, 179–80, 185
elder 45, 101–2, 107, 148–9, 162
ἐπίπνοιαν 142, 143, 146, 148
epistle 2, 4, 15, 37, 41, 47, 51, 66–7, 79–80, 83, 107, 145, 162
ἐπιστολή 65–7
εὐαγγέλιον 38–9, 41, 65–6, 68–9, 72–4, 77
Euangelium 38, 68, 103
Eusebius 10, 146, 190
evangelists 72, 75, 142, 161
exegesis 34, 56, 79, 82–3, 116
Eynde, Damien van den 2, 13, 38, 100–1, 106, 111, 117, 125, 127–8

face 70, 154, 168, 182
Farkasfalvy, Denis, M. 23, 27, 37, 39, 41, 48, 68, 73, 75, 157, 160, 162–3
Ferguson, Everett 23, 26–7, 33, 37, 41, 68, 70, 74–5, 92, 100, 103, 109, 136
Flesseman-van Leer, Ellen 2, 26–8, 33–34, 37, 39, 41, 100–1, 108, 111, 116, 125, 127–8, 141–2, 157, 159, 166–7
fourfold gospel 69–72, 74, 76–7, 166
fragment 9–10, 18, 66, 143, 148–9, 172, 175, 189

Gamble, Harry Y. 2, 31, 65, 92, 141, 145, 189
γραφή 2–3, 5–6, 13–25, 27, 29–31, 33–41, 43–5, 47–9, 51, 55, 64, 66–7, 91, 93
Grant, Robert M. 21, 73, 88, 142, 159

Hägglund, Bengt 100–101, 116, 125
Hahneman, Geoffrey M. 2, 31, 189
hands 171–2
Hanson, R. P. C. 84–5, 142
Harnack, Adolf von 1–2, 7, 51, 84, 115, 121, 141, 149
Harris, R. Laird 1–2, 140, 157, 159–60, 162
Harvey, W. Wigan 9–10, 28, 42, 66, 84, 149–50
heaven 20–1, 47, 58, 75–6, 111, 118, 122, 153, 162, 168, 172, 176
heretical teachings 60, 104, 120, 126

heretical writings 31, 43
heretics 8, 19, 45, 60–1, 69–70, 82–3, 103, 113, 120, 134, 142, 148, 157, 160, 162, 166
historical context 56–7, 62, 77, 86–7, 191
history 4, 22, 86, 93, 100–1, 127, 136, 146, 179
Hitchcock, F. R. Montgomery 2, 7–9, 13, 21, 23, 26–8, 31, 33, 37, 42, 45, 47–8, 59, 71, 73, 75, 82–3, 92, 100–1, 106, 111–13, 115, 121, 142, 157, 159, 162
Hoh, Josef 2, 4, 13, 16, 18, 23–4, 30–1, 34, 39, 41, 48, 51, 64, 68, 75, 84, 92, 157–60, 162
Holstein, Henri 103–6, 109
Homer 35, 61, 120, 126, 142

image 35, 60–1, 70, 84, 127–8, 170, 174
Incarnation 6, 57–8, 88, 100, 119, 130, 132, 136–7, 140, 153, 167, 169, 174–5, 178–83, 185, 187, 189, 191
inerrant 192
infallibility, infallible 183, 192
inspiration, inspired, etc. 1–3, 5, 7, 55, 139–71, 174, 176, 181, 183–5, 187, 190–1
instrument 14, 49, 102, 143, 154, 157–8, 181, 185
introductions to citations 53, 55, 63, 65, 67–8, 150, 152, 156–9, 163
invisible, invisibility 28, 46, 58, 117–18, 123, 153, 173, 175–8, 180, 185, 187

Jews 26, 28, 103, 113, 131–2, 167–8, 173
John 4, 28, 36, 39, 45, 67, 76, 80, 83, 84, 107, 110, 123, 126, 166–7, 173, 179–80
Justin Martyr 53, 69, 121, 133, 135, 146, 153–4, 167, 169, 171

Kalin, Everett R. 3, 143, 145, 147, 149, 165, 167–8
κανών τῆς ἀληθείας 60–1, 115, 117–18, 120, 124, 126, 128
Kelly, J. N. D. 115, 121
king 33, 35, 60–1, 70, 126–8, 148
kingdom 21, 58, 81, 83, 85, 131, 162

language 9, 29, 36, 38, 40, 56, 60, 67–8, 76, 102–3, 110–11, 120, 122, 133, 143, 147
law 4, 15, 26–7, 32, 36, 41, 55, 57, 62, 67–8, 75–6, 79, 104–5, 110–11, 122, 131–4, 173, 178, 181
Lawson, John 2, 13, 20–1, 23, 37, 41–2, 45, 48, 52, 56, 62, 71, 76, 83, 88, 91, 100–1, 106, 112–13, 115, 121, 133, 142, 155, 157, 161–2
letter 15, 21–2, 26, 30, 36, 40, 46, 51–2, 65–7, 78, 110, 122, 143, 146, 162, 166
literal 9, 56, 78, 81–2, 86, 142, 149
little treatise 106, 108
living tradition 93, 100–1
living voice 101, 110–11
Logos: 171; also see "Word"
Λόγος 146, 175
λόγους ἀποστολικούς 4, 32, 34
love 23, 27, 107, 122, 131, 133–4, 178–9
LXX 26, 45, 58, 107, 142–3, 165, 172; also see "Septuagint"

manuscript 9, 36, 42–3
Marcion, Marcionite 1, 17, 36, 51, 72, 83, 157, 161
Mark 39, 65, 76, 110, 165
Mary 83, 85, 148, 157–8
Massuet, R. 9, 42
McDonald, Lee M. 1, 4, 13, 23, 31, 35, 37, 39, 41, 51, 67, 69–70, 73, 92, 127, 141, 145, 159, 189
mediation, mediator, mediated 5, 7, 116, 140, 153, 176, 178, 182–3, 185, 187, 191–2
messianic prophecy 29, 153–5
metaphor, metaphorically 21, 33, 35, 62, 78, 81, 83
Metzger, Bruce M. 13, 31, 37, 70–1, 75, 93, 141, 145
Migne, J. P. 9, 146
Minns, Dennis 9, 133, 142, 159
Moses 19, 28, 33, 51, 53–5, 58–9, 65, 68, 104–5, 122, 155, 157, 171, 173
mouth 20, 168, 172
Muratorian fragment 70, 145, 189
mystery 78, 111–12, 147

narrative 59, 83, 127, 136, 150, 156, 165
nourish, nourishing 132, 169, 172–3, 176, 183
numerological 73

Ochagavia, Juan 3, 13, 31, 37, 92, 101–4, 106, 108–9, 113–16, 119–21, 123, 153, 169, 171, 176–9, 181
oracle 27–9, 35, 60, 62
oral, orally 37–9, 72–3, 77, 100–2, 106, 108–14, 142, 160, 168
oral traditions 101, 108, 113
Origen 88–9, 167, 190
orthodox, orthodoxy 17, 30, 72, 82, 93, 104, 117, 125–6, 128, 145
Osborn, Eric 23, 27, 41, 71, 82–3, 100–1, 113, 115–17, 142, 159, 163
ostensiones ex Scripturis 20, 23–6, 130

Papias 30
parable 32–6, 43–4, 56–7, 59, 61, 84–8, 104, 120, 126–7, 130
παραδίδωμι 102–5, 107
παράδοσις 100, 102–8, 113, 122
passion 57–8, 100, 118
Paul 4, 17, 21–2, 26, 33, 36, 39, 41, 45, 47–8, 51, 64–5, 67–8, 72, 75–6, 78–83, 107, 110–12, 133–4, 143, 145–6, 148, 157–8, 161–3, 165–7
Pentateuch 53–5, 151
Pentecost 167
perfect, perfection, etc. 21, 55, 58, 76, 110–12, 141–2, 144, 155, 159–61, 167, 169, 176, 188
person 62, 153–5, 182
perversion, perverting 17, 32, 43, 46, 60, 68, 75, 157
Peter 4, 36, 39, 45, 64–5, 76, 107, 110, 112, 146–7, 160, 165–6, 168
pillar 37–8, 69, 76, 109, 176
Plato 53
pleroma 32–4, 75, 79
pneumatology 164, 167, 169–70, 184
πνοή 143, 149
poem 35, 61, 120, 126–7, 149
Polycarp 105, 148
presbyters 44, 110, 113, 132
proofs from the scriptures 23, 25–6, 36, 37

prophecy 28, 57–8, 62–3, 82, 131–2, 135–6, 143, 147, 152–5, 163, 168–9
prophesy 56–7, 88–9, 119, 135–6, 147, 162, 168, 171, 182, 185, 187
prophet 4, 16, 18–20, 26–8, 31–4, 36, 41–4, 46, 48, 52–5, 57, 62–4, 67–8, 75–6, 87, 101, 104, 111, 118–19, 122, 126, 131–2, 134–5, 140–3, 150–5, 157, 161–4, 167–9, 171–4, 177–9, 181, 183, 185, 187, 191

recapitulation, recapitulate, etc. 3, 6, 82, 118, 132–7, 174
Reed, Annette Yoshiko 3, 41, 65, 68–9, 71–3
regula veritatis 61, 103, 115–17, 119, 124–5
Reilly, W. S. 62–3, 87, 143, 155
Rescher, Nicholas 5, 14
restore, restoring 61, 83, 127–8, 174
resurrection 22, 84, 100, 118, 130, 174
retroversion 9–10, 29, 148, 160–1, 166
Revealer of the Father 5, 7, 86, 95, 140, 176, 179, 181–2, 184–5, 187
revelation 1, 3–5, 7, 36, 38, 62, 66, 68, 86–7, 93, 101, 104, 116, 125, 129, 135, 137, 140, 142, 144, 149, 153, 156, 169, 171, 173–7, 179–83, 185, 187–9, 191
Reynders, D. B. 7, 18, 29, 100, 102–7, 109
righteousness 85, 119, 133, 157, 168
Roberts, Alexander and James Donaldson 10, 24, 27, 29–31, 37, 39, 41–2, 48, 59, 75, 119, 124, 126, 148–9, 151, 162
Rome 30, 76, 110, 112, 145
Rousseau, Adelin et al. 9–10, 24–25, 27–31, 34, 37–9, 41–2, 48, 59, 65–6, 119, 125–6, 135–6, 148–9, 151, 154, 160–2, 166, 172, 175, 183
rule of truth 1, 6, 20, 35, 61–3, 81–2, 88–9, 94, 99, 114–30, 132, 134, 136–7, 150, 172, 174, 187–8, 191; also see *"regula veritatis,"* "κανών τῆς ἀληθείας"

Sagnard, F. 9, 24, 30
Saieg, Paul 127

salvation 21, 29, 37–8, 40, 56, 76, 83, 85–6, 109, 118–19, 127, 135–6, 174–5, 179–83, 185
Savior 39, 79–80, 110, 122, 135, 154, 157
Schleiermacher 144
scriptura 15, 18–20, 22–32, 36–44, 47–9, 51, 64, 75, 93, 111, 130, 151
scripture 1–7, 13–49, 51–67, 69–71, 73–9, 81–95, 99–102, 106–10, 113–16, 119–21, 123, 125–38, 140–5, 147–60, 162–5, 169–73, 181–5, 187–91
scriptural text 2–3, 6, 51–7, 63–4, 75, 89, 91
Scripturis dominicis 20, 26–30
secret 39, 111–13
Seitz, Christopher R. 128, 131–2, 135
Septuagint 4, 45, 93, 101, 162–3, also see "LXX"
Sesboüe, Bernard 3, 13, 24–5, 37–9, 41, 45, 165
Shepherd of Hermas 3, 13, 16, 30–1, 53, 93, 146
speech 14, 83, 149, 158, 161
spurious writings 15, 31, 46
Steenberg, M. C. 2, 13, 16, 18, 23–8, 30–4, 36–9, 42, 48, 51, 59, 71, 91, 93–4, 101
story 54, 57, 60, 127, 135
succession 37, 39, 44, 110, 112, 132, 188
Sundberg, A. C. 1, 2, 4, 70, 145, 189
system 7–8, 17–18, 21, 29, 32, 34, 47–8, 58–60, 79–80, 100, 127–8, 137, 177, 191; also see "ὑπόθεσις"

Tertullian 141, 149, 190
testimony 5–6, 45, 52–3, 55, 64, 67–8, 71–2, 74–7, 88–9, 91, 99, 113, 123–4, 140, 157, 160, 185, 189
θεῖος 142–3, 149
theme 35, 59, 85, 108, 119–20, 126, 128, 132–3, 136, 189; also see "ὑπόθεσις"
θεόπνευστος 143, 149
Torrance, T. F. 75, 84, 182
traditio 102–3, 105–6, 108, 111
tradition 1, 5–7, 16, 25, 31, 39–40, 48, 68, 72–3, 76, 93, 99–117, 121–3, 130, 137, 142, 160–3, 168–9, 182; also see "παράδοσις," *"traditio,"* "apostolic tradition," "oral traditions"

trado 102, 104–5
transcendence 176, 178–9, 185
Truth, see "rule of truth"

Unger, Dominic J. 10, 19, 24, 28–9, 31, 37–9, 41–2, 48, 59, 75, 108, 124–6, 149, 151, 160, 162–3
unwritten tradition/unwritten teachings 100–1, 106, 108, 113
ὑπόθεσις 34, 56, 59–60, 80–1, 103, 113, 120, 126–32, 136–7

Valentinian 8, 17, 21, 29, 32–6, 47, 56, 71, 80–4, 117, 120, 126–7, 145, 161, 164
Virgin 85, 107, 118, 122, 148, 157, 162–3

Werner, Johannes 16, 21, 41–2, 48, 150, 157–8, 162–3
Wiegel, James 135–6
wisdom 110, 131, 135, 172
witness 1, 3, 30, 33, 45, 47, 70–2, 75, 77–8, 107, 113, 131, 140, 148, 157–8, 160, 165–8, 182, 185, 187, 189, 192
Wittgenstein, Ludwig 14, 49
Word 3–5, 7, 20, 54, 62–3, 69, 77, 86–7, 89, 95, 118, 123, 128, 140–1, 150–6, 159, 161, 166, 169–85, 187, 189, 191

Young, Frances 45, 56, 59, 117, 127

Zahn, Theodor 73, 115, 121

Index of References to Irenaeus' Works

Adversus haereses/Against Heresies

1.pre.1	17, 29	1.15.6	143, 149
1.pre.2	60, 120	1.18.1	18, 54, 58–9
1.1.3	18	1.18.1–3	19
1.3.1–5	32	1.18.1–1.19.1	59
1.3.4	133	1.18.2	18
1.3.6	4, 31, 32, 55, 59, 68, 75, 78	1.19.1	18–19, 46
		1.19.2	179
1.4.4	60	1.20.1	18, 31, 46, 54
1.5.2	104	1.20.2	46, 68
1.6.3	18, 20–3	1.20.2–3	17
1.7.3–4	82	1.20.3	60, 124, 177
1.8–9	30	1.21.1	102, 104
1.8.1	4, 16–18, 27, 29–35, 41, 48, 59–60, 67–8, 103, 105, 128	1.21.2	104, 169
		1.21.5	102
		1.22.1	18–20, 55, 117, 124–6, 172
1.8.1–2	33–4		
1.8.1–1.9.4	32, 34, 36, 60	1.23.3	142–3
1.8.2	18, 32, 65, 66–7, 79–80	1.25.5	105
1.8.2–5	79	1.26.2	68
1.8.3	80	1.26.3	67, 156
1.8.4	68, 104	1.27.2	29, 36, 55, 67–8, 104–5
1.9.1	18, 32, 34, 67	1.27.2–4	30, 36
1.9.2	80, 167, 172	1.27.4	18, 29, 32, 36, 41, 67
1.9.3	18, 32, 34, 67, 103	1.30.4	143
1.9.4	17–18, 35–6, 60–1, 117, 120–1, 124–5, 127–8	1.30.11	17, 79, 82, 155
		1.31.4	103
1.9.5	103	2.pre.1	18, 59, 103
1.10.1	35, 103, 118, 121, 133, 165, 174	2.pre.2	60, 103
		2.2.5	18, 41, 48, 54, 75, 155
1.10.1–2	103, 125	2.2.6	4, 29
1.10.2	103, 105, 122	2.6.1	177
1.10.3	18, 60, 105, 151	2.9.1	18, 47, 55, 68, 103, 107, 173
1.11.1	104		
1.13.2–5	155	2.9.2	59
1.13.4	105	2.10.1	18
1.14.1	104	2.10.1–2	59
1.14.8	59	2.10.2	18
1.15.4	143	2.11.1	29, 55, 181

Reference	Pages
2.11.2	29
2.12.3	60
2.12.8	60
2.13.3	18
2.14.1	60
2.14.4	142
2.14.7	177
2.18.4	60
2.19.8	60
2.20–24	30, 36, 43
2.20.1	36, 43
2.20.9	68
2.21.2	104
2.22	113
2.22.1	62
2.22.1–2	36, 59, 78
2.22.2	18, 36, 65, 75, 81
2.22.3	55, 68, 113
2.22.3–5	36
2.22.4	113
2.22.5	101, 105, 113
2.22.6	113, 142
2.23.1–2	36
2.24–25	73
2.24.1–3	36
2.24.3	18, 36, 59, 73
2.24.4	18, 32, 36, 55, 67
2.25.1	60–61, 117, 127–8
2.25.1–2	120
2.25.2	62, 117, 127
2.26.1	143
2.27–28	59
2.27.1	18, 61, 117, 127
2.27.1–2	128
2.27.2	18, 30, 32, 40–3, 67
2.27.3	17
2.28.1	117, 124
2.28.2	18, 55, 76, 140, 149, 152, 155, 159, 173
2.28.2–3	62, 159
2.28.3	18–19, 55, 128, 159
2.28.4	18, 47, 55, 74
2.28.7	18, 31, 48, 55, 75, 151–2
2.30.6	18, 20, 27–8, 155
2.30.7	18, 47, 55, 75
2.30.9	41, 48, 104, 119, 172, 176
2.31.3	142
2.32.4	147
2.32.5	26
2.33.3	62
2.33.4	143
2.34.4	54, 149
2.34.5	130
2.35.2	18, 26
2.35.3	18–19, 143
2.35.4	18, 20, 23, 26–8, 31, 41, 48, 68
3.pre	18, 20, 23, 26, 37, 103, 108, 130, 166, 183
3.pre–3.1.2	76, 109–10
3.pre–3.4.3	26
3.pre–3.5.1	31
3.pre.1	17
3.1	39
3.1–3	103
3.1–4	30, 36–7, 40, 71
3.1–5	106, 108–13
3.1.1	18, 32, 37–41, 67–8, 74, 103, 107, 140, 144–5, 160–2, 165, 167, 176, 183
3.1.1–3.4.3	108
3.1.2	55, 82, 105, 110–11, 119, 181
3.2	39
3.2–4	113
3.2.1	18, 32, 67, 102–4, 112, 117, 126, 140
3.2.1–2	110
3.2.2	18, 32, 67–8, 103, 111, 161, 166
3.2.3	103, 111
3.3	39
3.3–4	76
3.3.1	68, 103, 111–12
3.3.1–2	74
3.3.2	68, 103, 105
3.3.2–4	112
3.3.3	15, 18, 30, 37, 65–6, 68, 103, 112, 122
3.3.4	68, 105, 167
3.4	39
3.4.1	18, 32, 39–40, 67–8, 101, 103, 112, 128
3.4.2	40, 103, 119, 122, 174

3.4.3	167	3.12.10	54
3.5.1	18, 20, 24–6, 68, 103, 108, 111, 113, 129–30, 166	3.12.11	64, 68, 78
		3.12.12	17–18, 30, 32, 36, 65, 67–8, 161
3.5.2	166, 183	3.12.13	161
3.5.3	29, 120, 164	3.12.14	168
3.6.1	18–19, 22, 31, 54, 151–2, 164–5	3.12.15	166, 168, 182
		3.13–15	76, 147
3.6.2	28, 150	3.13.1	65, 83
3.6.3	18	3.13.3	64–5, 67, 83
3.6.4	18, 31	3.14.1	65, 165–6
3.6.5	54, 150–1	3.14.1–2	111
3.7	83	3.14.1–4	65
3.7.1	65, 78–9	3.14.2	106, 167, 183
3.7.1–2	162	3.14.4	68, 130, 140
3.7.2	65, 82, 143, 161	3.15.1	68, 117, 120
3.8.1	31, 41, 48, 68, 78	3.15.2	60
3.8.2	79, 172	3.15.3	68
3.8.3	169, 172	3.16.1	74, 78, 114, 145, 157–8
3.9–11	71, 74	3.16.2	140, 142, 157–9, 163, 165, 167, 170
3.9.1	31, 41, 48, 68, 71, 164		
3.9.1–3	79	3.16.2–4	114
3.9.2	41, 48	3.16.3	18, 45, 65
3.9.3	62, 152	3.16.4	18, 45, 145
3.10.1	165	3.16.5	18, 65
3.10.2	55, 68, 181	3.16.6	60, 133, 174
3.10.3	151, 181	3.16.7	83
3.10.4	55	3.16.8	60, 65–6
3.10.6	41, 65, 156, 165	3.16.9	65, 83, 158
3.11.1	117, 119–20, 123, 126–7, 172	3.17.1	168–9, 175
		3.17.1–3.18.4	176
3.11.2	65, 172	3.17.2	168–9
3.11.3	172	3.17.3	57, 84, 85, 168
3.11.6	153, 179	3.17.4	18, 31, 41, 48, 60
3.11.7	17, 69	3.18.1	170, 172
3.11.7–9	68–74, 77	3.18.1–2	174
3.11.8	65, 70, 145, 147, 166, 173	3.18.2	84
		3.18.3	18, 83, 151, 176
3.11.9	18, 29, 31, 64–5, 68, 70–2, 105–6, 120, 147	3.18.5	156
		3.18.7	54
3.12.1	18, 168	3.19.1	151, 156
3.12.2	68	3.19.1–3.20.3	174
3.12.3	176	3.19.2	18, 26, 41, 45, 68
3.12.5	18, 30, 32, 36, 64, 68, 160	3.19.3	85
		3.20.1	18
3.12.6	111, 117, 125	3.20.2	175
3.12.7	55, 68, 111, 160	3.21.1	18–19, 45, 55
3.12.8	18, 45, 55	3.21.1–3	4, 19
3.12.9	18, 20, 25–6, 67, 167	3.21.1–5	45

Index of References to Irenaeus' Works

3.21.2	18, 55, 142–3, 149, 163	4.10.1	18–19, 28, 55, 131, 152, 171
3.21.3	18, 45, 68, 103, 107, 162–3, 167	4.10.1–2	44, 79
3.21.4	41, 151, 162–3, 165, 167, 170	4.10.2	54
		4.11.1	18–19, 22, 44, 54–5, 62, 152
3.21.5	18, 148, 158, 163		
3.21.8	57	4.11.3	18, 79, 105
3.21.9	151–2	4.12.1–5	79
3.21.10	171–2	4.12.1	102
3.22.1	65, 156	4.12.2	133–4
3.22.4	85	4.12.3	41
3.23.2	18–19, 54	4.12.4	102, 150
3.23.3	18–19, 54, 65	4.12.12	55
3.24.1	41, 55, 143, 168–9	4.13.4	156
3.24.2	172	4.14.1	156
3.25.5	53	4.14.2	66
3.25.7	29, 120	4.15.1	54, 150
4.pre	120	4.16.1	18–19, 22, 54, 75, 150
4.pre.1	29	4.16.2	54
4.pre.2	60	4.16.3	54
4.pre.3	60, 103, 145, 158, 167, 182	4.16.4	18–19, 54
		4.16.5	54
4.pre.4	18, 150, 171	4.17.1	55, 151
4.pre.4–4.1.1	165	4.17.2	151
4.1.1	31, 165	4.17.3	151
4.2.1	54	4.17.4	151
4.2.3	28, 55, 65, 155, 173	4.17.6	66
4.2.4	151	4.18.3	54, 150–1, 171
4.2.5	28, 156	4.18.4	54
4.5.1	18, 55, 176, 181	4.18.6	66
4.5.2	18, 28, 173	4.19.2	151, 179
4.5.5	62	4.20.1	18–19, 54, 150, 171–2
4.6.1	177	4.20.1–3	179
4.6.1–3	79	4.20.1–12	179
4.6.1–7	177	4.20.2	18, 30, 53, 172
4.6.2	53	4.20.3	151, 155
4.6.3	175–7	4.20.4	62, 152, 155, 172, 174, 179–80, 182
4.6.4–5	178		
4.6.5	175	4.20.4–8	152
4.6.6	55, 62, 165, 173, 175, 178, 181–2	4.20.5	55, 62, 152, 165, 176, 179
4.6.7	177–8	4.20.6	54, 65, 151, 180
4.7.4	28, 54, 150, 171, 177	4.20.7	152, 173–4, 180
4.8.1	79, 157	4.20.8	54, 62, 152, 155
4.8.3	54	4.20.9	28, 54, 150, 152, 171, 173
4.9–11	131		
4.9.1	28, 105	4.20.9–10	155
4.9.2	65–6, 156	4.20.10–12	62, 150
4.9.3	55, 102	4.20.11	66, 156, 180

4.21.1	18, 65–6	4.36.6	41, 65–6, 85, 168
4.21.2	65–6, 151	4.36.7	85
4.21.3	57, 66, 151–2, 171	4.36.8	68, 152, 156, 173–4
4.23.1	18–19, 55, 131	4.37.1	65–6
4.23.2	18–19, 44	4.37.7	105, 107
4.24.1	18, 25–6	4.38.1–3	169–70
4.24.1–2	19	4.38.3	169, 172
4.24.2	18, 44, 179	4.38.4	151
4.25.2	18, 54	4.40–1	85, 86
4.25.3	57, 131	4.40.3	18, 54, 75
4.26.1	18, 22, 44, 57, 85, 88, 128, 130–2	4.41.2	18, 30, 32, 36, 67, 151
		4.41.4	29, 66–8, 120
4.26.2	132	5.pre	18, 31, 41, 48, 66–8, 103, 105–6
4.26.4	68, 132		
4.26.5	18, 44, 132	5.1.1	175
4.27.1	18–19, 44, 62, 155	5.1.3	143, 150, 170–1
4.27.3	65–6	5.2.3	65–6
4.27.4	65–6, 105	5.3.1	65–6, 104
4.28.3	65–6	5.5.1	18–19, 54–5, 171
4.29.1	65–6	5.5.2	18–19, 75
4.29.2	54, 150	5.6.1	65–6, 147, 170–1, 176
4.30.2	18–19, 54	5.7.1	65–6
4.30.3	29	5.8.1	65–6, 79, 169–70
4.30.4	67	5.8.1–4	79
4.31.1	18–19, 44, 54–5	5.8.2	143, 148
4.31.1–3	57	5.9.1–4	79
4.31.2	54, 151	5.10.1	83, 170
4.32.1	18, 54, 65–6, 68, 172	5.10.2	65–6
4.32.2	68, 103	5.11.1	65–6, 79
4.33.7	119	5.11.2	65–6
4.33.8	18, 68, 105	5.12.1–4	79
4.33.10	57	5.12.3	65–6, 68, 86
4.33.10–15	62	5.12.4	65–6
4.33.11	79	5.12.5	65–6
4.33.15	18	5.13.2	78, 81
4.34.1	41, 68, 131	5.13.3	65–6
4.34.2	65–6	5.13.4	65–6
4.34.3	62, 143, 149	5.13.5	81
4.34.3–5	182	5.14.1	150
4.34.4	68, 151	5.14.2	65
4.34.5	18, 25–6	5.14.3	66–7
4.35.1	17–18, 44	5.14.4	18, 65–6, 150
4.35.1–4	79, 82	5.15.2	18–19, 22, 54, 75, 83, 172
4.35.2	183		
4.35.4	18, 44, 55, 82, 117, 119, 123, 126–7	5.15.3	86, 151
		5.15.4	18, 54
4.36.2	104–5	5.16.1	18–19, 22, 54
4.36.3	171	5.16.2	175
4.36.5	151	5.17.1	18, 54, 156

5.17.2	55	*Dem.* 30	62, 135, 152
5.17.4	57	*Dem.* 31–42a	136
5.18.2	65, 168, 176	*Dem.* 32	18, 19, 54, 170
5.18.3	53, 54, 172, 174	*Dem.* 34	151, 173
5.20.1	68, 103–6, 119	*Dem.* 37–8	174
5.20.2	18, 20, 27–8, 54, 132–3, 150–1, 169	*Dem.* 38	151
		Dem. 41	134, 168
5.21.1	54, 65–6, 150	*Dem.* 42	135, 152, 168
5.21.2	18, 174	*Dem.* 43	54, 57, 79, 134, 155, 172
5.22.1	65, 156	*Dem.* 44	18, 54, 171
5.23.1	18–19, 54	*Dem.* 45	151, 153, 174
5.23.3	66	*Dem.* 46	54, 68, 134, 150
5.24.1	79, 151, 155	*Dem.* 47	134, 175
5.24.4	65–6, 156	*Dem.* 47–50–7	
5.25.1	65–6	*Dem.* 49	62, 152–5, 163
5.25.3	65	*Dem.* 50	151
5.26.1	67, 78, 85	*Dem.* 52	18, 135
5.28.2	66–7	*Dem.* 53–89	57, 151
5.28.3	18, 54	*Dem.* 55	54
5.28.4	171	*Dem.* 56	78
5.30.1	15, 18, 32, 36	*Dem.* 57	54
5.30.1–2	30, 67	*Dem.* 58	54
5.30.2	18, 32, 36, 67	*Dem.* 62	18
5.32.1	65–6	*Dem.* 67	18, 62, 151
5.32.2	18, 65–6, 150	*Dem.* 68	151
5.33.4	18, 30	*Dem.* 71	18
5.34.2	66	*Dem.* 73	151
5.34.3	151	*Dem.* 75	58
5.35.2	67	*Dem.* 79	54
		Dem. 86	68, 103, 134

The Demonstration of the Apostolic Preaching

		Dem. 87	79, 133–4
		Dem. 89	168
		Dem. 90	18
Dem. 1	18, 31	*Dem.* 92	57, 151
Dem. 2	54, 126, 150–1, 171	*Dem.* 93	150–1
Dem. 3	104, 117, 121, 125–6, 136	*Dem.* 94	134
		Dem. 95	54
Dem. 5	169–70, 172	*Dem.* 97	18
Dem. 6	62, 117–19, 121, 136, 165, 168, 172, 174	*Dem.* 98	68, 103–5, 135
		Dem. 99	68, 104
Dem. 7	121, 153, 175		
Dem. 8	134	*Fragments from Lost Writings*	
Dem. 8–30	136		
Dem. 8–42a	136	frg. 2	18
Dem. 9	57	frg. 19	18
Dem. 12	171	frg. 20 (ANF 22)	54
Dem. 24	18, 19, 54, 150–2, 171	frg. 38 (ANF 37)	66
Dem. 26	54	frg. 39 (ANF 40)	18–19
Dem. 29	54, 150